OFFICIAL HISTORY OF THE INDIAN ARMED FORCES IN THE SECOND WORLD WAR 1939–45

ATLAS

CAMPAIGNS IN THE EASTERN THEATRE

THE ARAKAN OPERATIONS
1942–45

THE RETREAT FROM BURMA
1941–42

CAMPAIGNS IN SOUTH-EAST ASIA
1941–42

THE RECONQUEST OF BURMA
Volume 1

THE RECONQUEST OF BURMA
Volume 2

The Naval & Military Press Ltd

Published by

The Naval & Military Press Ltd

Unit 5 Riverside, Brambleside
Bellbrook Industrial Estate
Uckfield, East Sussex
TN22 1QQ England

Tel: +44 (0)1825 749494

www.naval-military-press.com
www.nmarchive.com

In reprinting in facsimile from the original, any imperfections are inevitably reproduced and the quality may fall short of modern type and cartographic standards.

OFFICIAL HISTORY OF THE INDIAN ARMED FORCES
IN THE SECOND WORLD WAR
1939-45

Campaigns in the Eastern Theatre

THE ARAKAN OPERATIONS
1942-45

Maps and Sketches

The Arakan Operations 1942–45
List of maps

1. General Map of Burma
2. Topography of Arakan
3. Rainfall in Burma. Mid-May to mid-October
4. Japanese dispositions facing 47 Ind Inf Bde. 17 January, 1943
5. Dispositions of forward troops of 55 Ind Inf Bde and Japanese troops. 31 January, 1943
6. 123 Ind Inf Bde attack–North of Rathedaung. 3 February, 1943
7. Japanese defences in Akyab Island. January, 1943
8. Japanese dispositions in Burma in December, 1942 and movement of 55 Div to Arakan
9. Japanese dispositions—end of Phase I and development of Phase 2. February, 1943
10. Japanese dispositions—end of Phase 2 and development in Phase 3. March, 1943
11. Japanese dispositions—end of Phase 3 and development in Phase 4. March-May, 1943
12. Arakan. Situation first week in November, 1943
13. Japanese counter-offensive. February, 1944
14. Sketch of 7 Ind Div Admin Box after arrival of 89 Ind Inf Bde. February, 1944
15. Arakan. Situation third week in February, 1944
16. Battle for Hill 551
17. Arakan. Situation third week in June, 1944
18. Myebon and adjacent area
19. Myebon Peninsula
20. Myebon Operations, January, 1945
21. Kangaw area
22. Kangaw Blockade
23. Invasion of Ramree Island. January-March, 1945
24. Capture of Akyab–Myebon–Kangaw–Myohaung–Ruywa and operations towards AN. January-March, 1945
25. Arakan

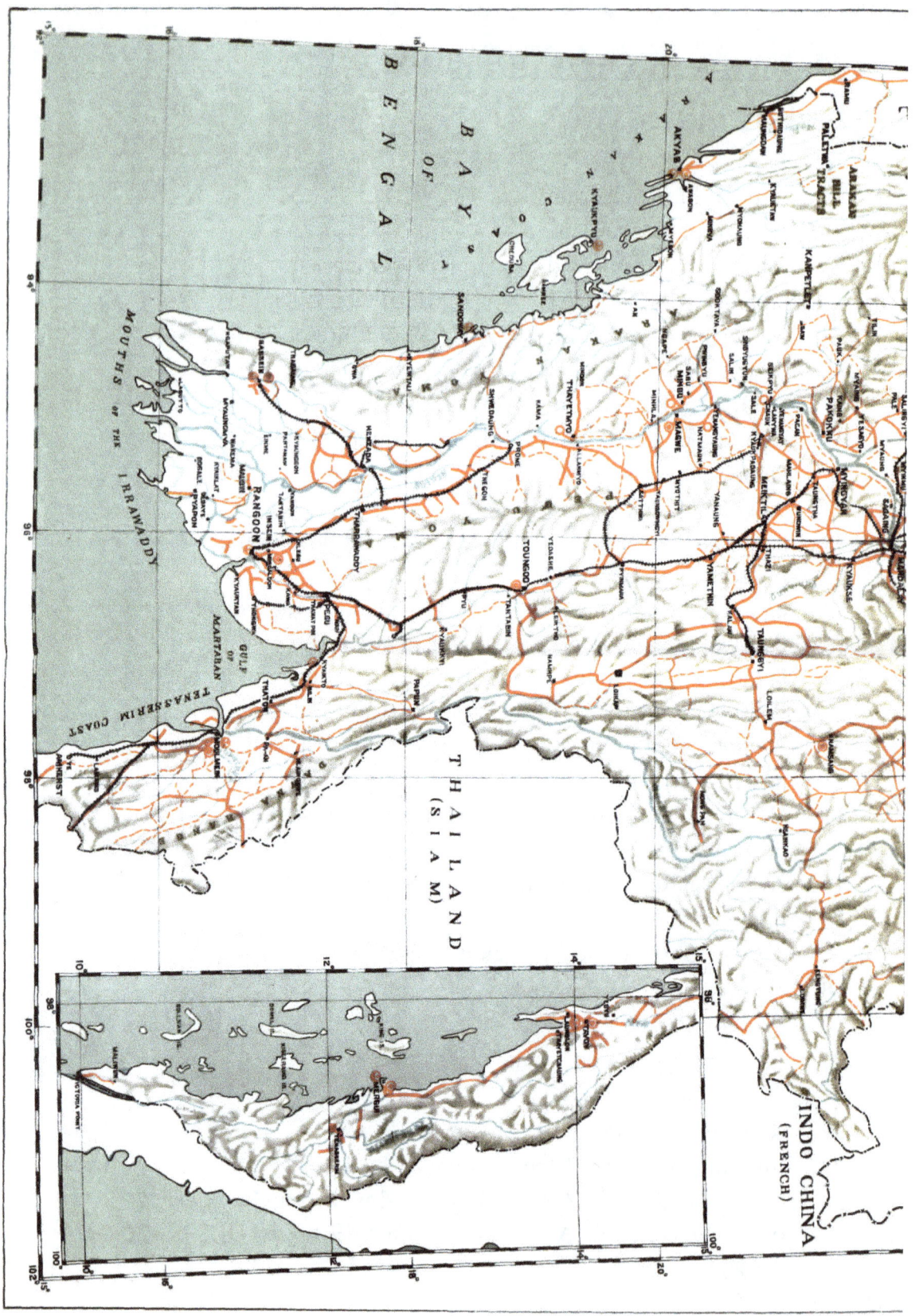

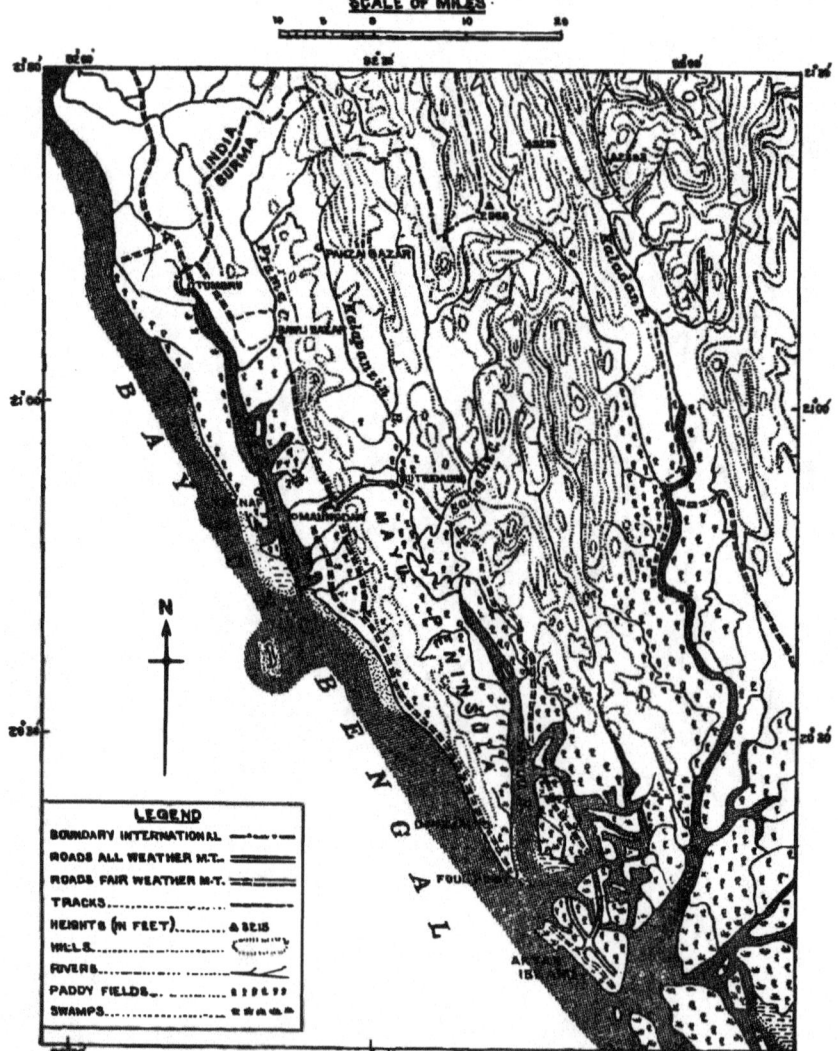

JAPANESE DISPOSITIONS
FACING 47 IND. INF. BDE.
17 JANUARY 1943
SCALE OF YARDS

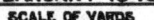

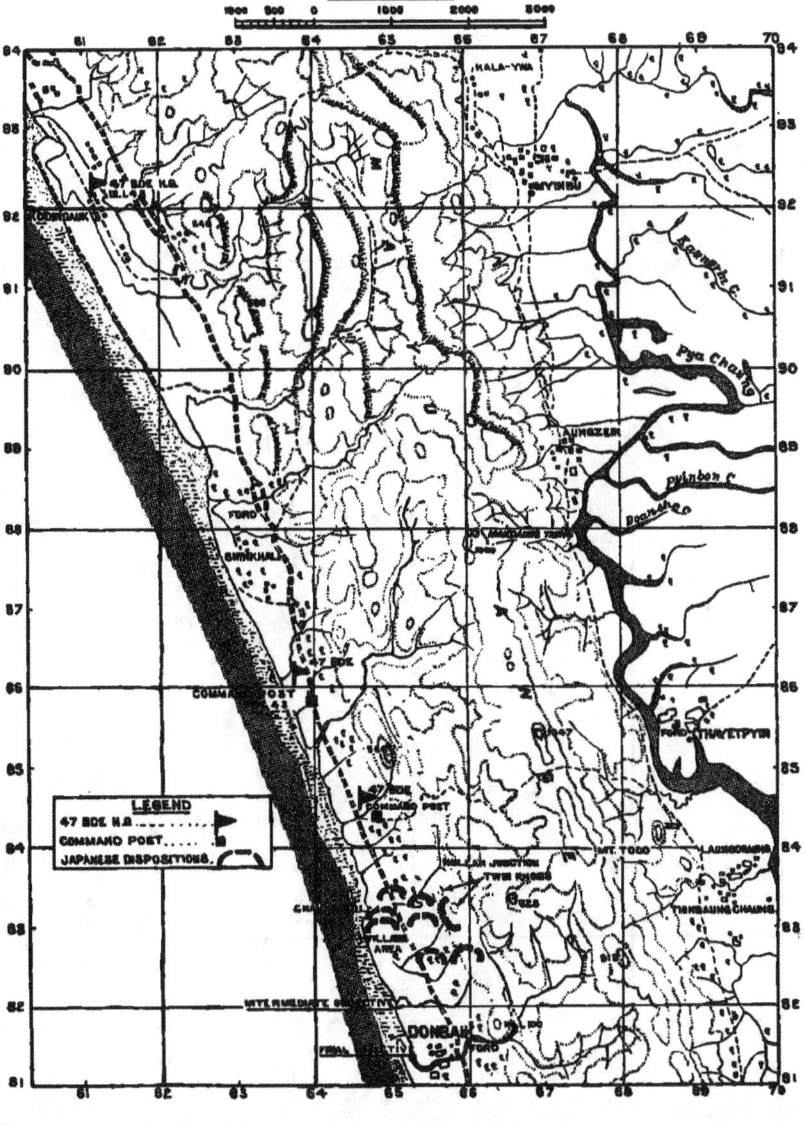

DISPOSITIONS-FORWARD TROOPS OF 55 IND. INF. BDE. AND JAPANESE TROOPS
31 JANUARY 1943.

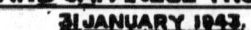

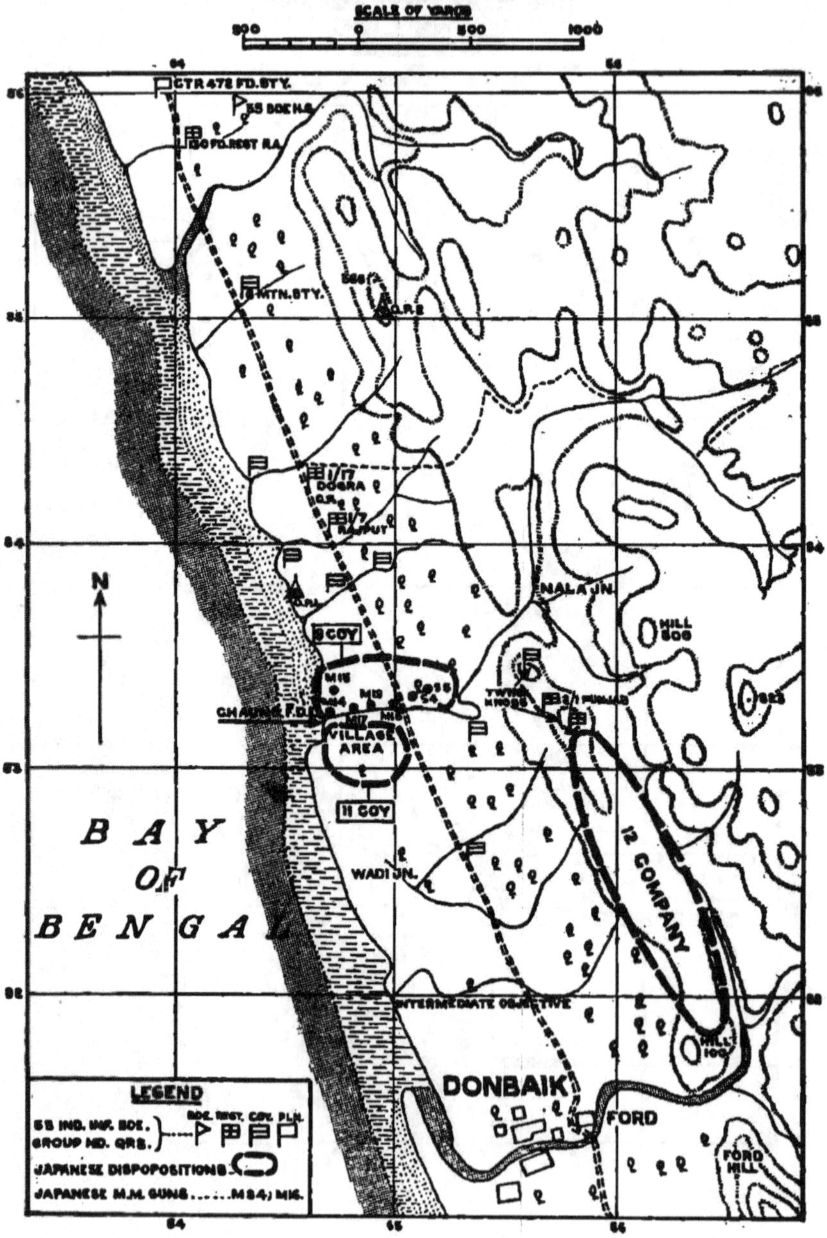

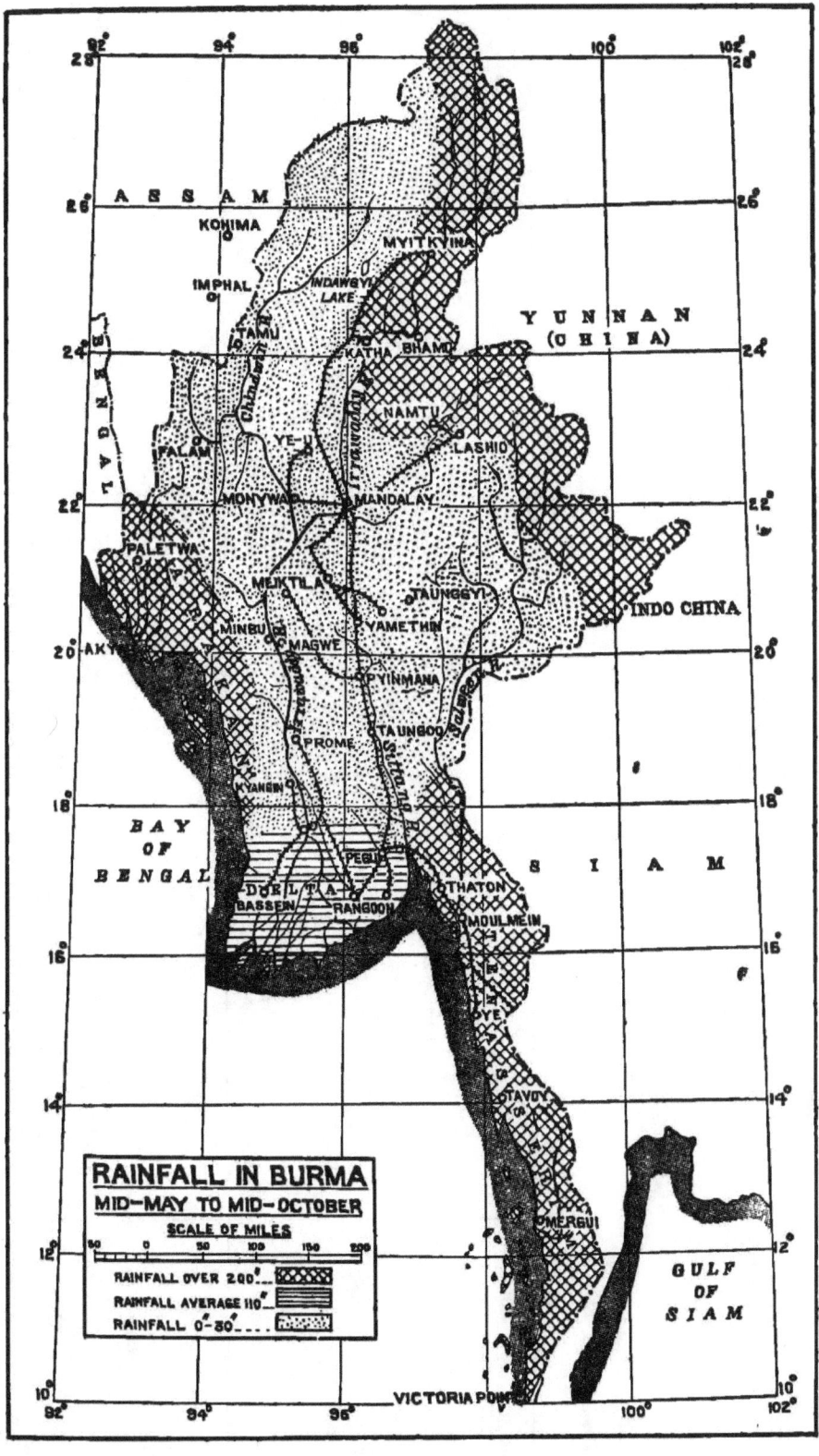

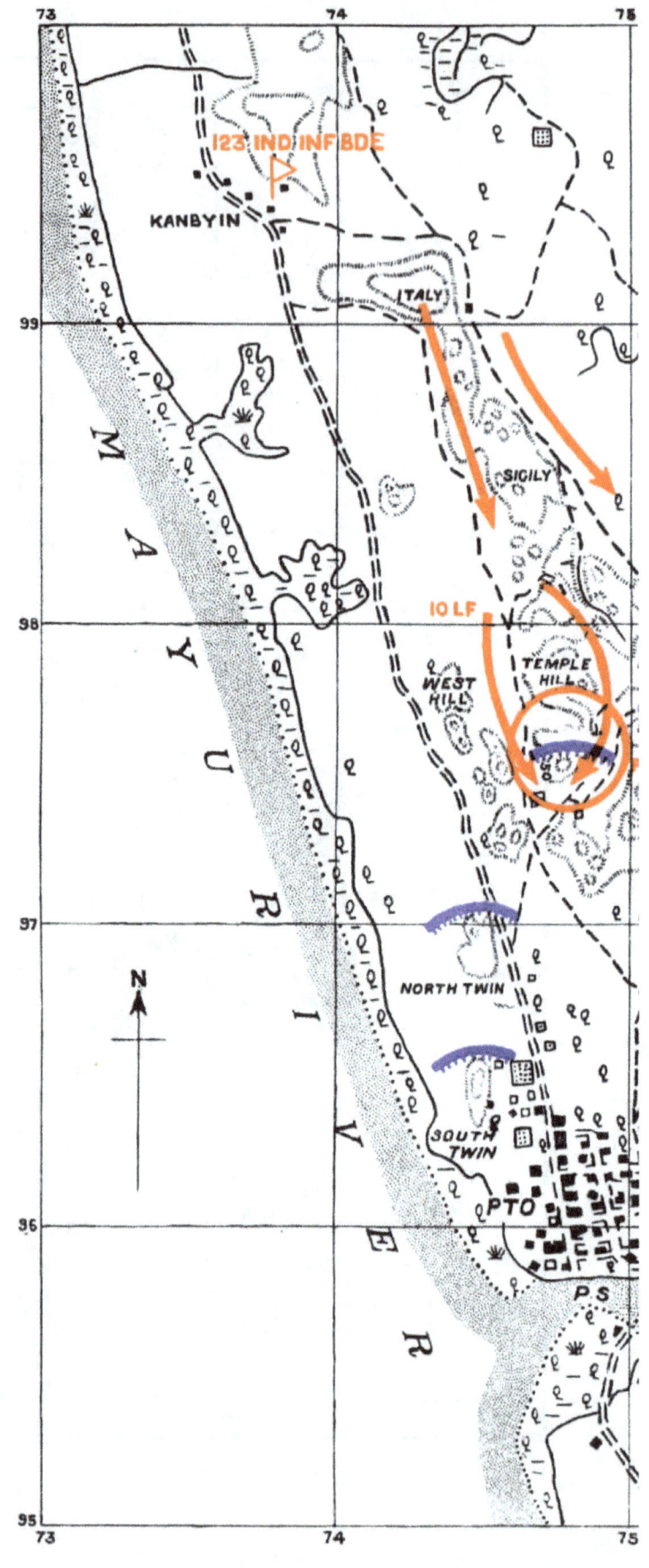

123 IND INF BDE ATTACK
NORTH OF RATHEDAUNG (3 FEB. 1943)
SCALE OF YARDS
500
0
500
1000
MOVEMENT OF TROOPS
BRIGADE OBJECTIVES
JAPANESE FOREMOST DEFENDED LOCALITIES
76
77
NGATAUKTUSHE
8/6 RAJ RIF
HILL NORTH 75
1/15 PUNJAB
PHASE 1
PHASE 2
PHASE 3
TAUNGHLAMAW
RATHEDAUNG
FERRY
RATHEDAUNG CHAUNG
98
97
96
95

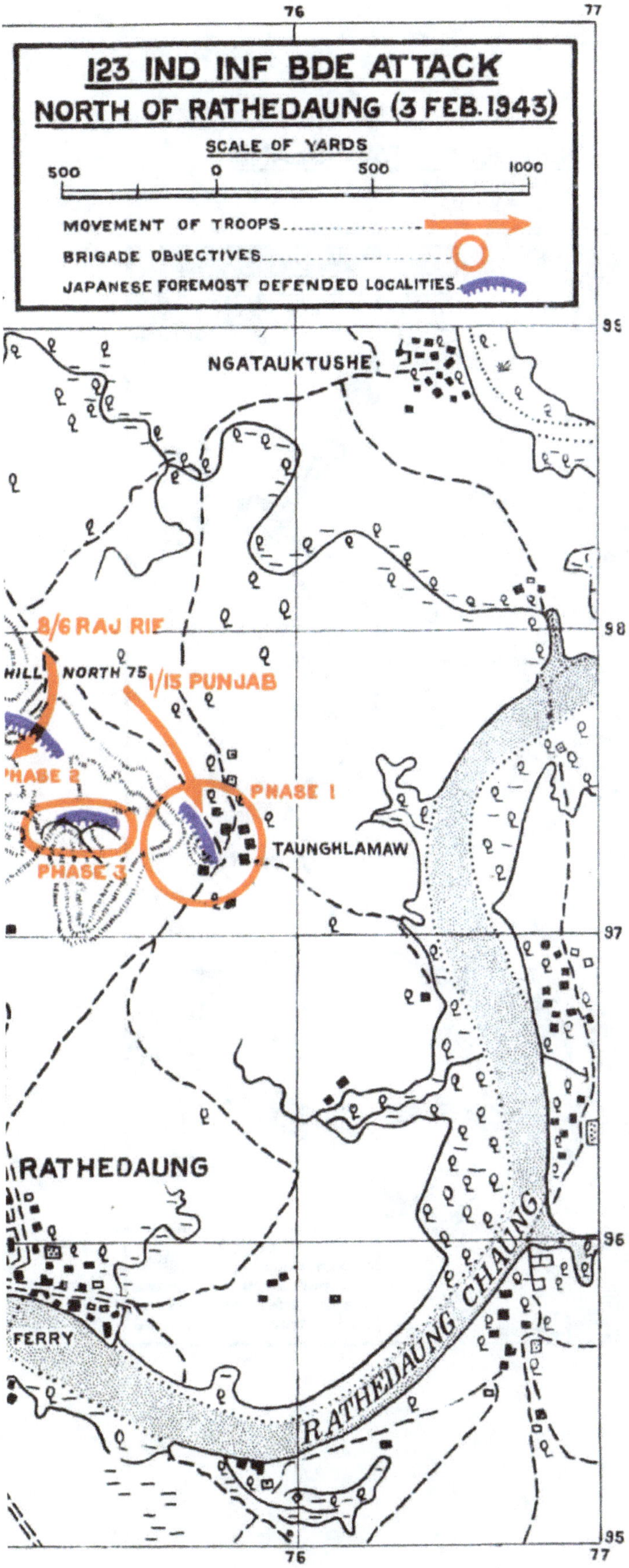

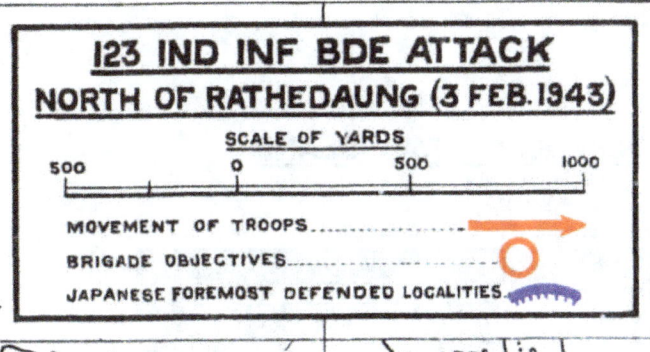

JAPANESE DEFENCES AKYAB ISLAND
JANUARY 1943
SCALE OF MILES

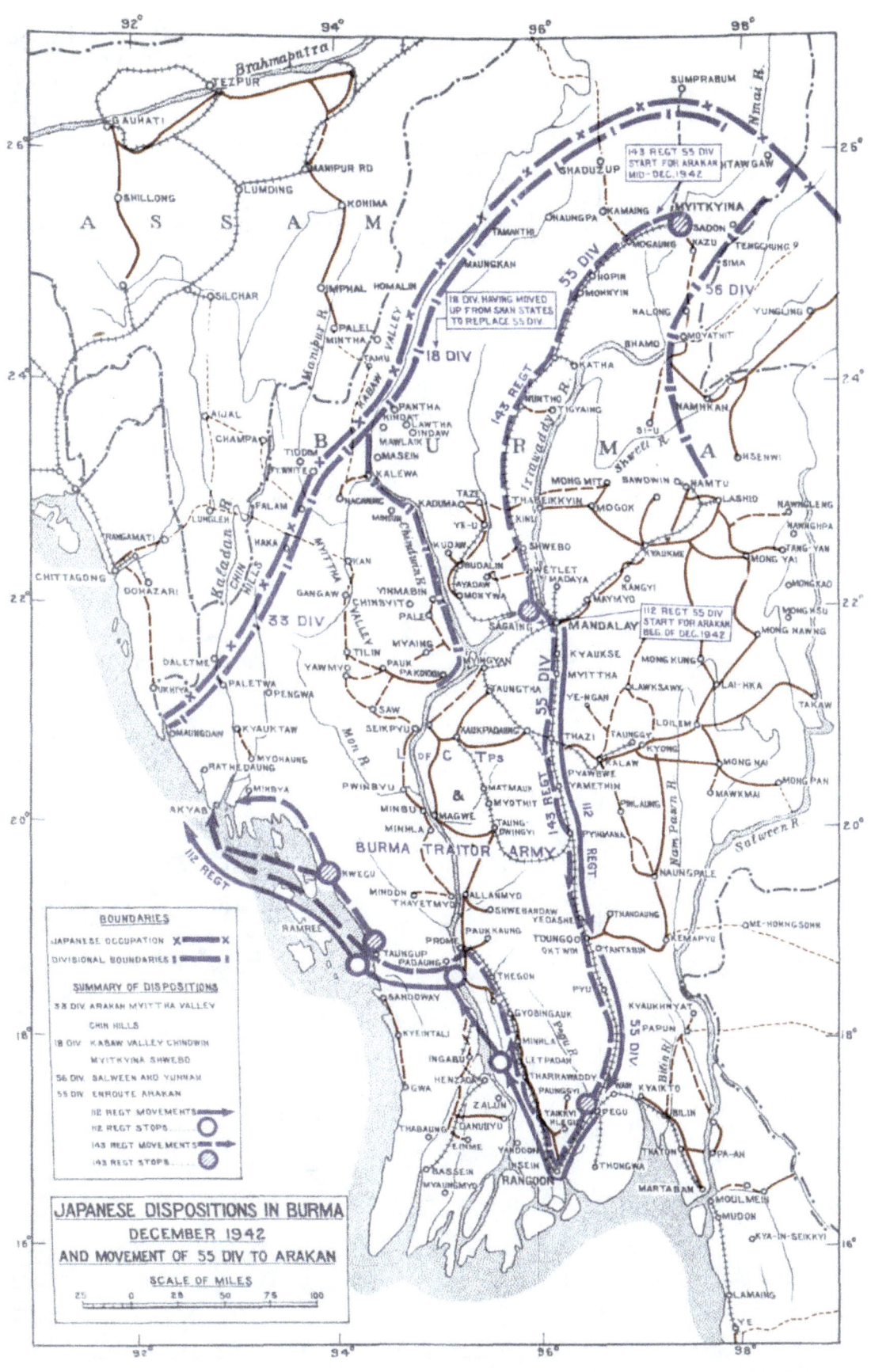

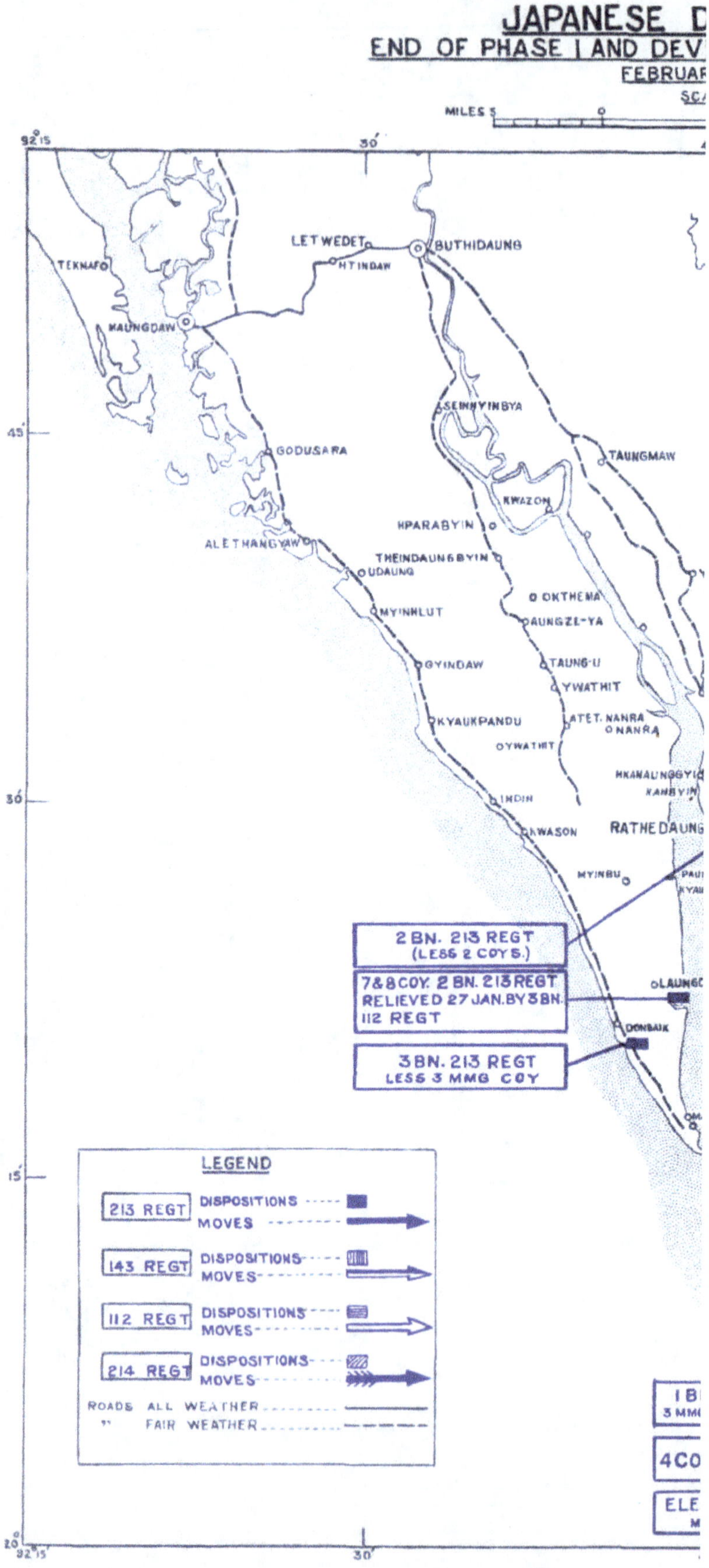
JAPANESE D
END OF PHASE I AND DEV
FEBRUAR
MILES 5 0
LETWEDET
BUTHIDAUNG
HTINDAW
TEKNAF
MAUNGDAW
SEINNYINBYA
TAUNGMAW
GODUSARA
KWAZON
HPARABYIN
ALETHANGYAW
THEINDAUNGBYIN
UDAUNG
OKTHEMA
MYINHLUT
AUNGZE-YA
GYINDAW
TAUNG-U
YWATHIT
KYAUKPANDU
ATET. NANRA
NANRA
OYWATHIT
HKANAUNGGYI
KANBYIN
INDIN
AWASON
RATHEDAUNG
MYINBU
2 BN. 213 REGT
(LESS 2 COYS.)
7&8 COY. 2 BN. 213 REGT
RELIEVED 27 JAN. BY 3 BN.
112 REGT
DONBAIK
3 BN. 213 REGT
LESS 3 MMG COY
LEGEND
213 REGT DISPOSITIONS
MOVES
143 REGT DISPOSITIONS
MOVES
112 REGT DISPOSITIONS
MOVES
214 REGT DISPOSITIONS
MOVES
ROADS ALL WEATHER
" FAIR WEATHER
4CO
ELE

DISPOSITIONS
DEVELOPMENT OF PHASE 2
...RY 1943

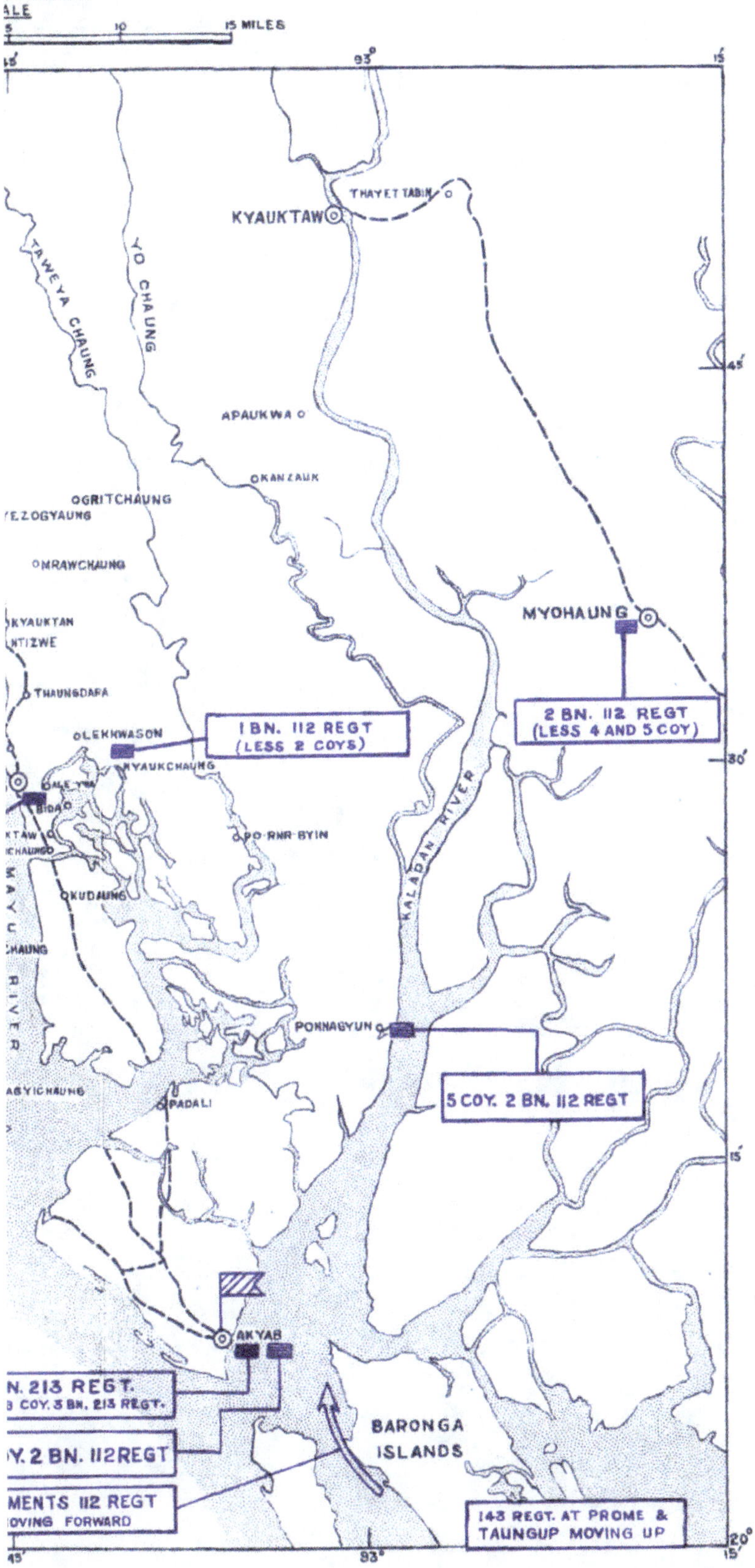

0   5   10   15 MILES

- THAYETTABIN
- KYAUKTAW
- TAWEYA CHAUNG
- YO CHAUNG
- APAUKWA
- OKANZAUK
- OGRITCHAUNG
- YEZOGYAUNG
- OMRAWCHAUNG
- KYAUKTAN
- NTIZWE
- THAUNGDARA
- OLEKKWASON
- KYAUKCHAUNG
- DALE TAW
- BIDAO
- KTAW
- CHAUNGO
- OKUDAUNG
- PO RWR BYIN
- MYOHAUNG
- MAYU RIVER
- KALADAN RIVER
- AGYICHAUNG
- PADALI
- PONNAGYUN
- AKYAB
- BARONGA ISLANDS

1 BN. 112 REGT (LESS 2 COYS)

2 BN. 112 REGT (LESS 4 AND 5 COY)

5 COY. 2 BN. 112 REGT

...N. 213 REGT.
... COY, 3 BN. 213 REGT.

...Y. 2 BN. 112 REGT

...MENTS 112 REGT
...OVING FORWARD

143 REGT. AT PROME & TAUNGUP MOVING UP

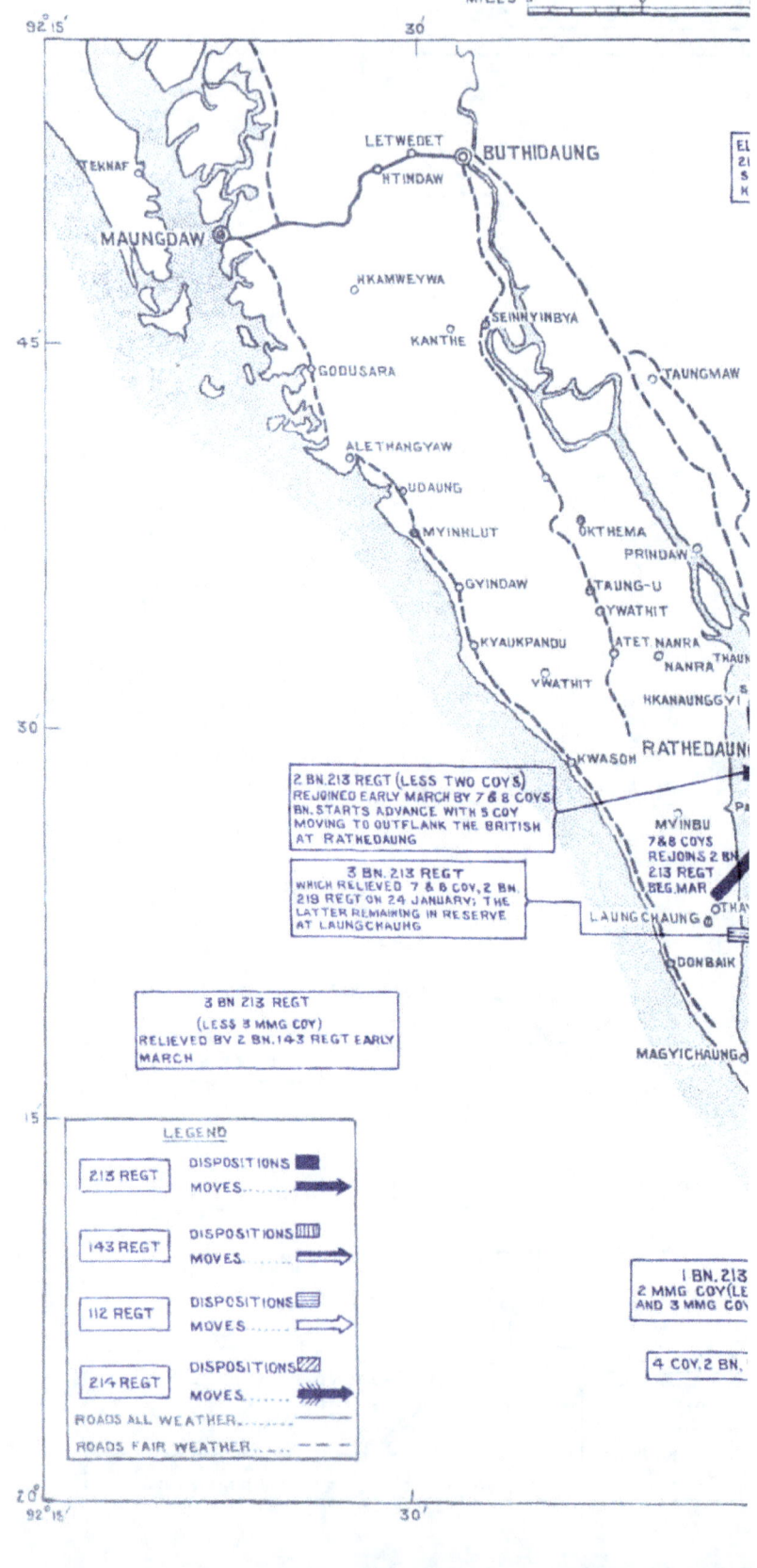

DISPOSITIONS
[D]EVELOPMENT IN PHASE 3
[MA]RCH 1943

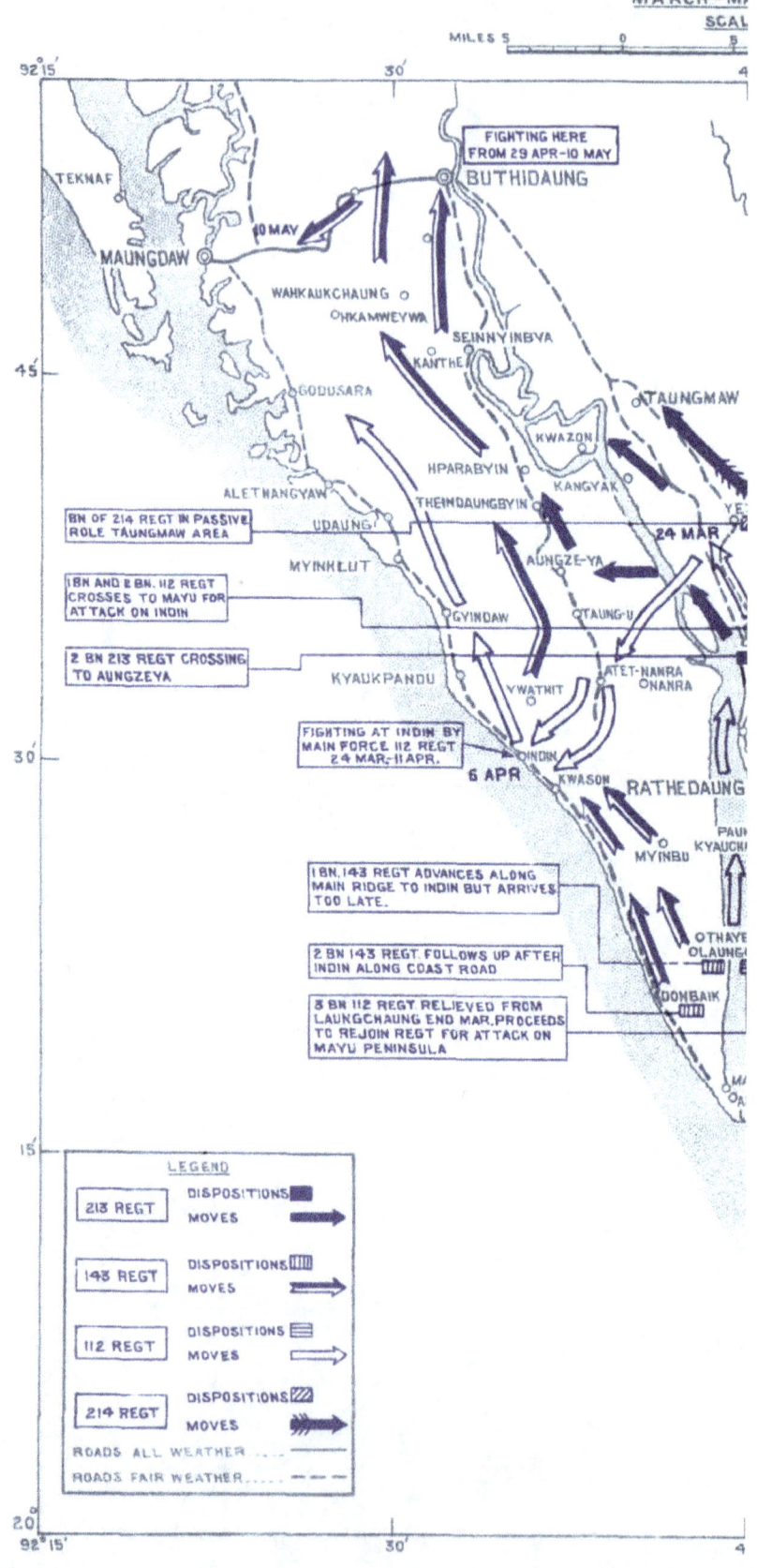

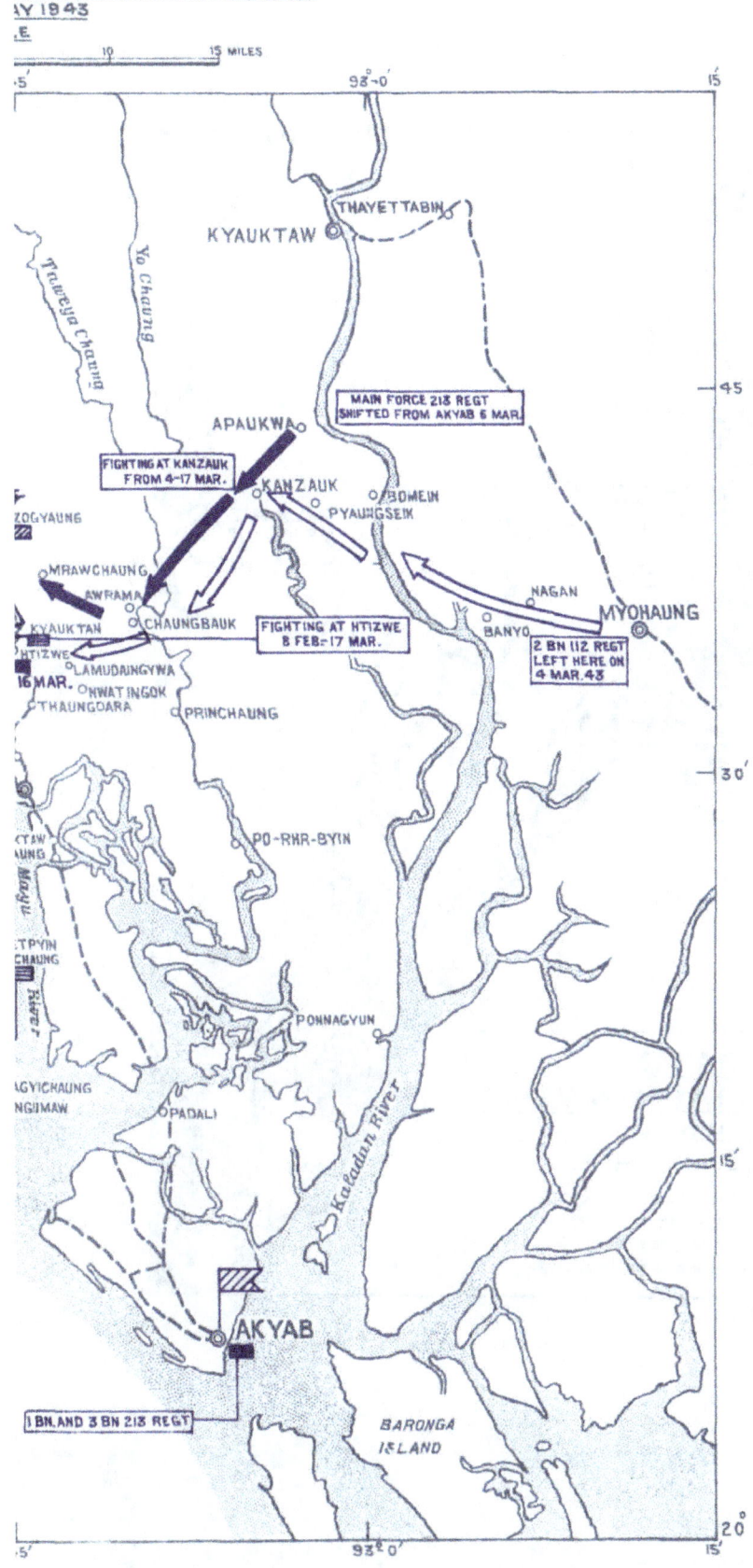

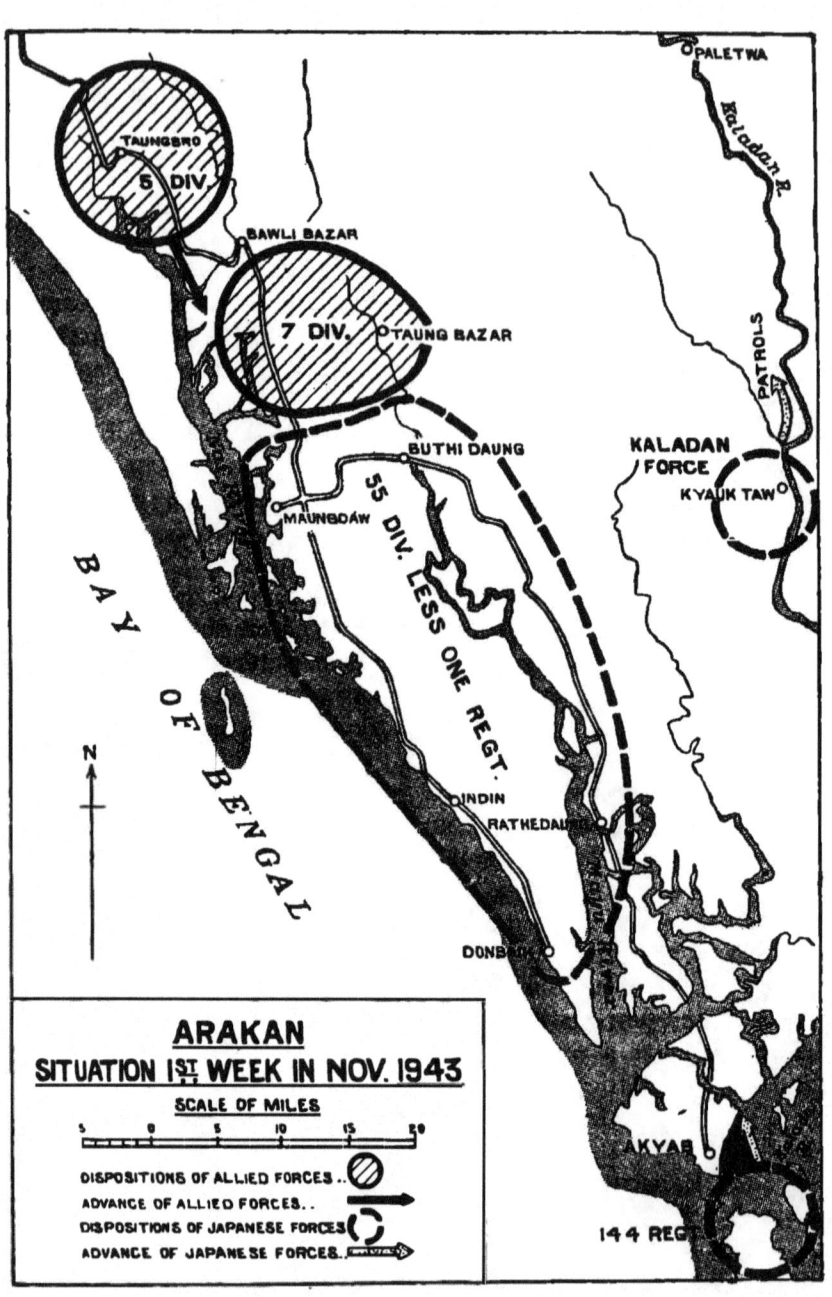

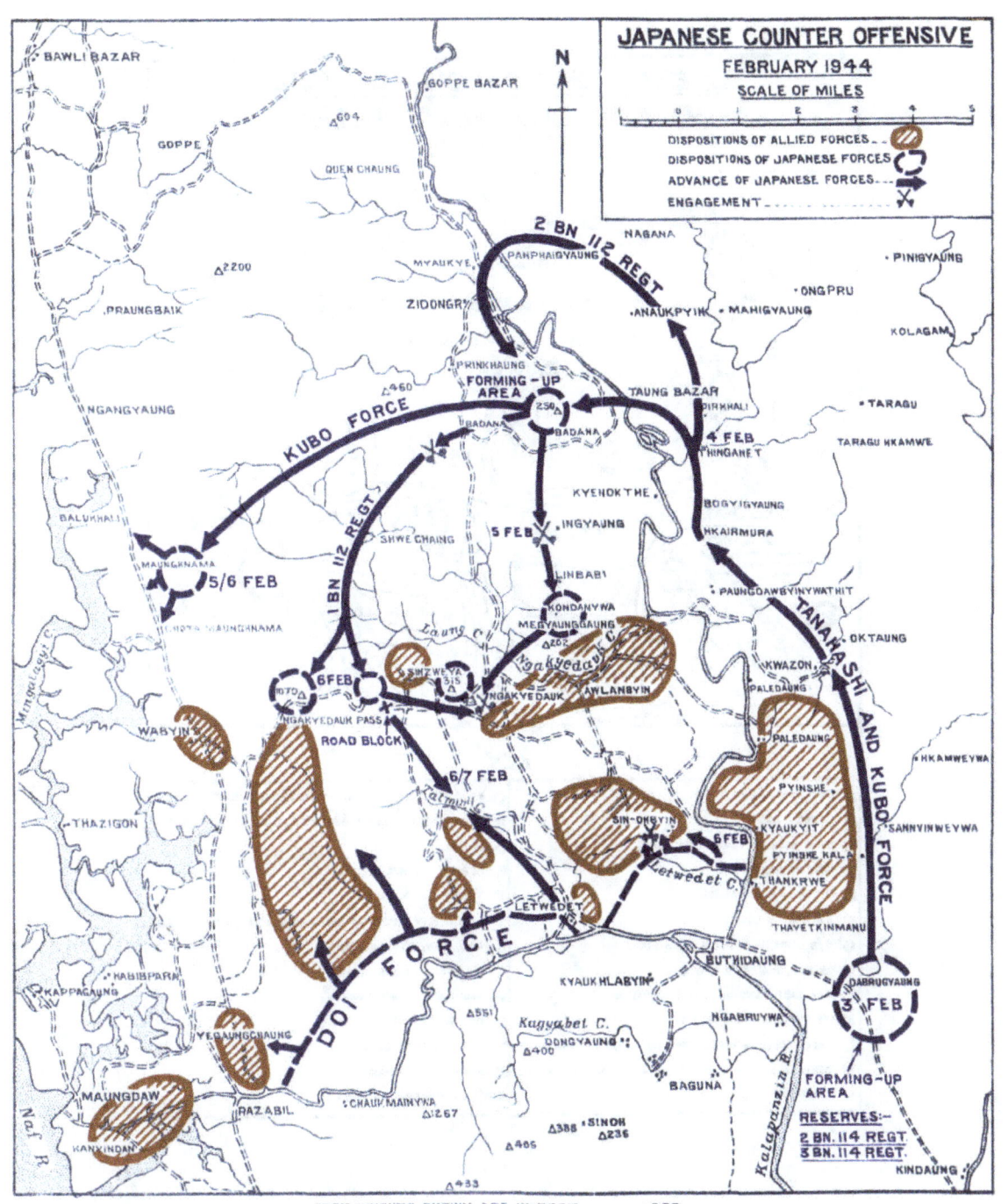

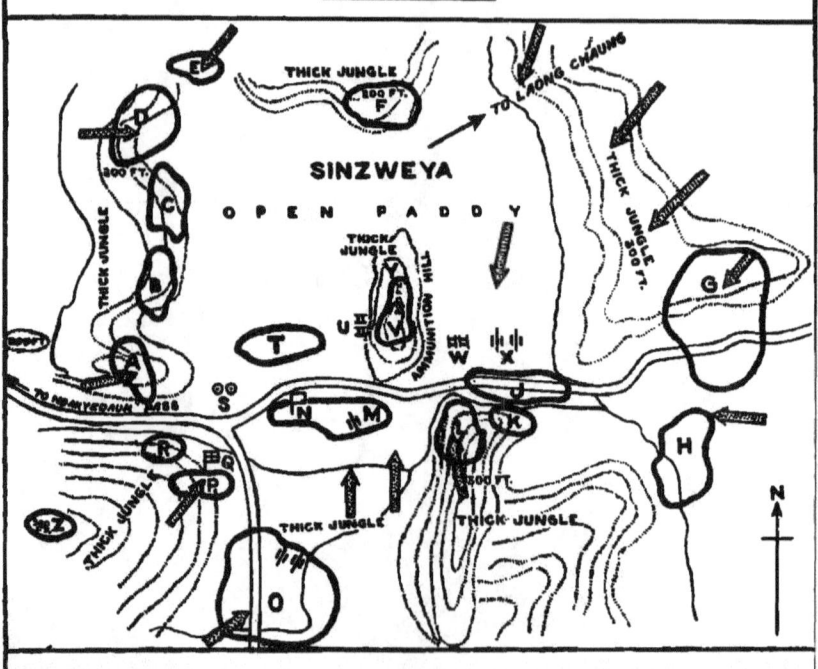

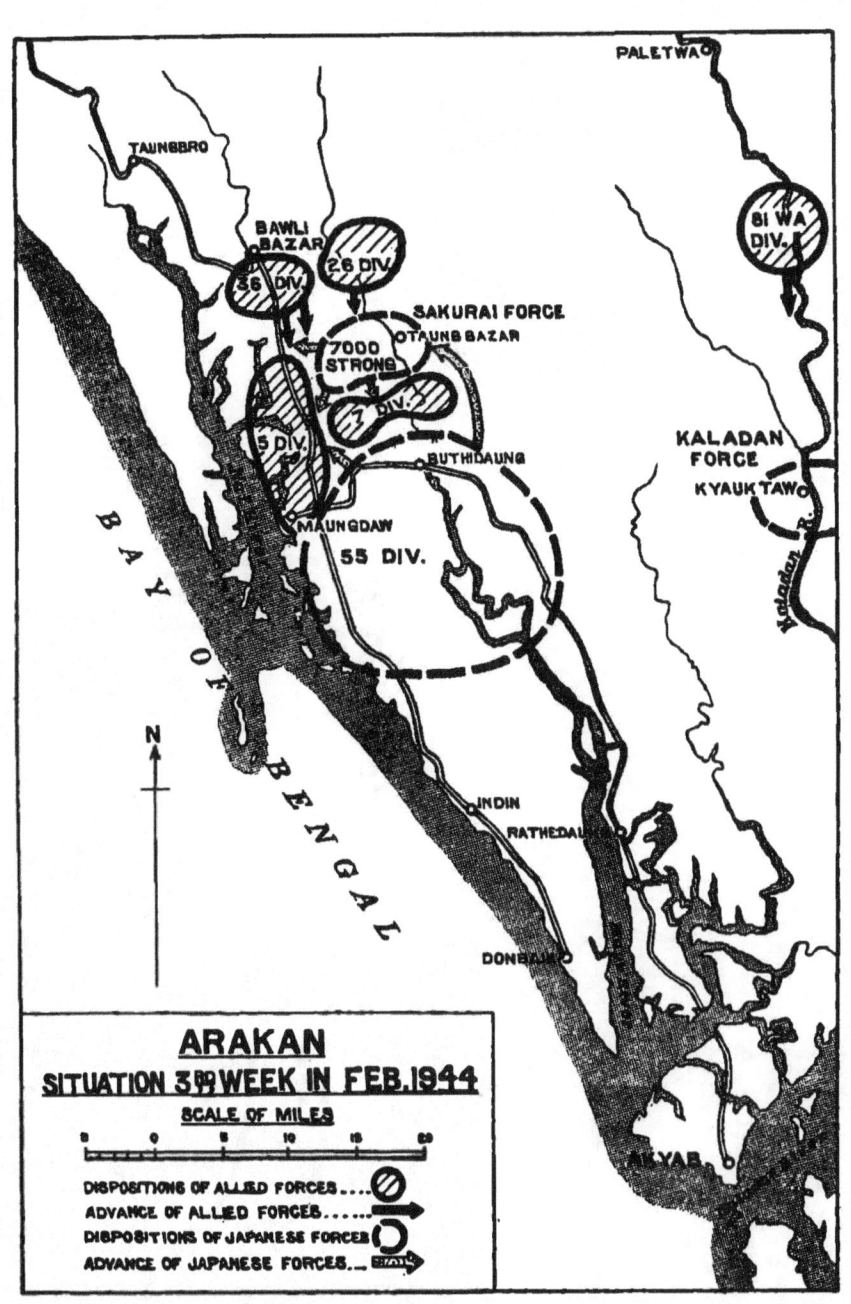

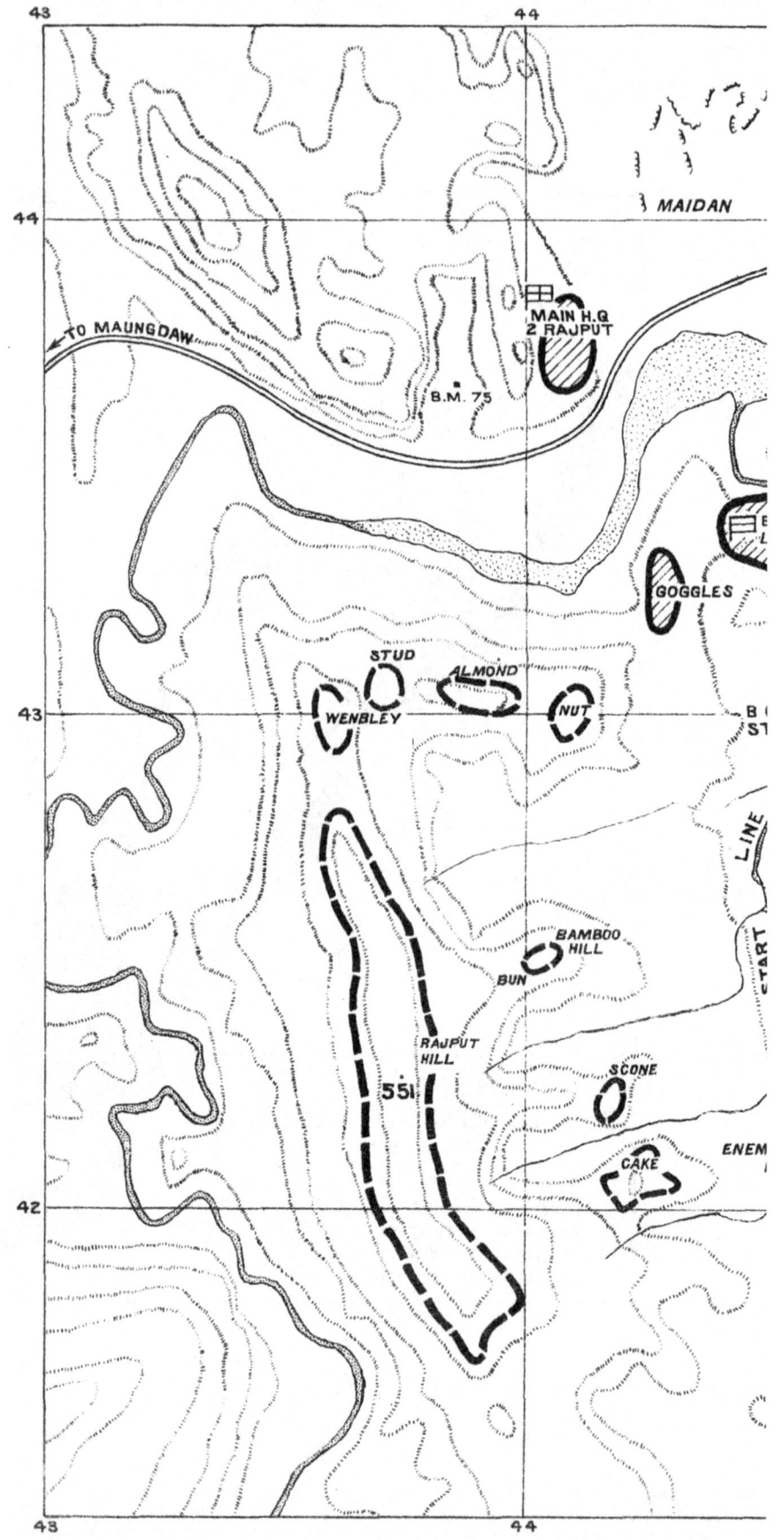

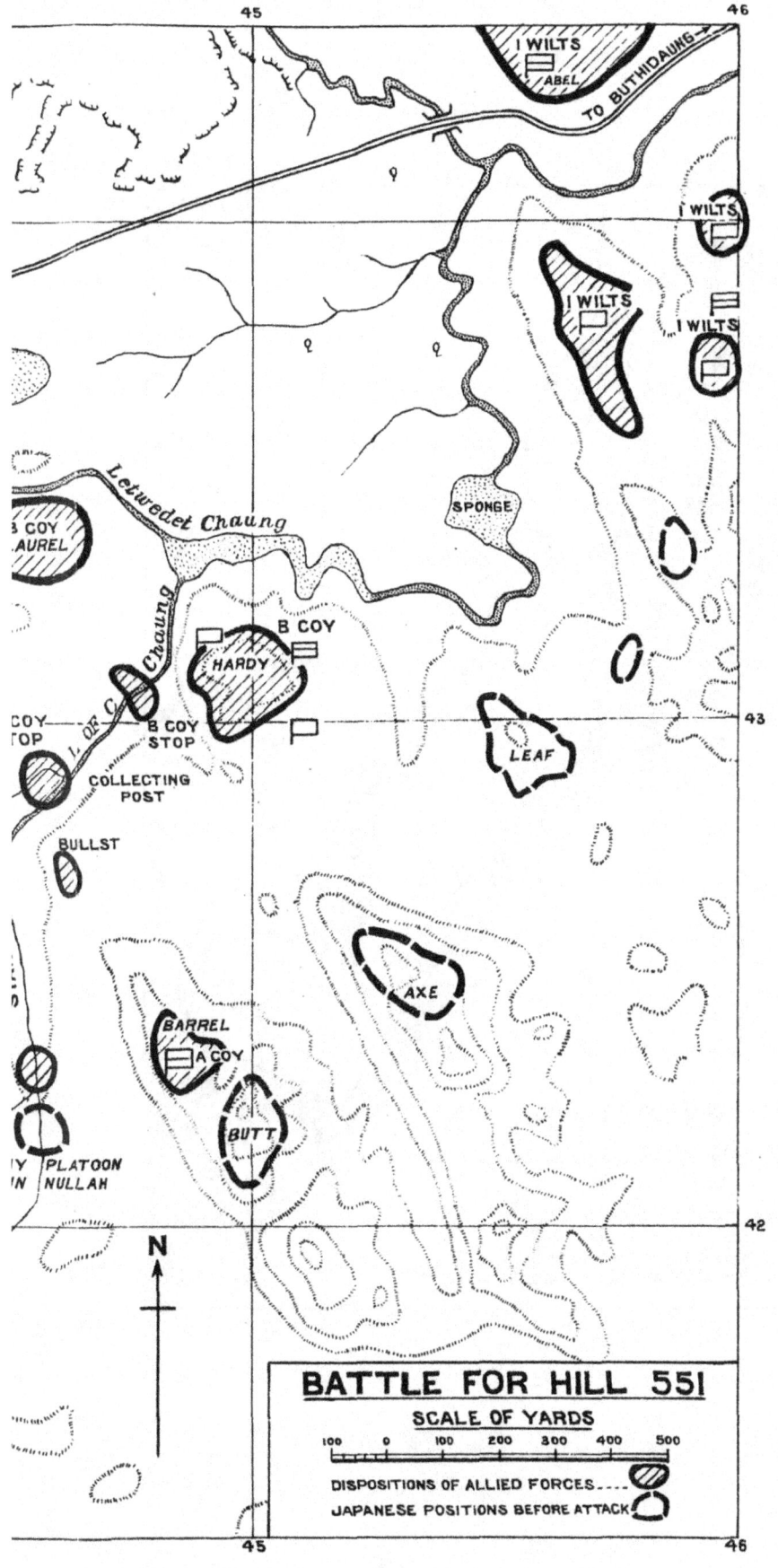

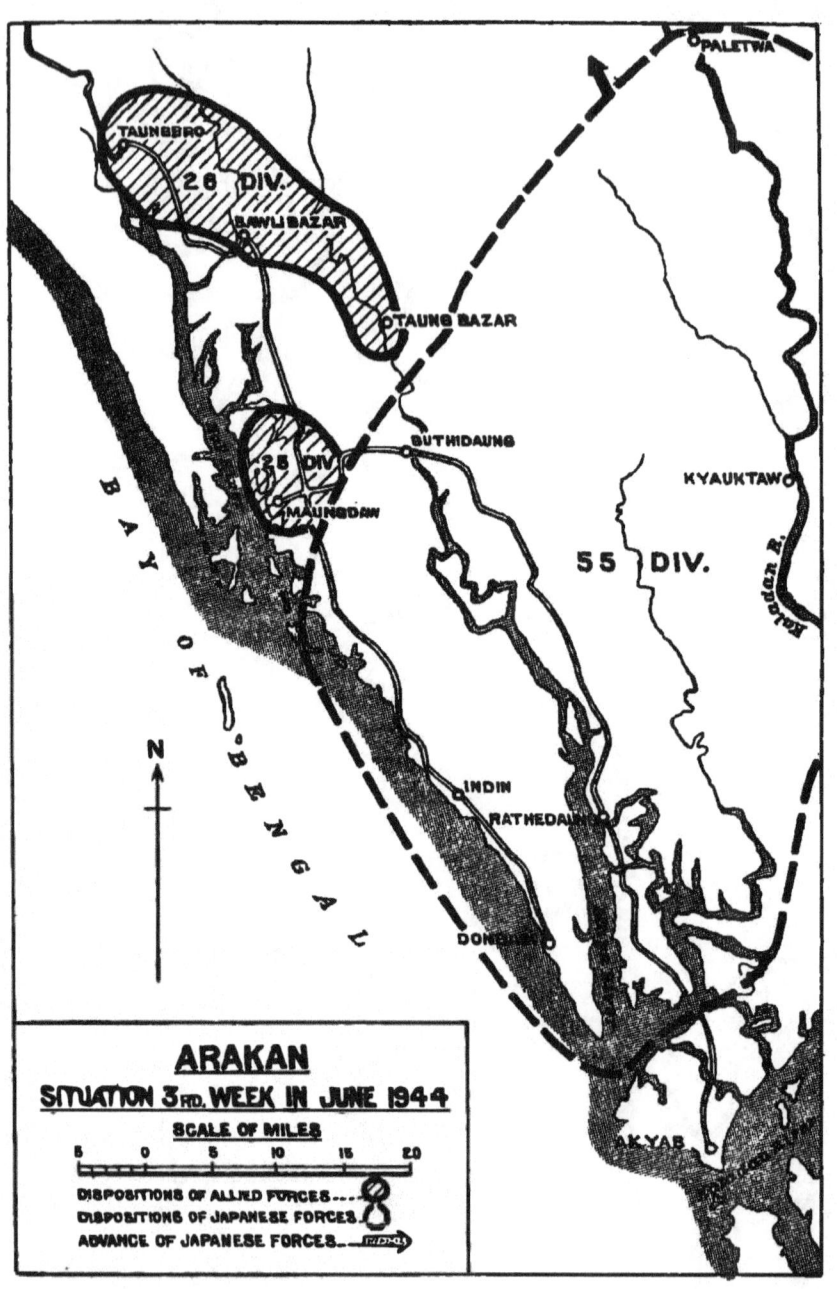

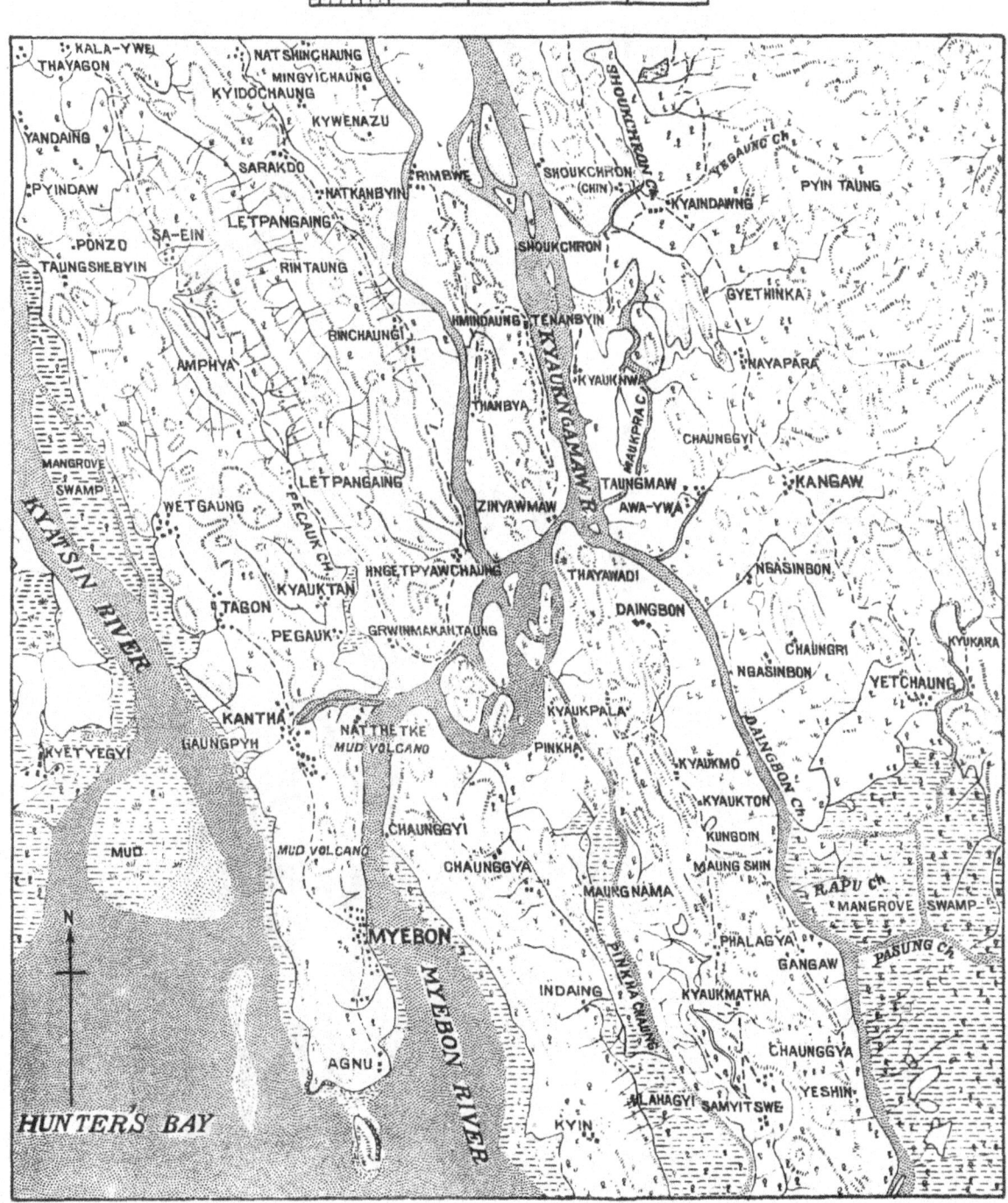

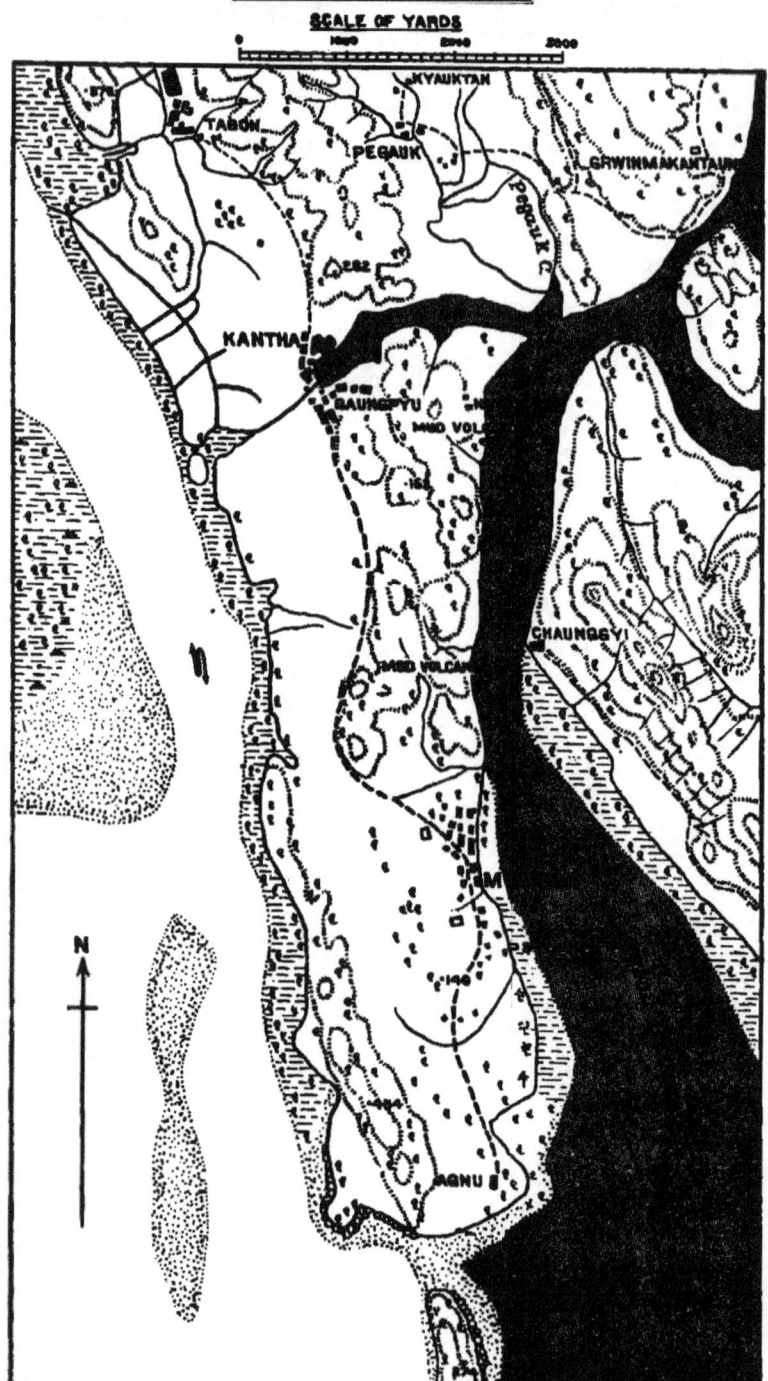

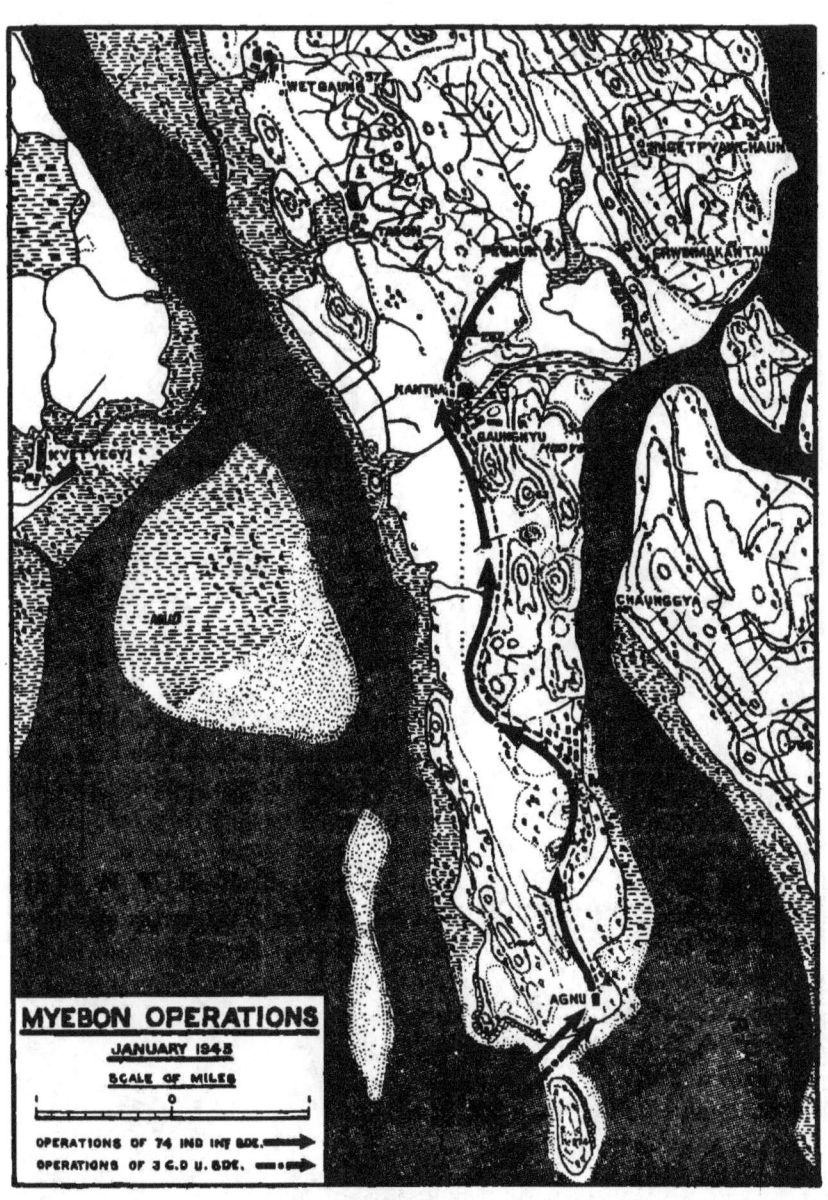

KANGAW AREA
SCALE OF MILES

SPOT HEIGHTS SHOWN ARE IN FEET...... ·148

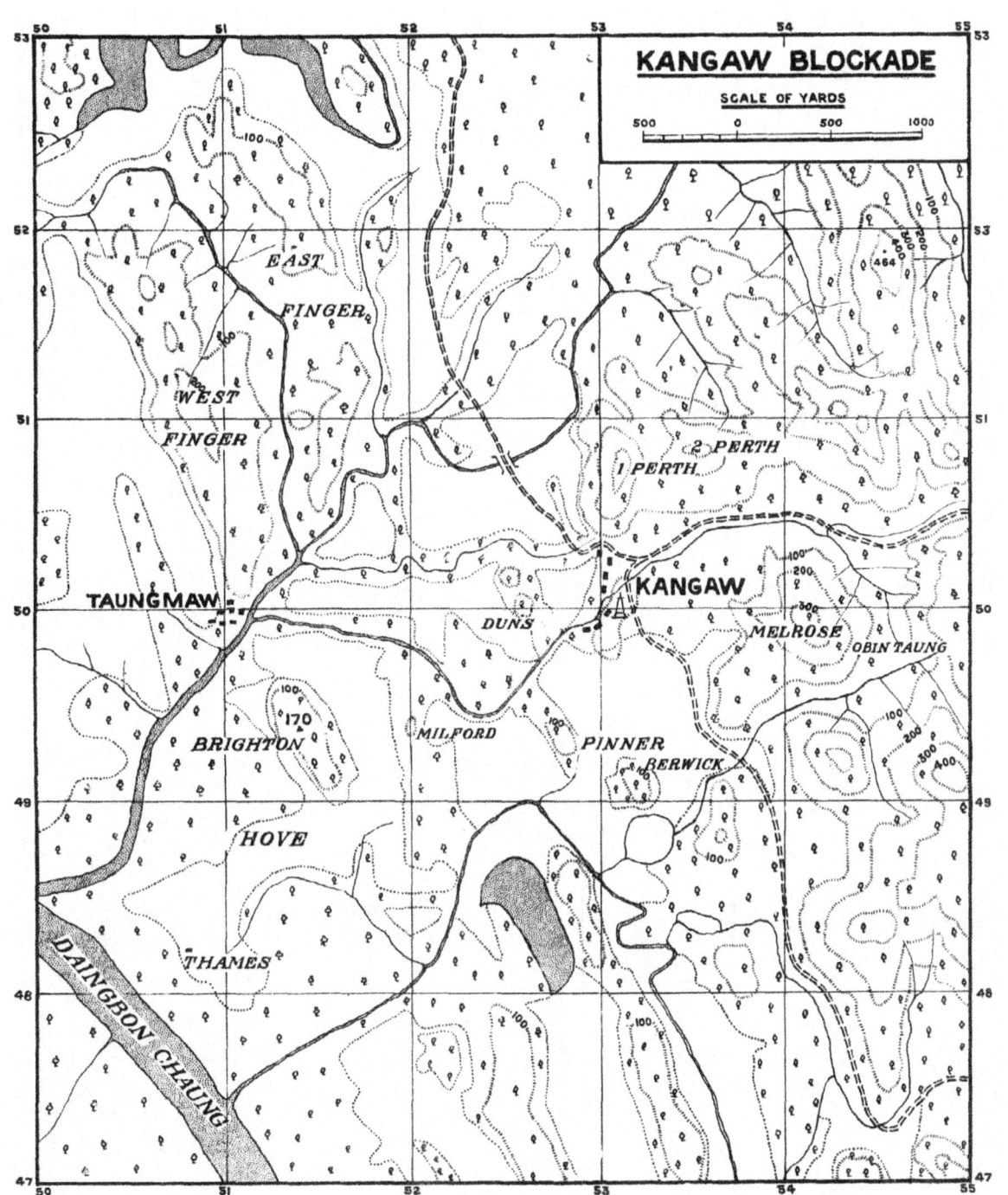

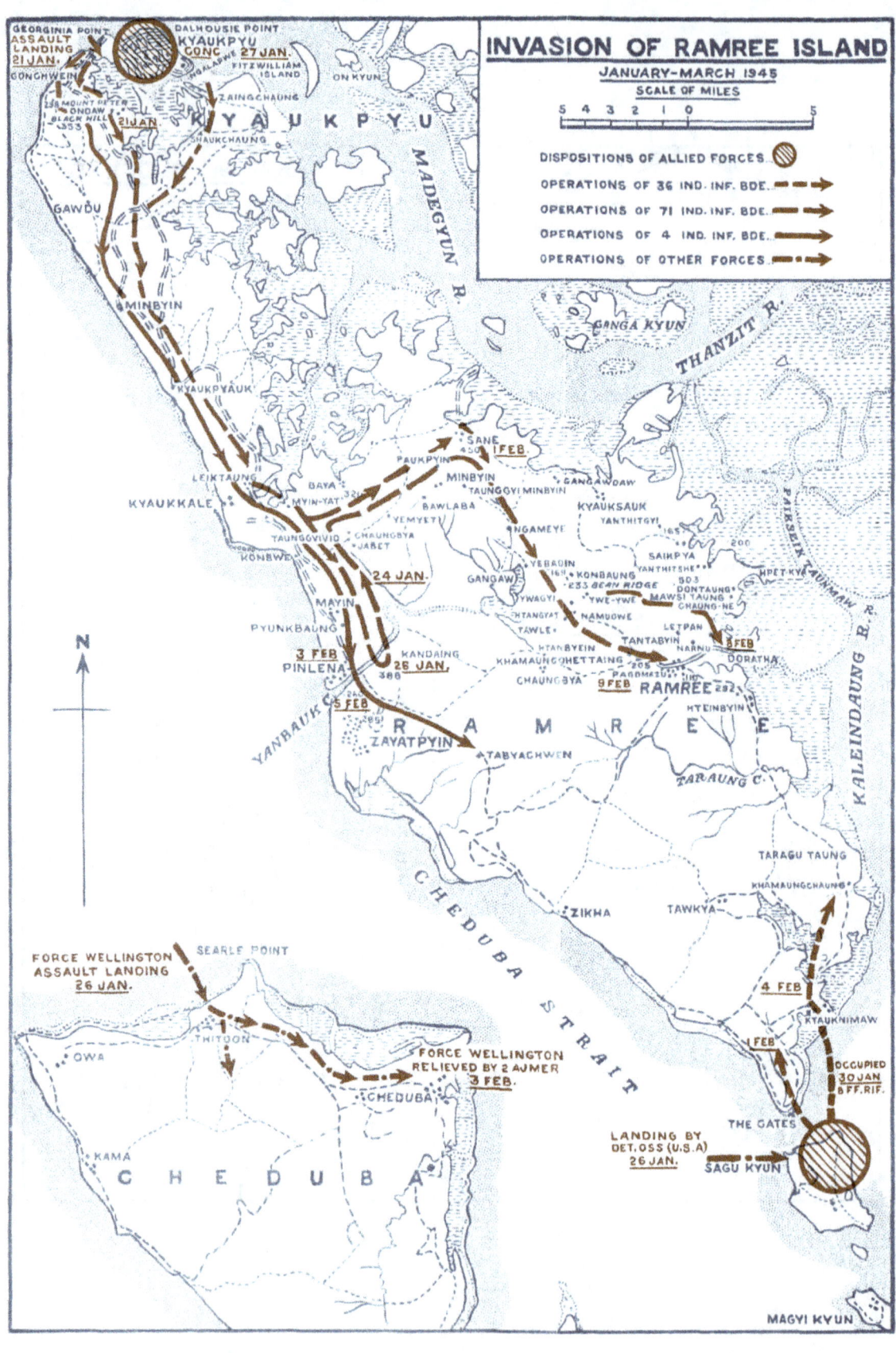

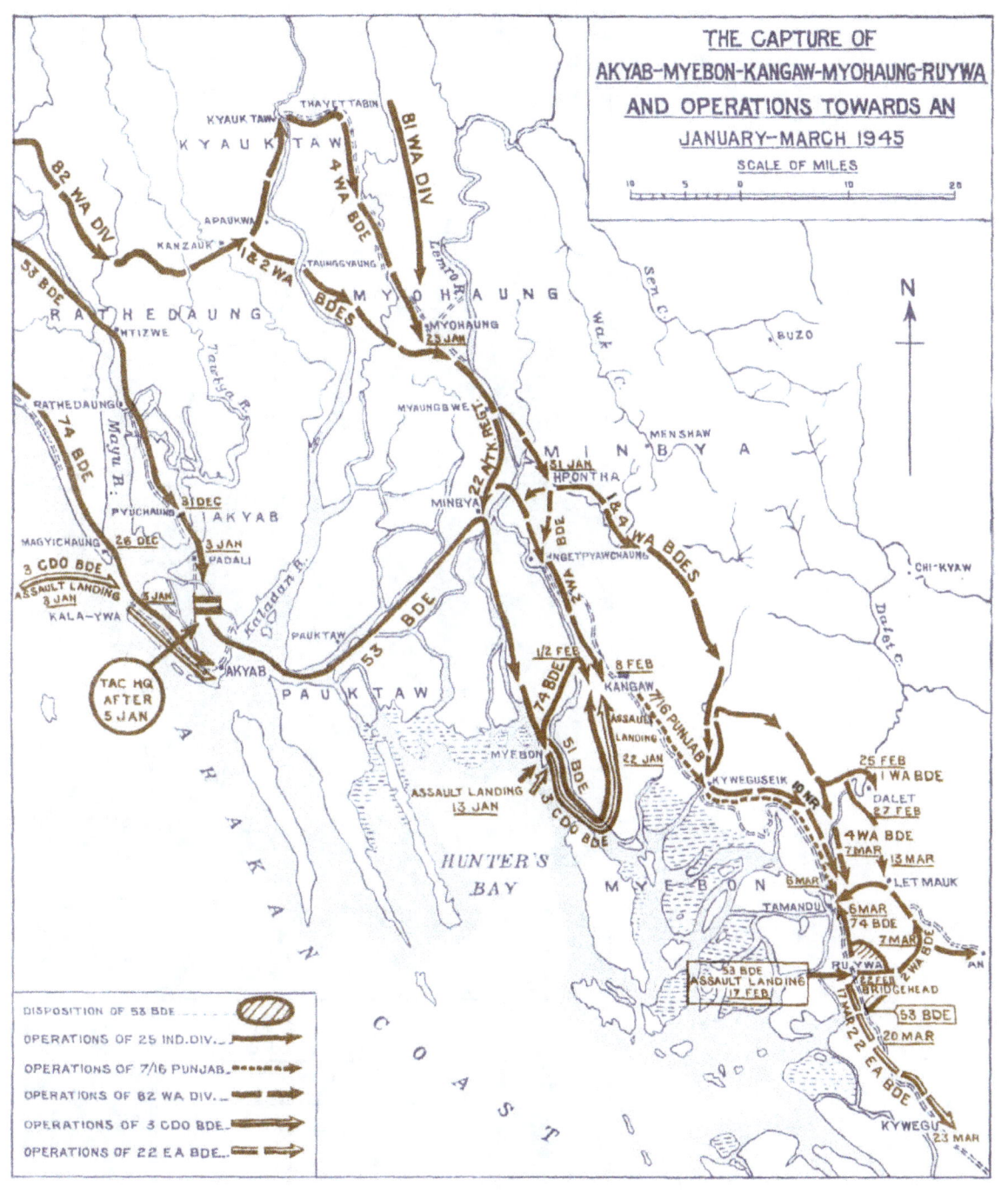

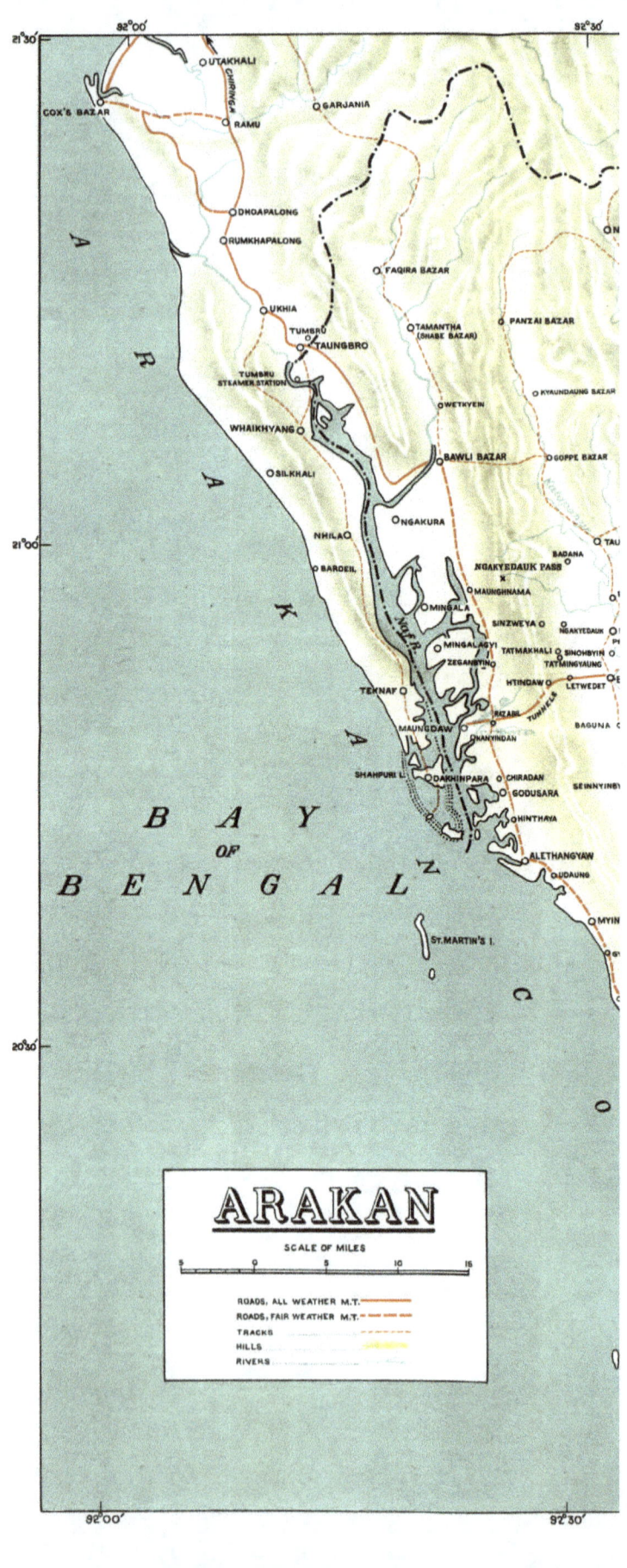

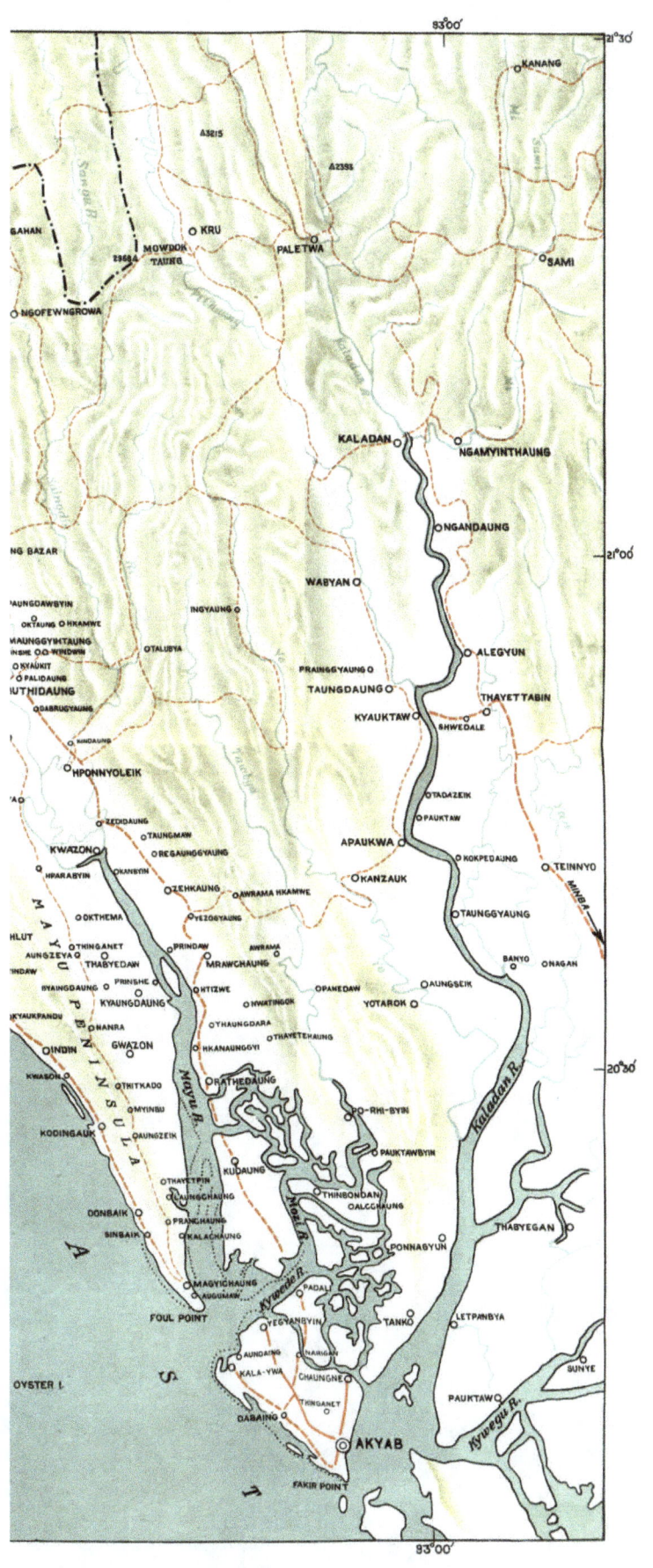

OFFICIAL HISTORY OF THE INDIAN ARMED FORCES
IN THE SECOND WORLD WAR
1939-45

Campaigns in the Eastern Theatre

THE RETREAT FROM BURMA
1941-42

Maps and Sketches

The Retreat from Burma 1941–42
List of Maps

1. Rainfall in Burma. Mid-May to mid-October
2. Dispositions of troops for defence of Central Burma and Tenasserim area. December, 1941
3. Action at Tavoy. 13-19 January, 1942
4. Brigade area of responsibility. 1 February, 1942
5. Dispositions of forces. 5-9 February, 1942
6. Dispositions of forces defending Bilin river line. 15-16 February, 1942
7. Retreat from Rangoon. 7-10 March, 1942
8. Operations in the Shan States and withdrawal of 1 Burma Division. 23 February-24 March, 1942
9. 1 Burcorps defence zone. 10-14 March, 1942
10. Dispositions 1 Burcorps. 28 March, 1942
11. 1 Burcorps counter offensive plan (Phase 1). 29 March, 1942
12. Minhla-Taungdwingyi area. Dispositions of 1 Burcorps. 9 April, 1942
13. Japanese thrust to the oilfields. 8-10 April, 1942
14. Yin Chaung dispositions. 14-16 April, 1942
15. Situation on 26 April, 1942 following Japanese break-through in Shan States
16. Battle of Monywa. 30 April-2 May, 1942
17. Kalemyo, Kalewa & Tamu area. Route of withdrawal of Allied Forces. 5-11 May, 1942
18. Action at Shwegyin. 9-11 May, 1942
19. The Japanese Advance from Mawchi to Myitkyina. April-May, 1942
20. Dispositions on Chinese Front. 5 April. 1942
21. Japanese advance and withdrawal of Indian forces. 1-4 May, 1942
22. Sketch of Martaban from Akyab
23. South-west Pacific & South-east Asia. Showing extent of Japanese occupation

24. Tenasserim-Siam Area. Showing routes of Japanese attack. 27 November to 28 December, 1941
25. Map of Mayawadi-Kawkareik area. Operations of 16 Ind Inf Bde. 20-25 January, 1942
26. Defence of Moulmein. 26-29 January, 1942
27. Moulmein Town and Environs. Operations of 2 Burma Brigade. 30-31 January, 1942
28. Operations Kuzeik-Duyinzeik-Thaton. 11-13 February, 1942
29. Withdrawal from Ouyinzeik-Thaton. 14-15 February, 1942
30. Operations in Danyingon. 16-17 February, 1942
31. Withdrawal from Bilin line. 20 February, 1942
32. Pegu dispositions on 5 March, 1942. Operations by 17 Div & 7 Armoured Bde in Waw area
33. Defence of Pegu by 48 Ind Inf Bde. 5 March, 1942
34. Action at Shwedaung. 29-30 March, 1942
35. Prome dispositions. 29 March-2 April, 1942
36. Kokkogwa-Thadodan. Operations of 48 Bde and 7 Armoured Bde. 11-14 April, 1942
37. Action by 1 Burma Div. 9-13 April, 1941
38. Operations in the Yenangyaung area. 16-17 April, 1942
39. Yenangyaung and Environs. Operations of 1 Burma Div., 7 Armoured Bde and Chinese 38 Div. 18-19 April, 1942
40. Battle of Kyaukse
41. Burma. Showing geographical details of mountains. rivers, communications, ports, airfields, mines and oil wells etc.

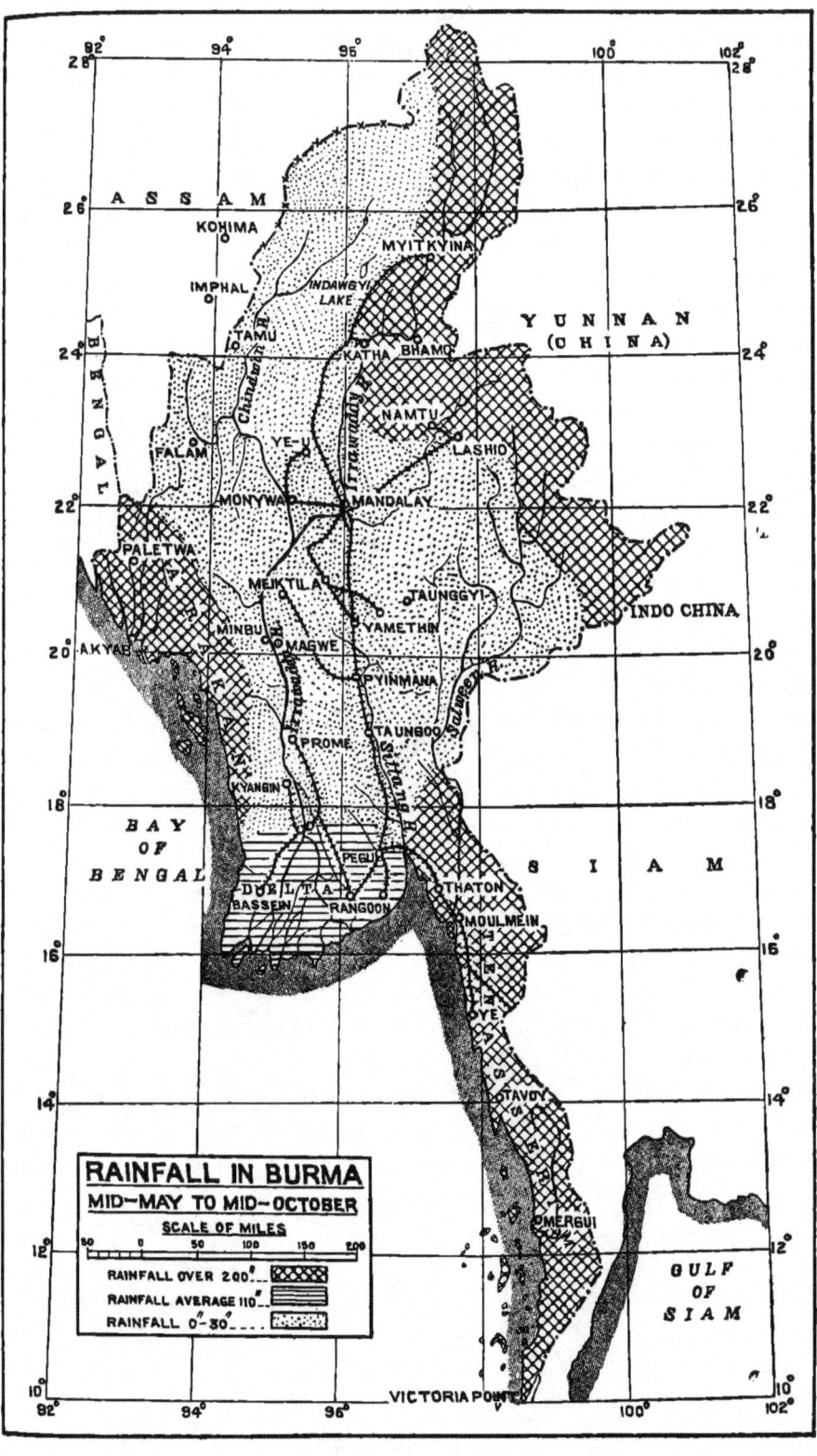

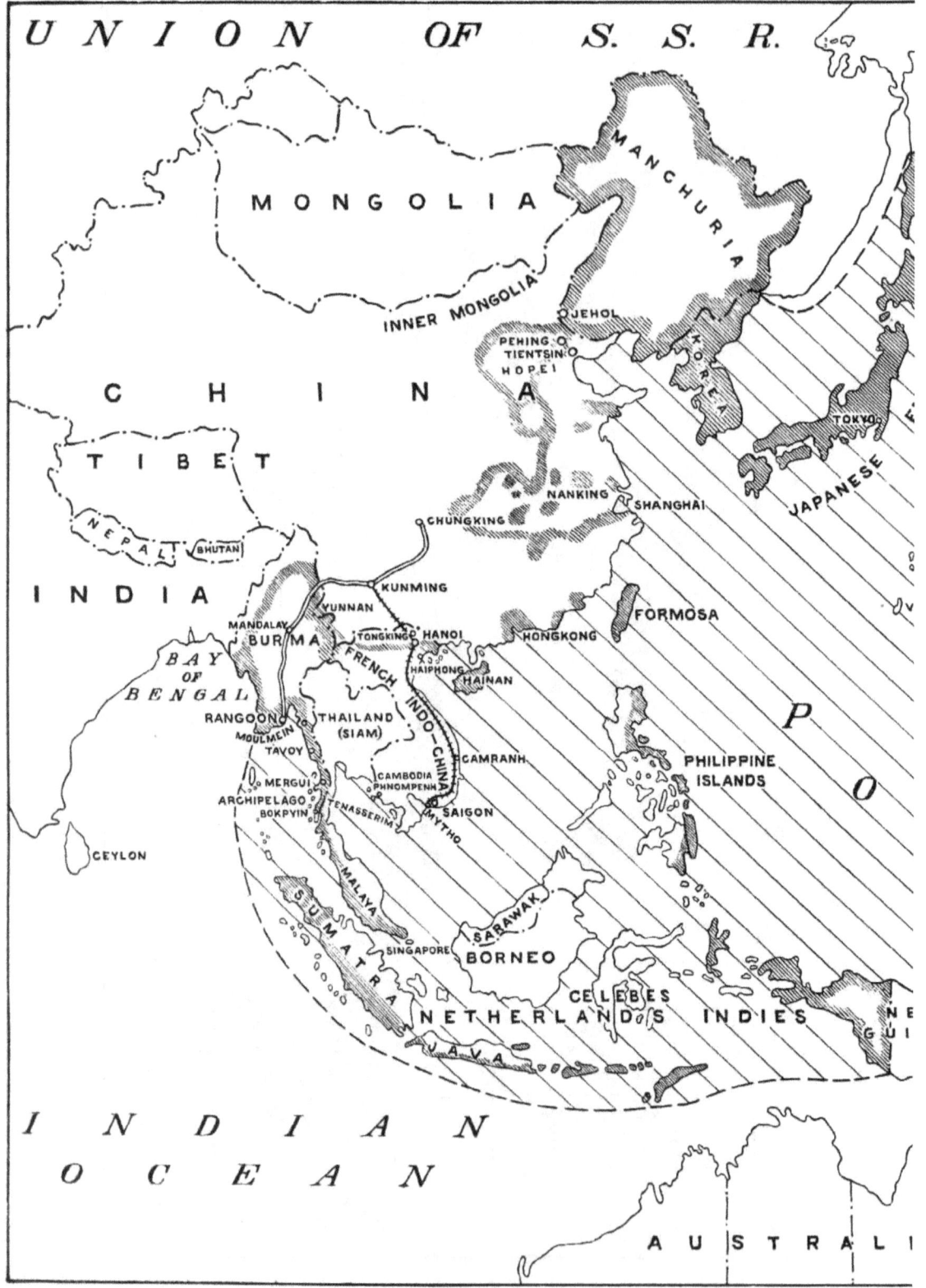

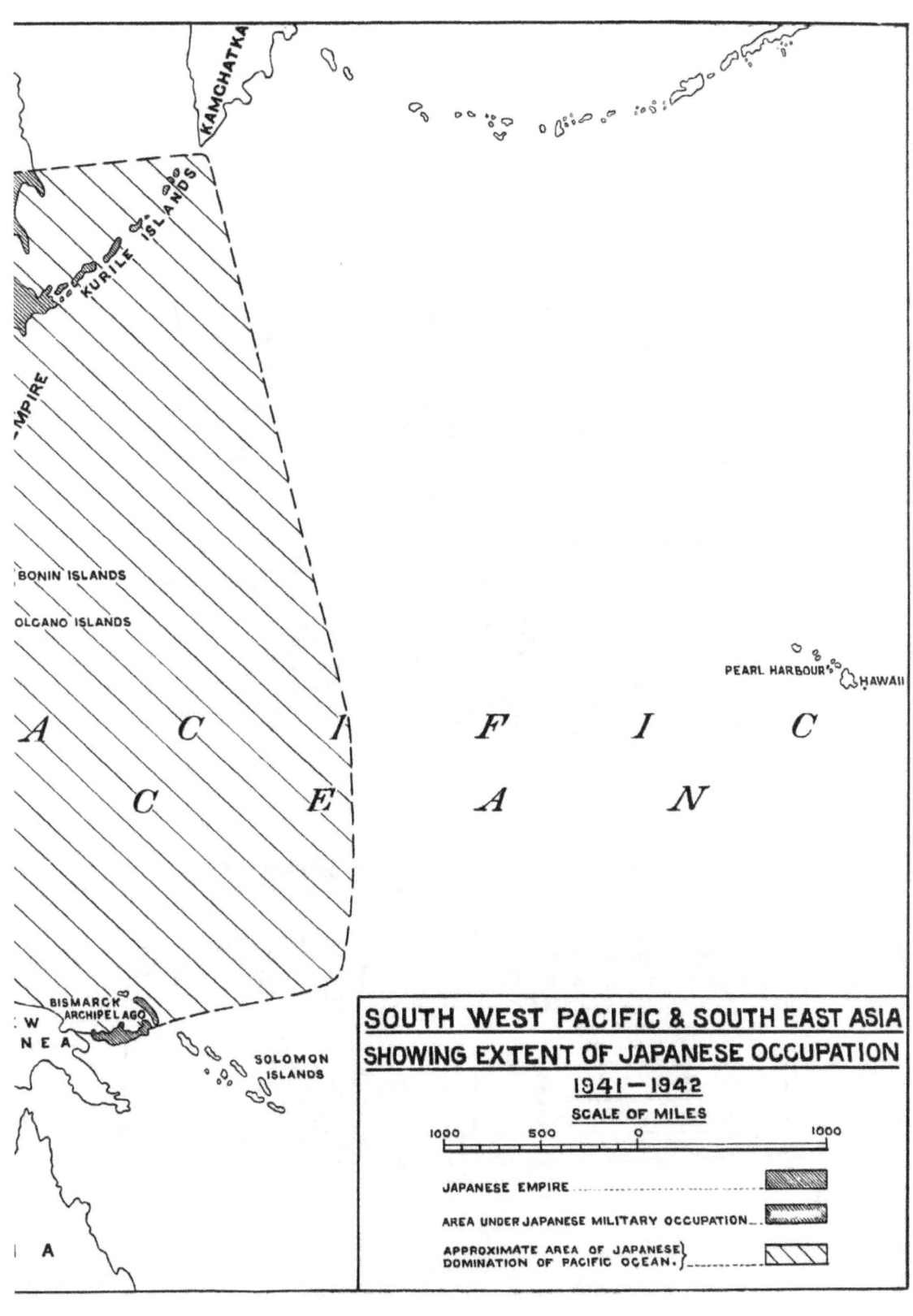

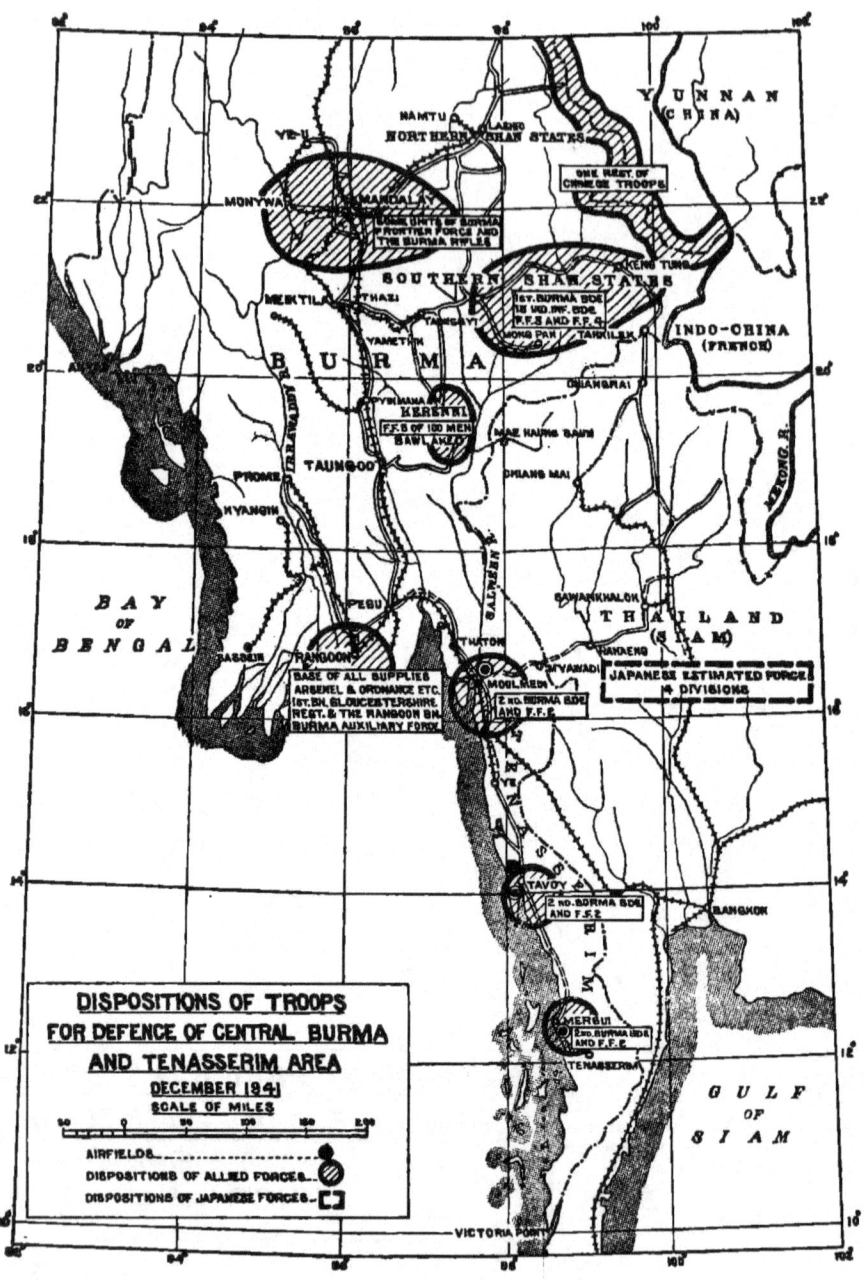

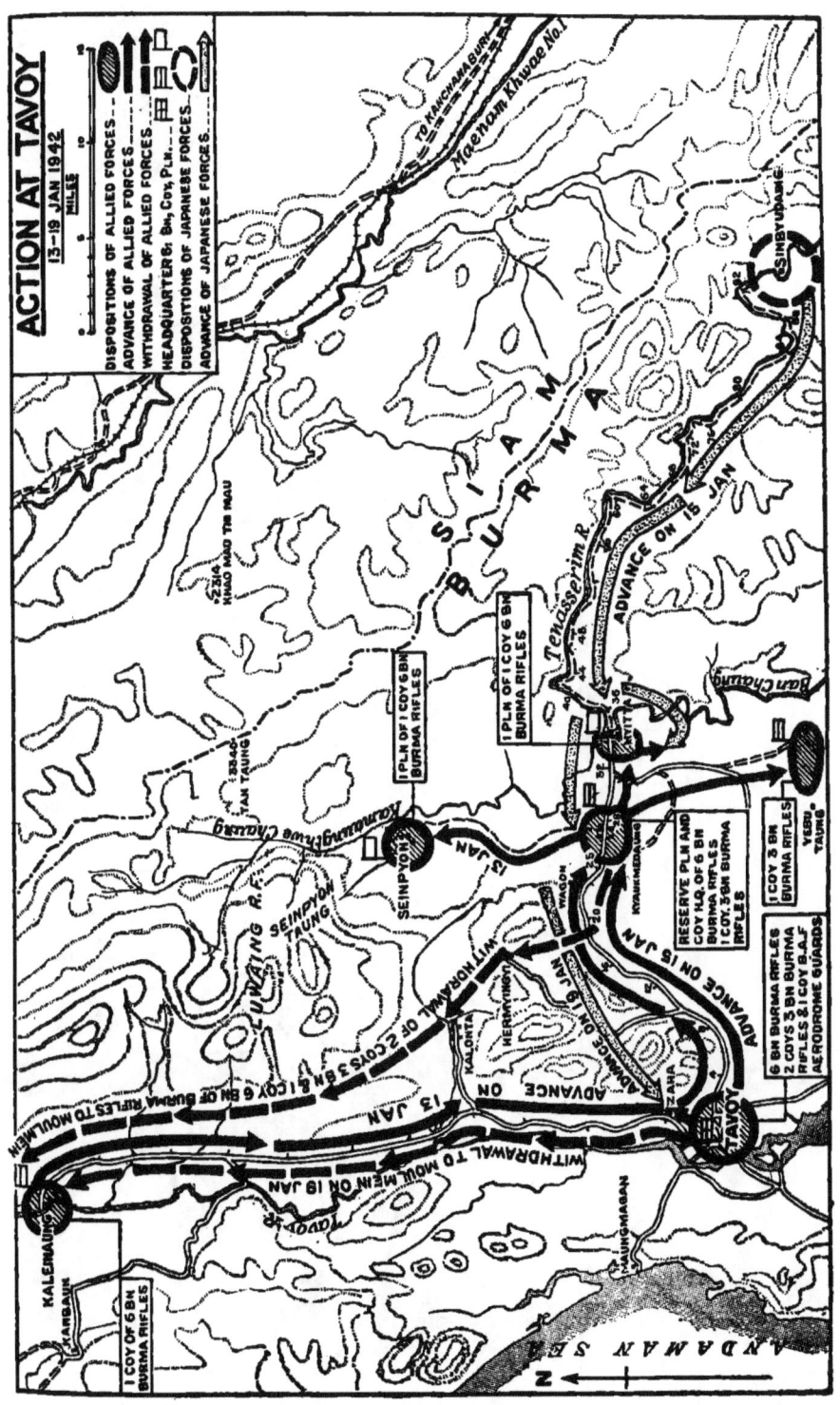

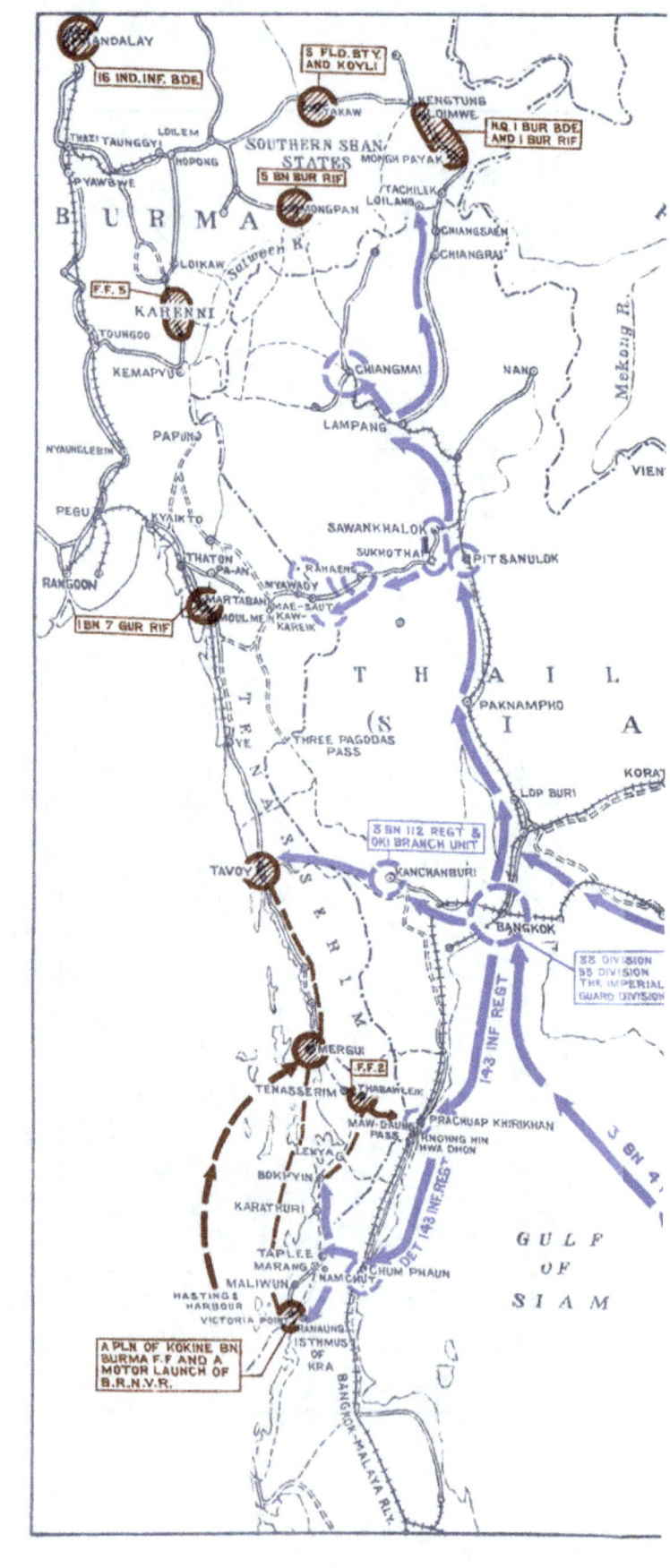

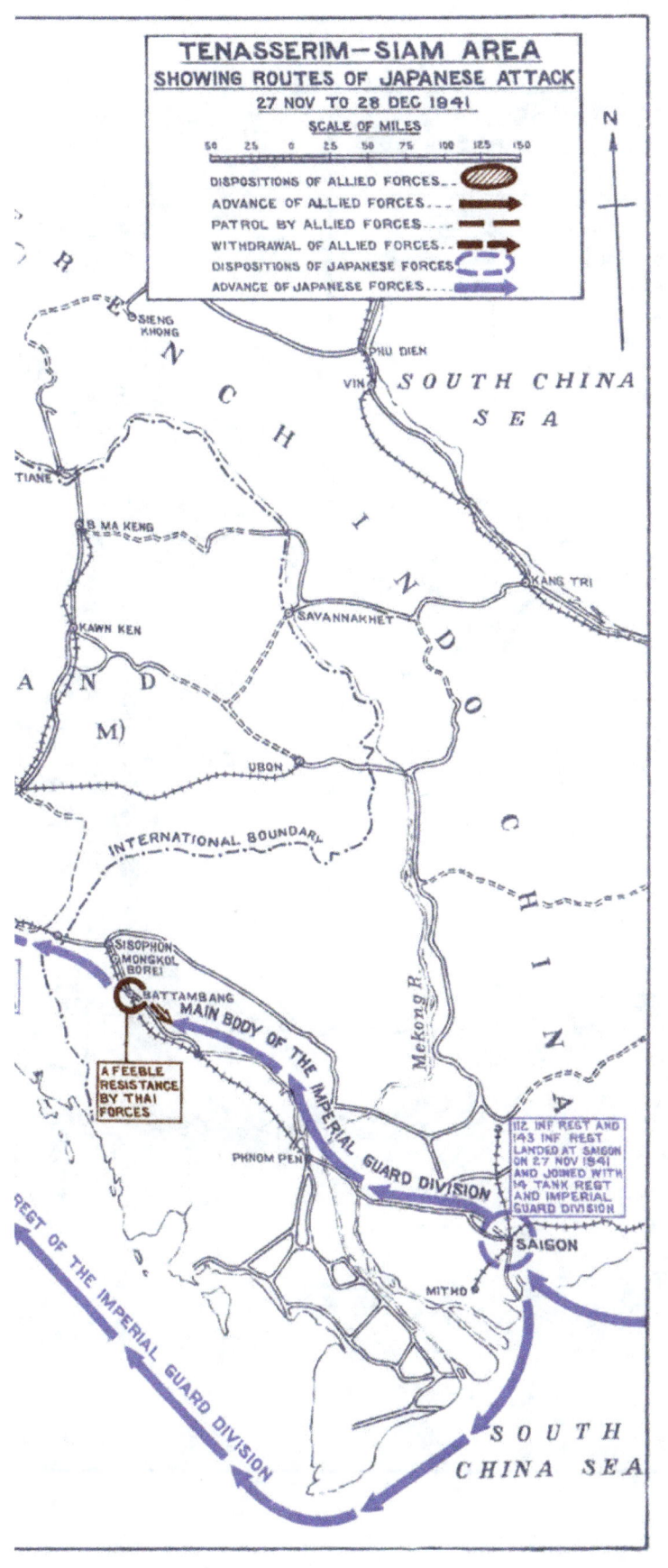

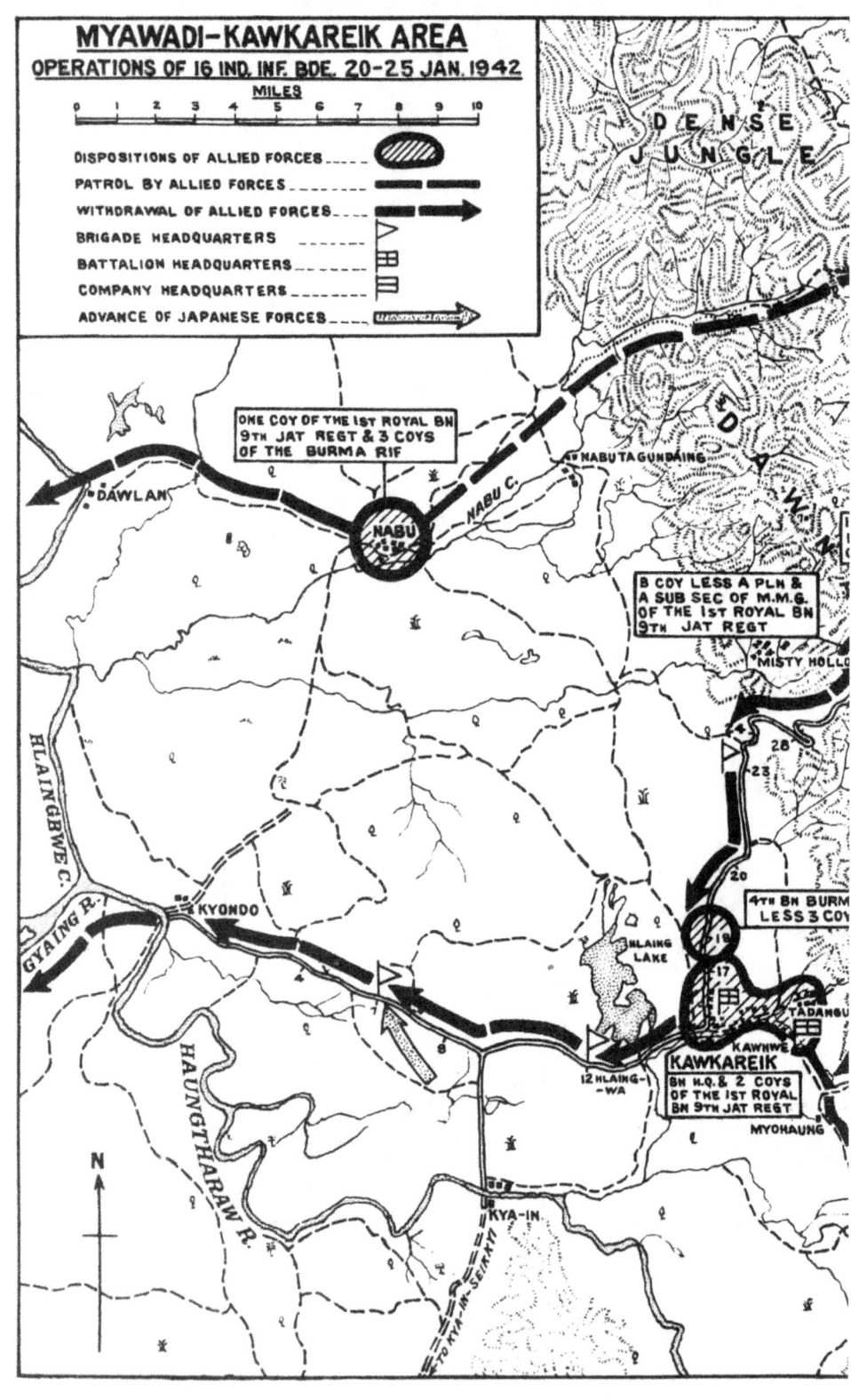

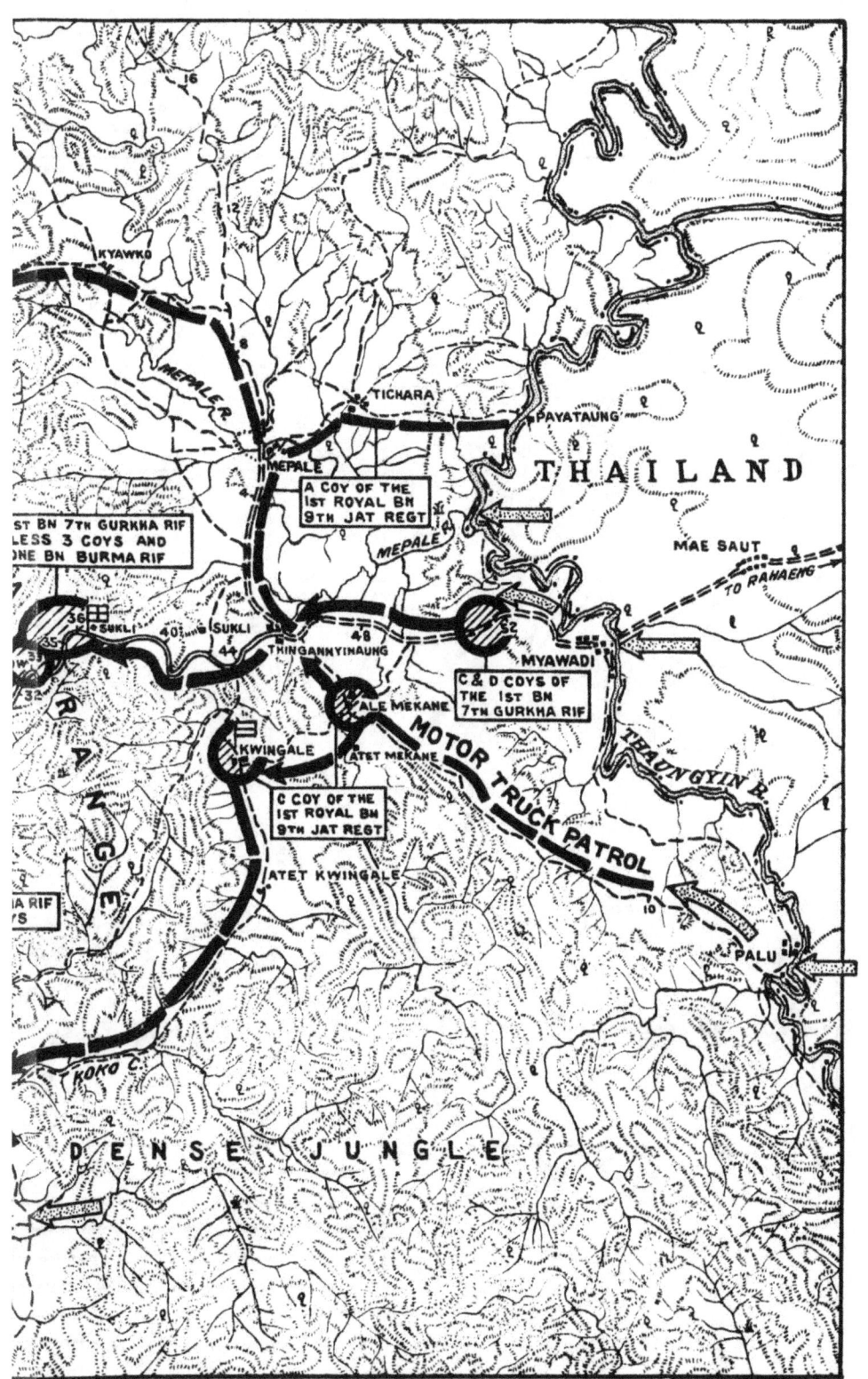

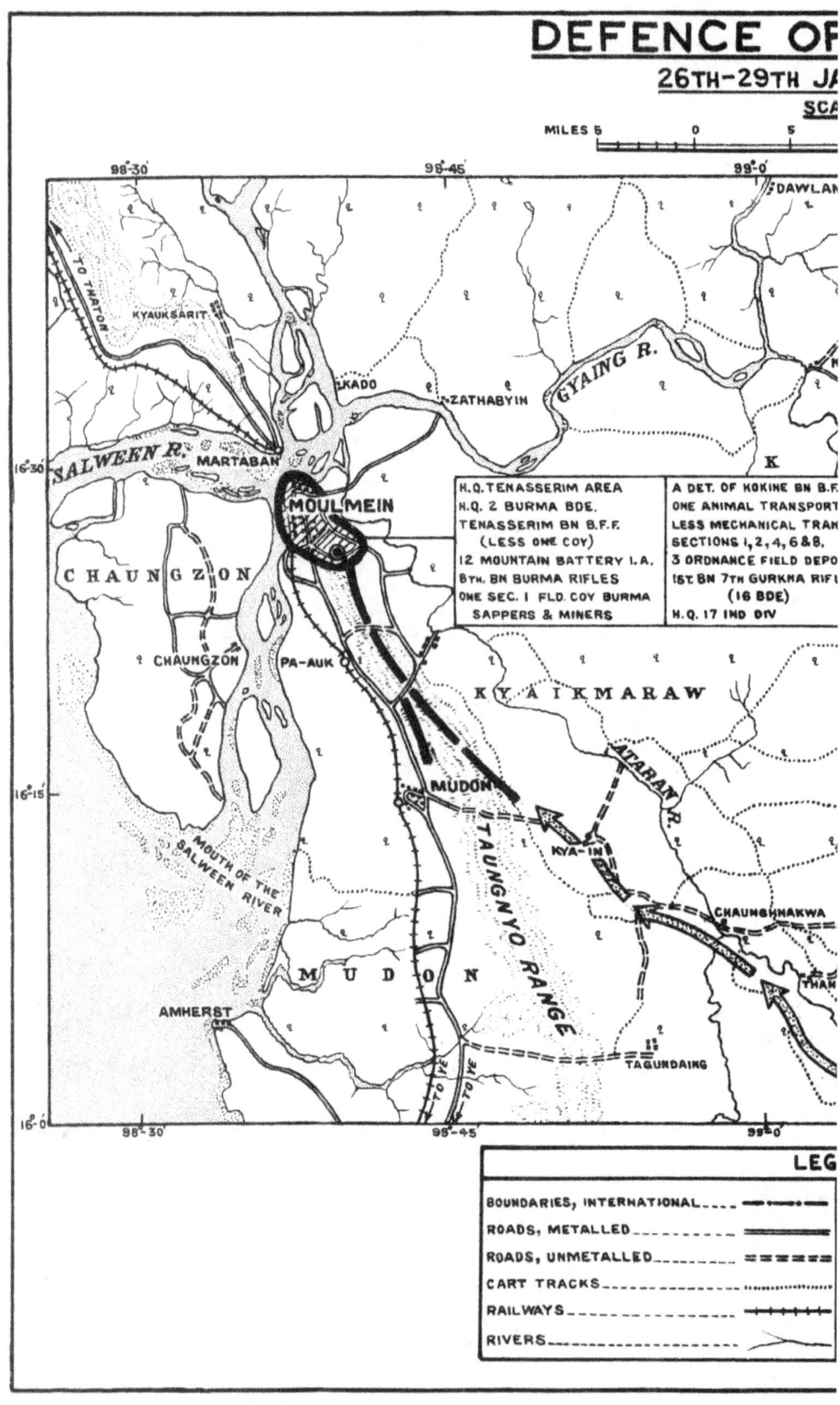

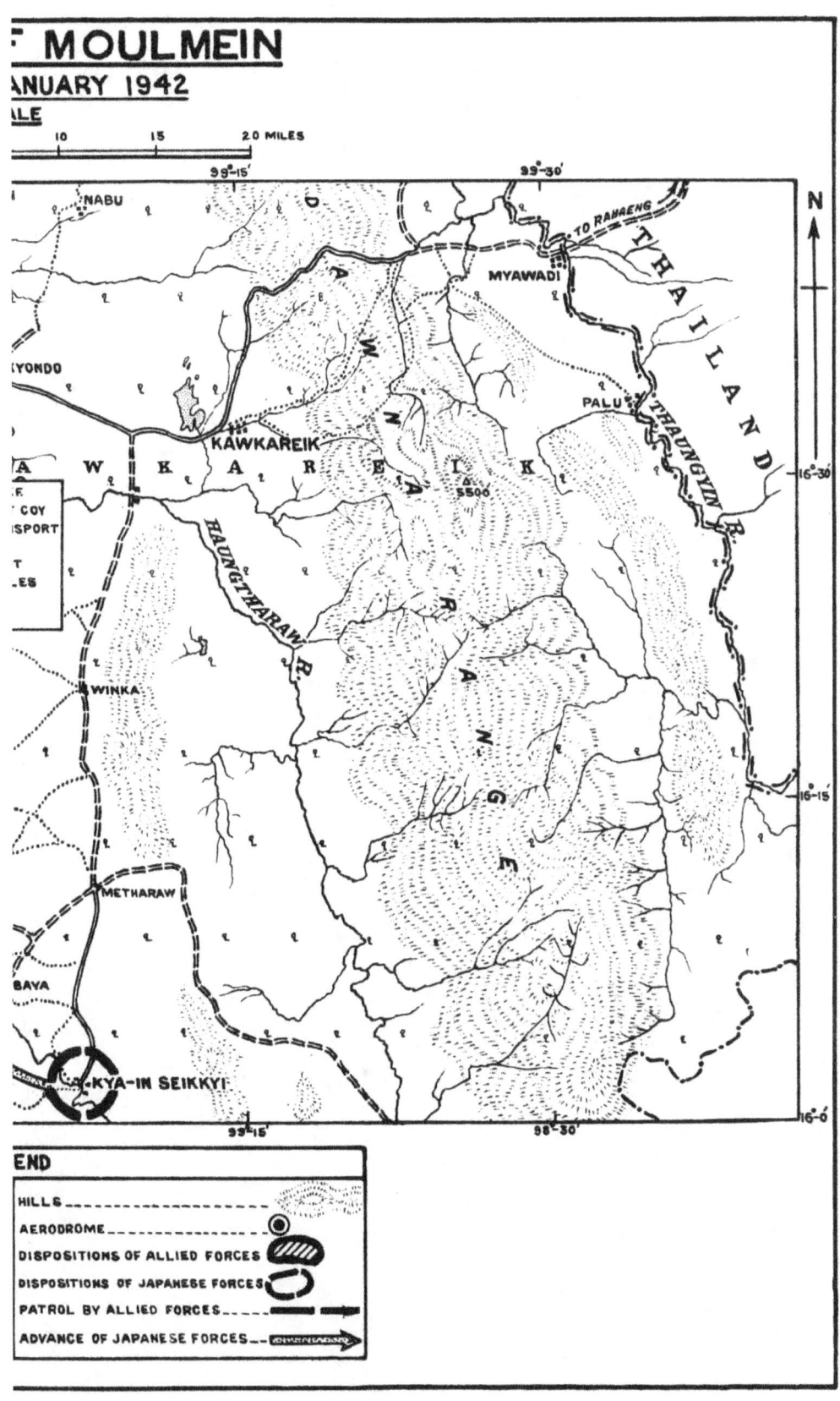

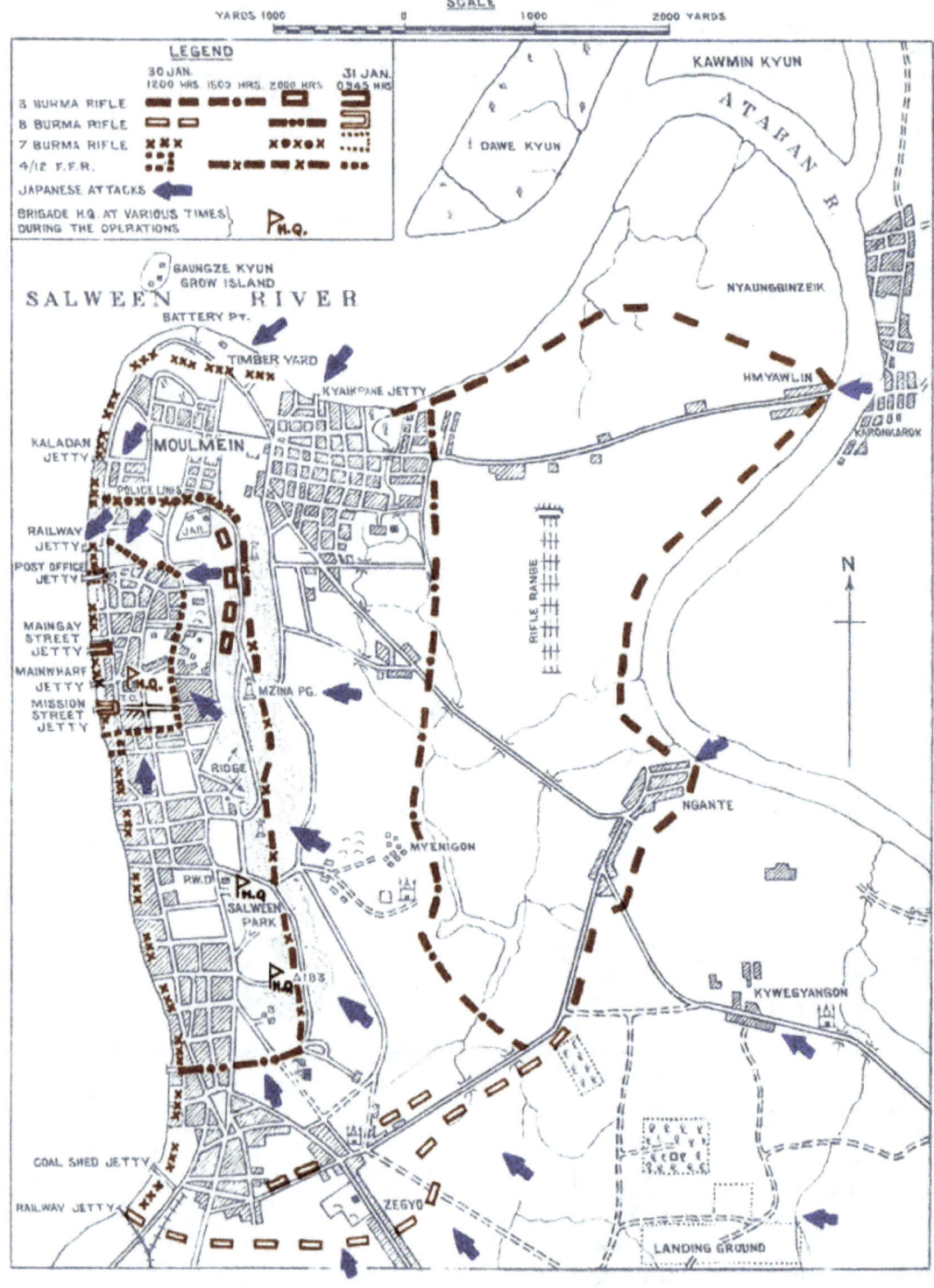

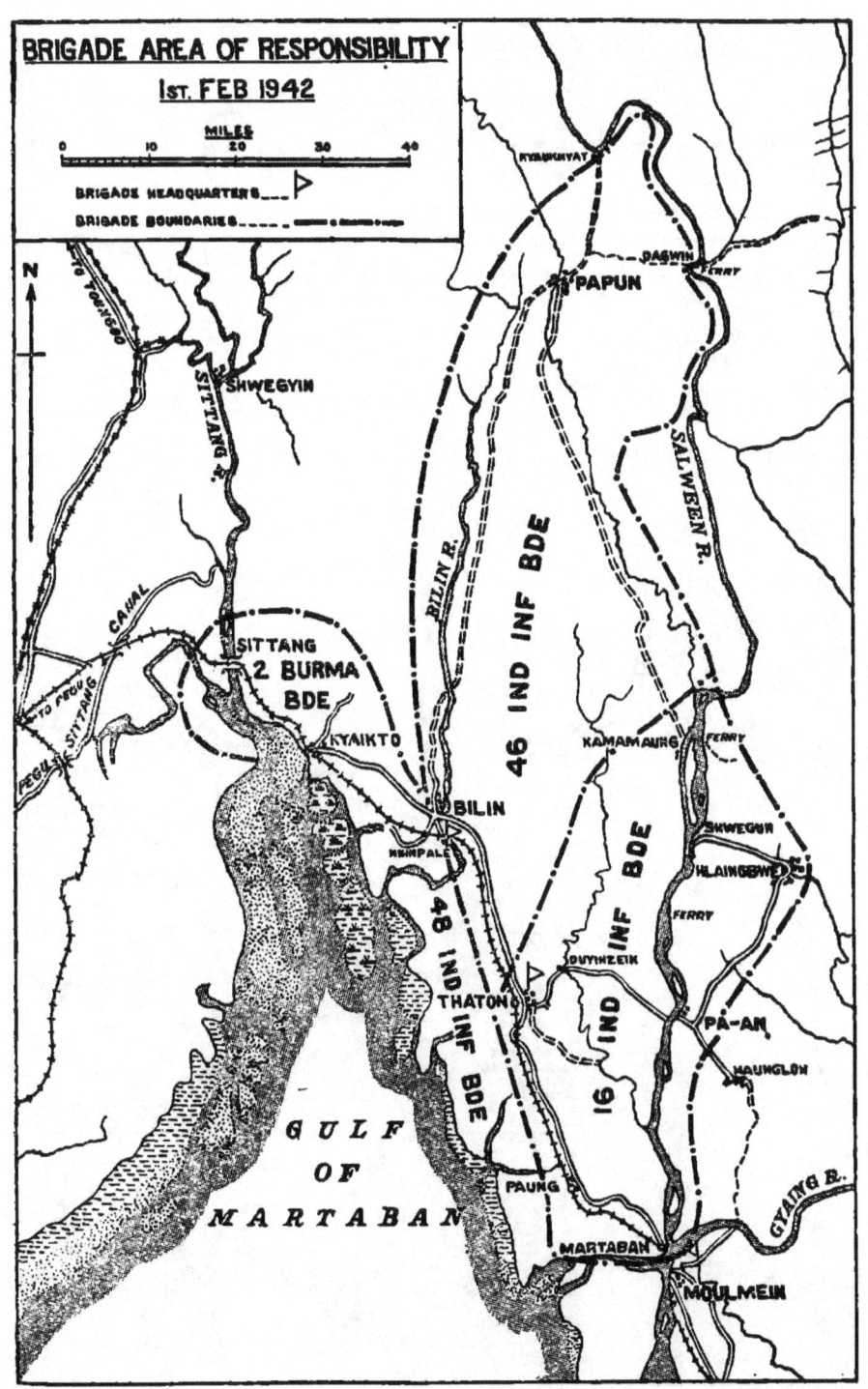

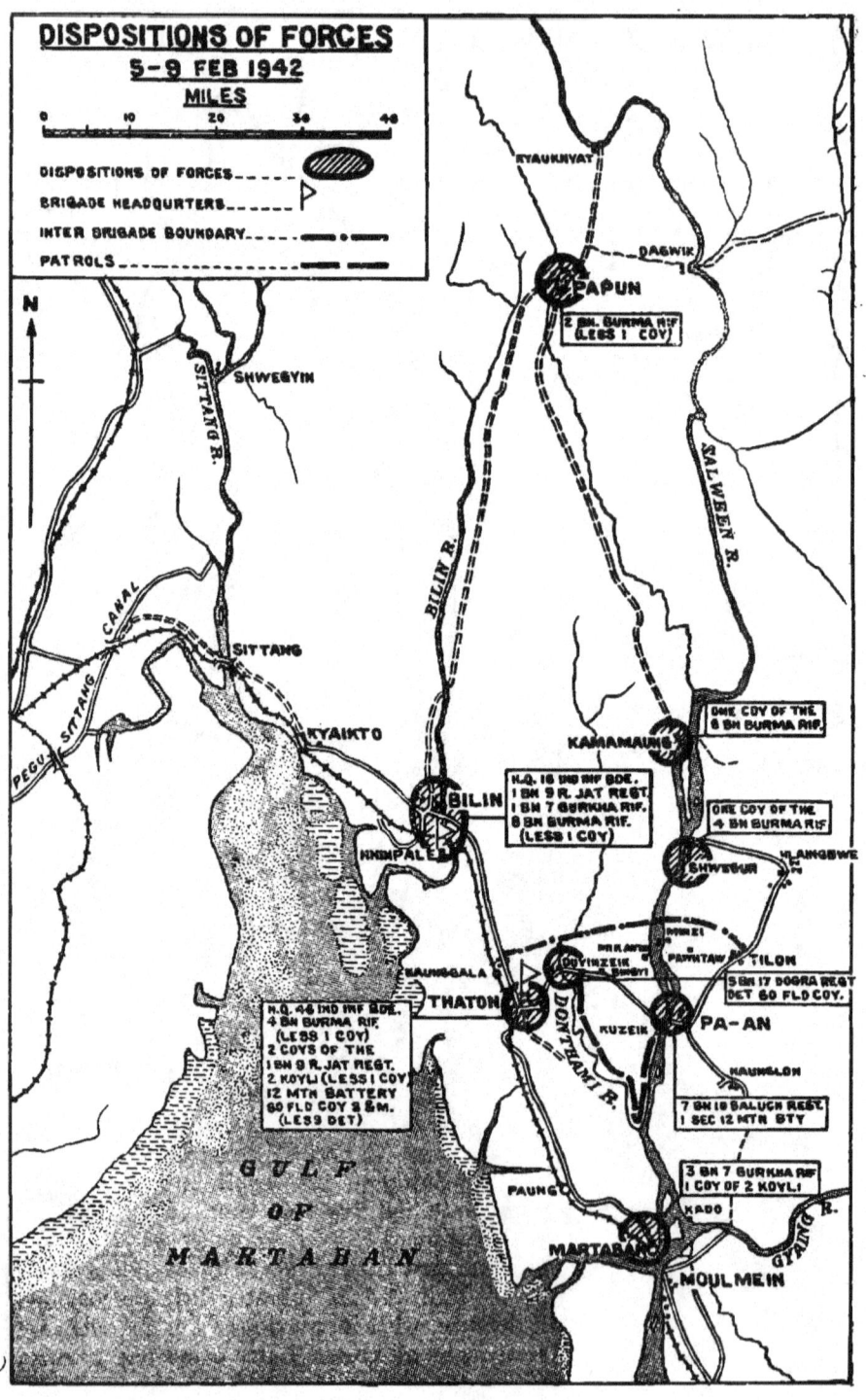

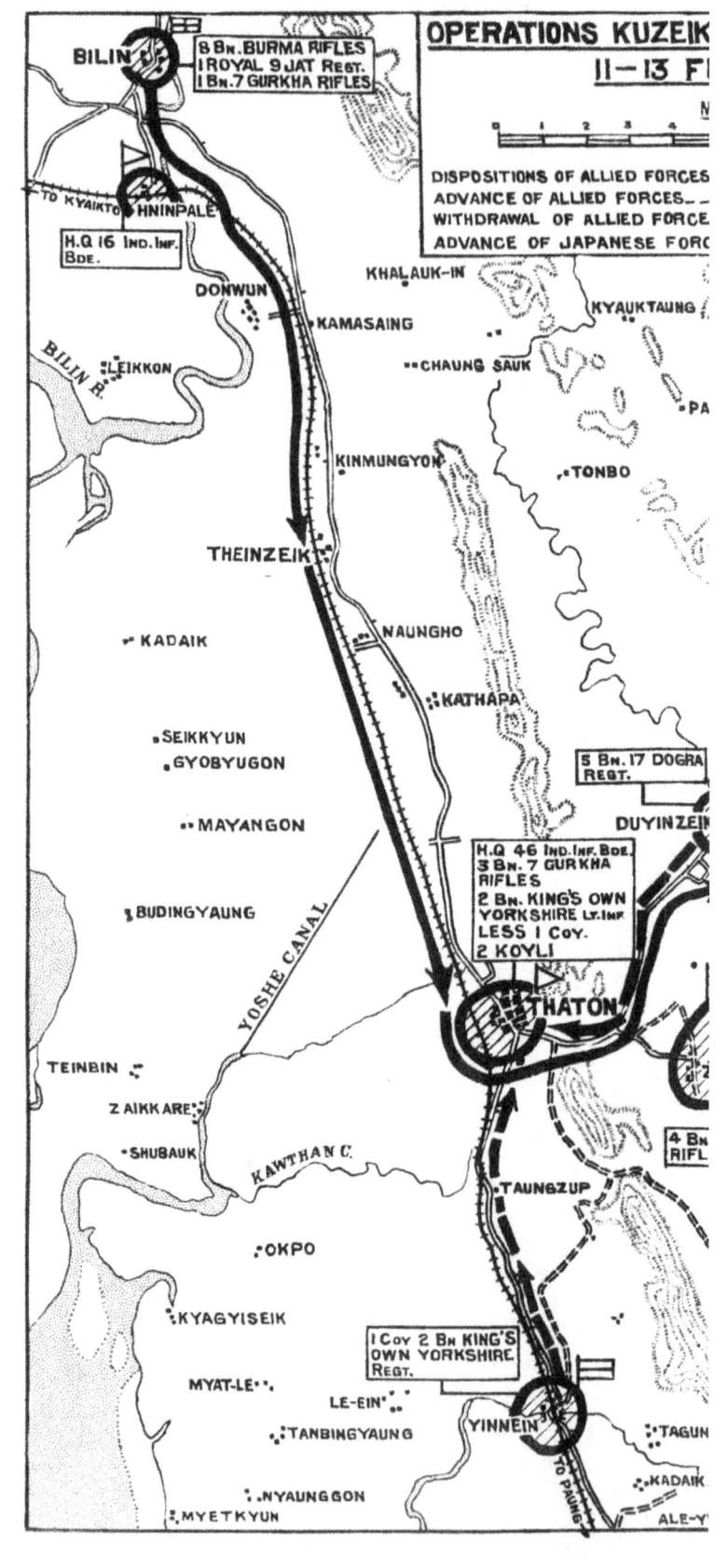

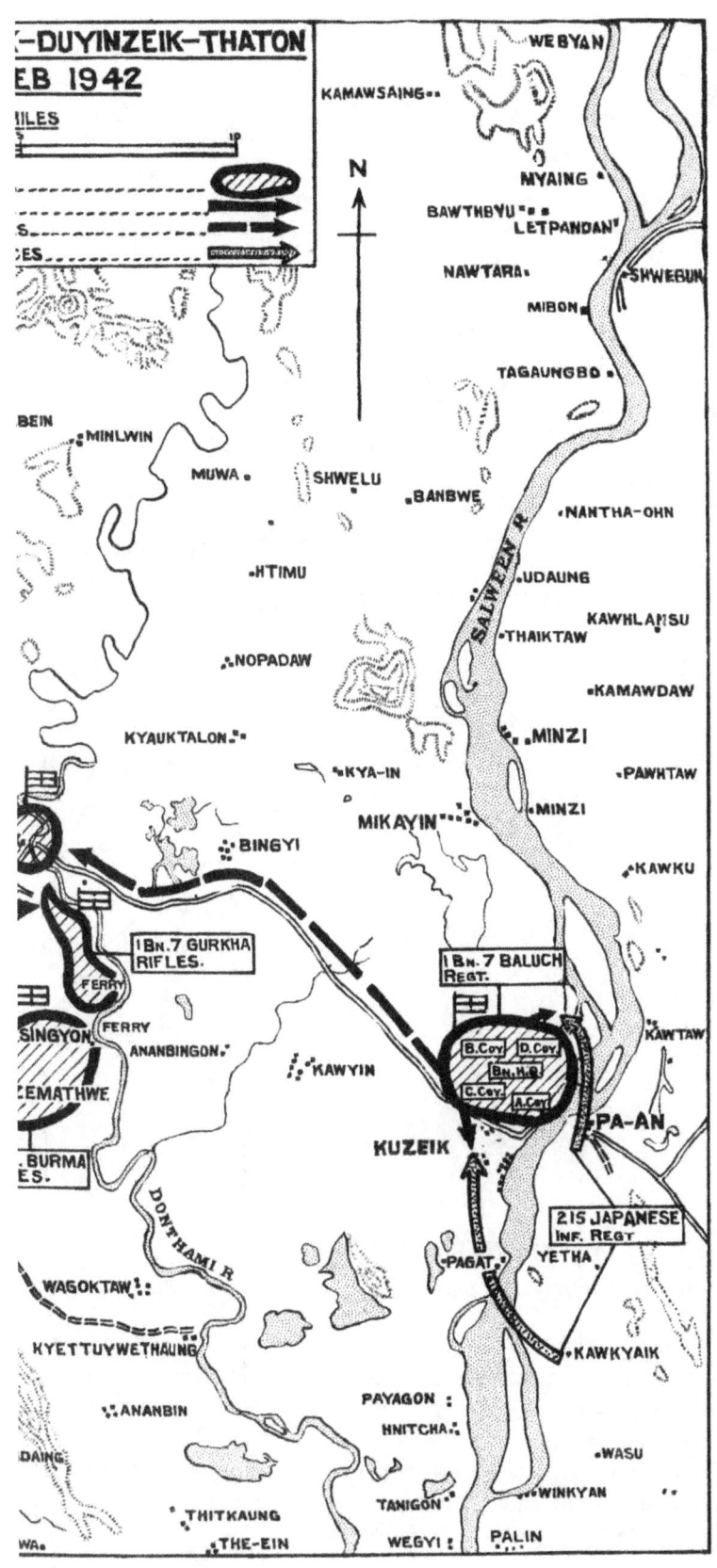

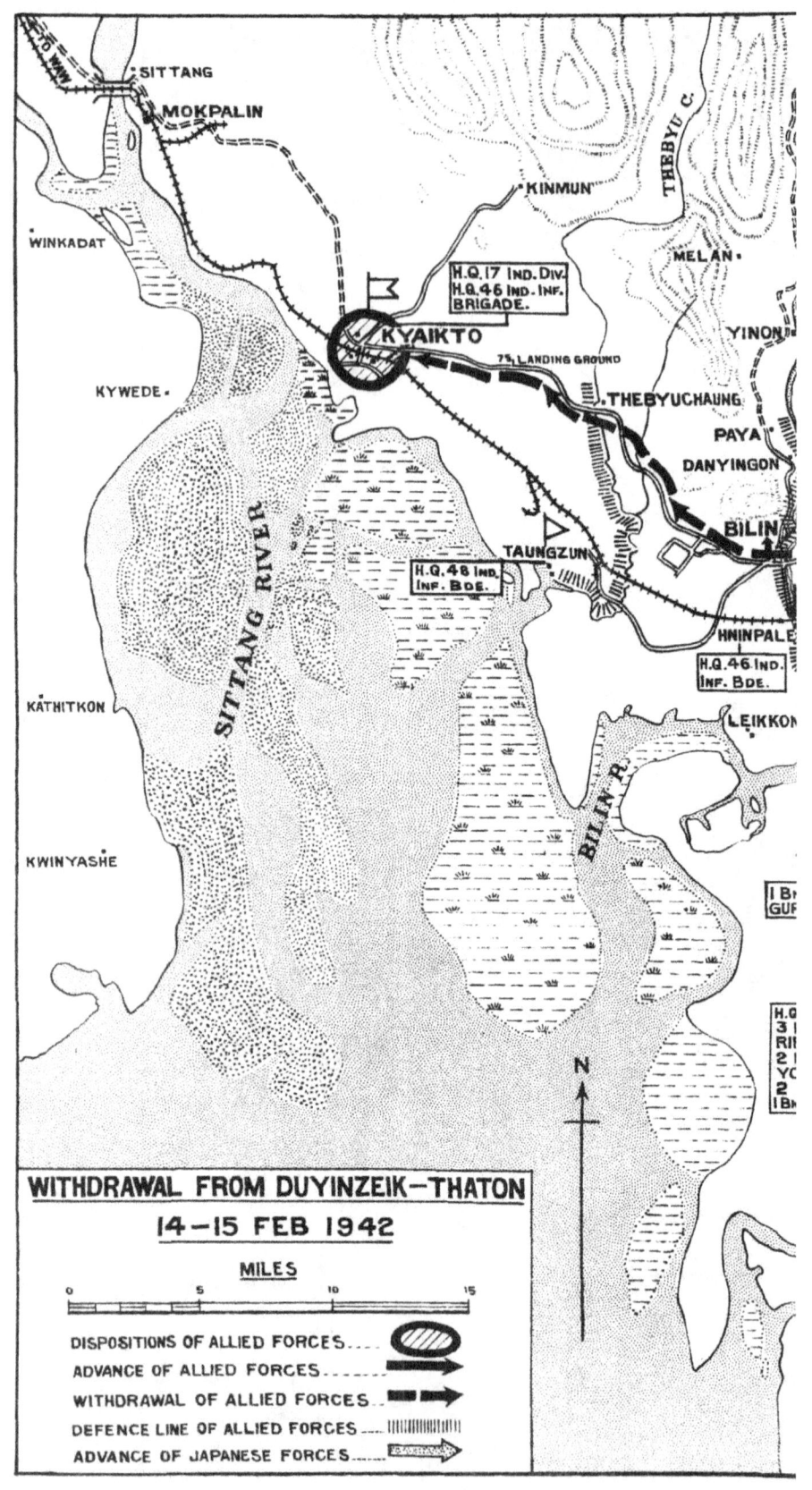

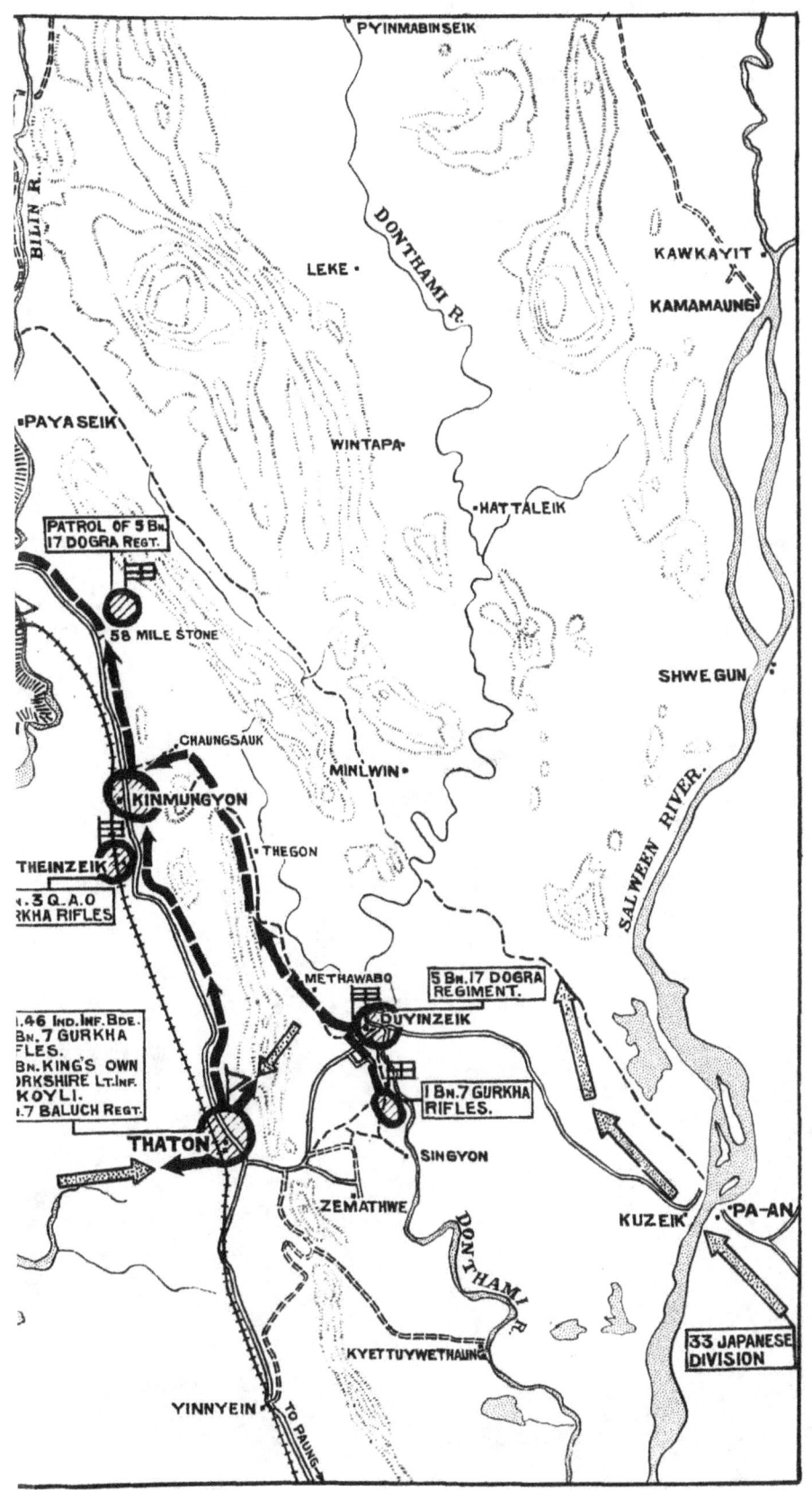

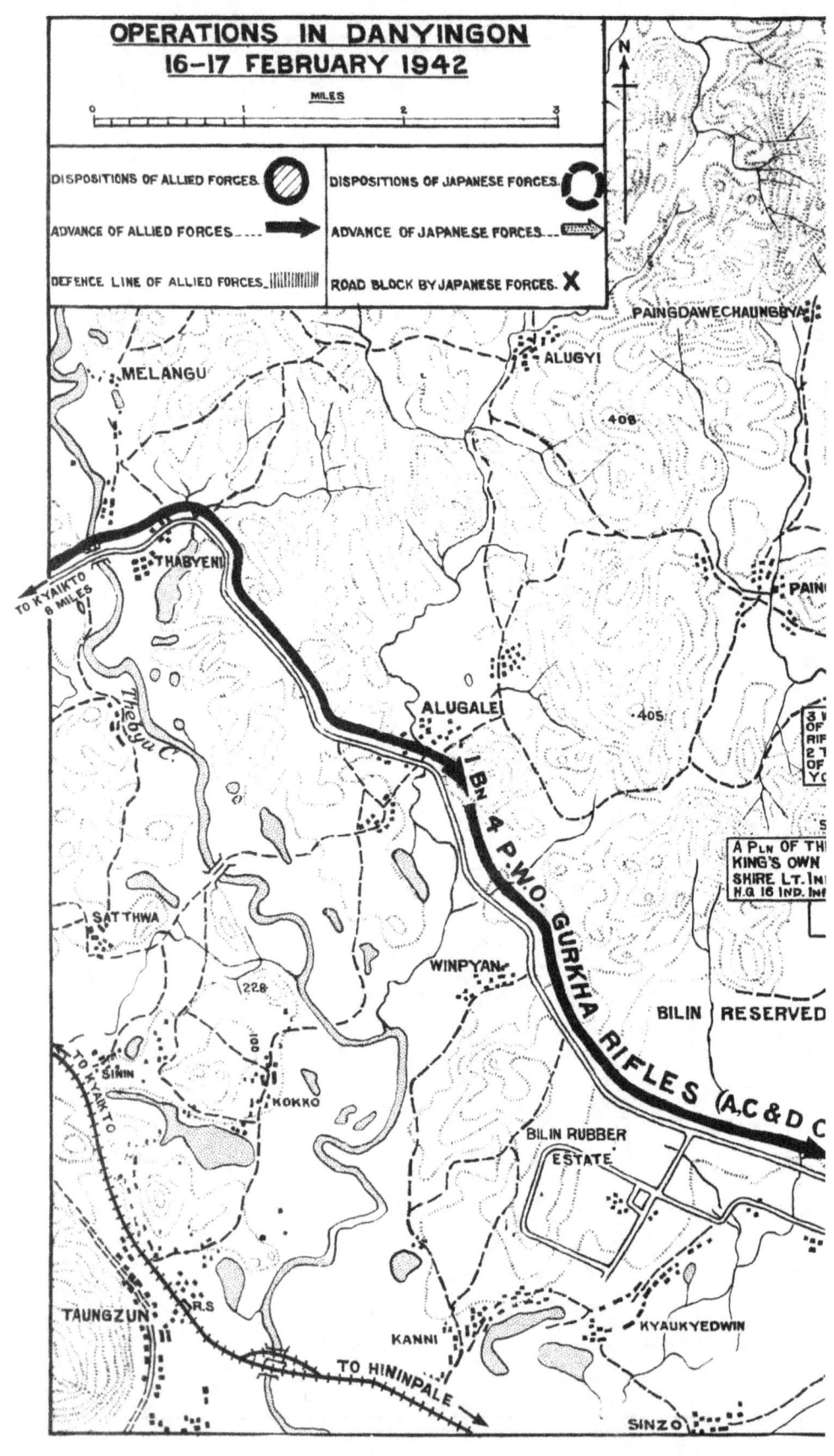

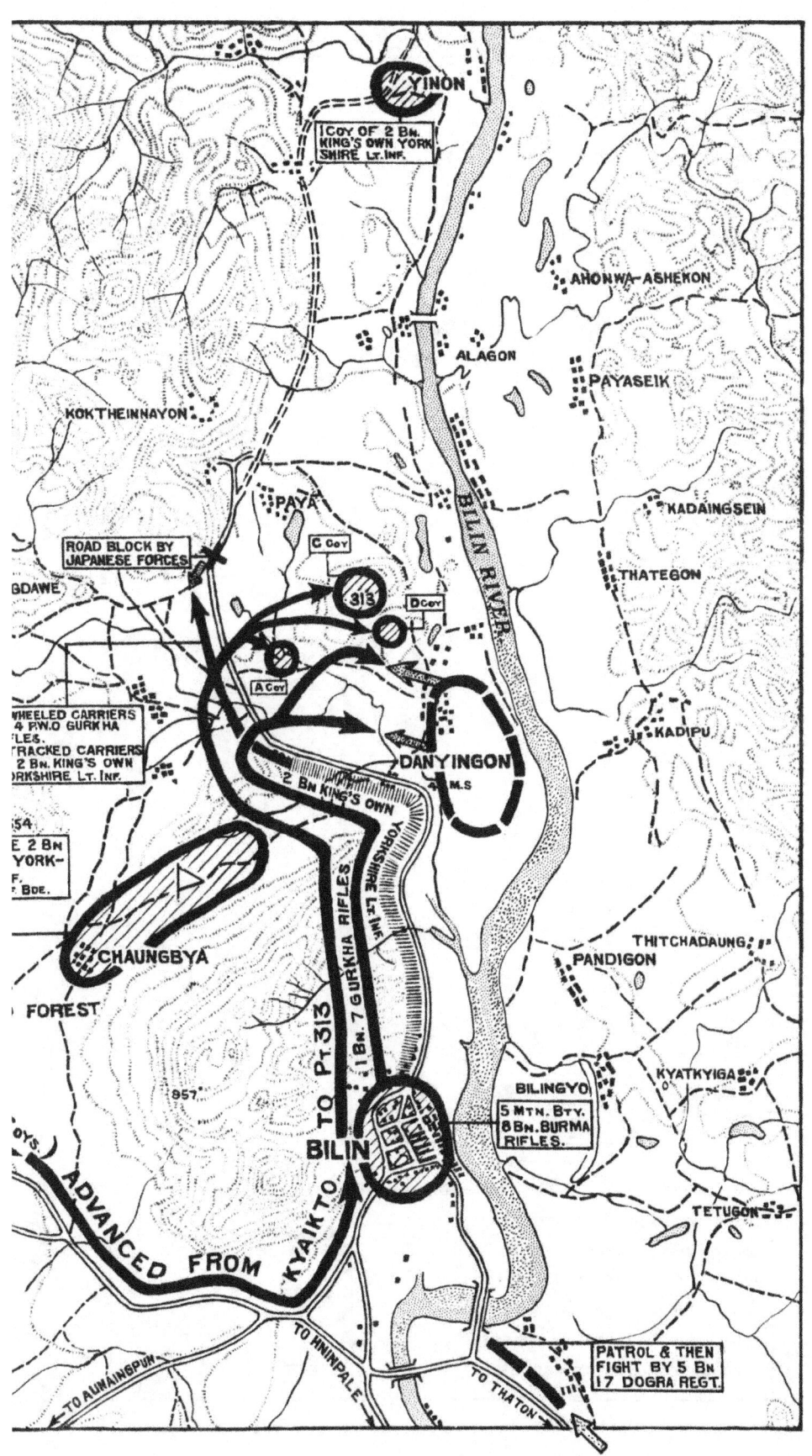

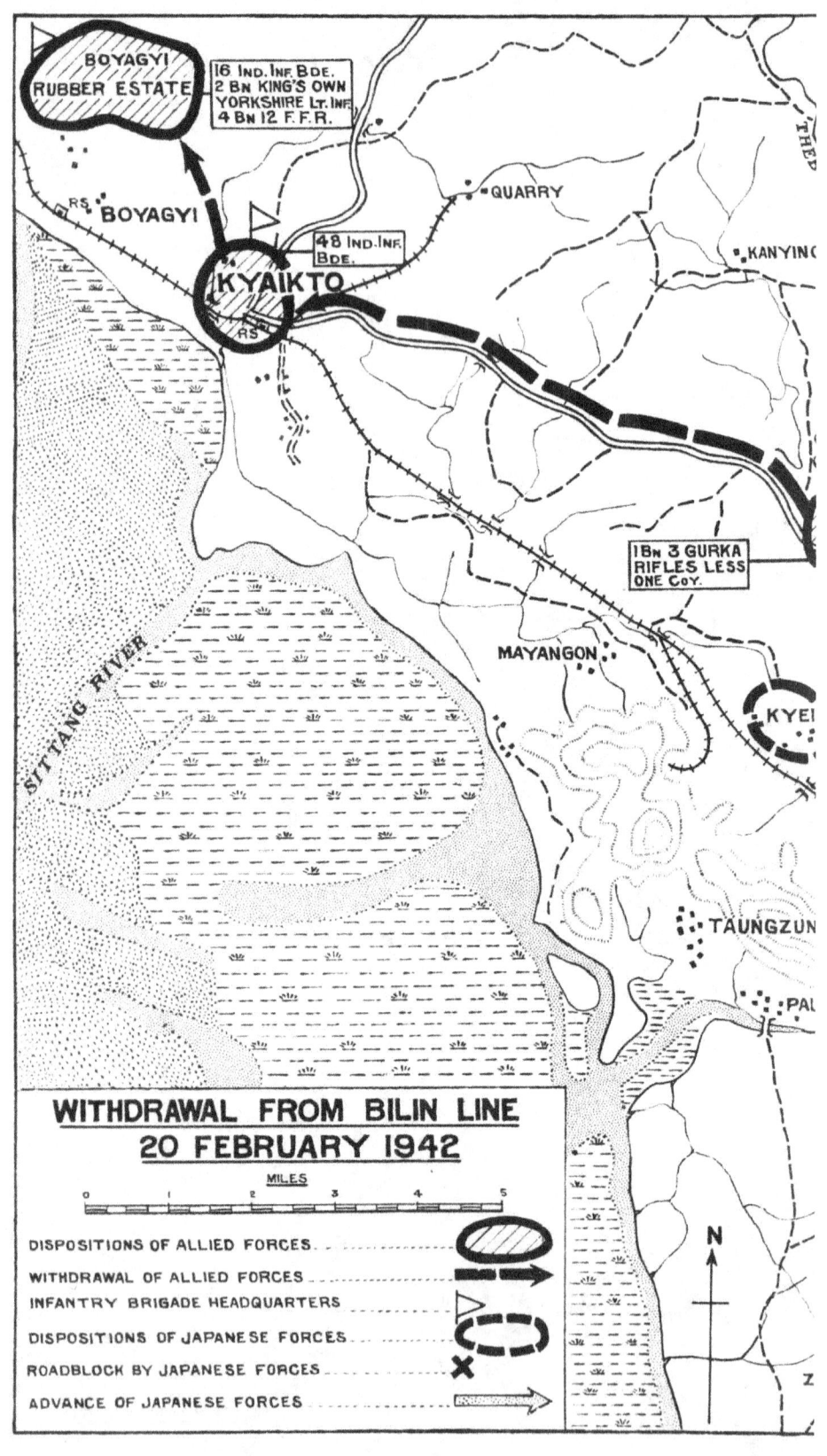

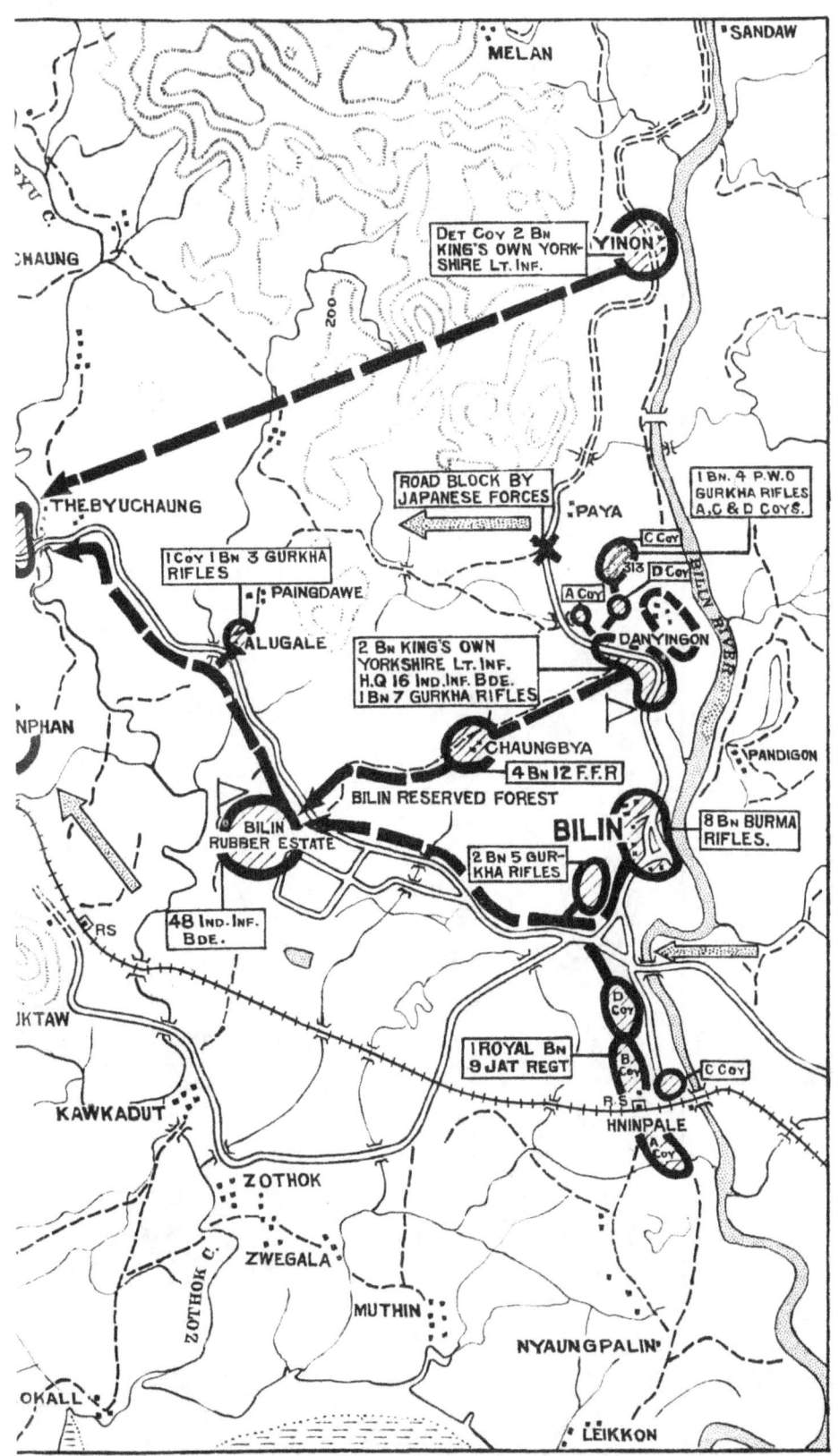

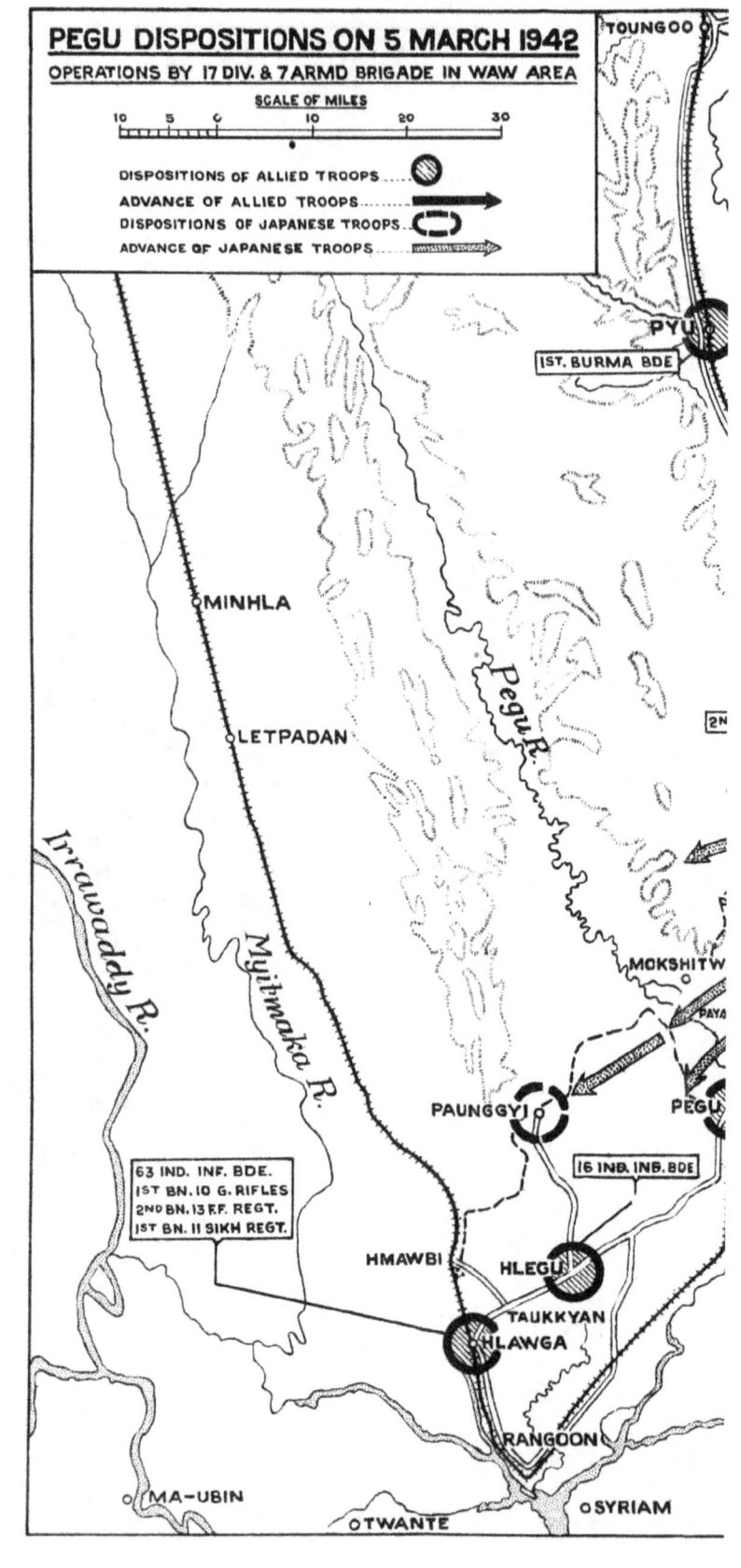

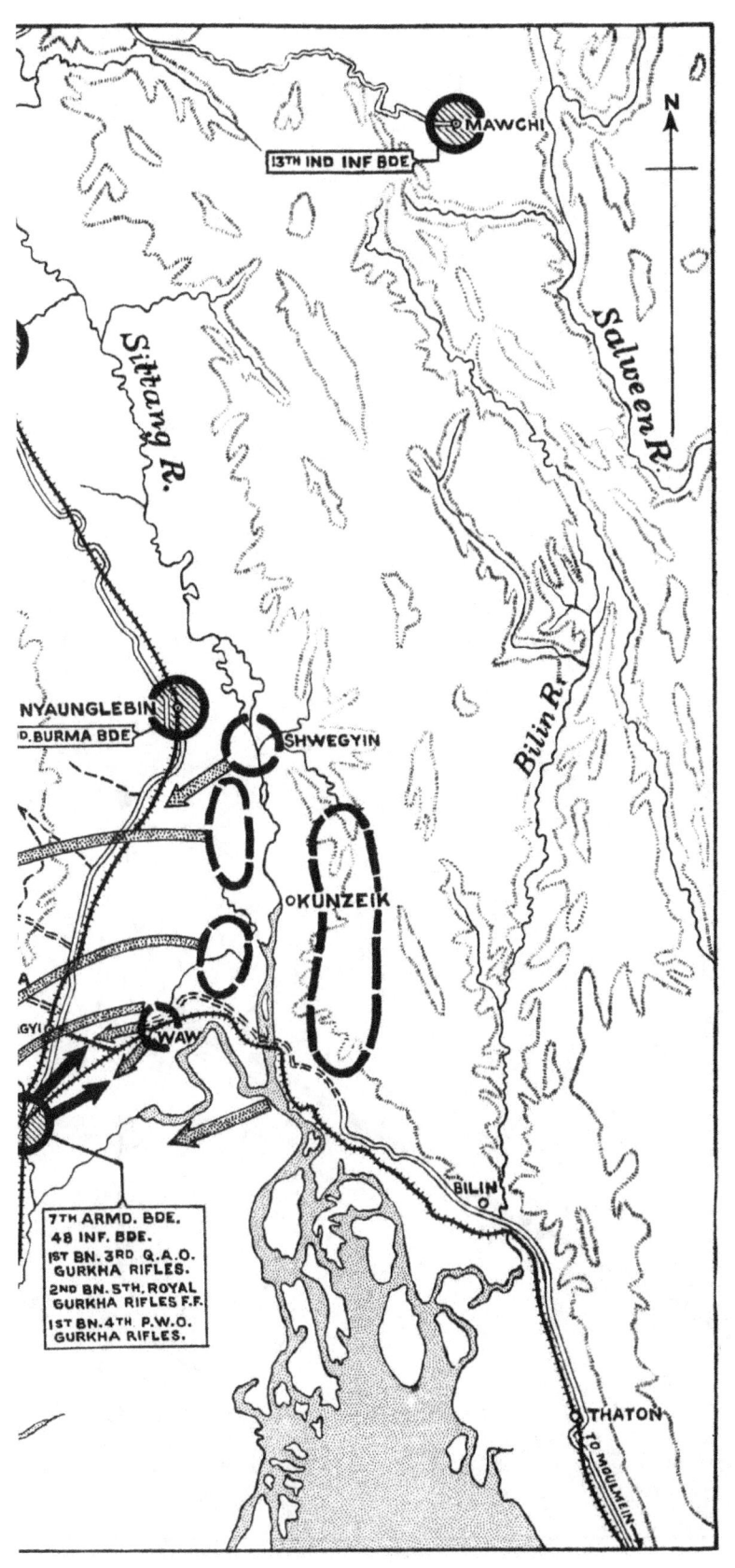

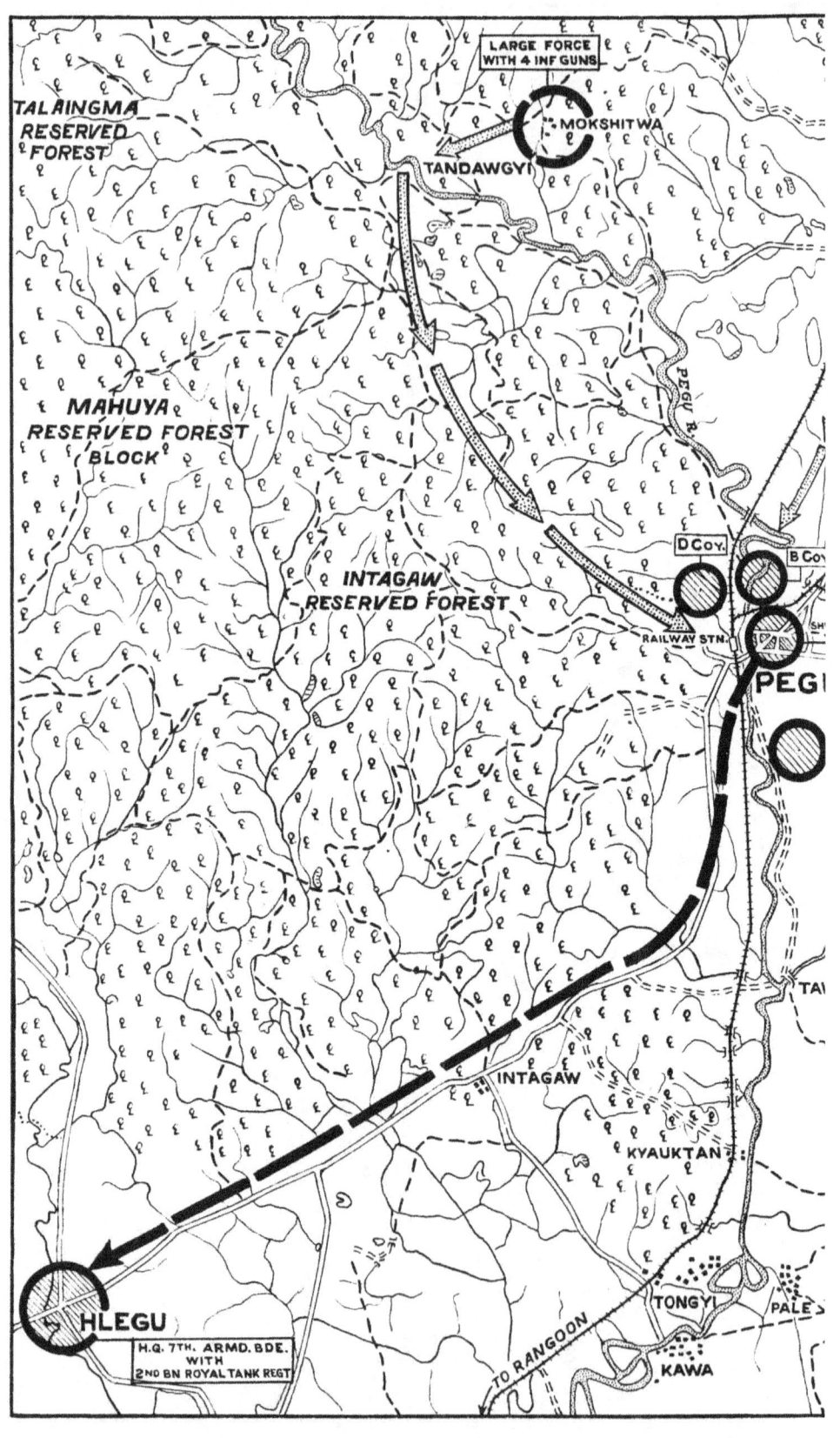

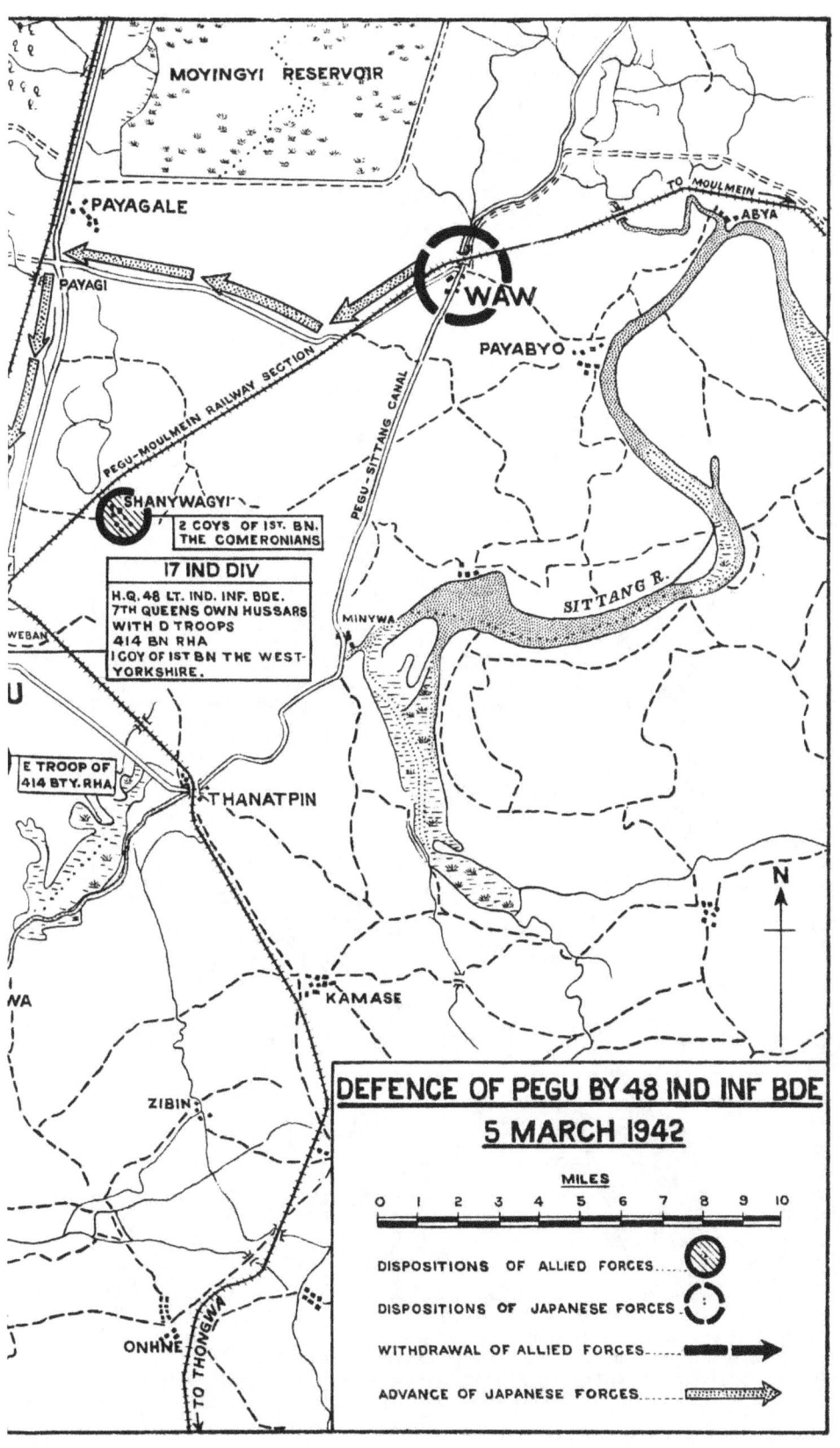

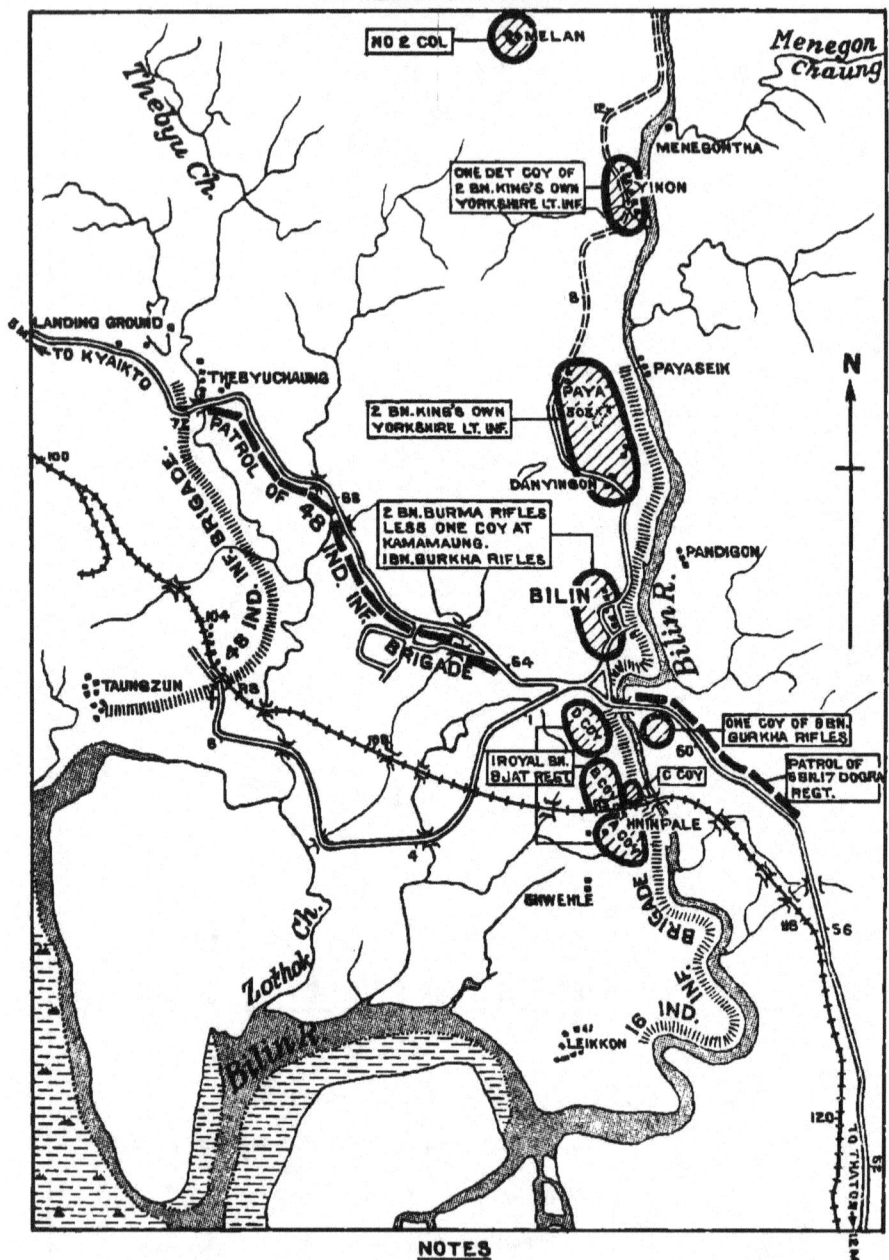

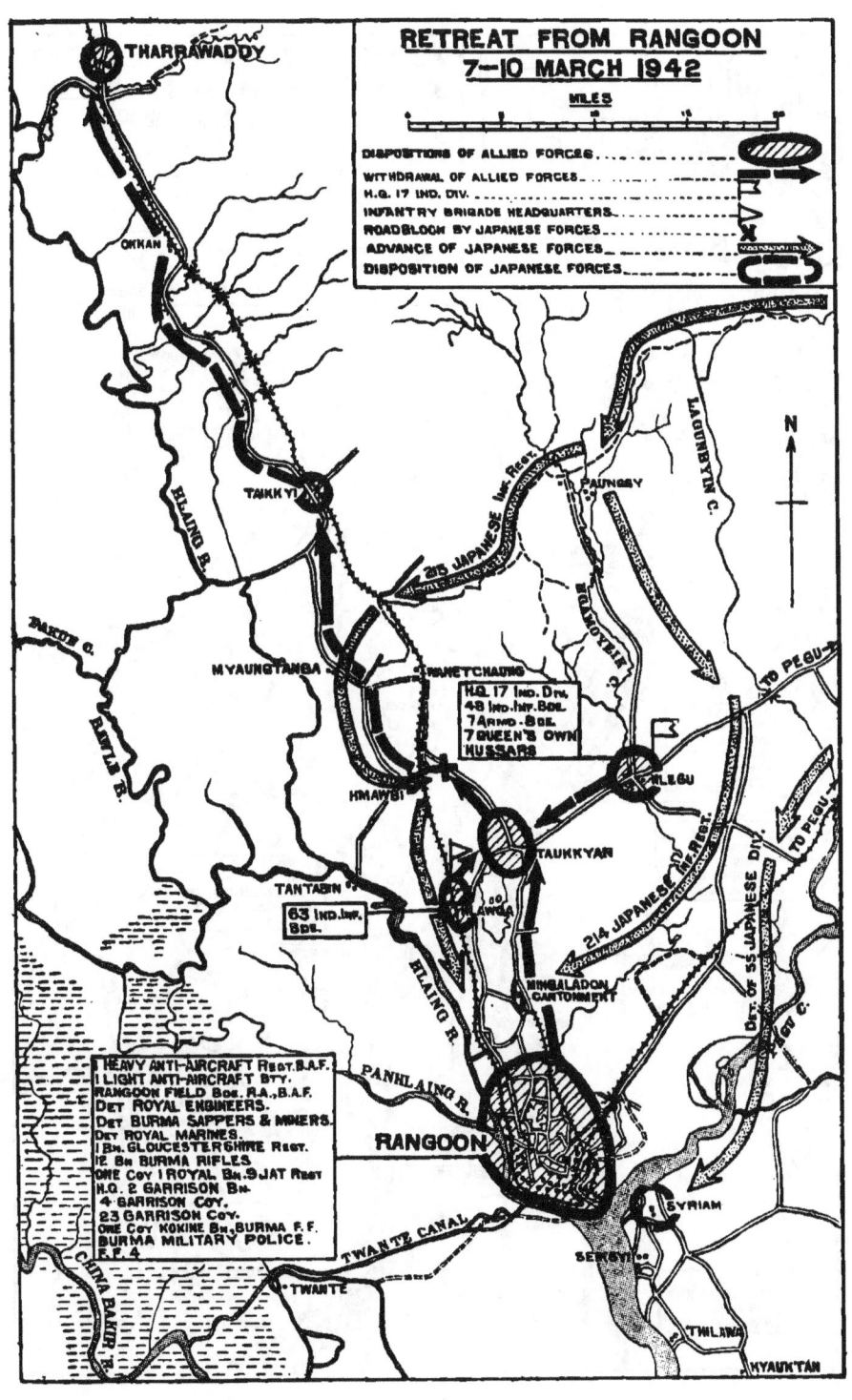

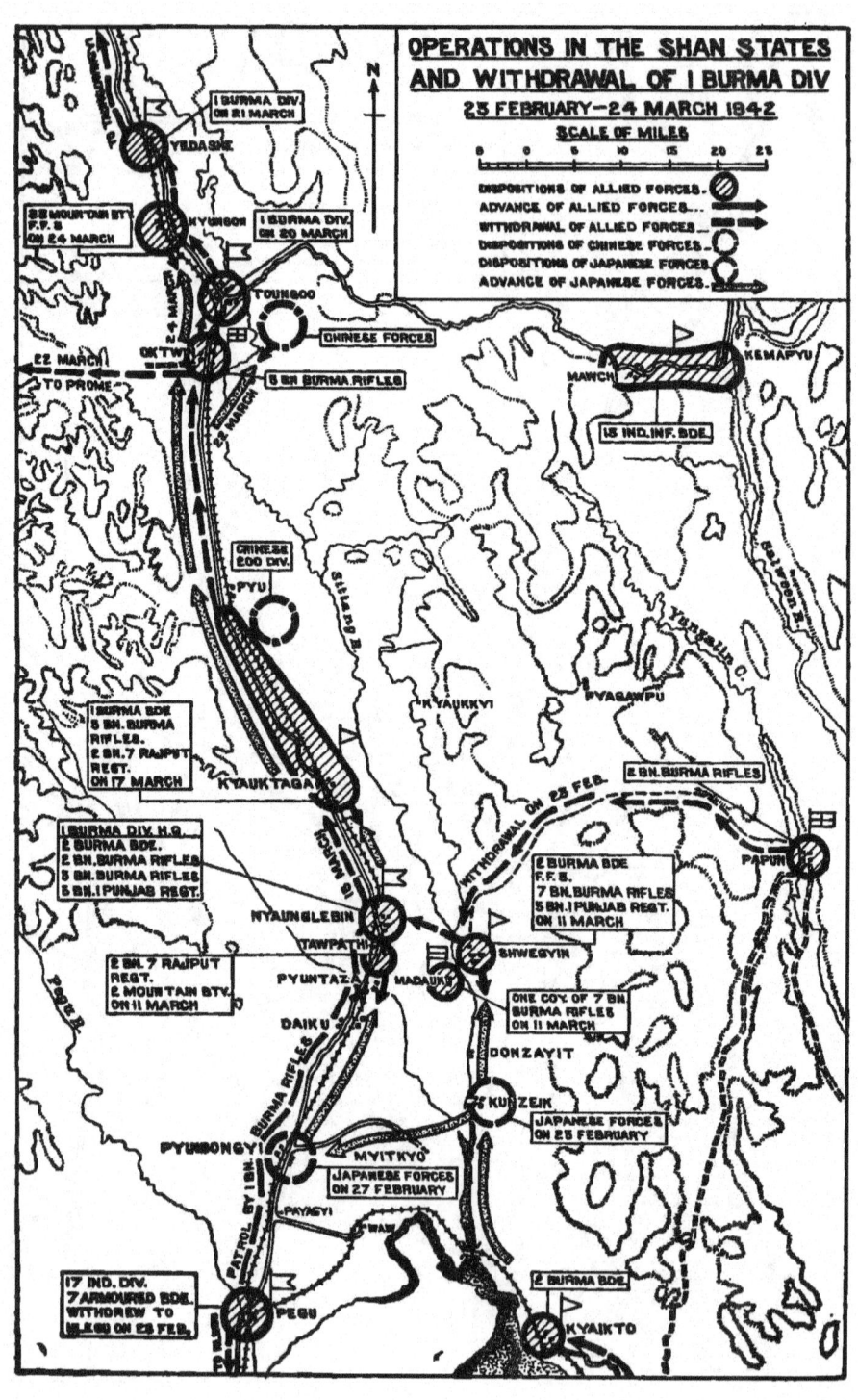

I BURCORPS DEFENCE ZONE

10–14 MARCH 1942

SCALE OF MILES

5 0 5 10

DISPOSITIONS OF ALLIED FORCES

PATROL BY ALLIED TROOPS

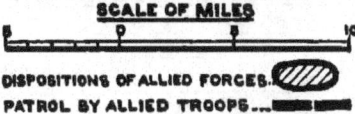

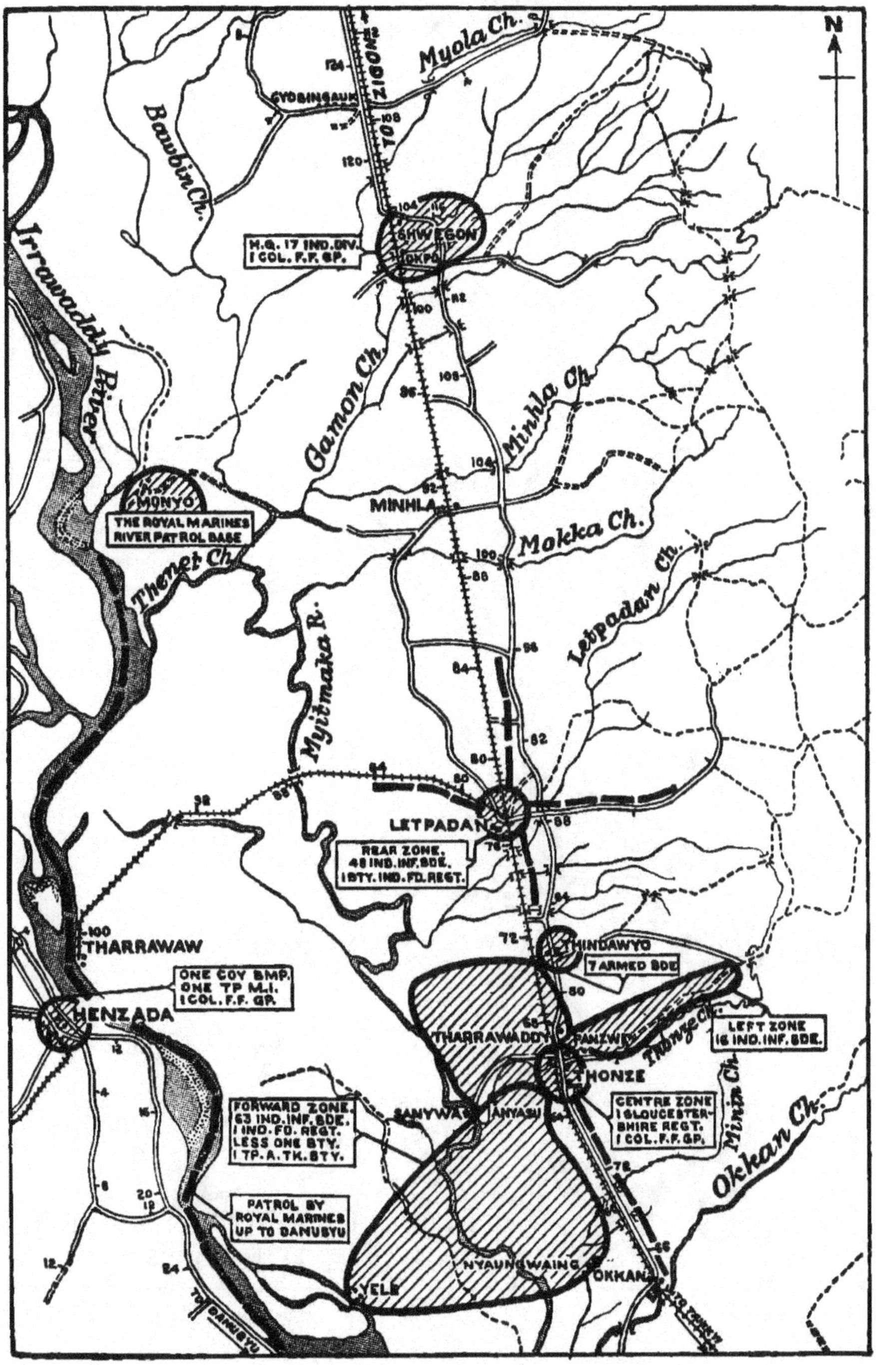

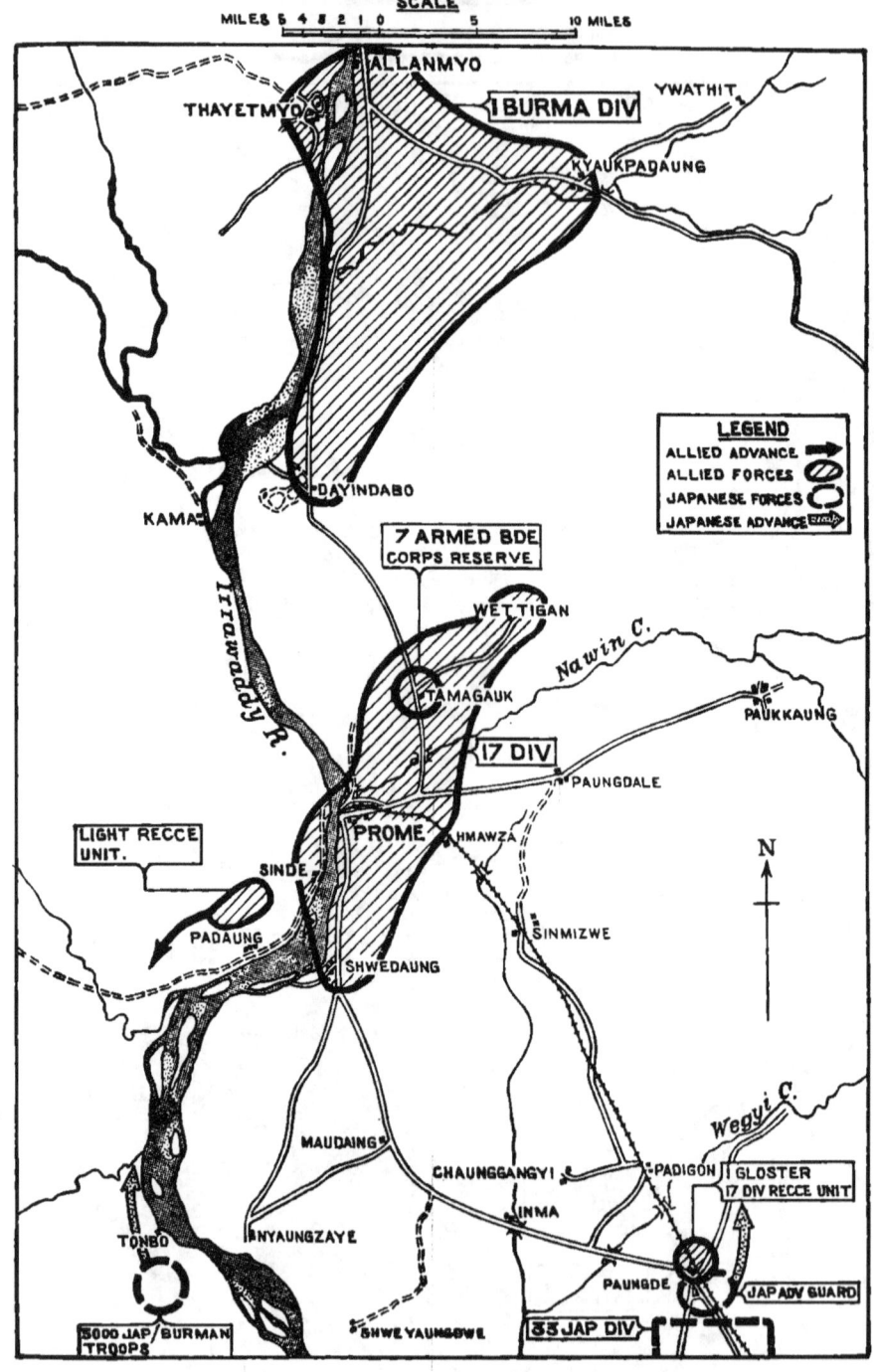

I BURCORPS COUNTER OFFENSIVE PLAN (1ST PHASE)

29 MARCH 1942

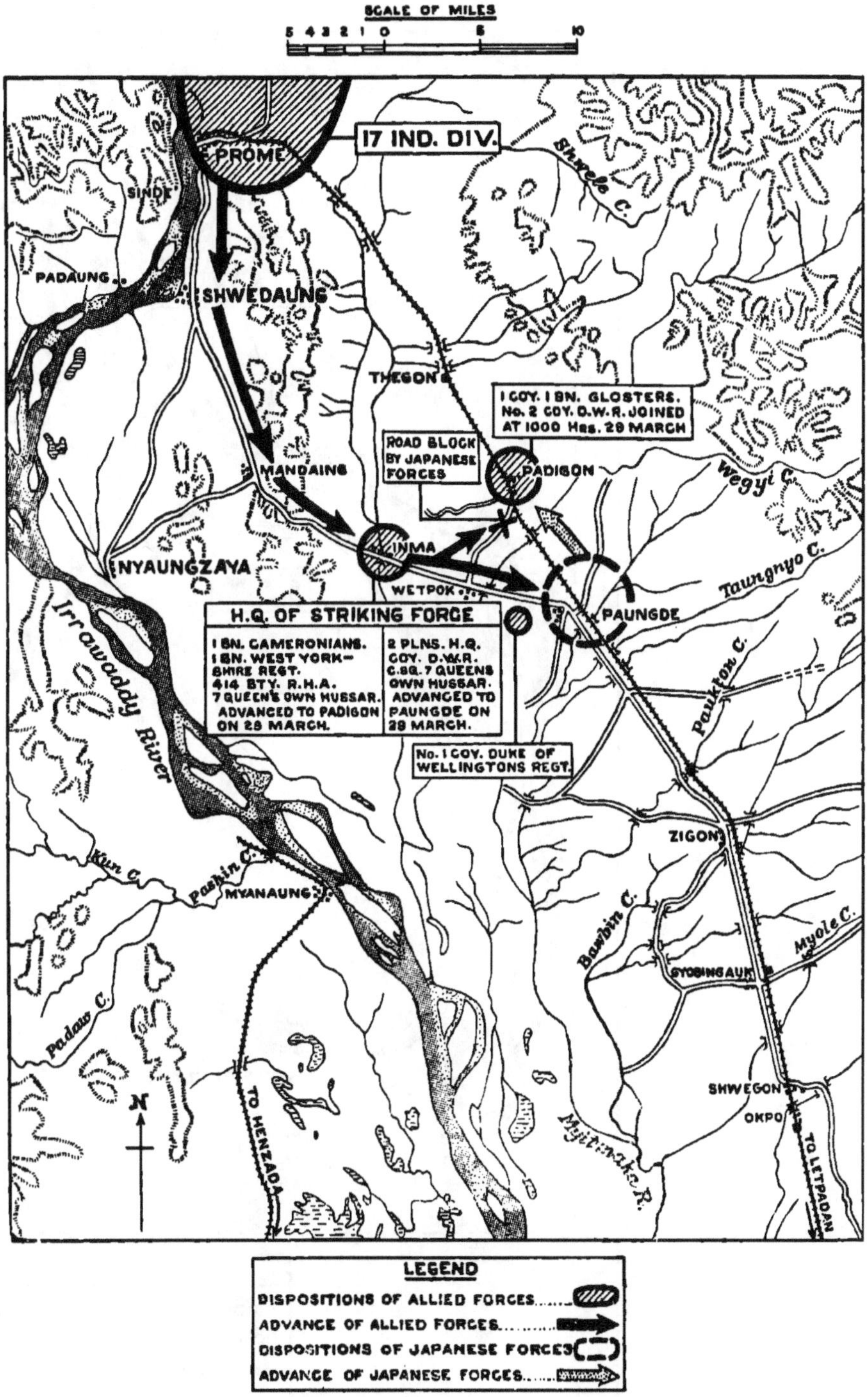

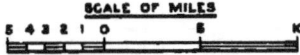

ACTION AT S[HWEDAUNG]
29–30 MA[R]
SCA[LE]

MILES 5 4 3 2 1 0

- PROME
- SINDE
- 2 PLN. & VICKERS SEC. ROYAL MARINE
- COMMANDO & B.M.P. LANDED ON 28/29.
- PADAUNG
- SHWEDAUNG
- 214 INF. REGT.
- IRRAWADDY RIVER
- JAPANESE ATTACKED AT 00.30 HRS. 30 MAR
- TONBO
- NYAUNGZAYE

17 IND D[IV]
- 1 SQ 2 BN ROYA[L] REGT.
- 1 COY. 1 BN. WEST SHIRE REGT.
- 1 BN. 4 P.W.O G[URKHA] RIFLES.
- ADVANCED T[O] SINMIZW[E]
- 4 BN 12 F.F. REG[T]
- 2 BN 13 F.F. RIF[LES]
- 1 BTY. 11 IND. FD.
- ADVANCED [TO] SHWEDAUN[G]

LEG[END]
ROADS METALLED	————
ROADS UNMETALLED	=====
RAILWAYS	+++++
RIVERS	~~~~
HILLS	......

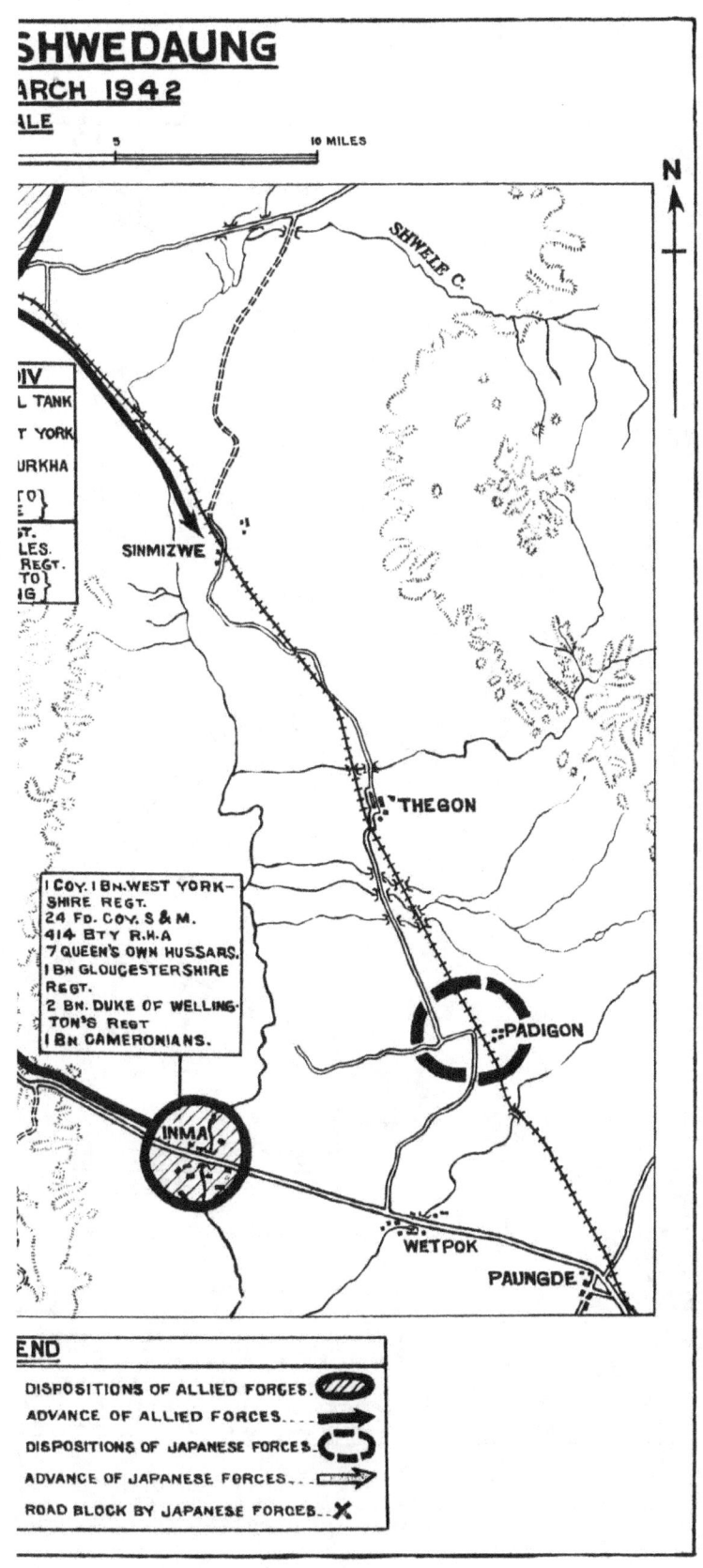

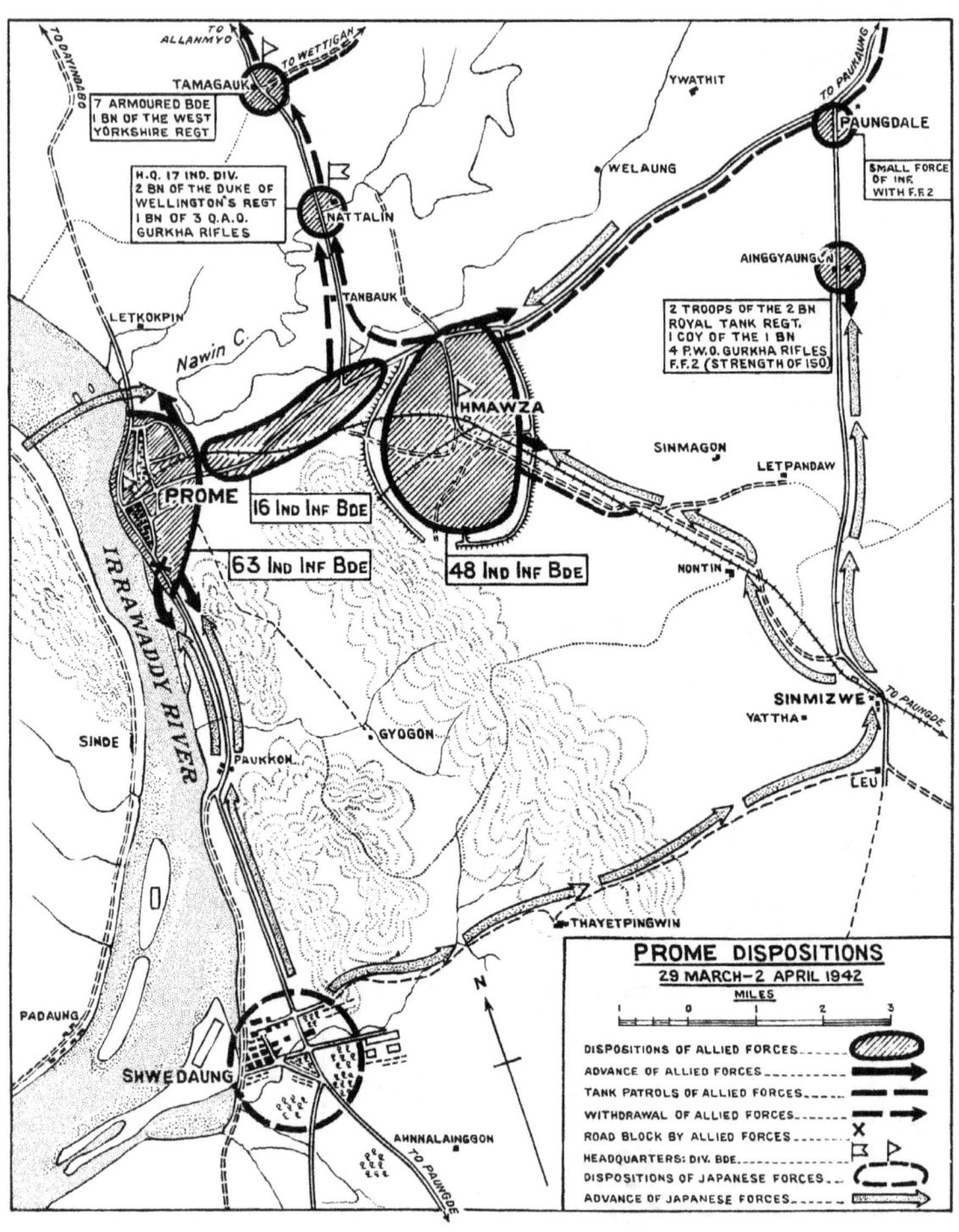

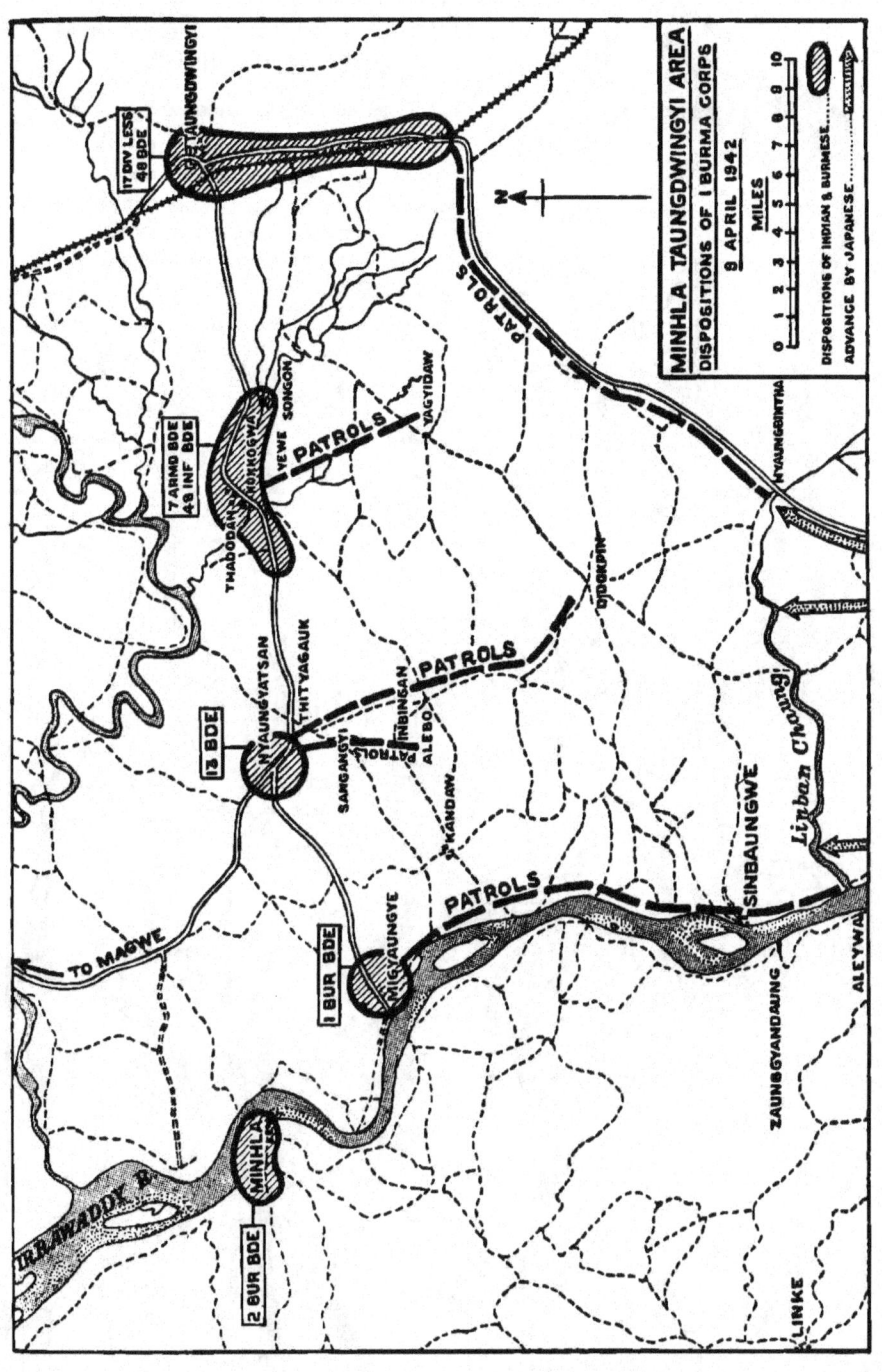

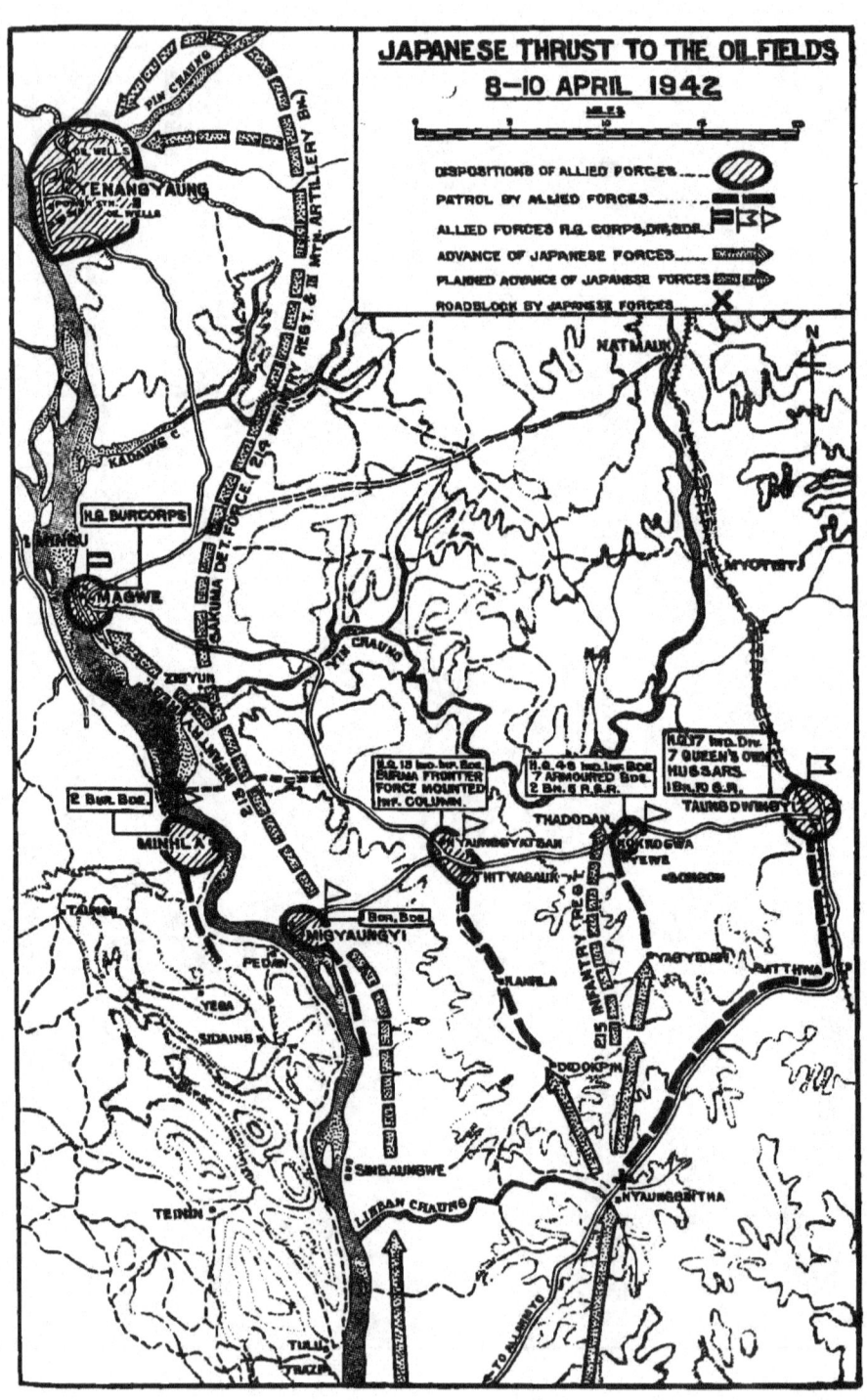

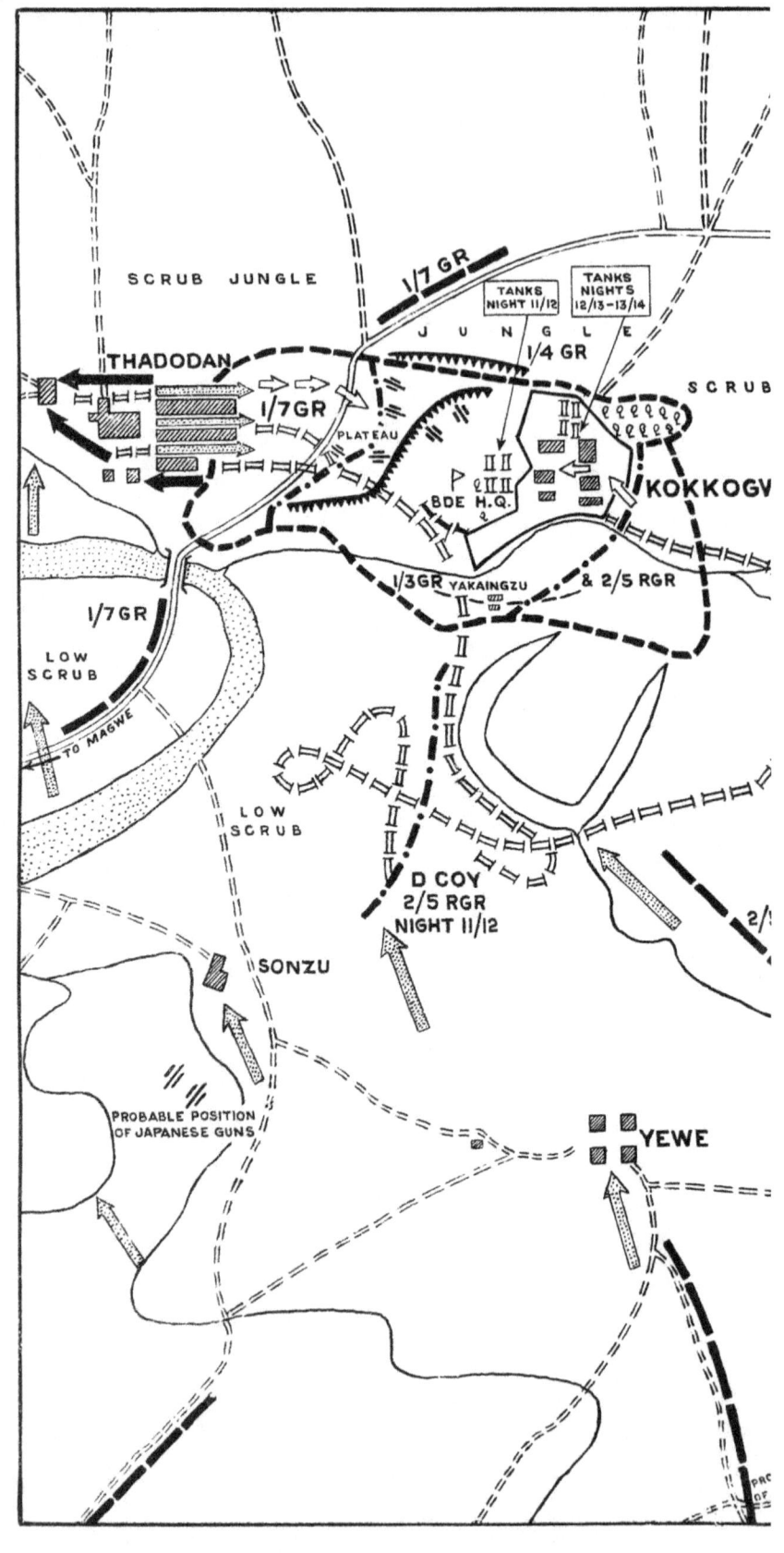

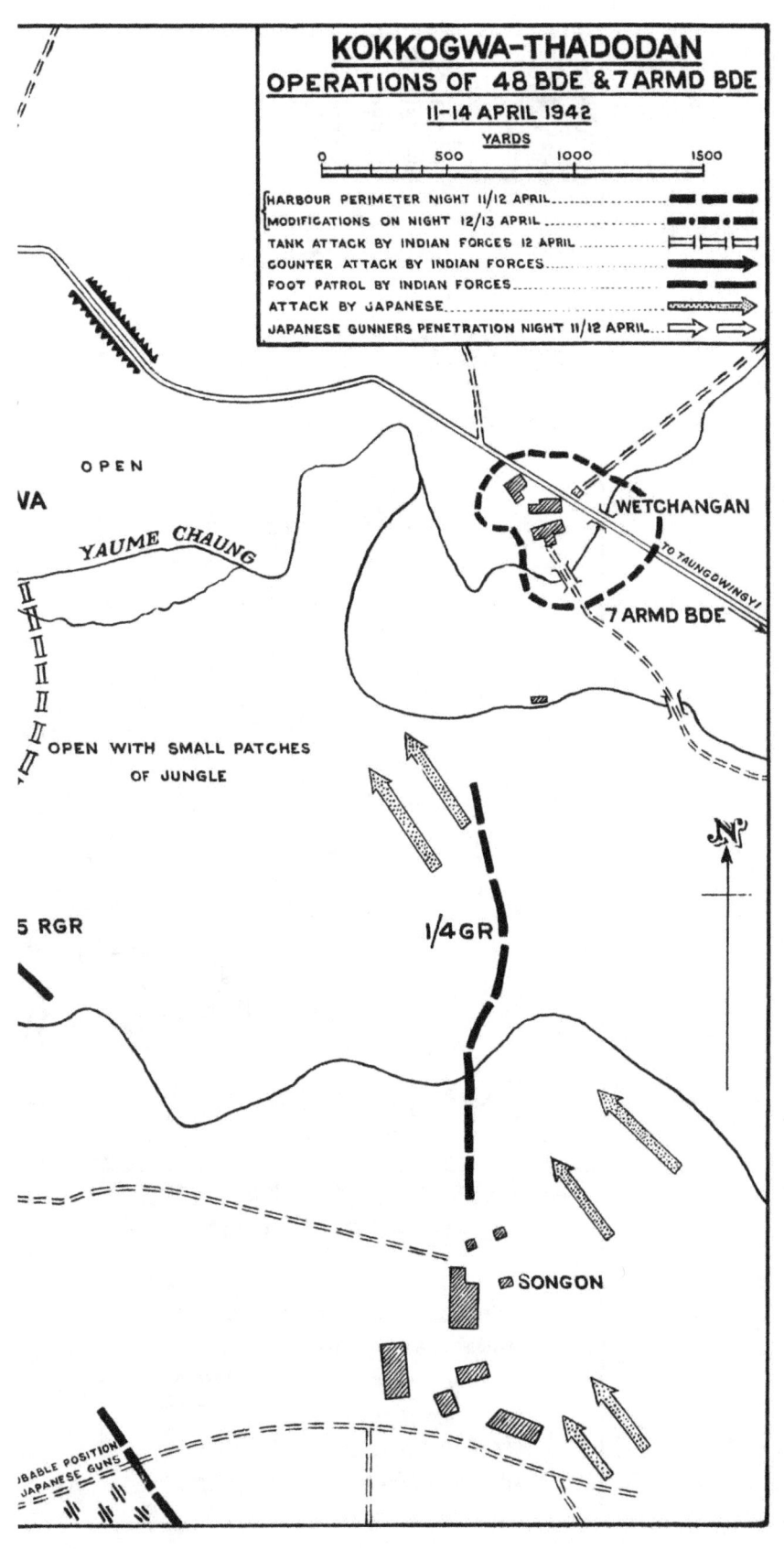

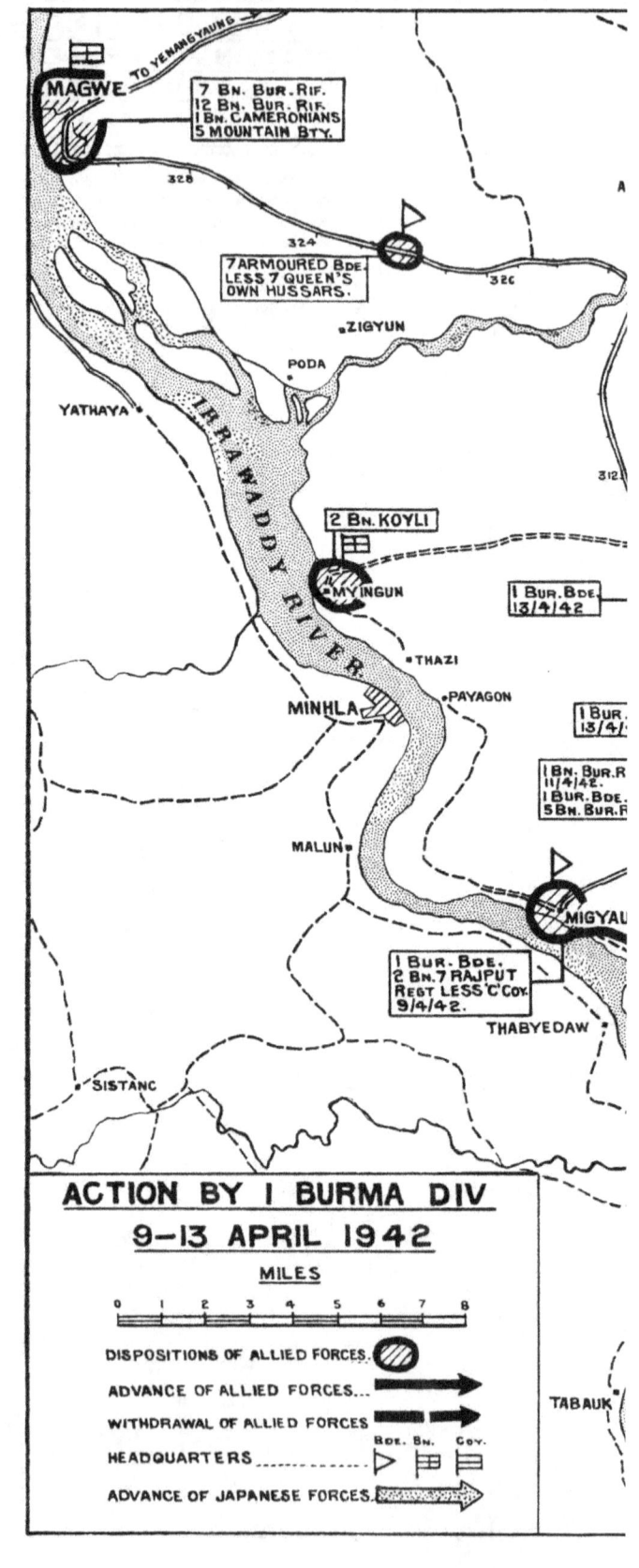

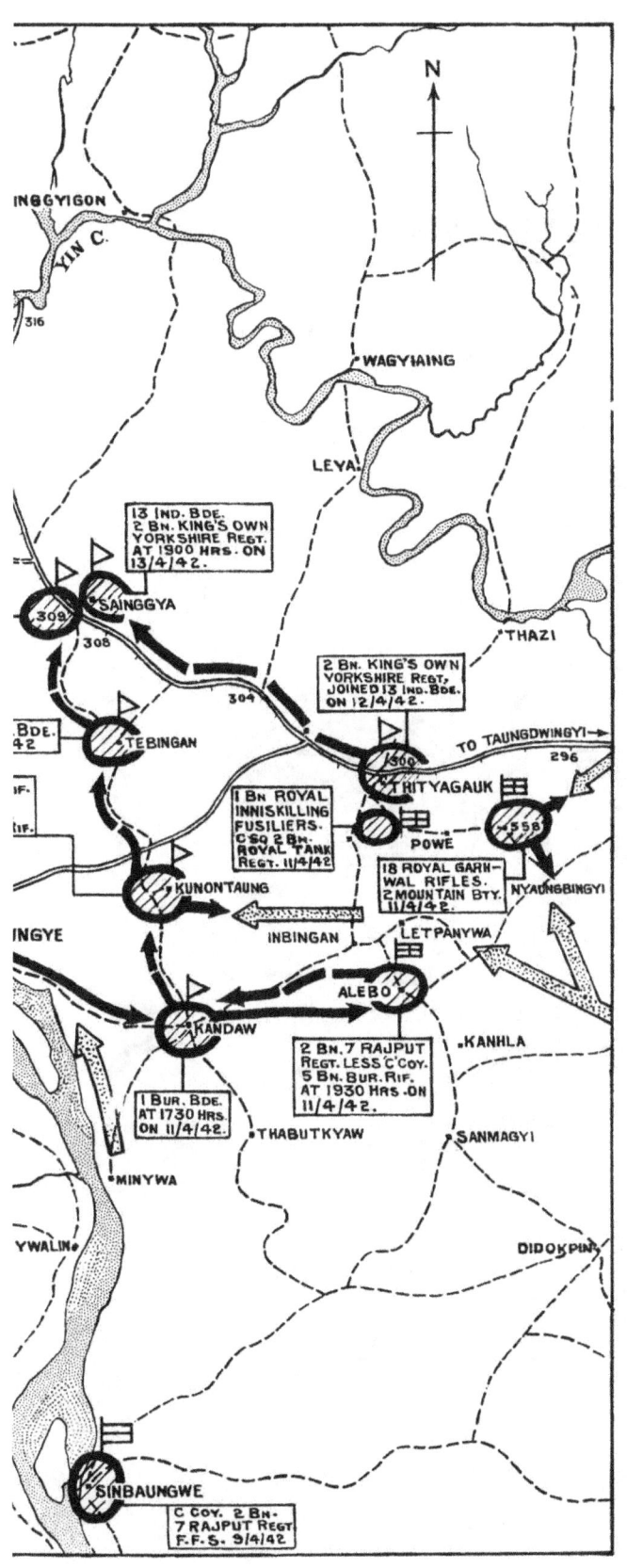

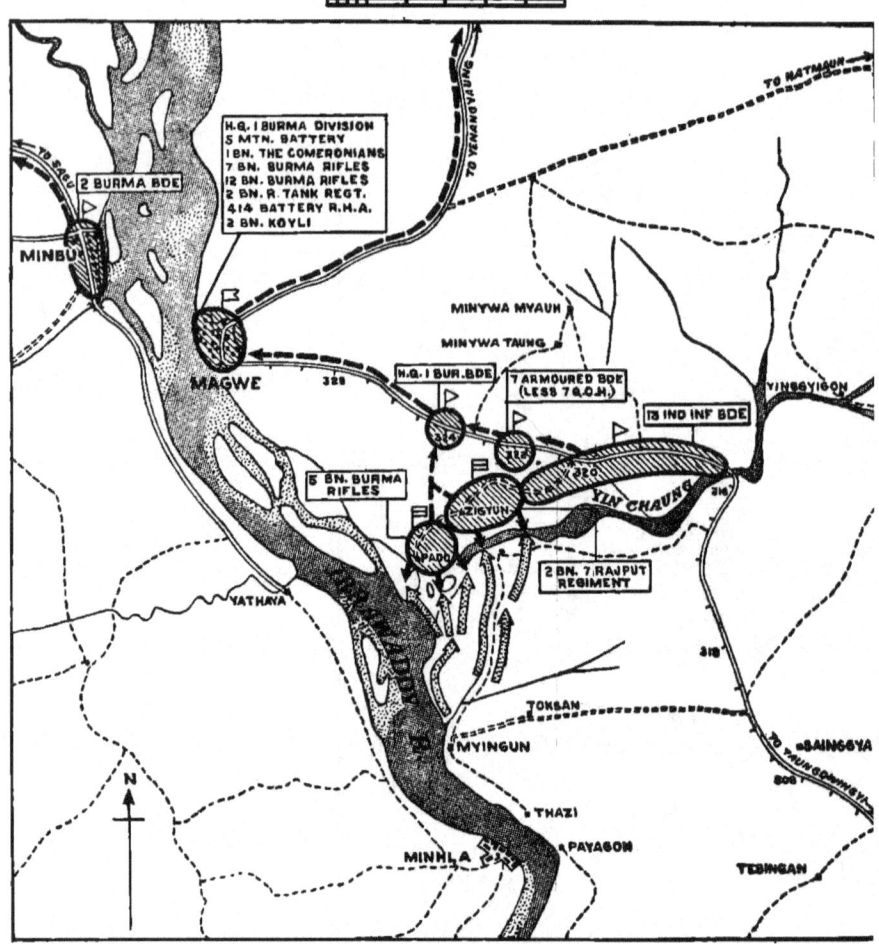

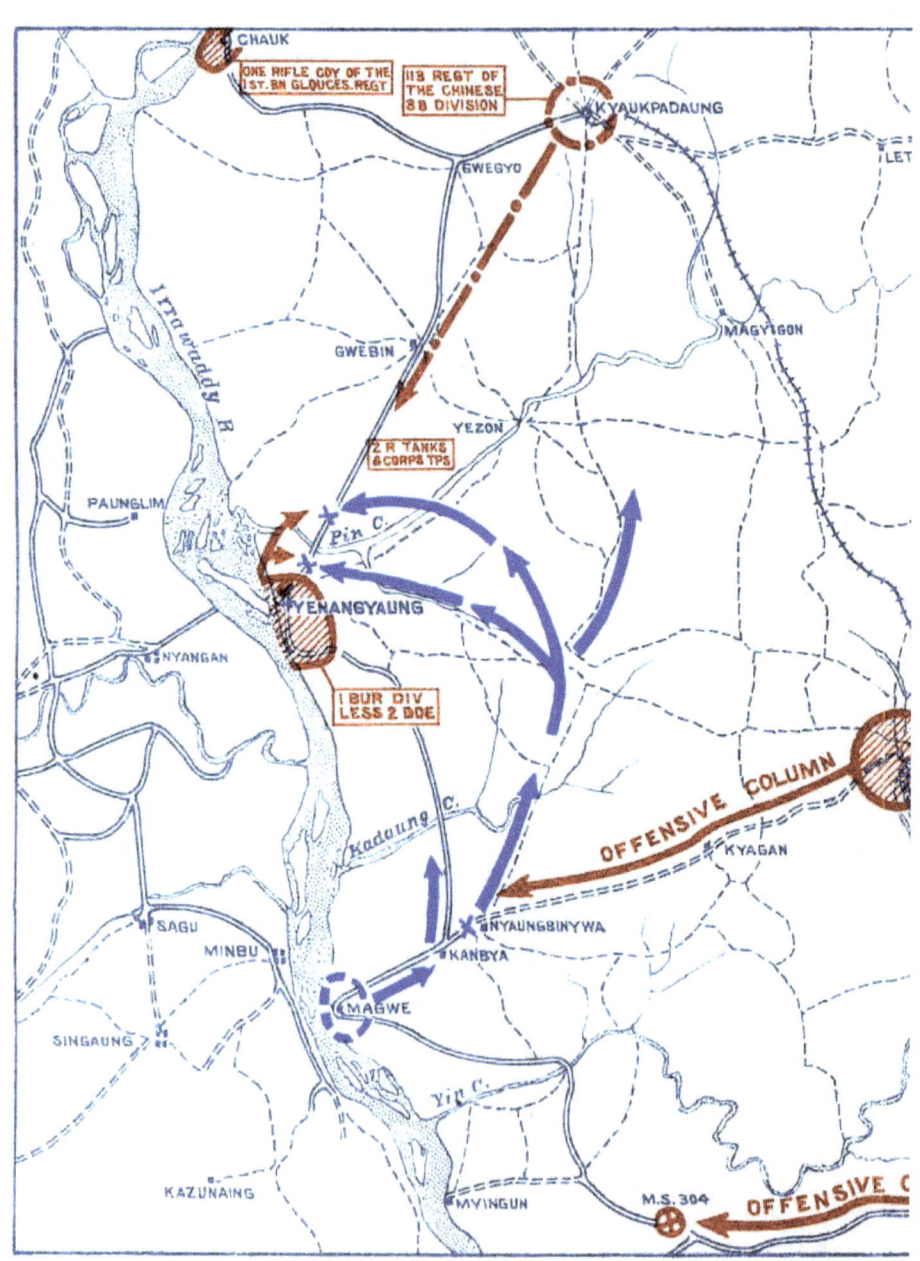

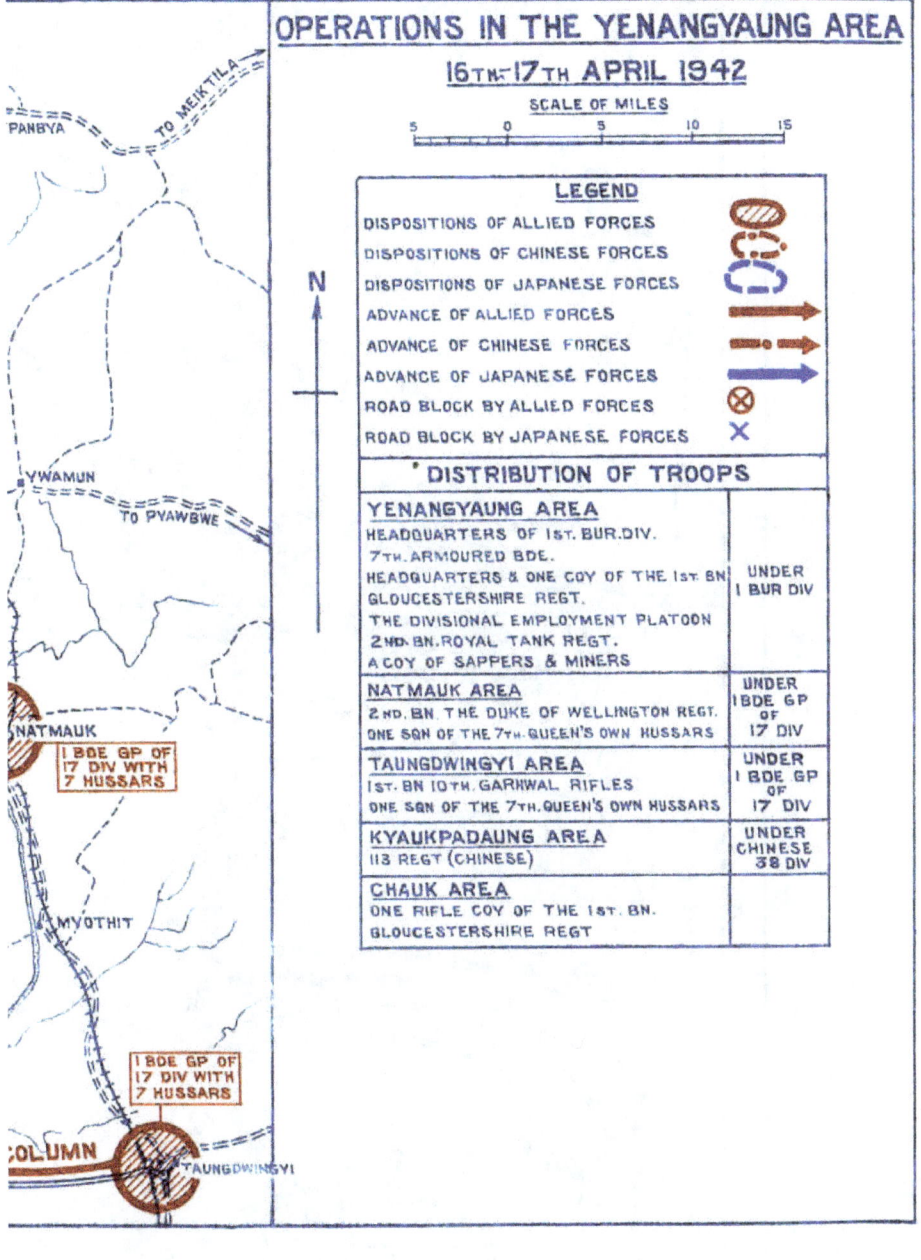

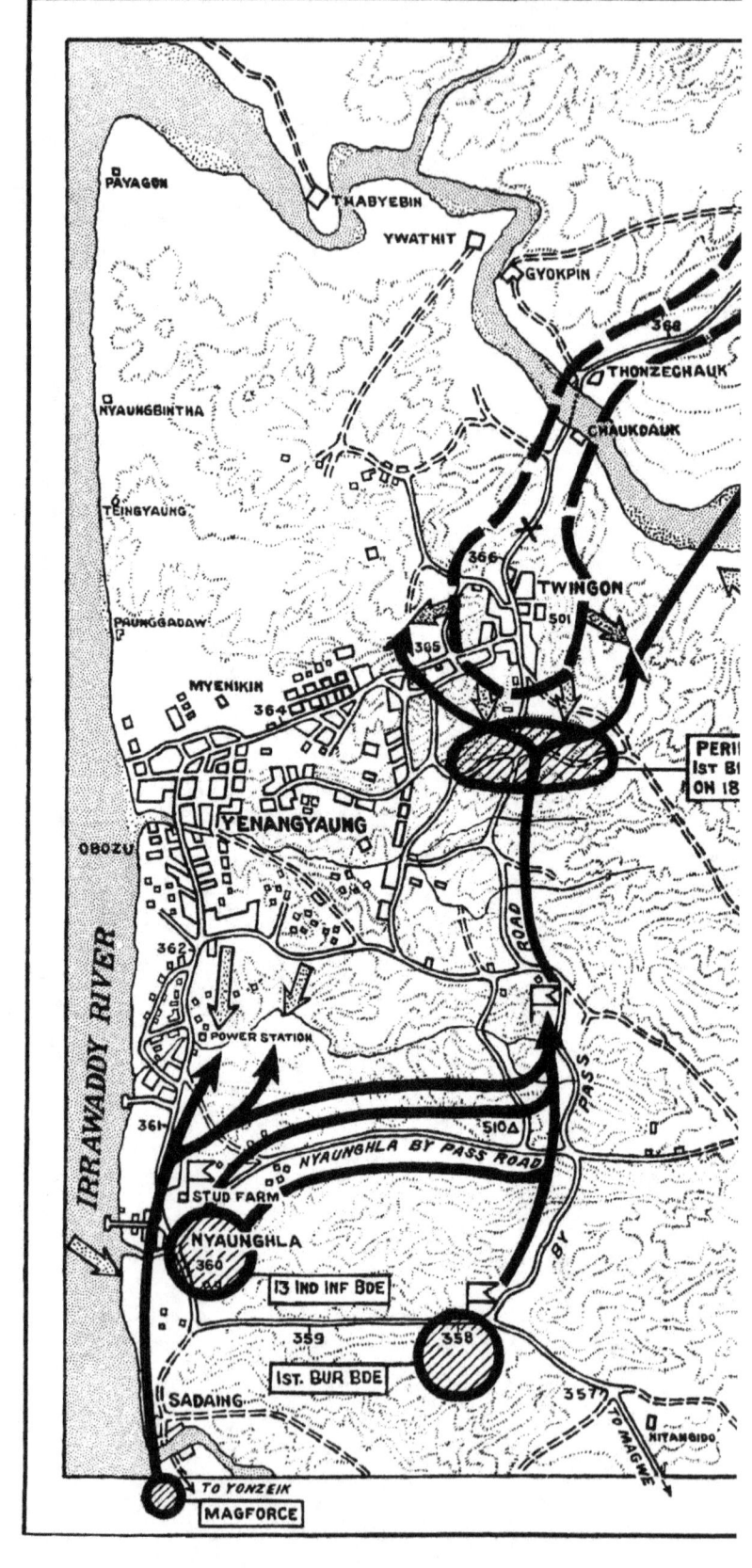

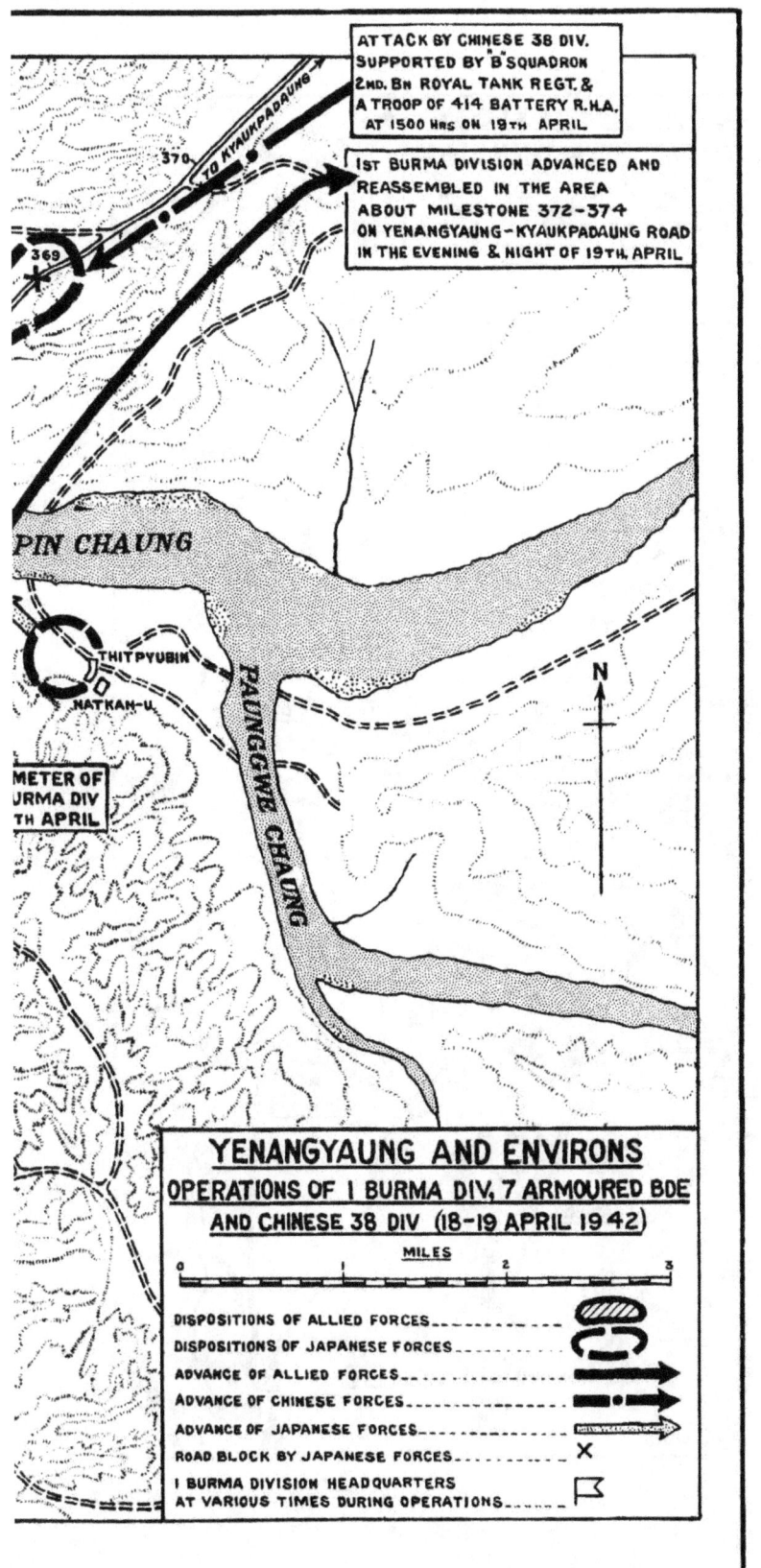

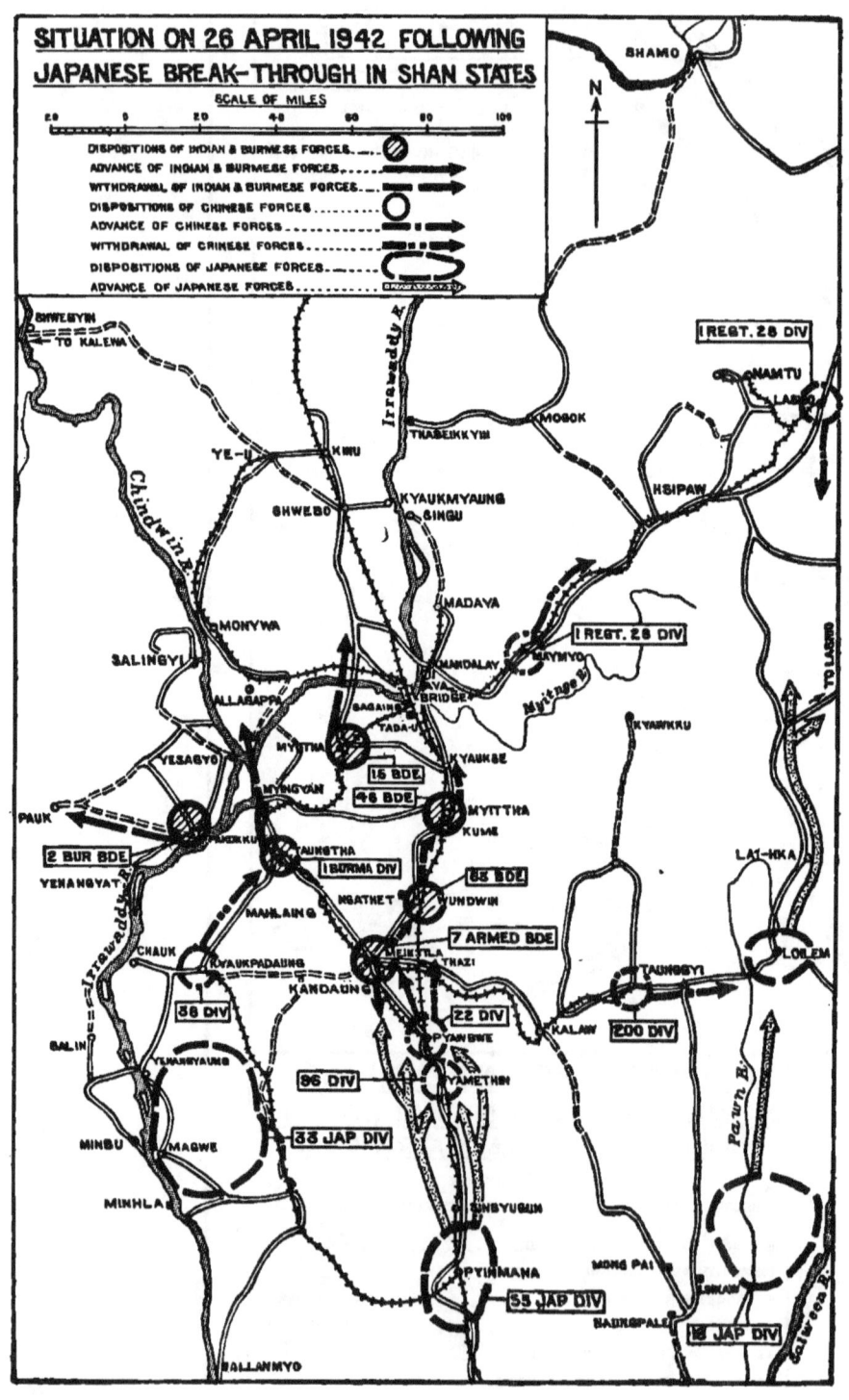

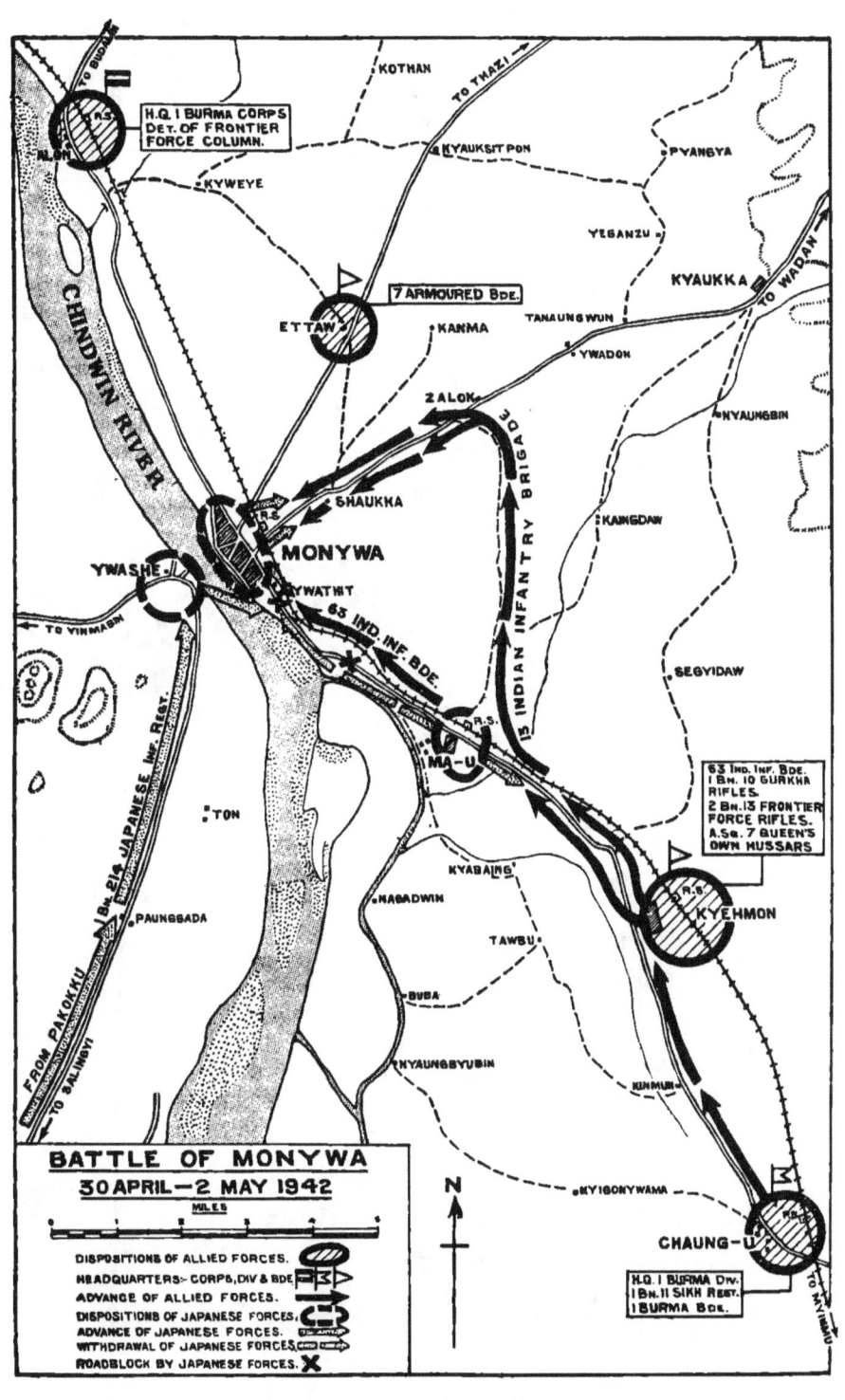

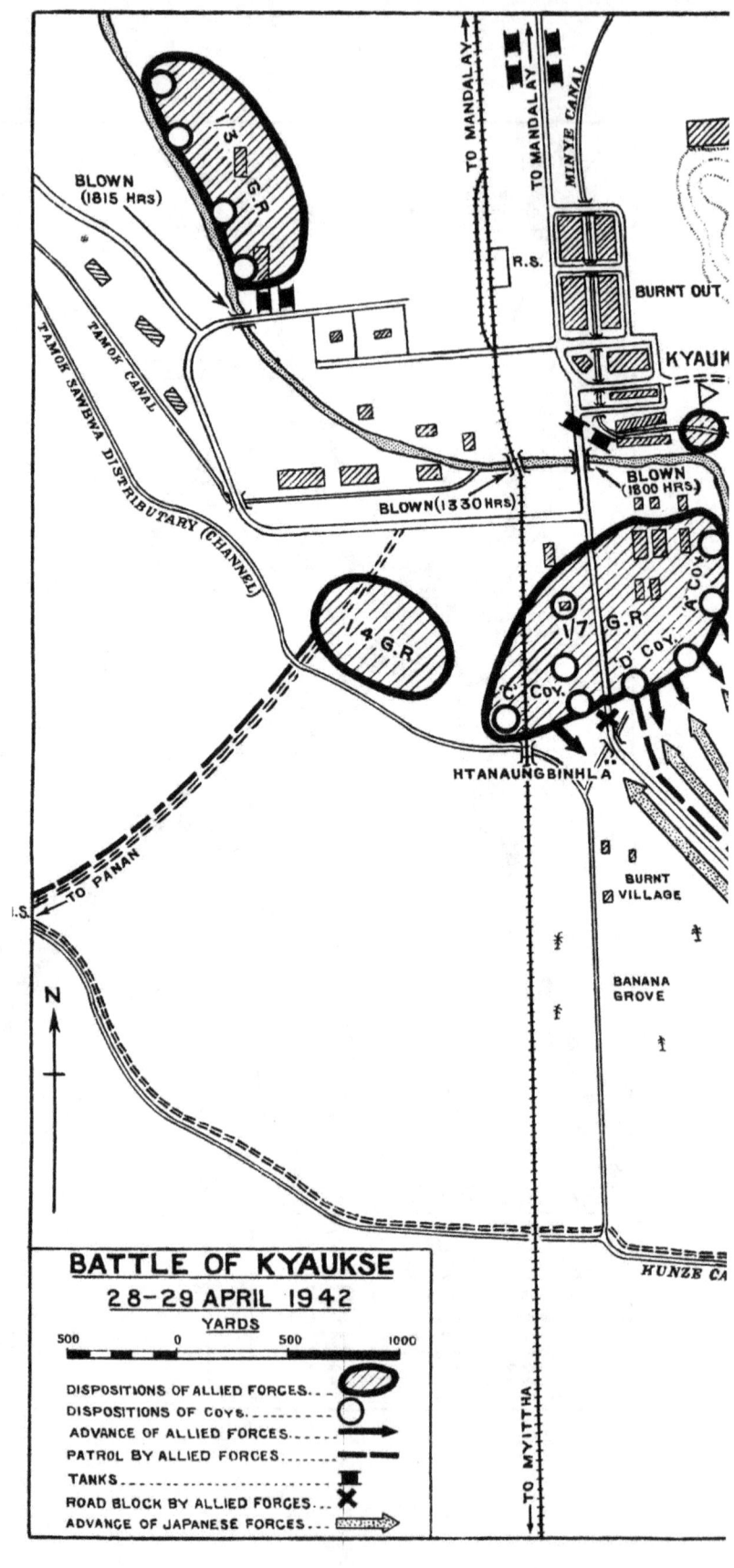

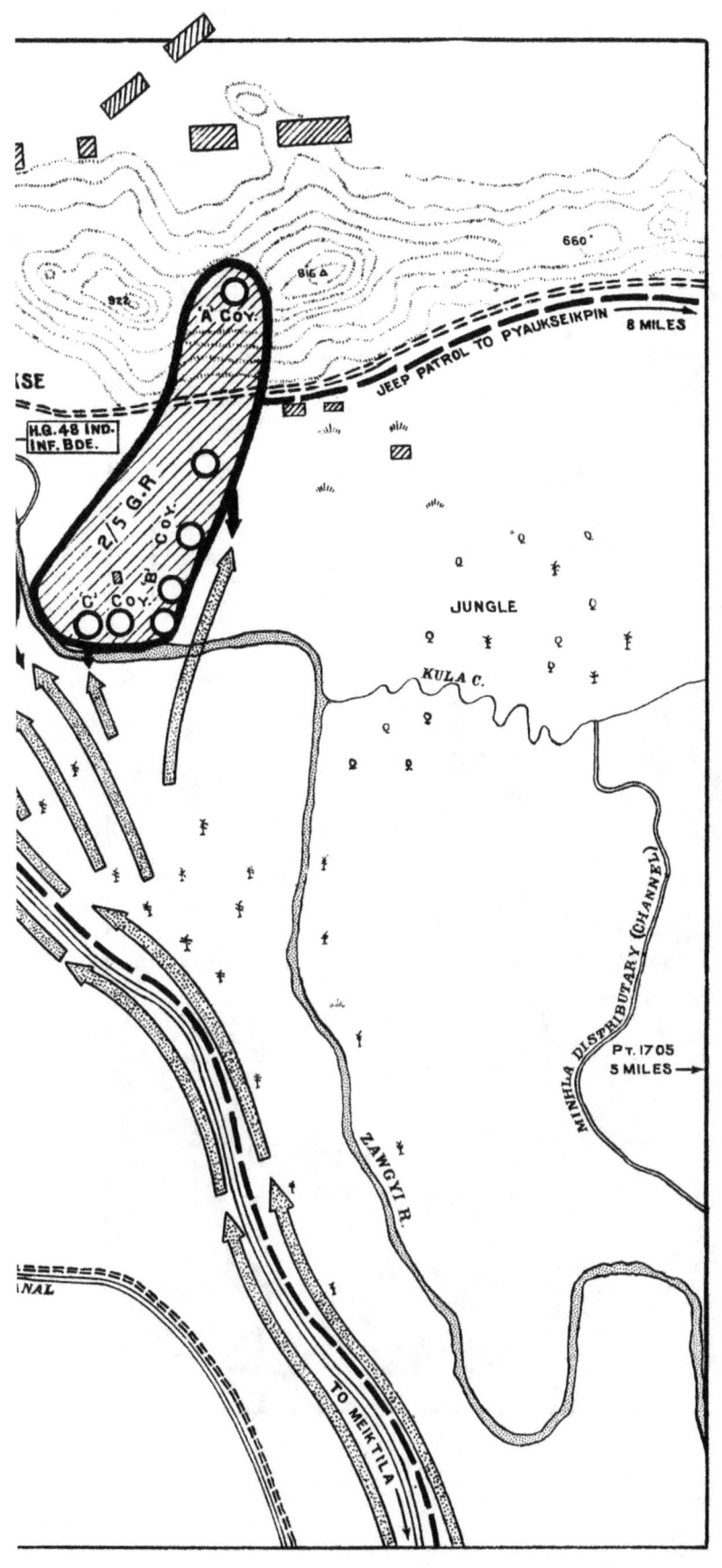

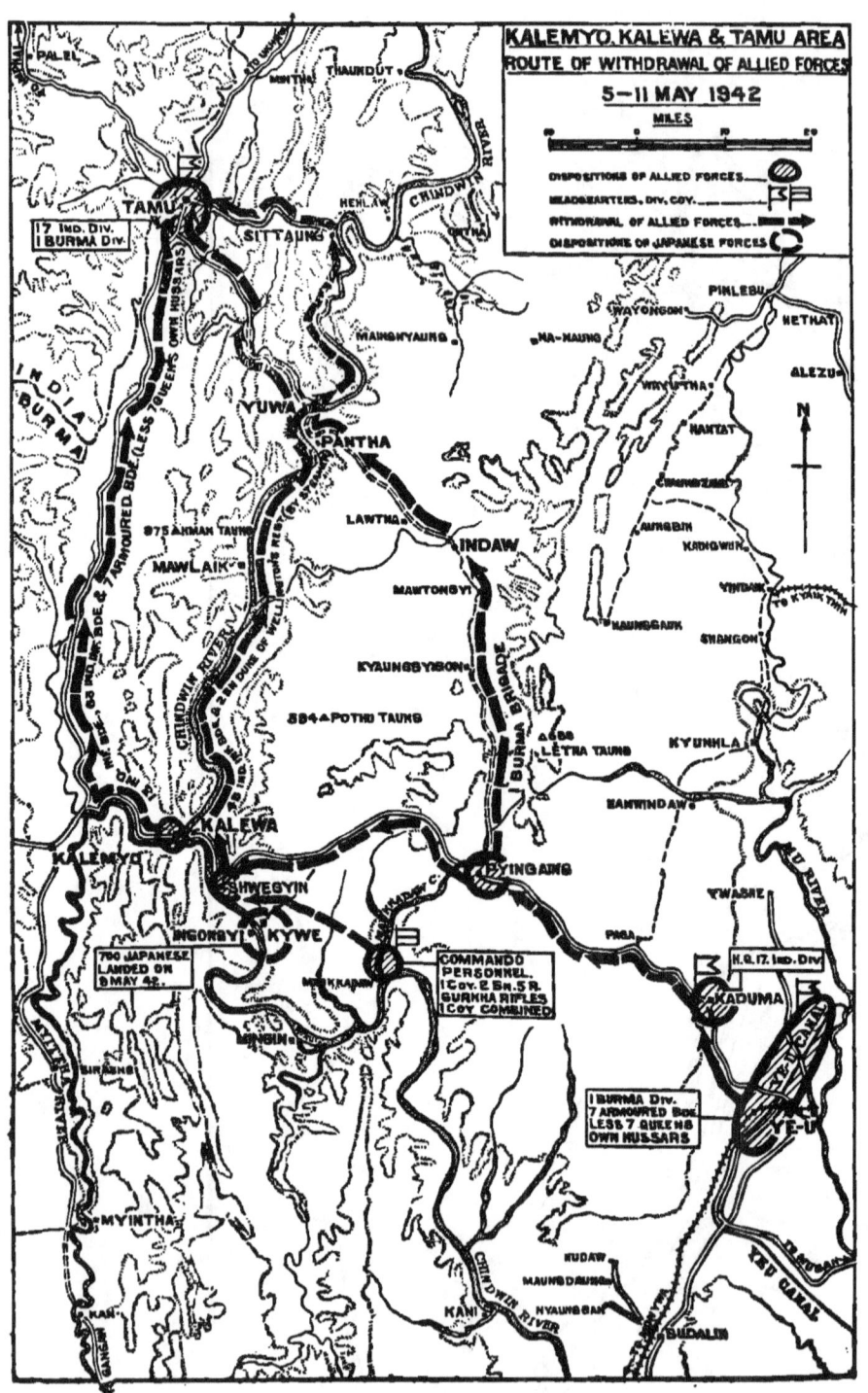

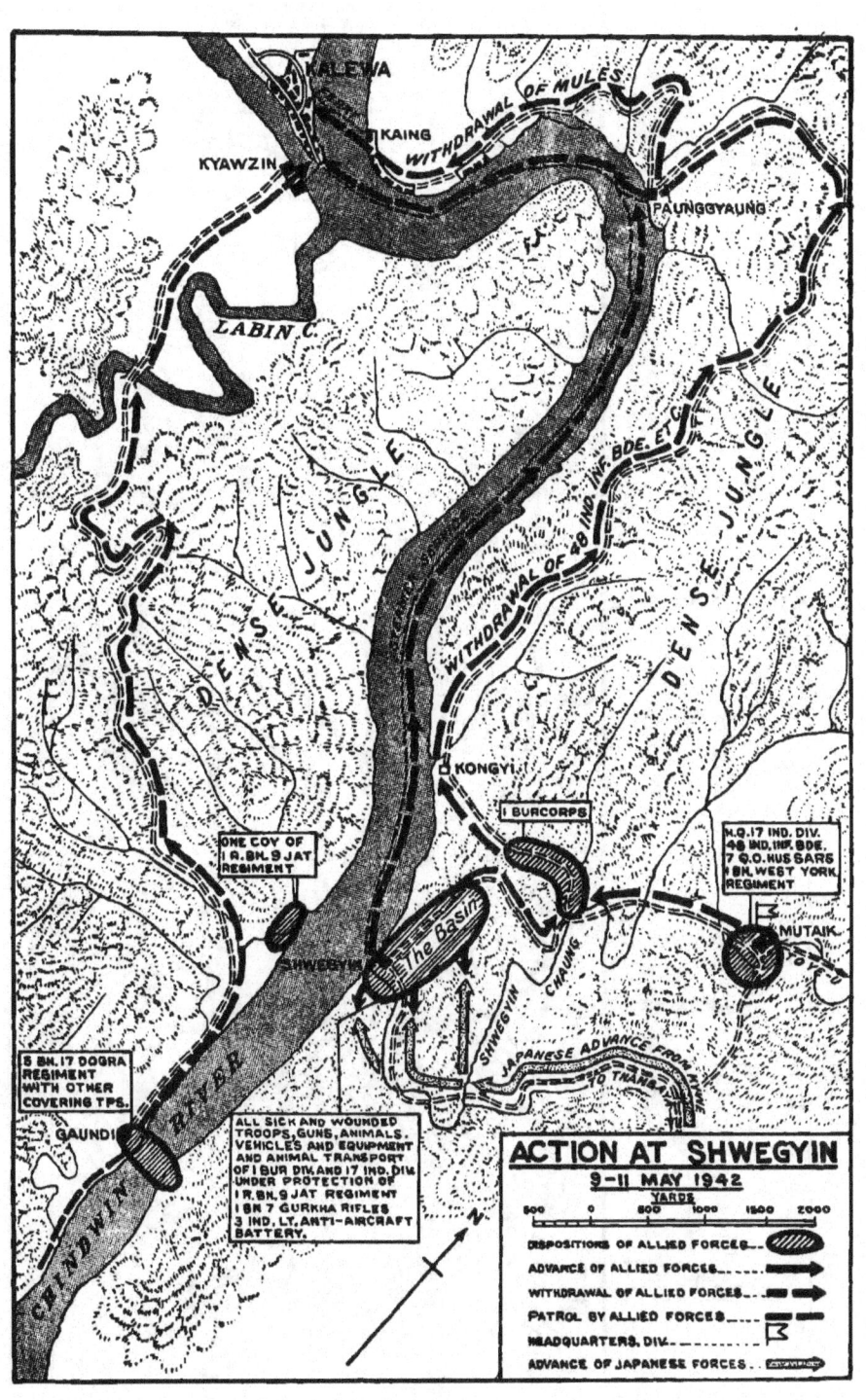

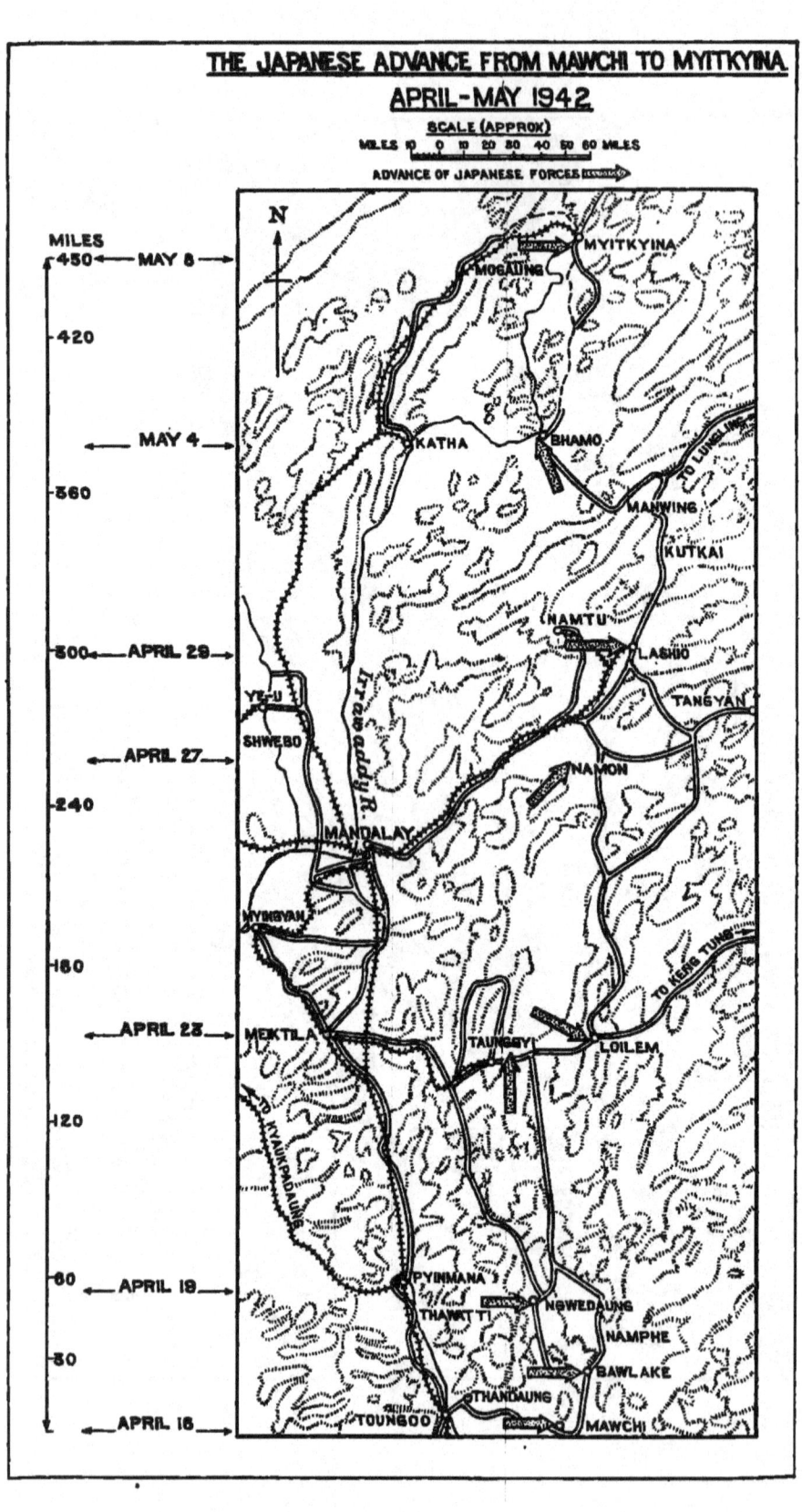

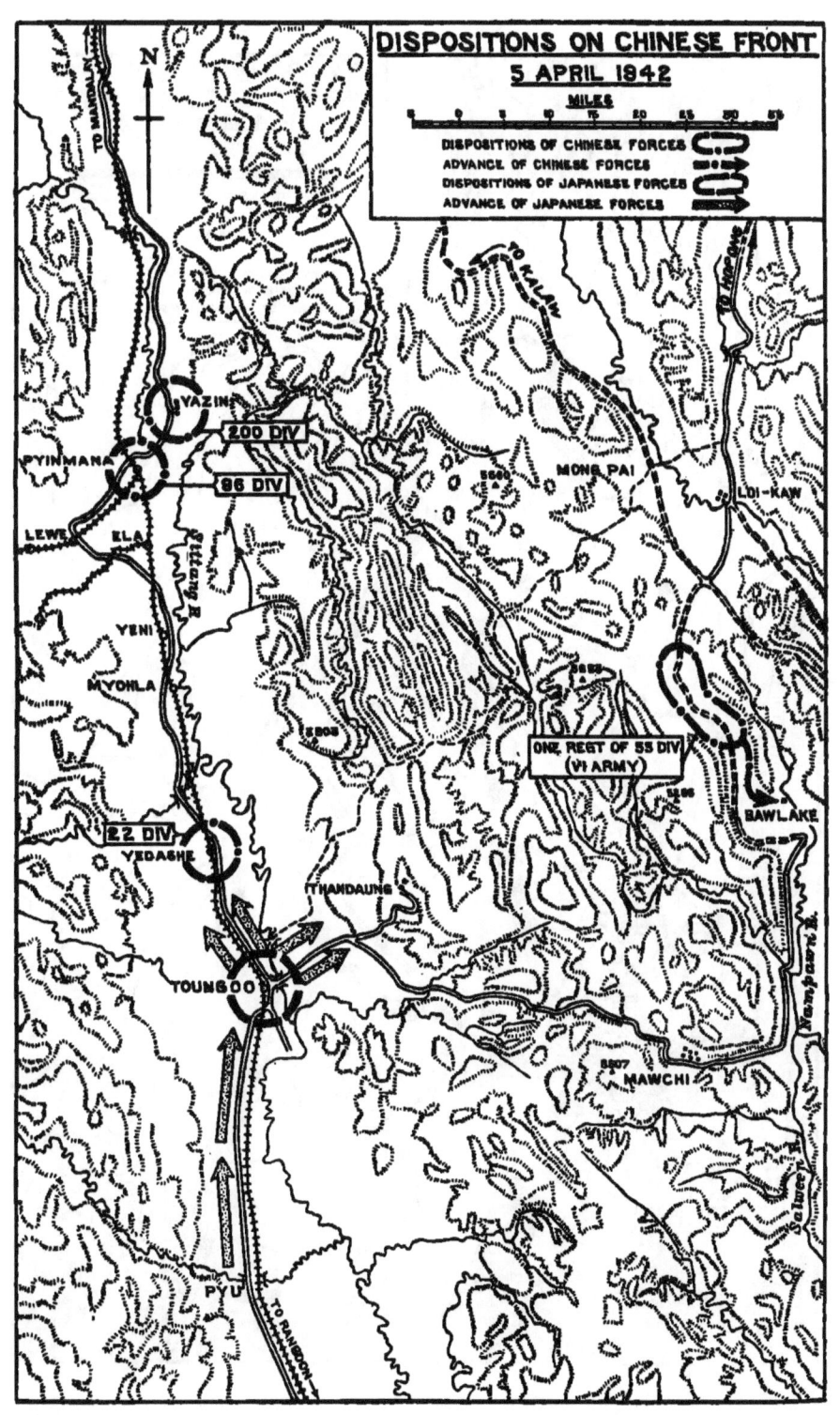

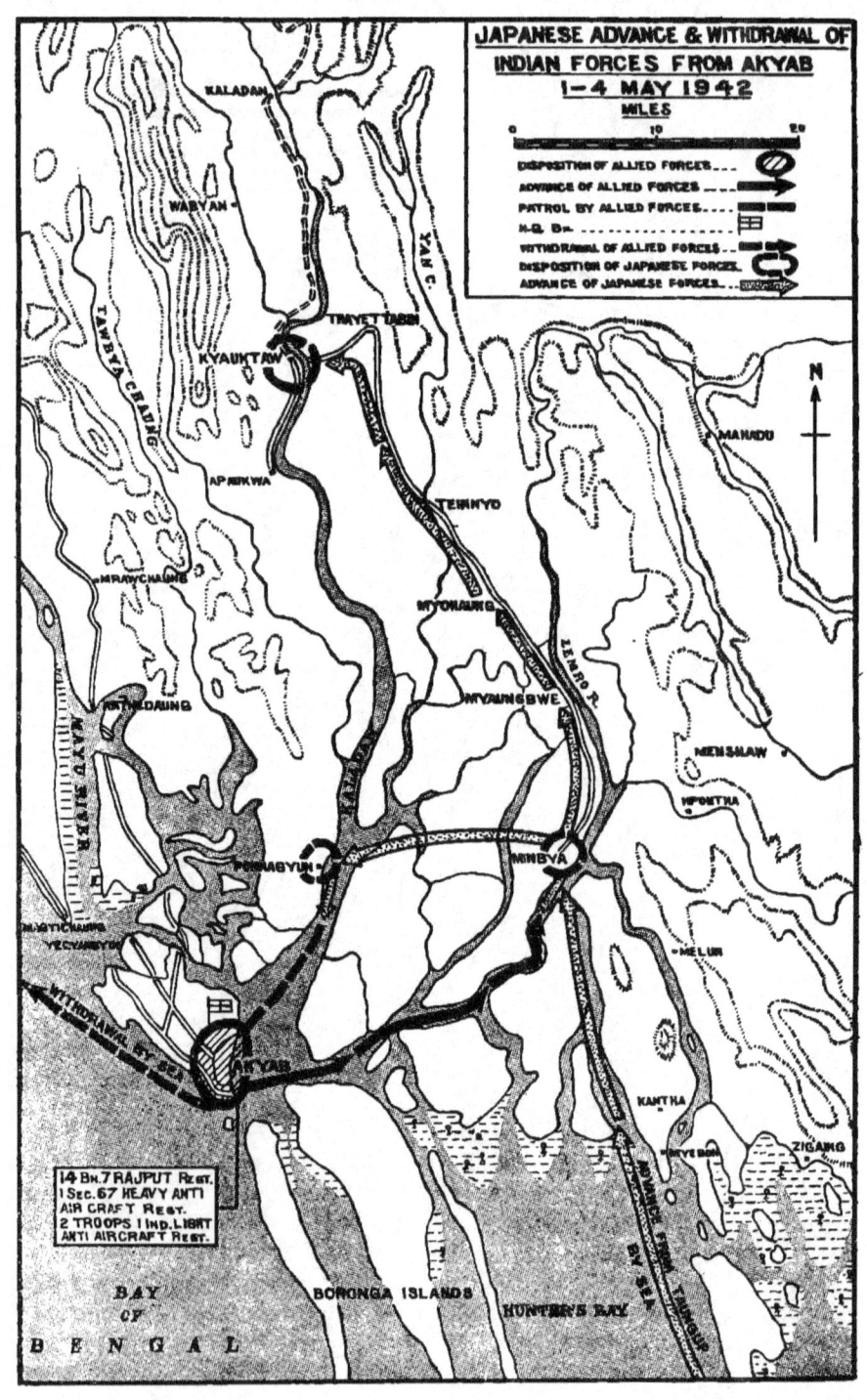

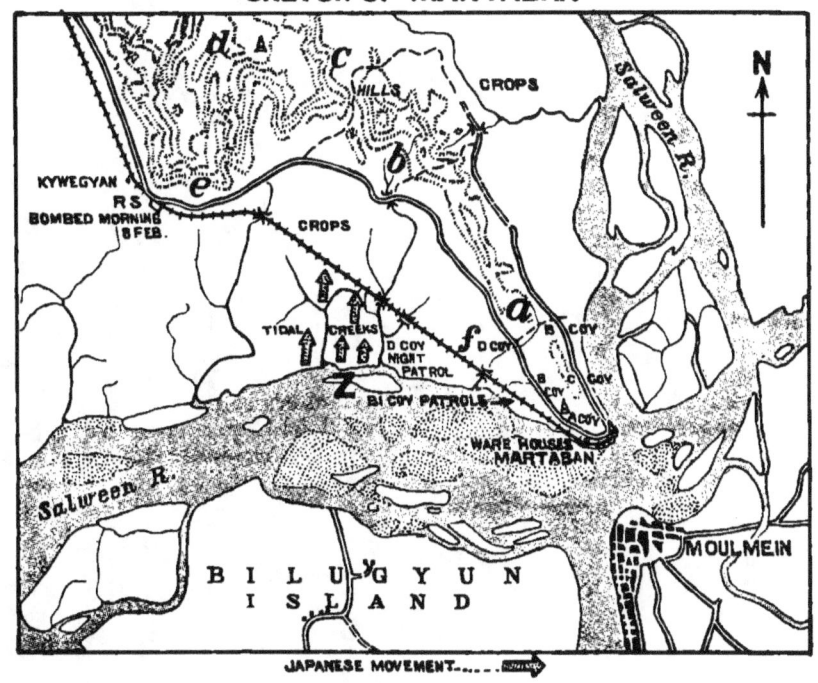

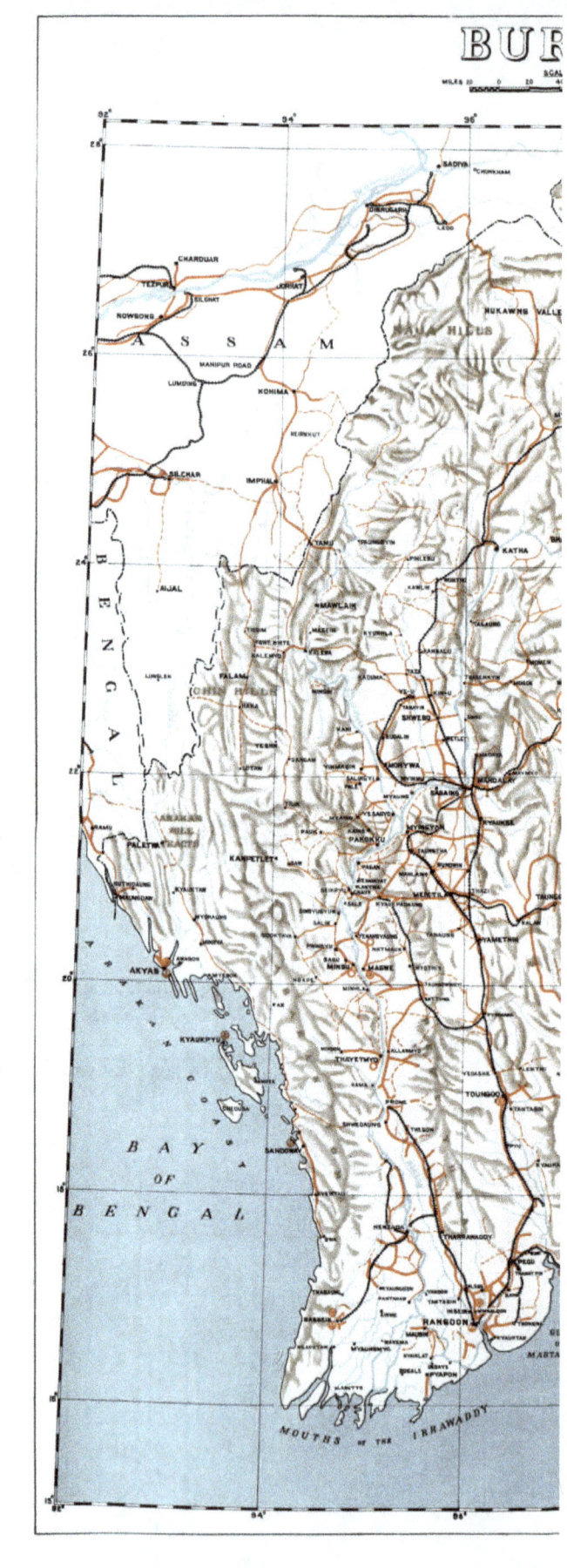

OFFICIAL HISTORY OF THE INDIAN ARMED FORCES
IN THE SECOND WORLD WAR
1939-45

CAMPAIGNS IN SOUTH-EAST ASIA
1941-42

Maps and Sketches

Campaigns in South-East Asia 1941–42
List of maps

1. South-East Asia
2. Hong Kong and New Territory showing Japanese advance
3. The Mainland—South of Tide Cove showing original inner line position of Mainland Brigade
4. Panoramic Section of Devil's Peak
5. Hong Kong Island showing dispositions of Allied Troops
6. Malaya, showing progress of Japanese Operations
7. Kelantan Troop Dispositions
8. Kota Bharu Area
9. Kota Bharu Beach Defences
10. Jitra Area
11. Malaya, Kedah State
12. GurunArea
13. Malaya, Kampar to Kuala Lumpur
14. Kampar–Telok Anson Area
15. Action at Trolak
16. Positions on the Slim River
17. Kuantan and Surrounding Area
18. Malaya, Tampin to Rengam
19. MuarArea
20. Malaya, Batu Pahat to Singapore
21. Singapore Island—Dispositions of Troops, 8 February 1942
22. Singapore Island (South-West Sector)
23. Singapore-Fighting in MacRitchie Reservoir Area, 12-15 February 1942
24. Borneo
25. Kuching Area (Sarawak) showing Dispositions of Sarfor on 22nd December, 1941 and line of withdrawal of 2/15 Punjab Regt. into Dutch Borneo
26. Dutch N. W. Borneo (Bengkajang-Sanggau Area)
27. Kuching (Sarawak) and Dutch West Borneo showing withdrawal route of 2/15 Punjab, 23 December 1941-29 March 1942

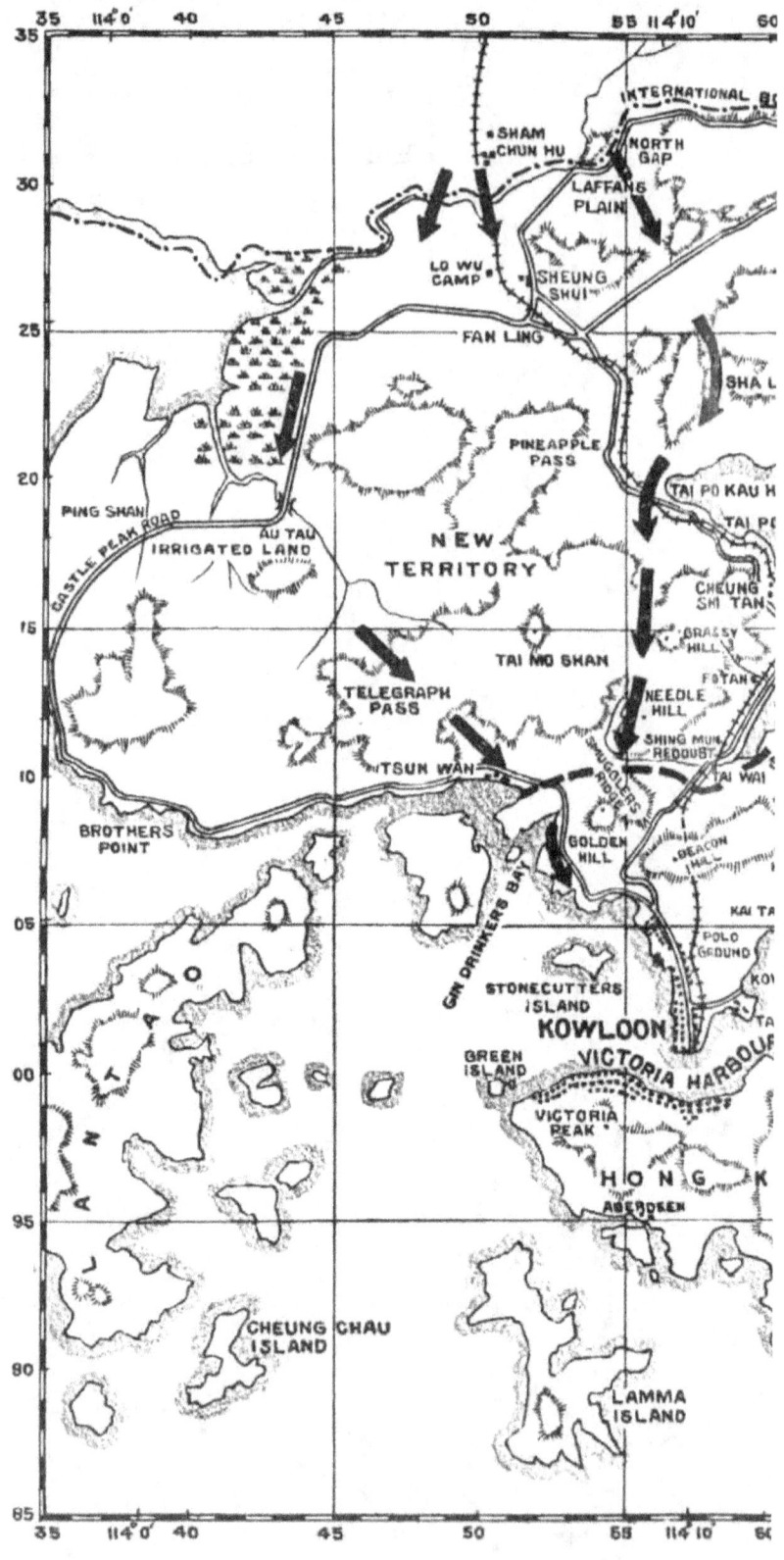

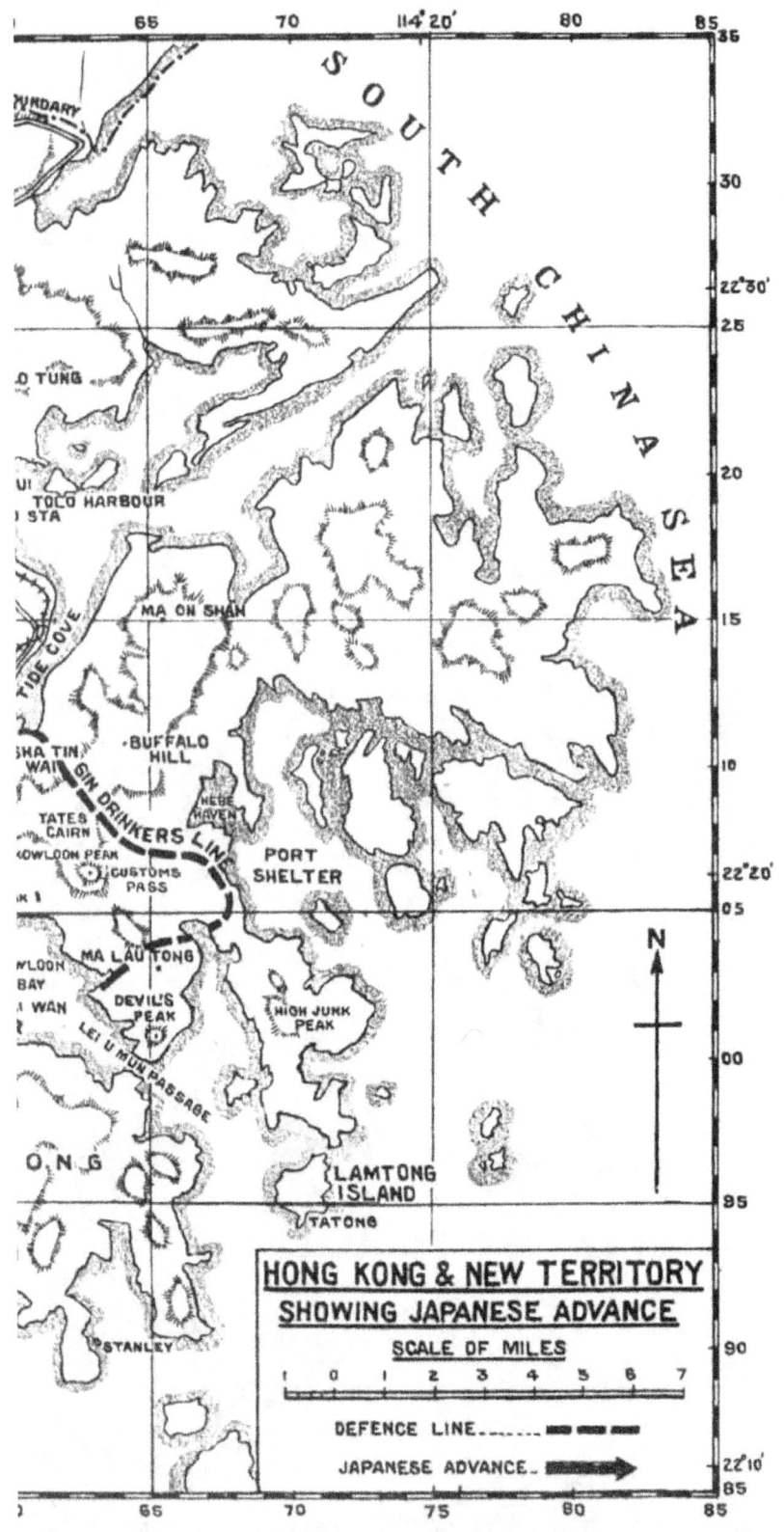

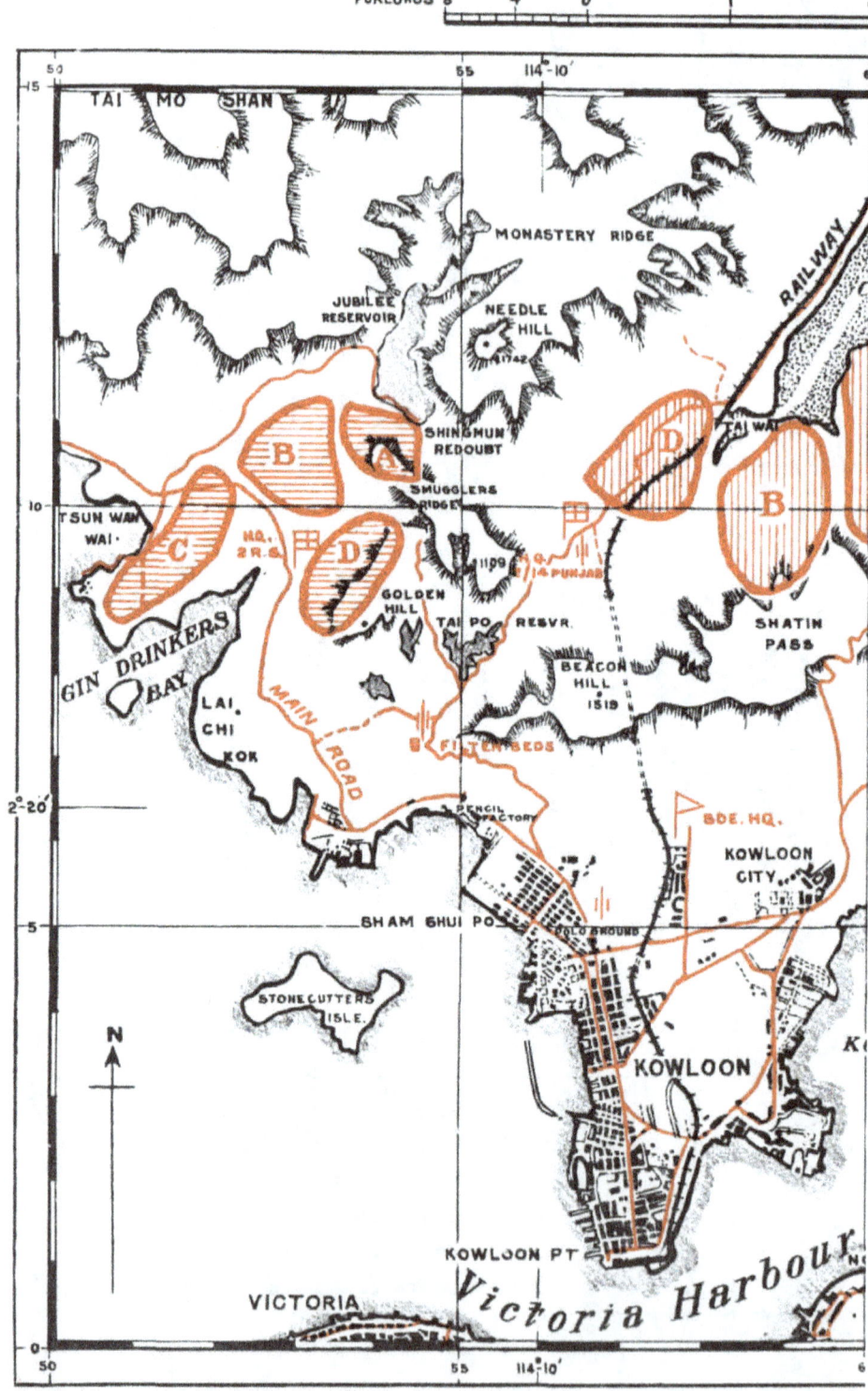

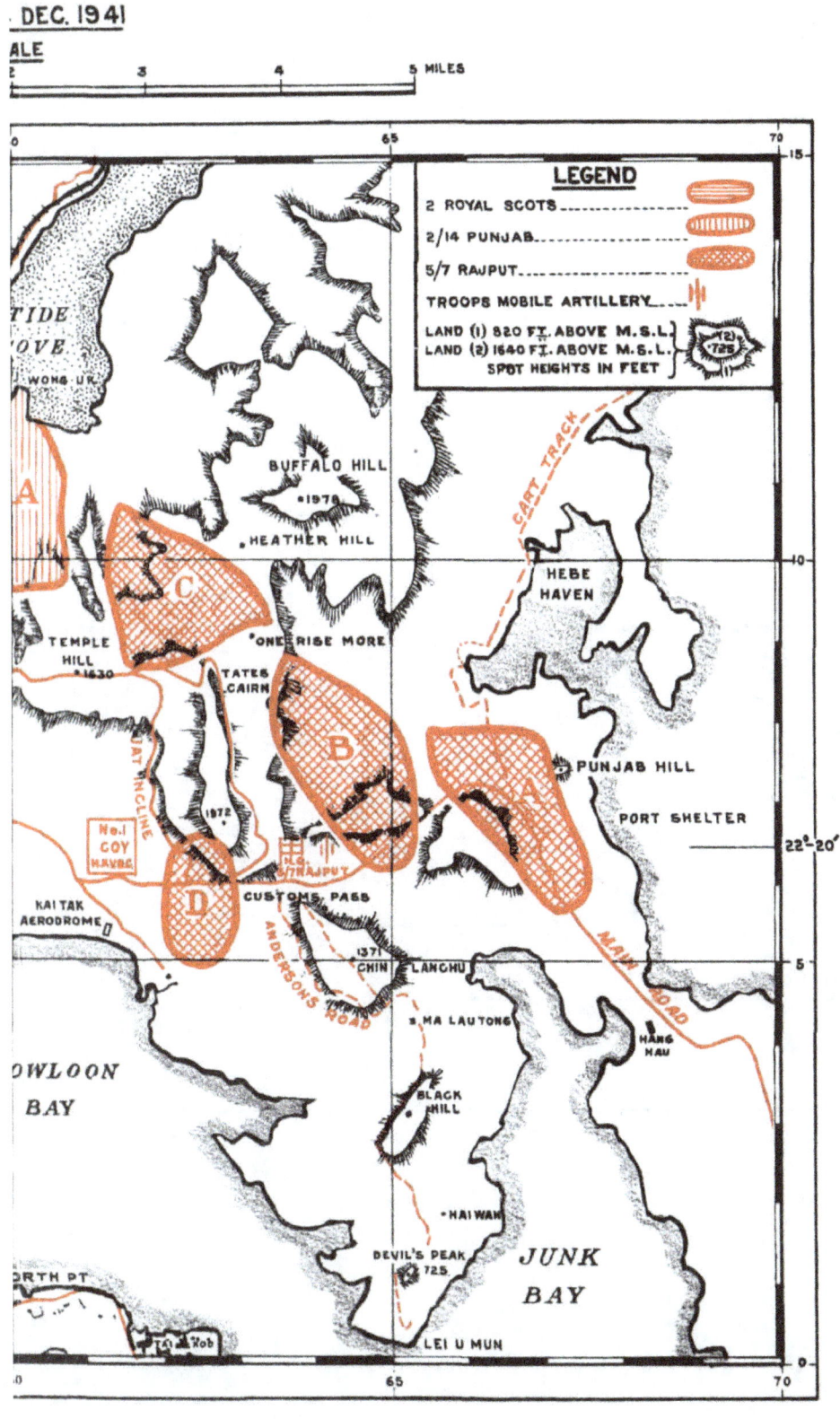

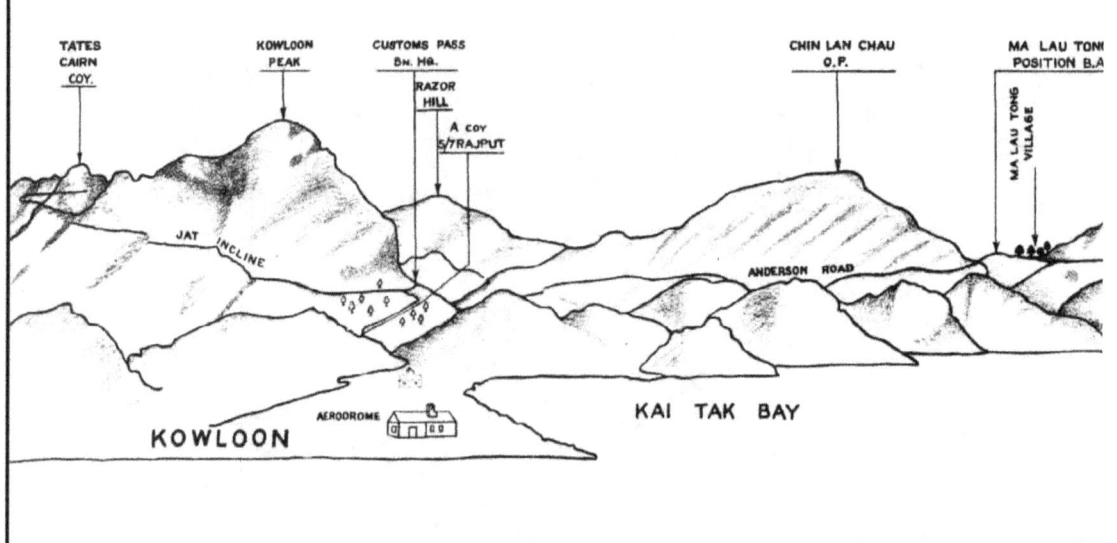

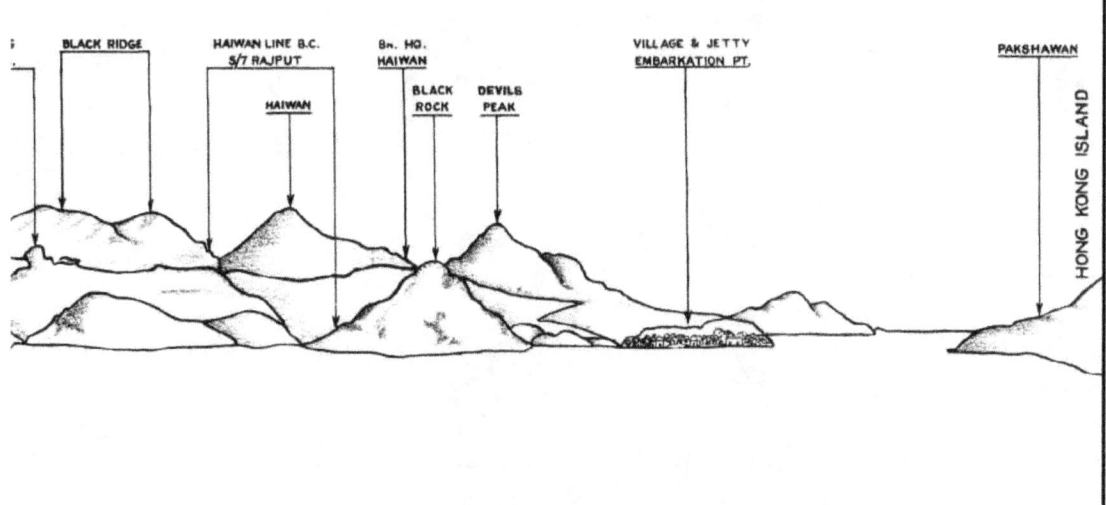

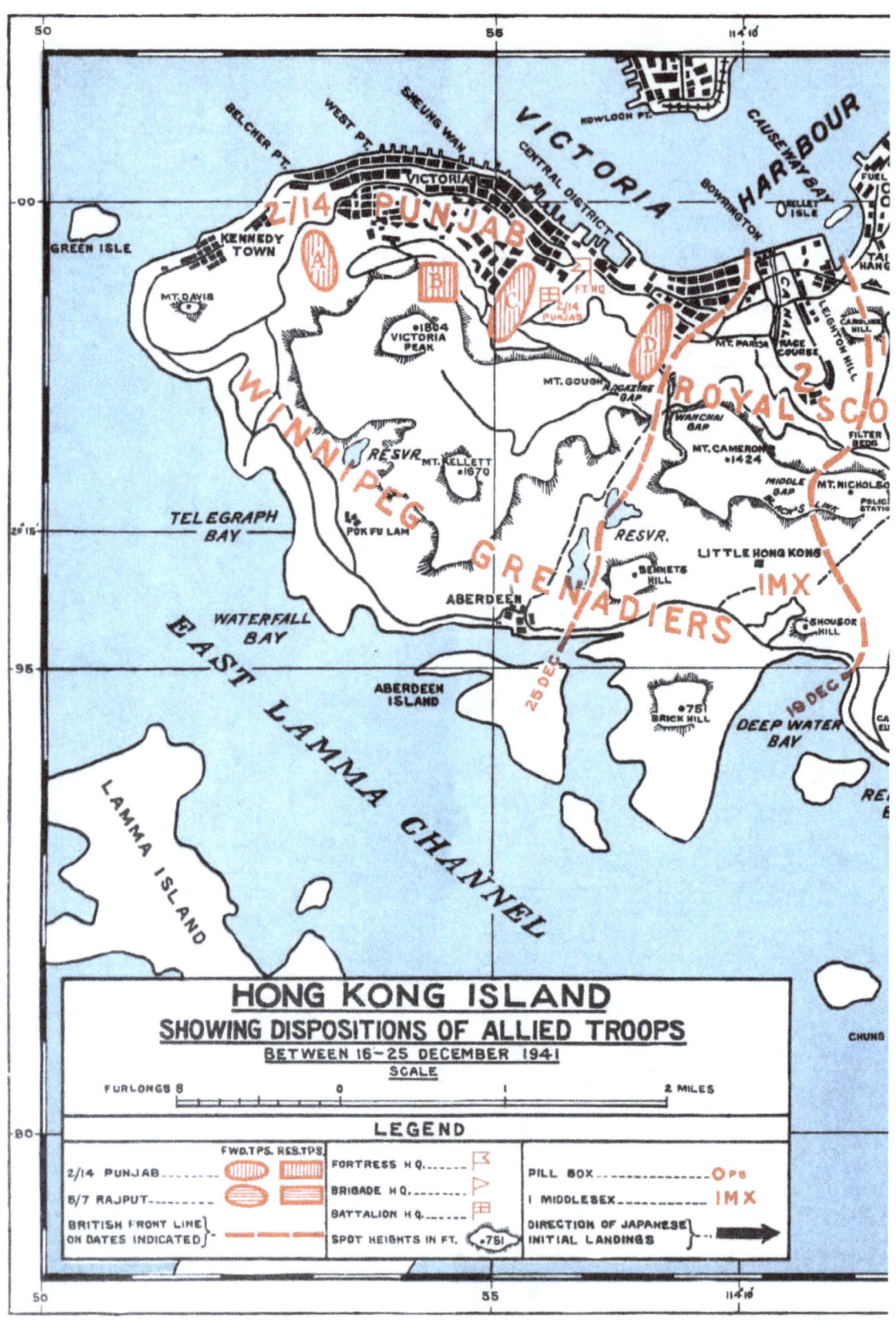

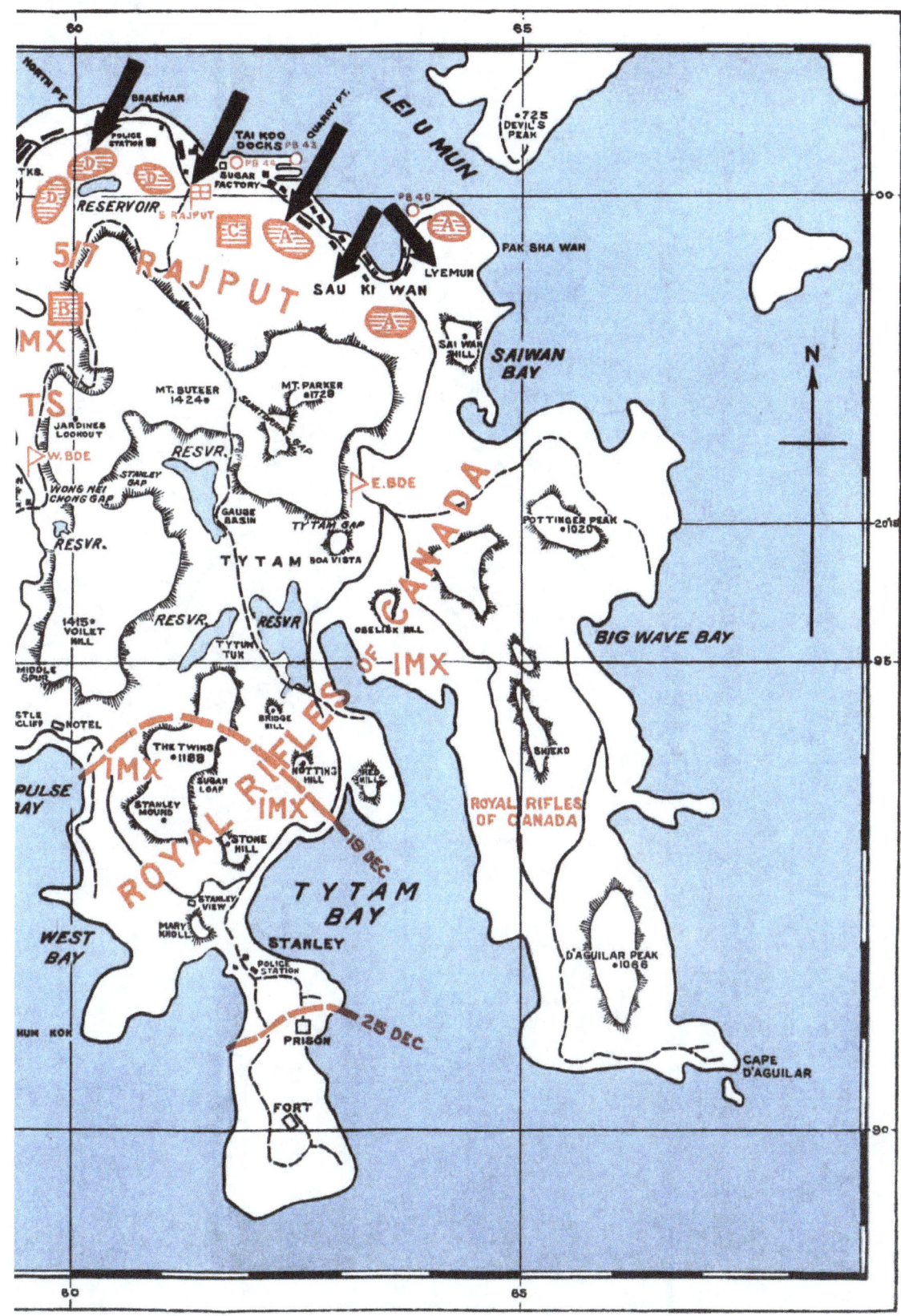

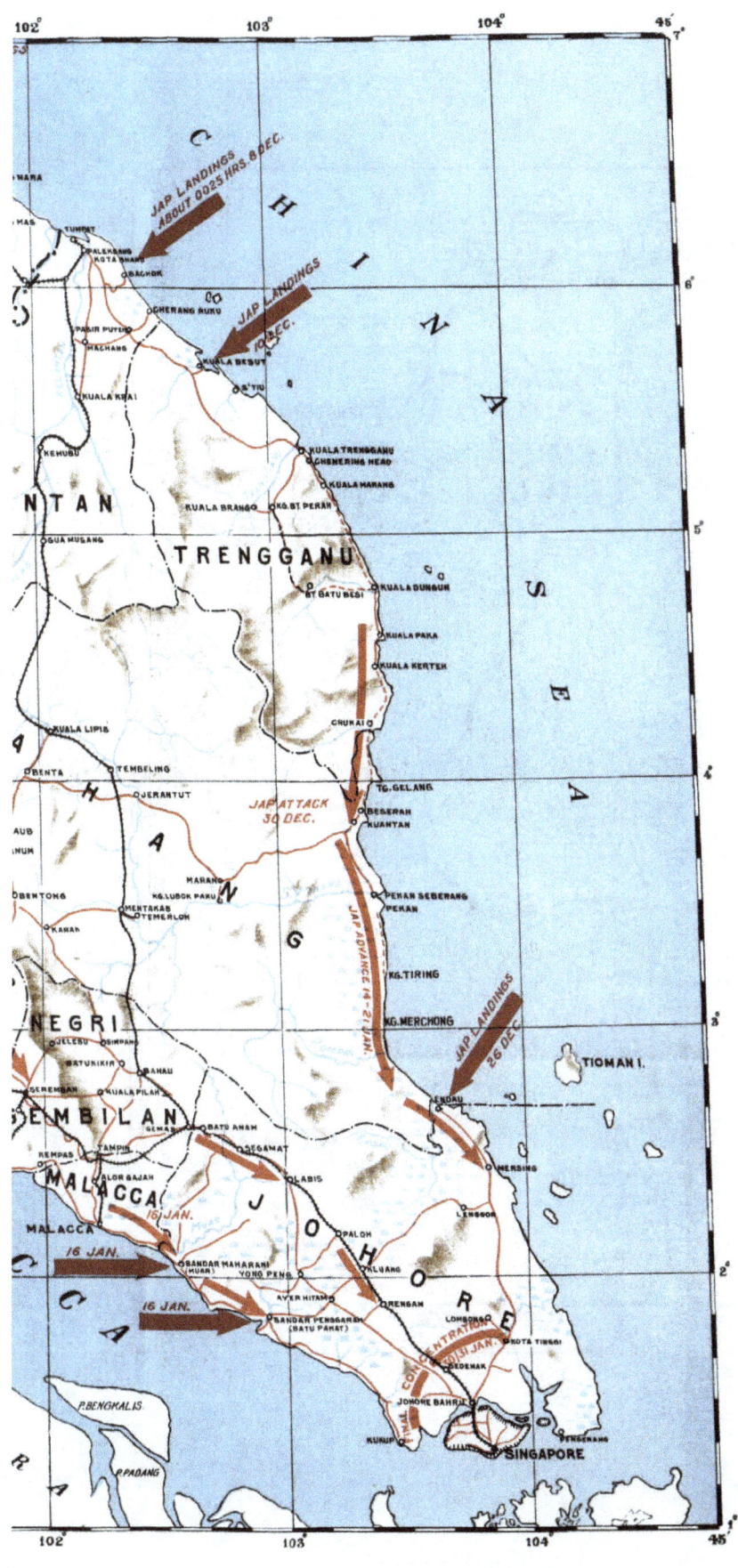

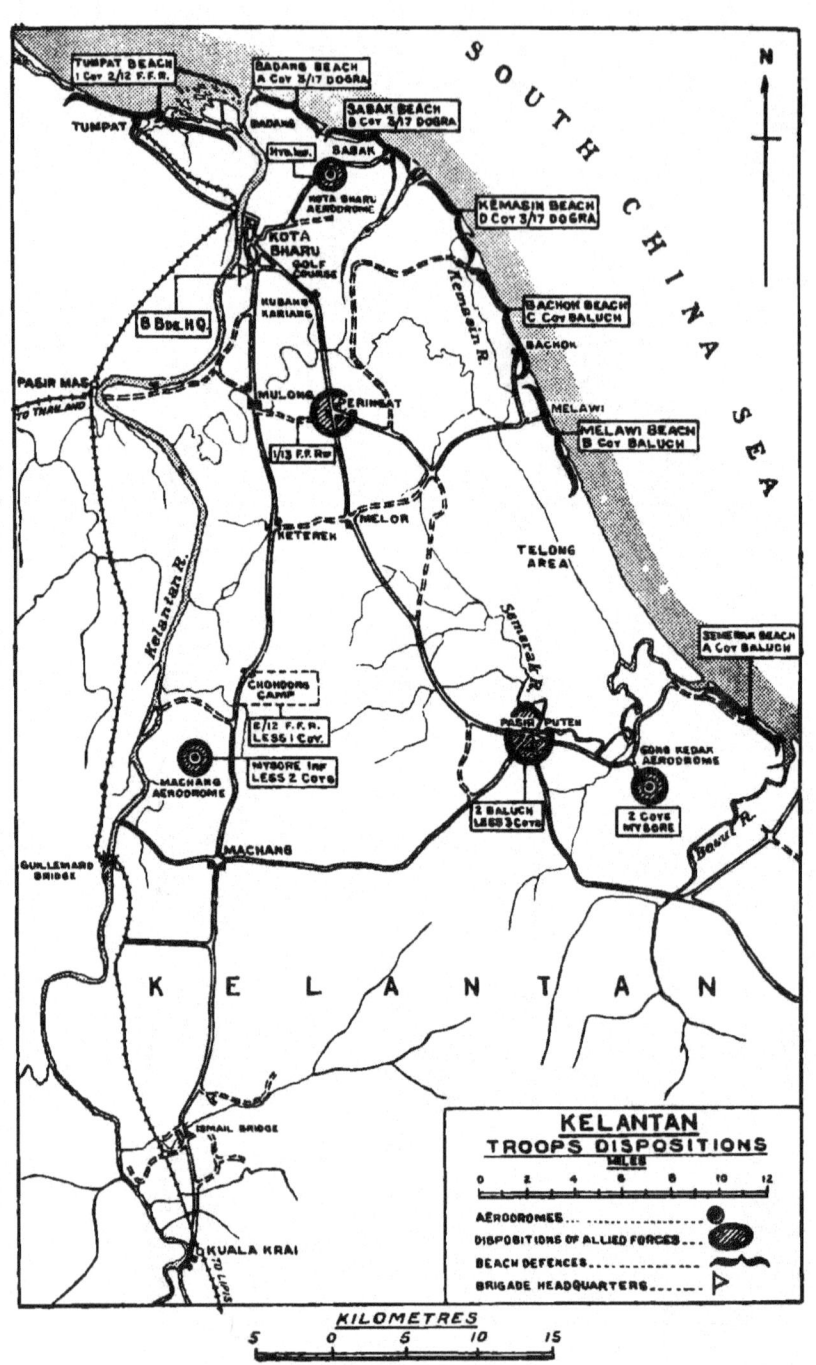

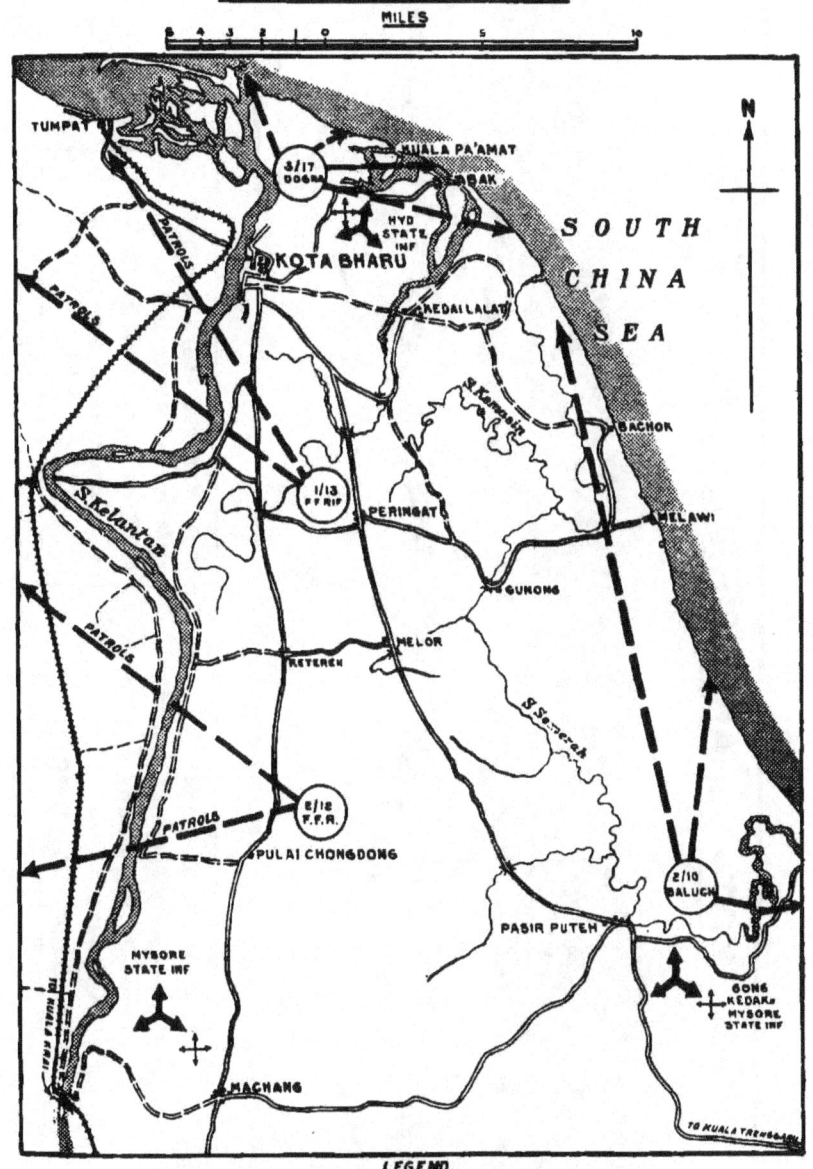

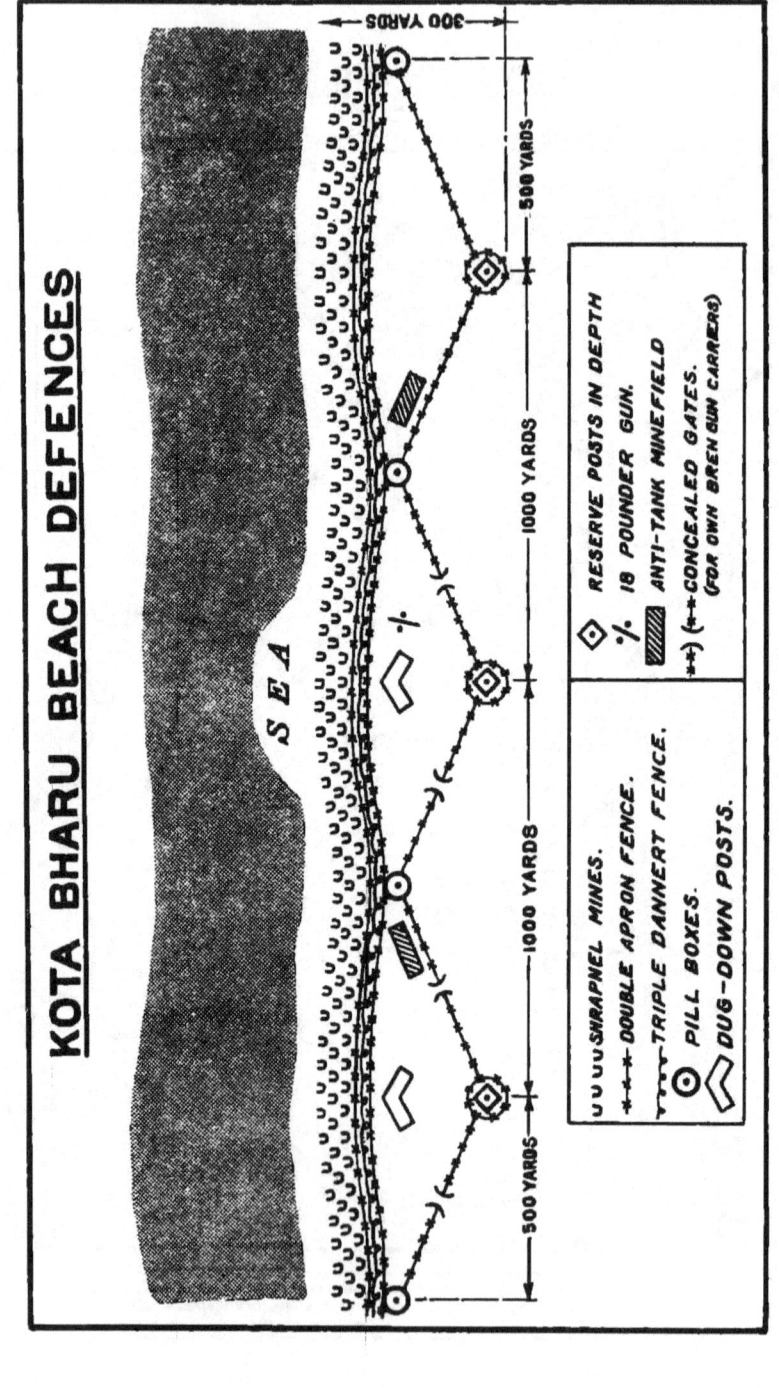

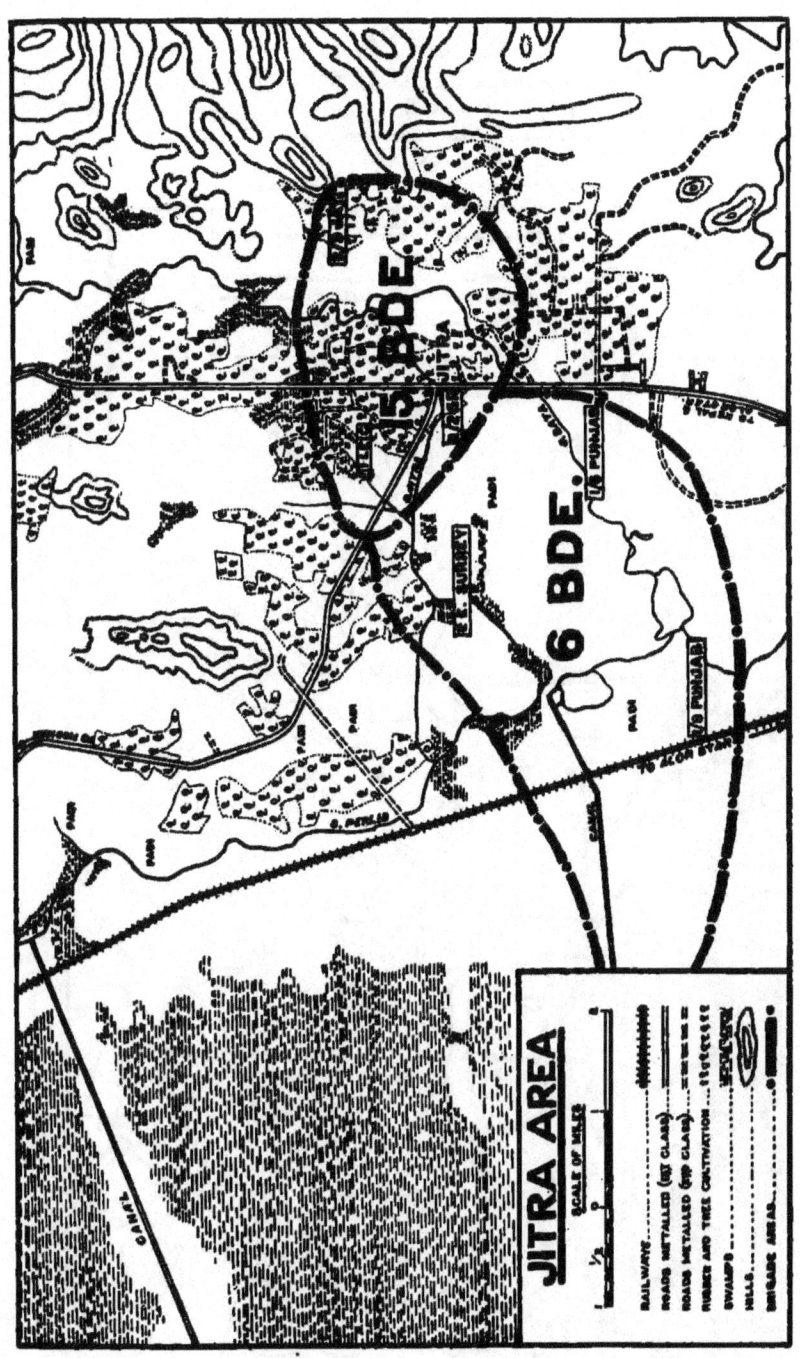

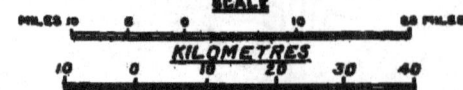

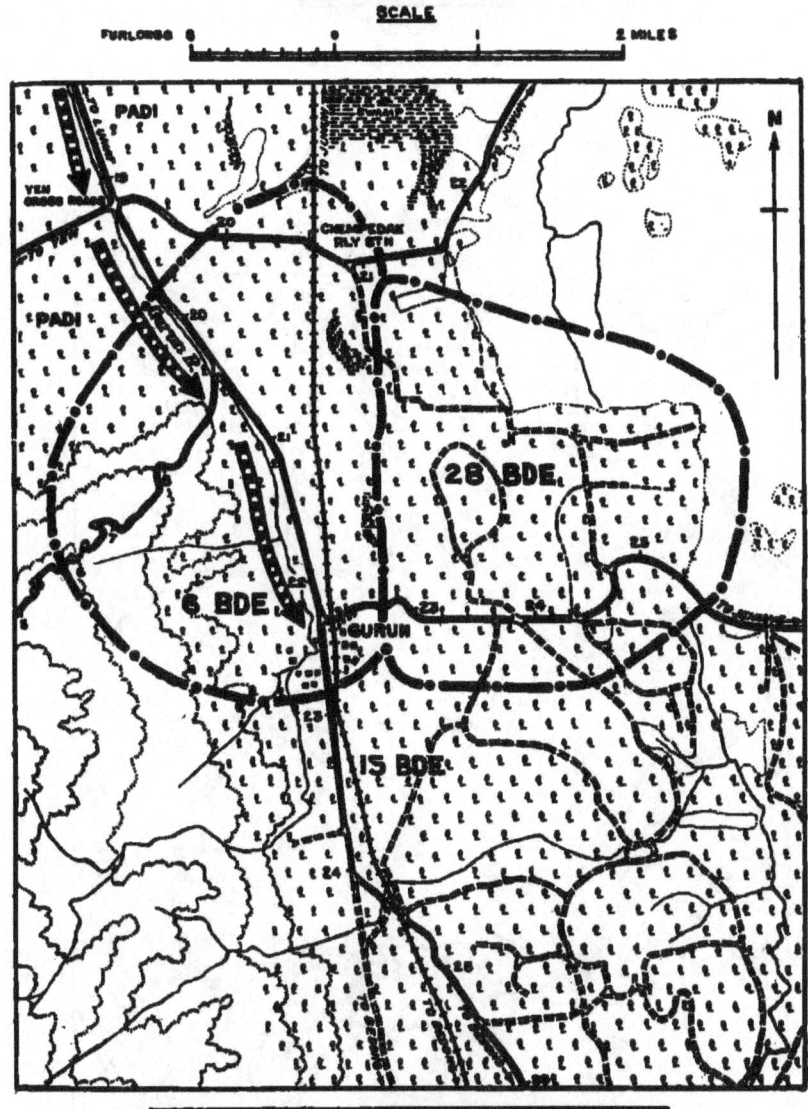

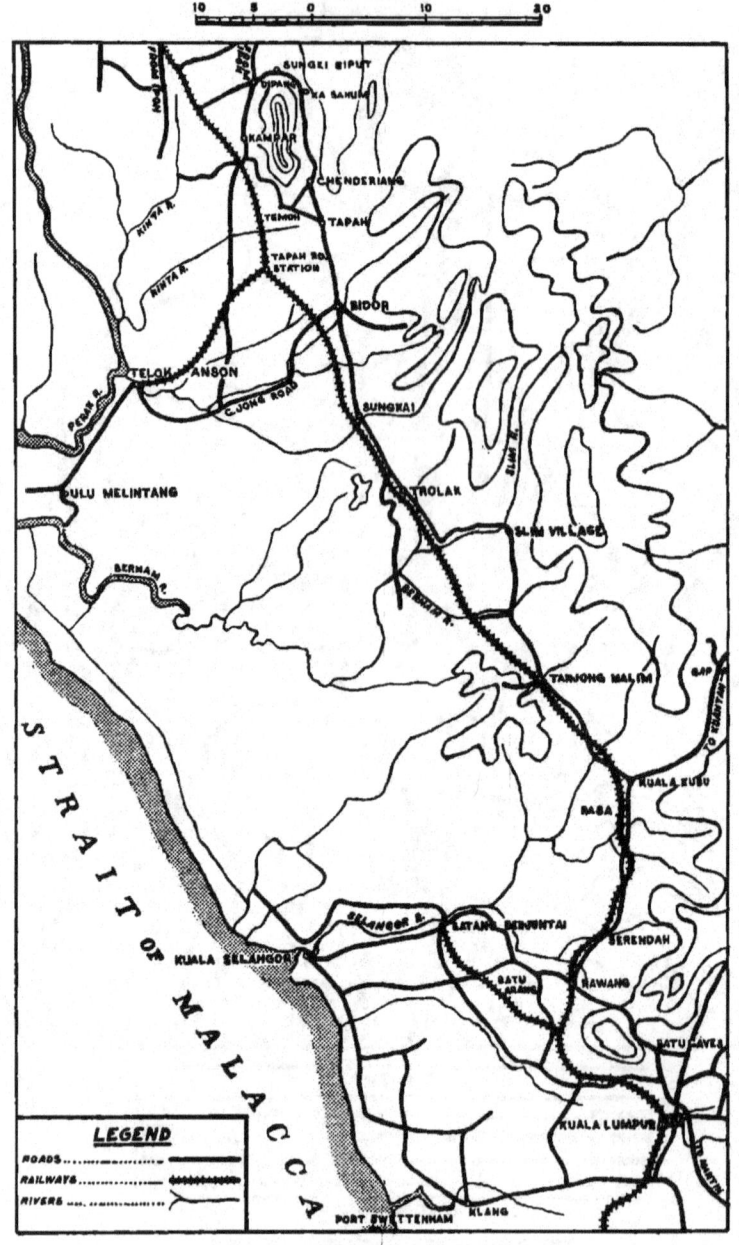

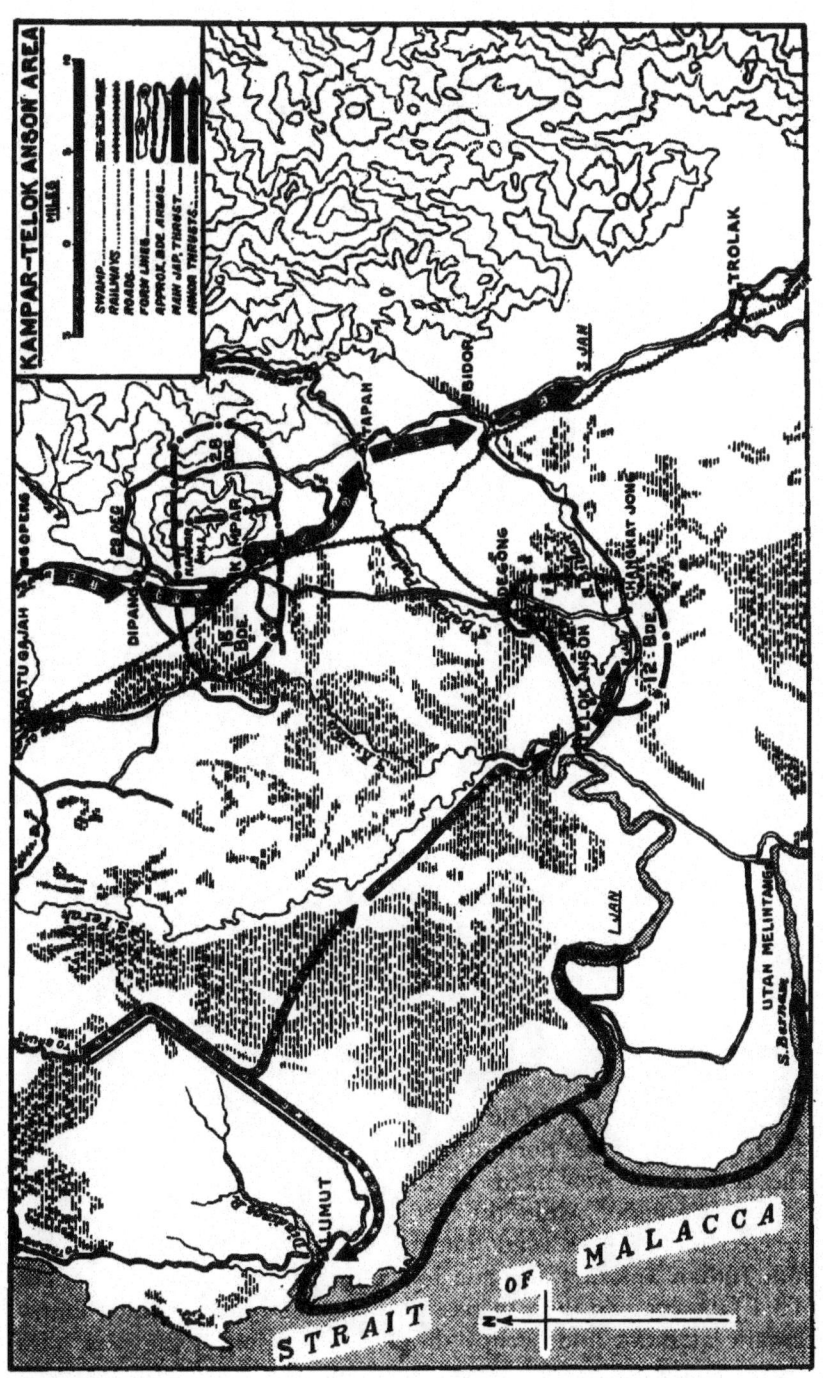

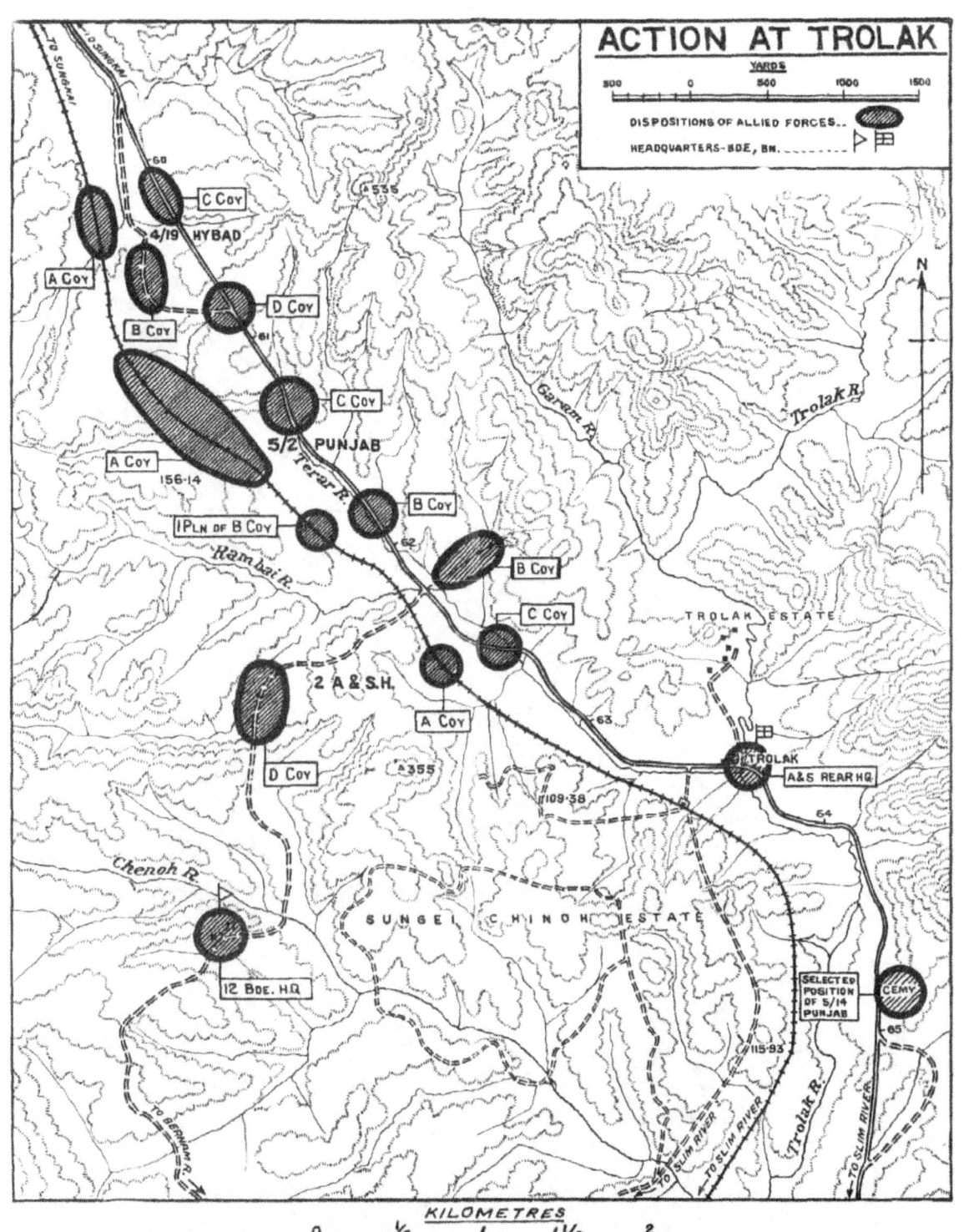

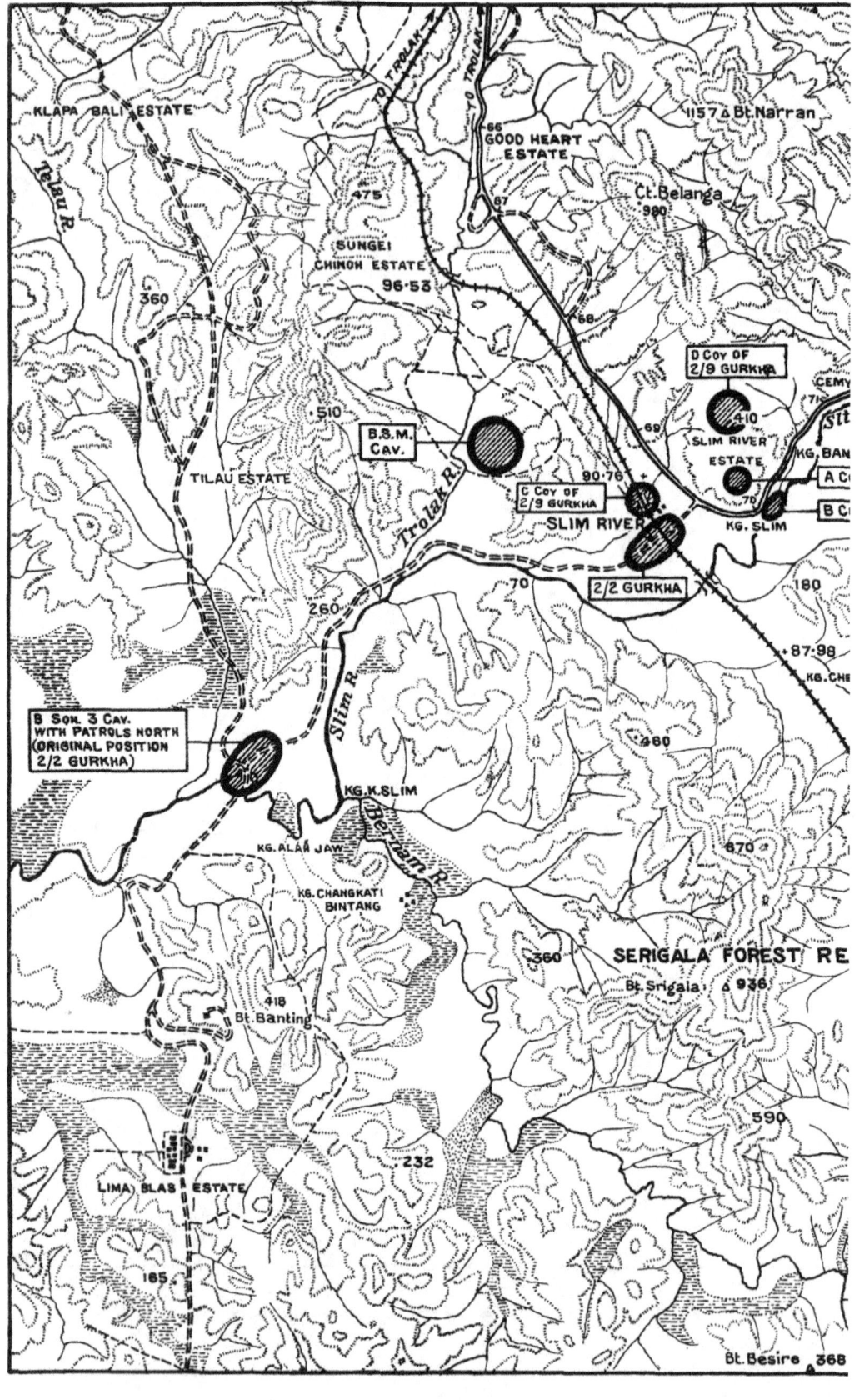

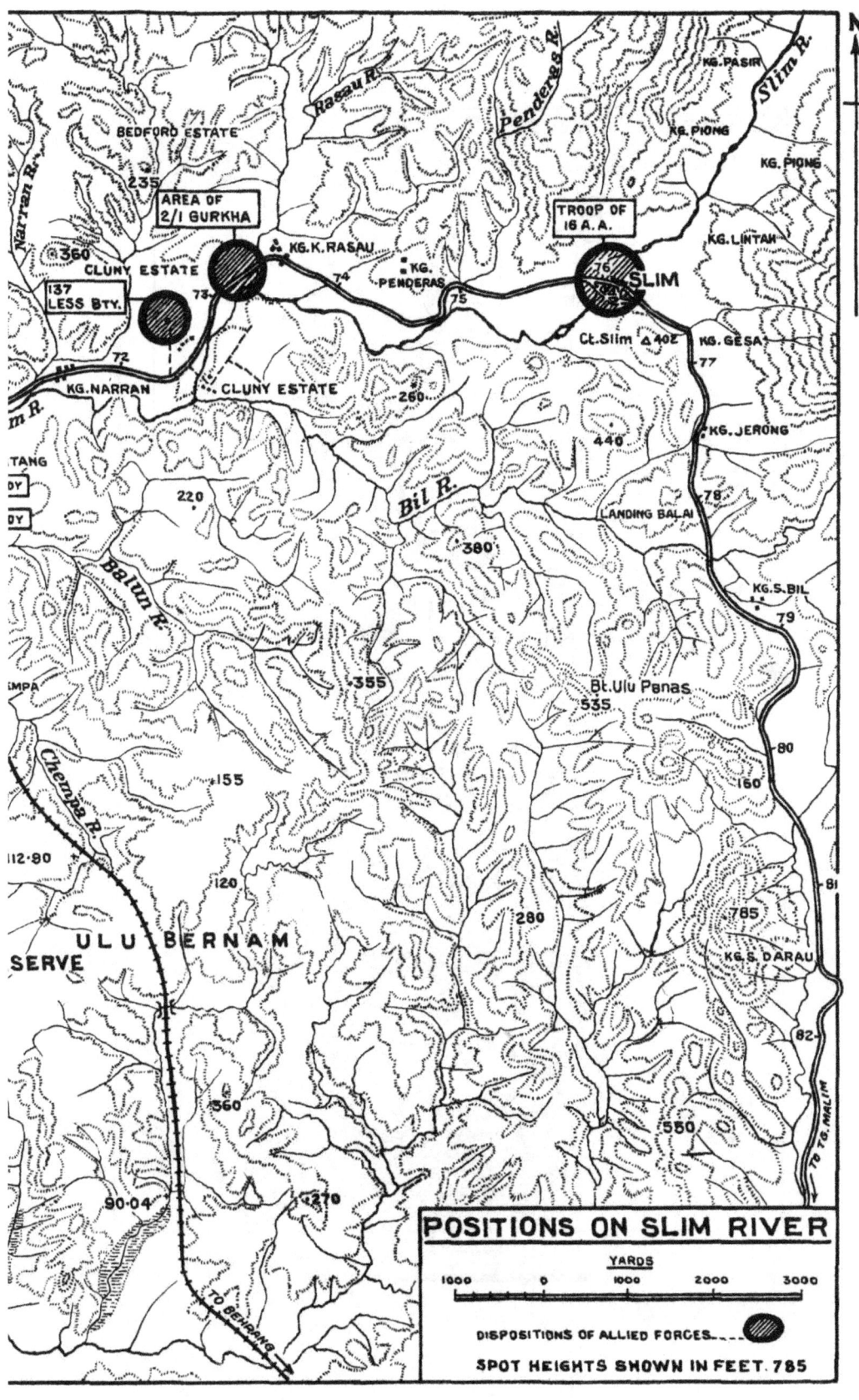

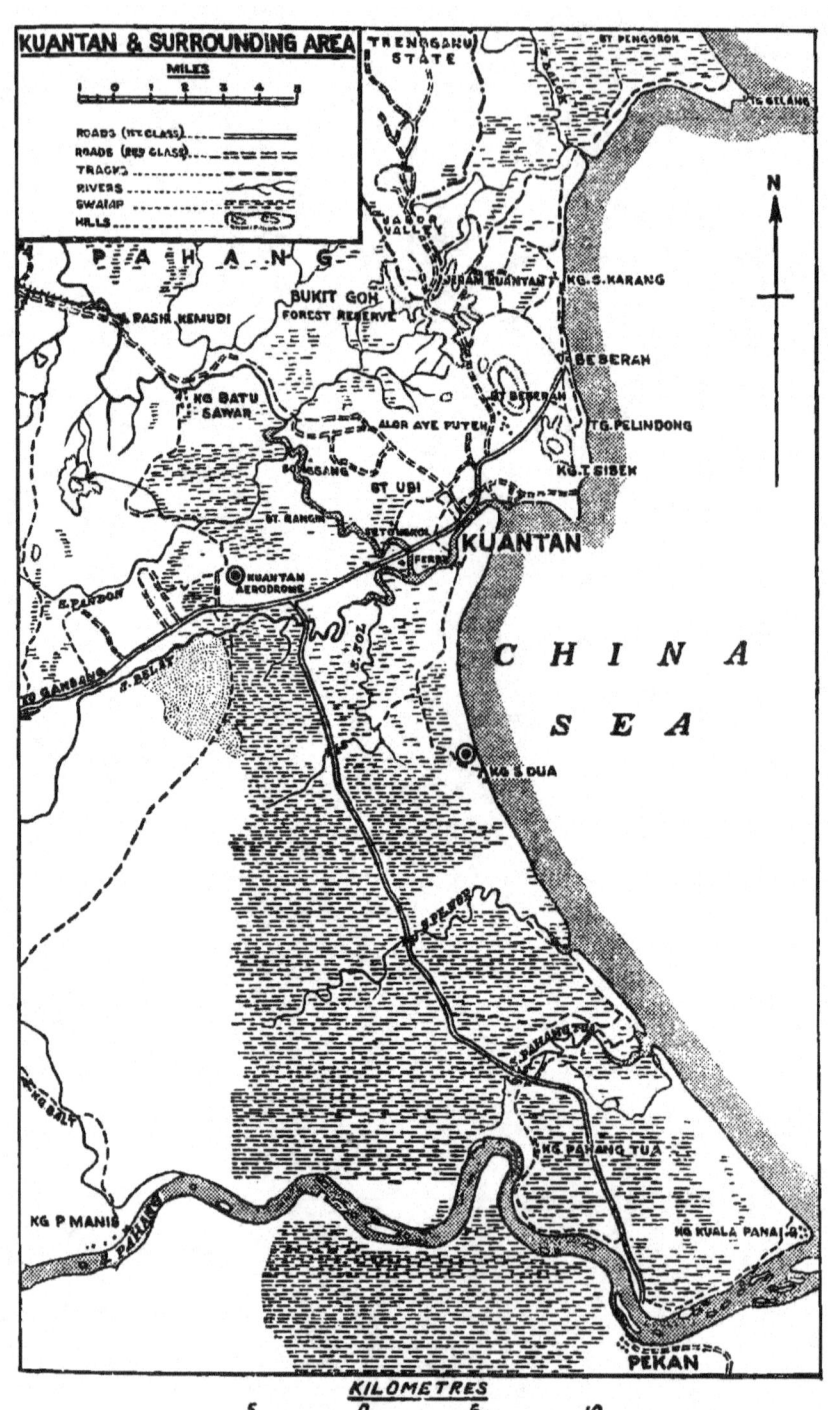

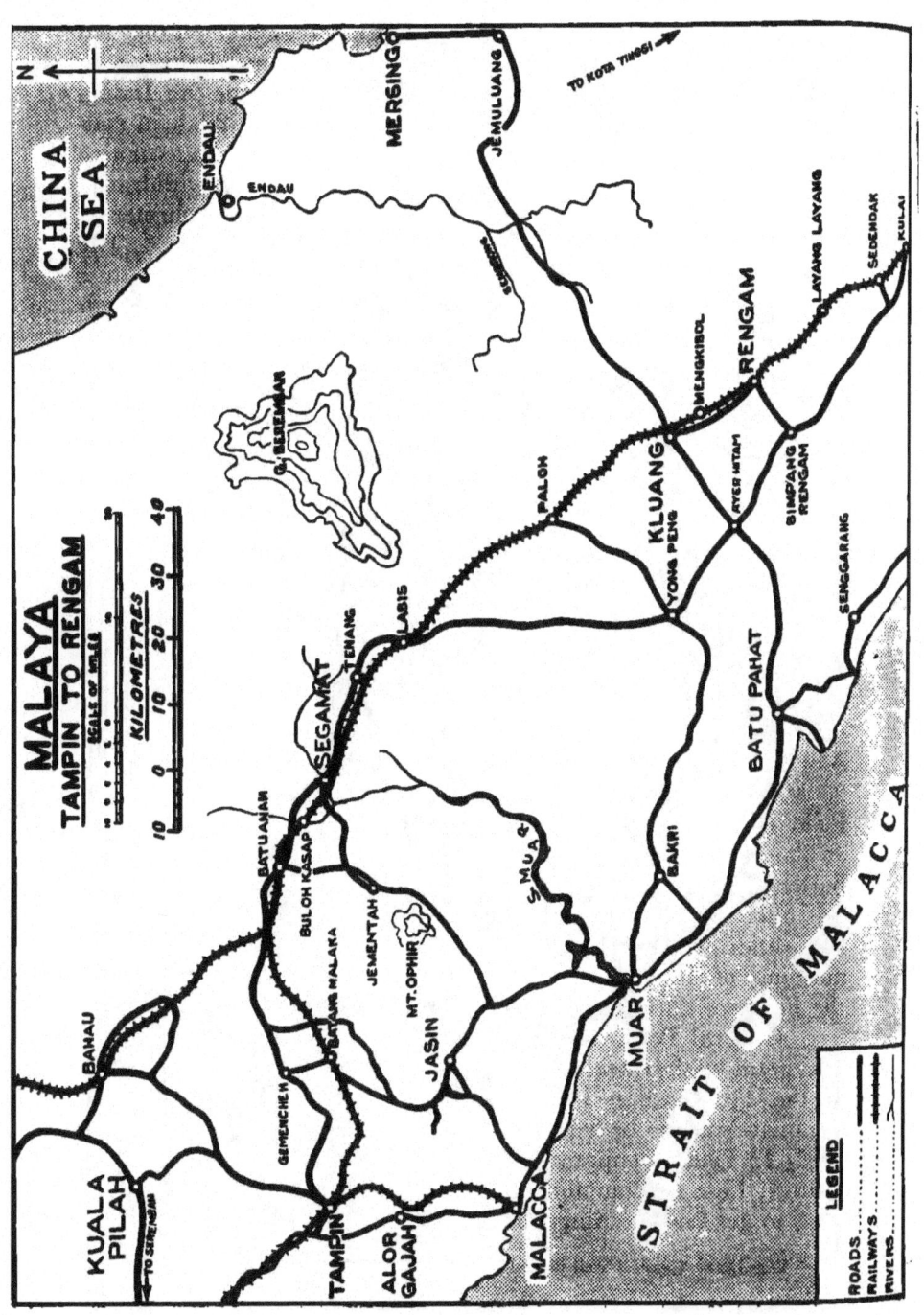

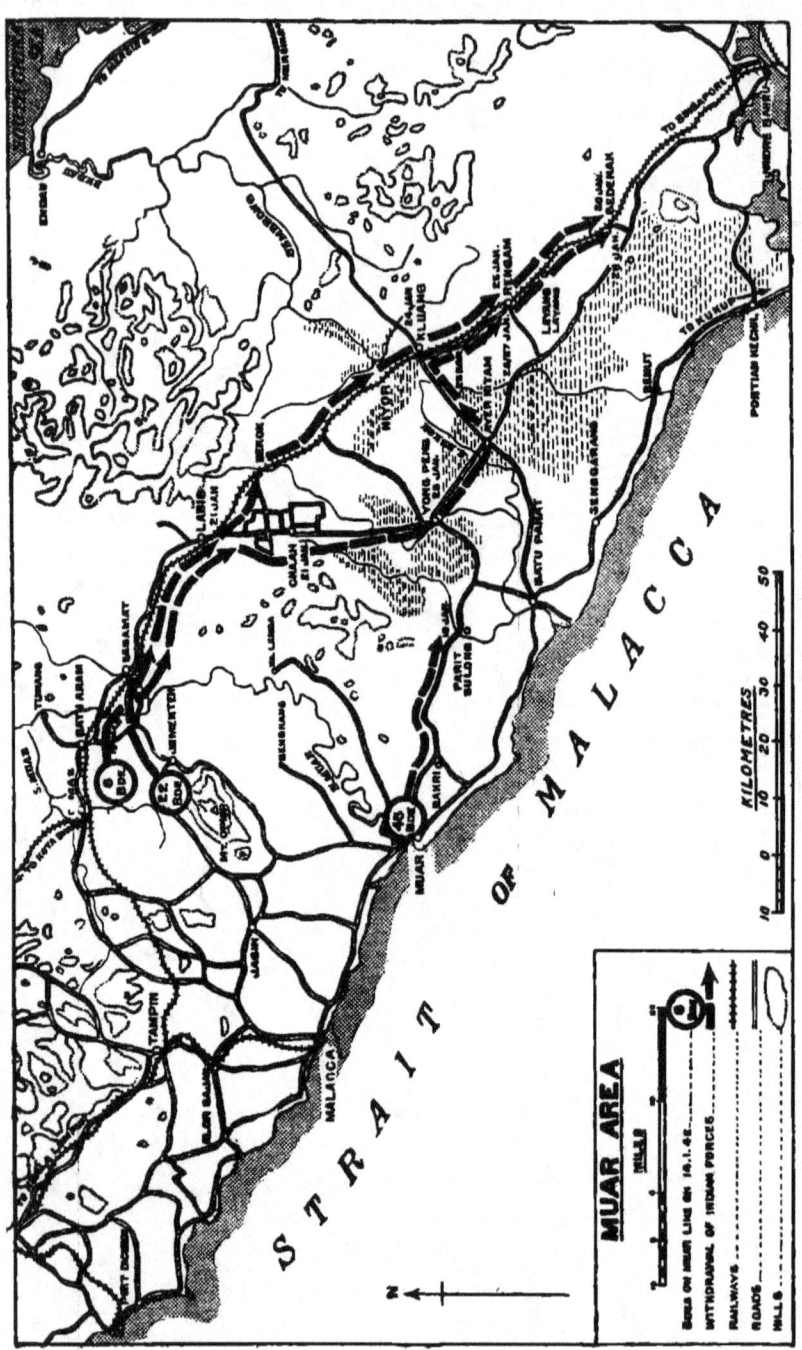

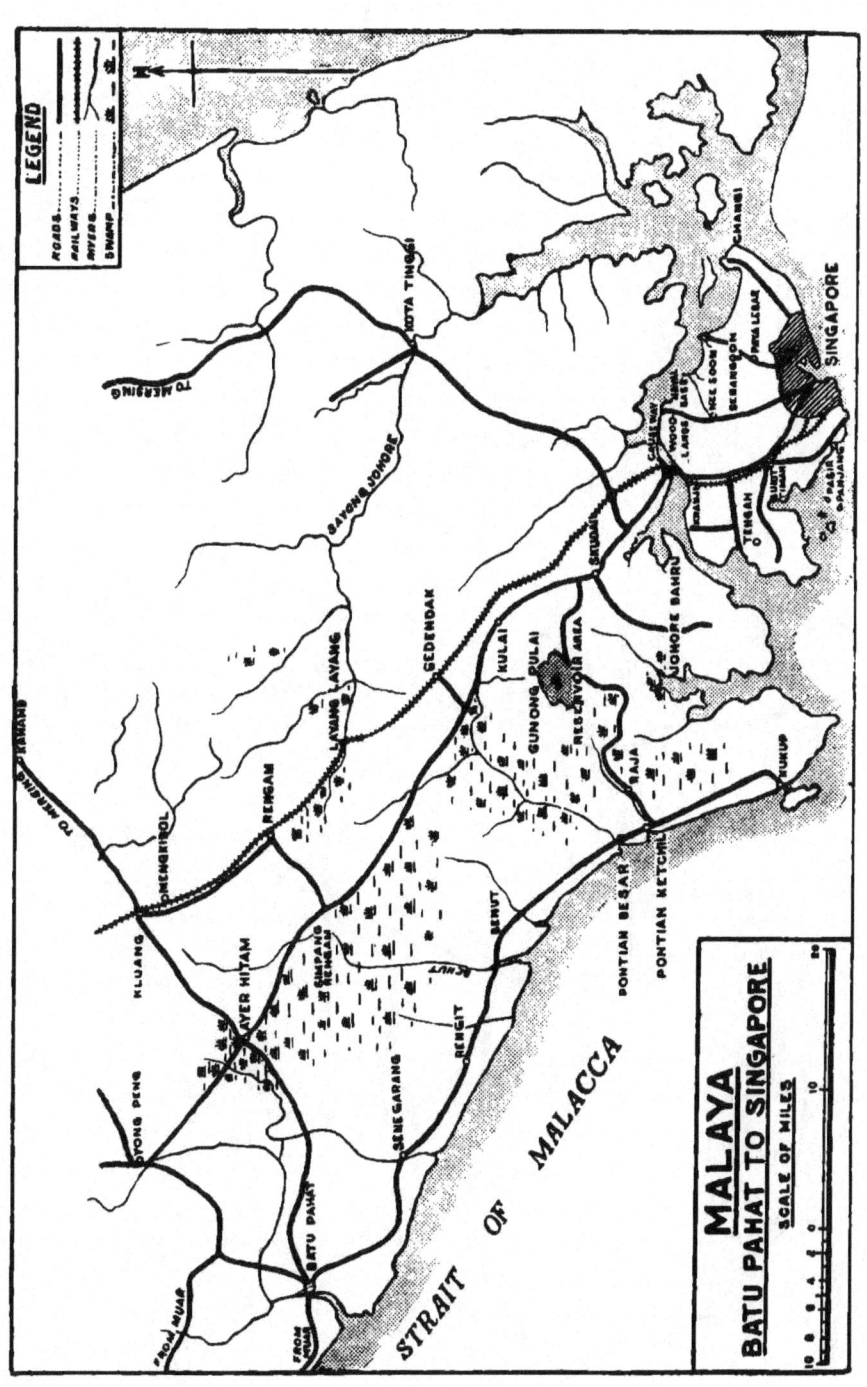

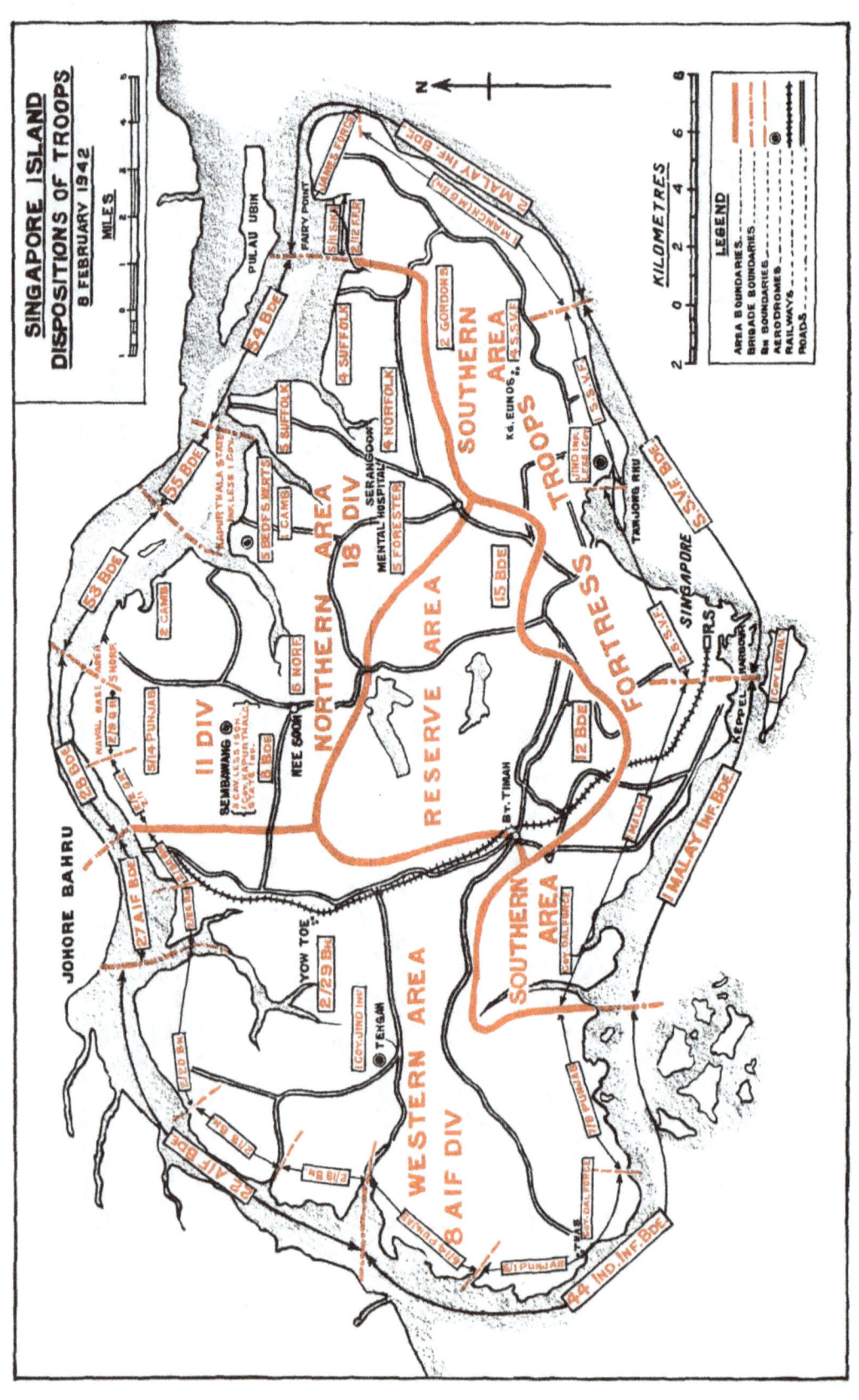

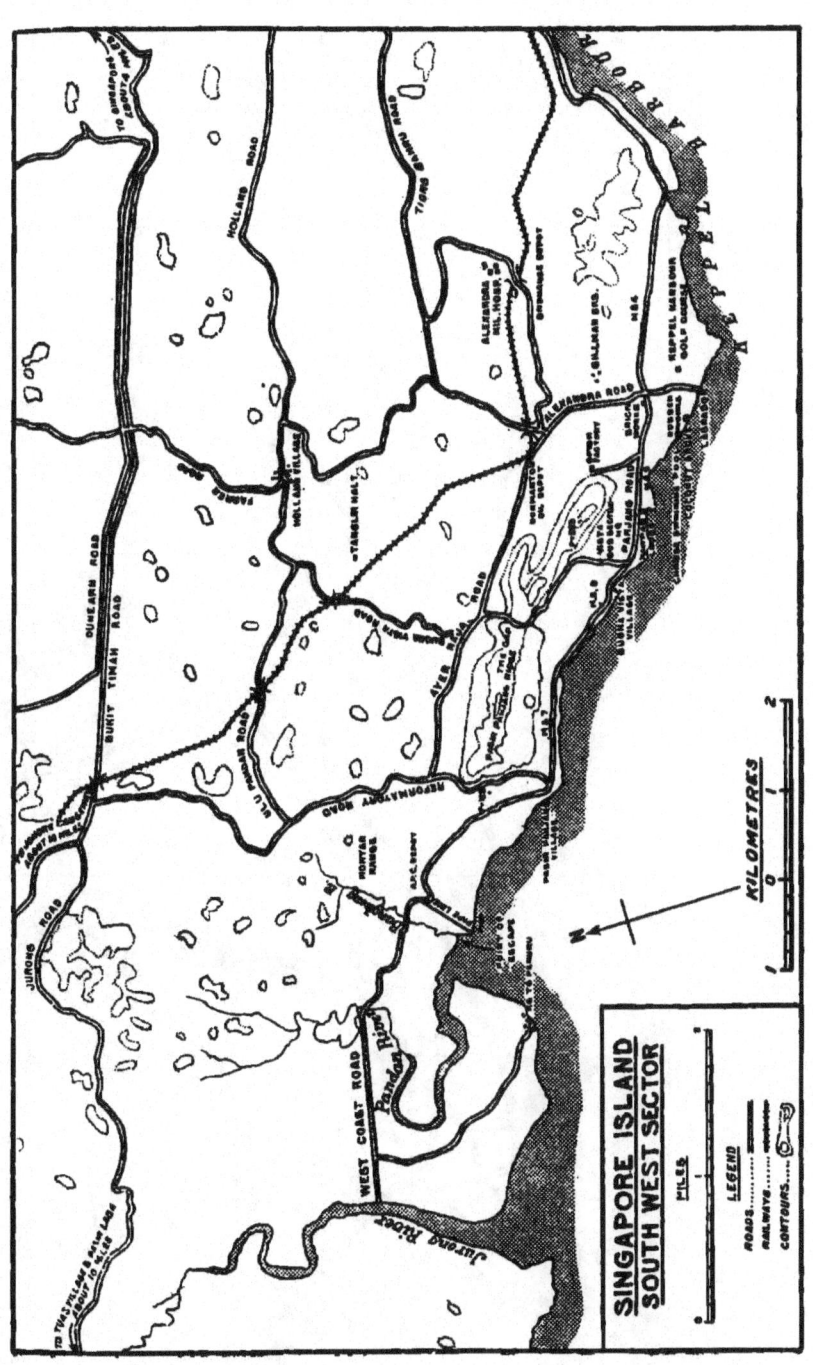

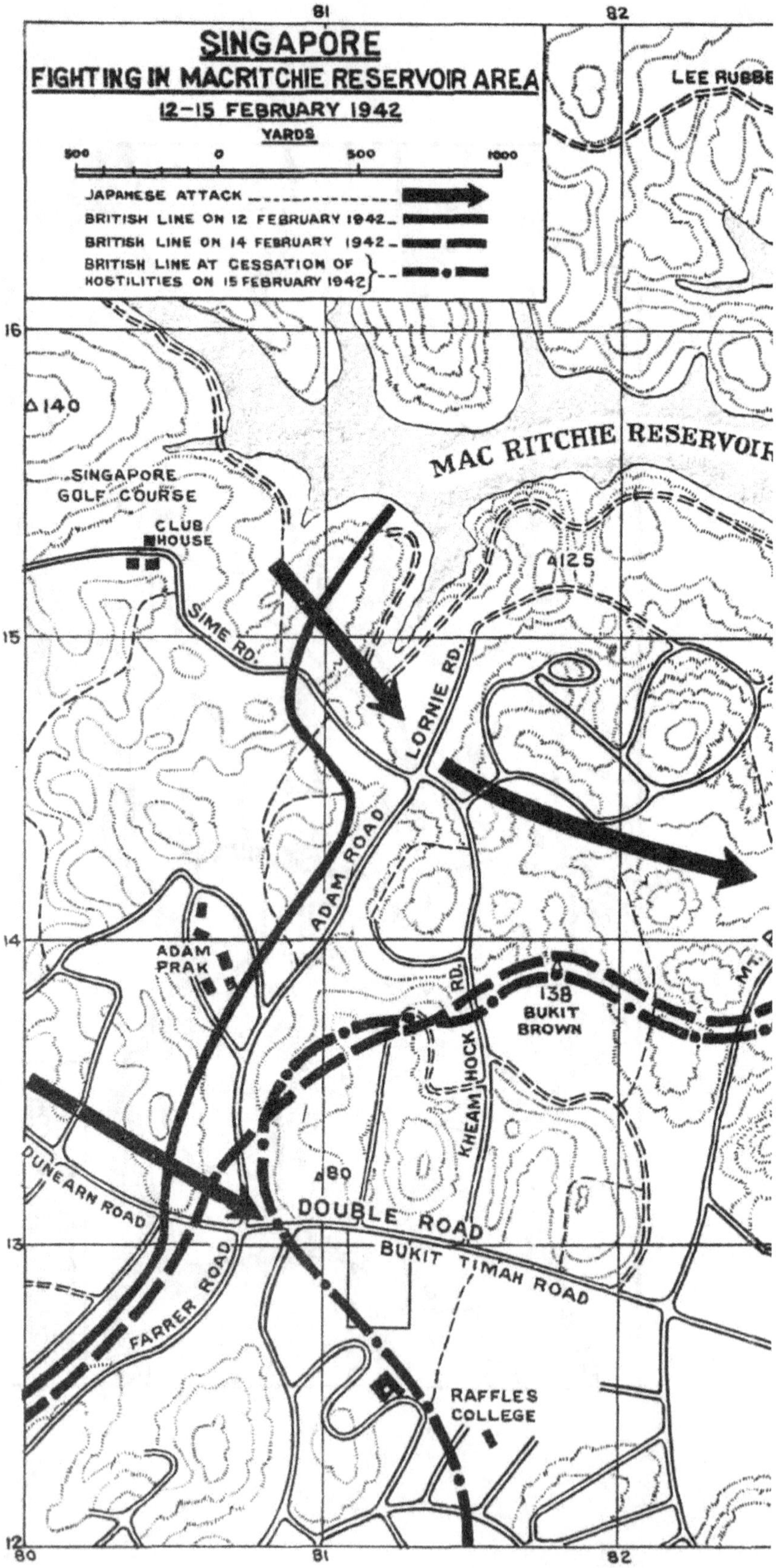

SINGAPORE
FIGHTING IN MACRITCHIE RESERVOIR AREA
12–15 FEBRUARY 1942
YARDS
500 0 500 1000
JAPANESE ATTACK
BRITISH LINE ON 12 FEBRUARY 1942
BRITISH LINE ON 14 FEBRUARY 1942
BRITISH LINE AT CESSATION OF HOSTILITIES ON 15 FEBRUARY 1942
LEE RUBBE
MAC RITCHIE RESERVOIR
SINGAPORE GOLF COURSE
CLUB HOUSE
SIME RD.
LORNIE RD.
ADAM ROAD
ADAM PRAK
KHEAM HOCK RD.
138 BUKIT BROWN
DUNEARN ROAD
DOUBLE ROAD
BUKIT TIMAH ROAD
FARRER ROAD
RAFFLES COLLEGE
SPOT HEIGHTS SHOWN IN FEET THU

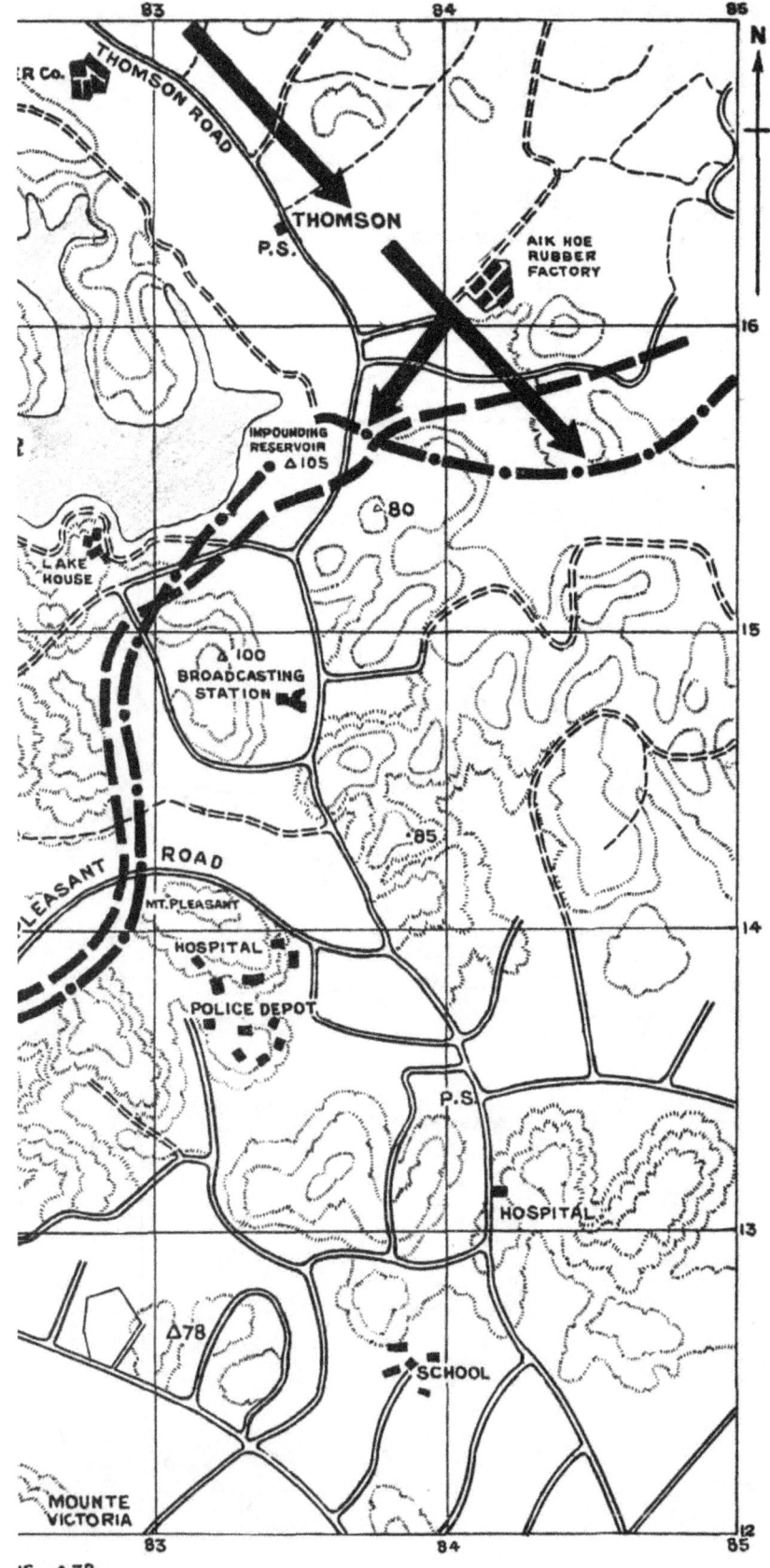

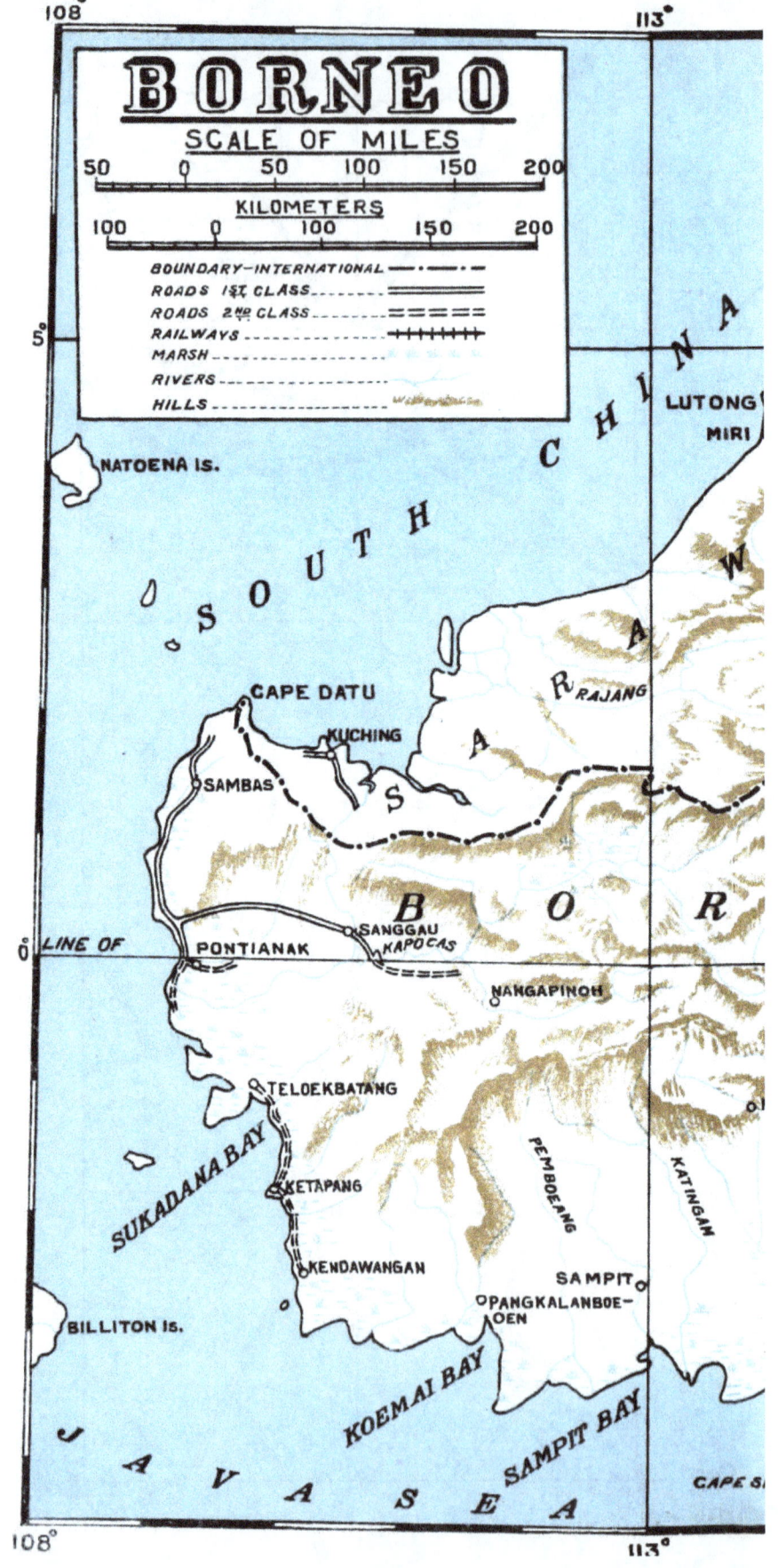

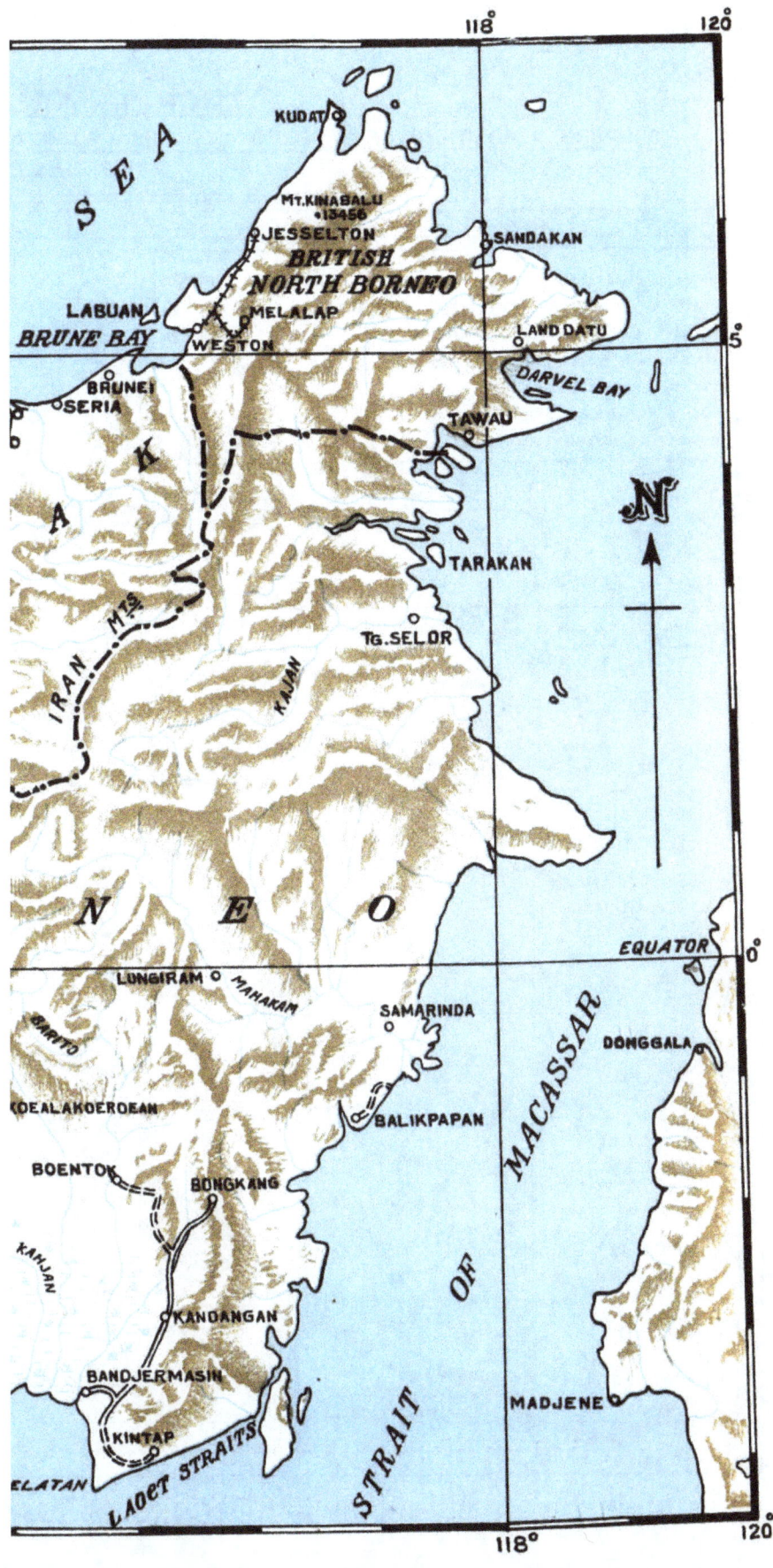

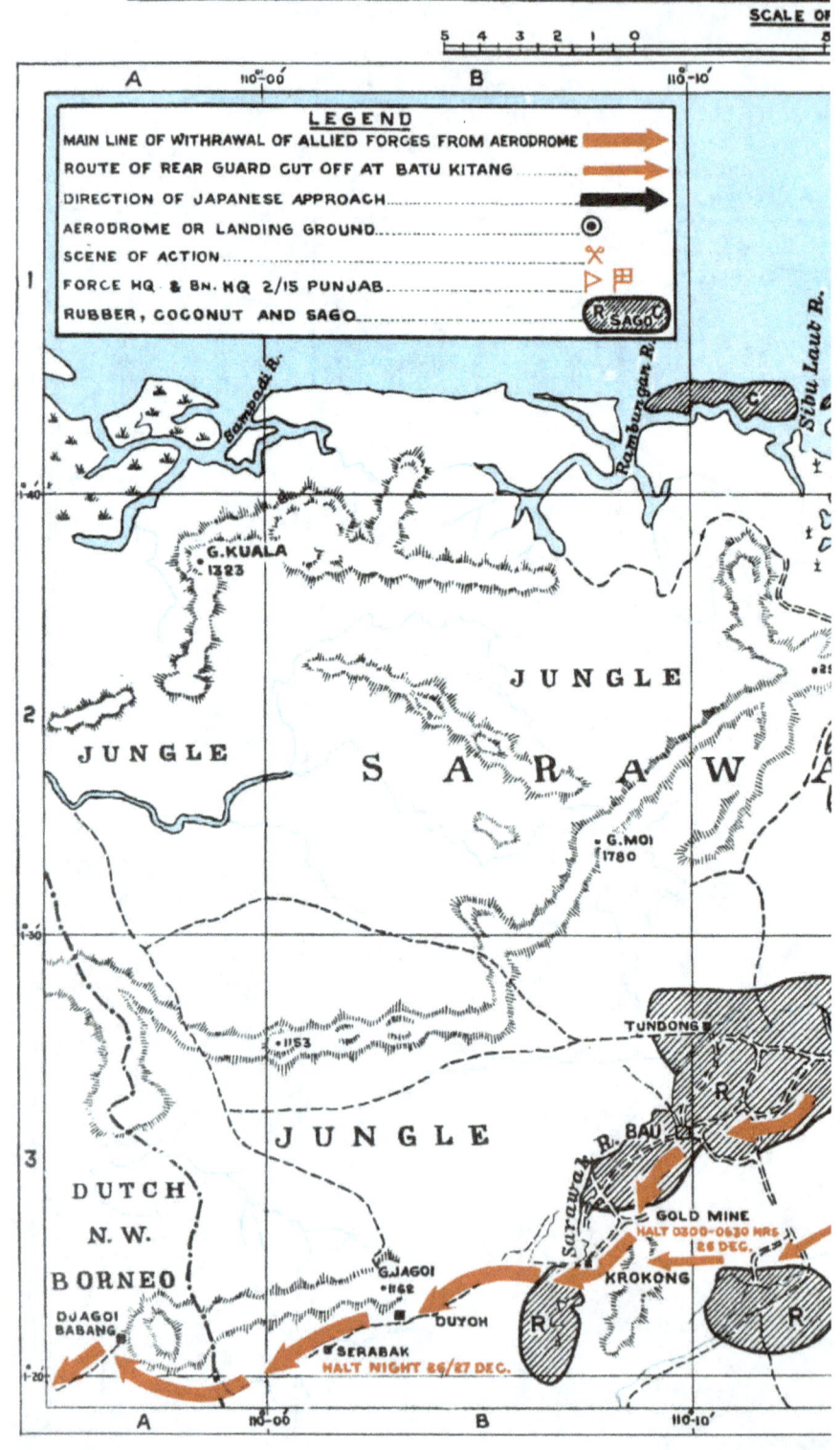

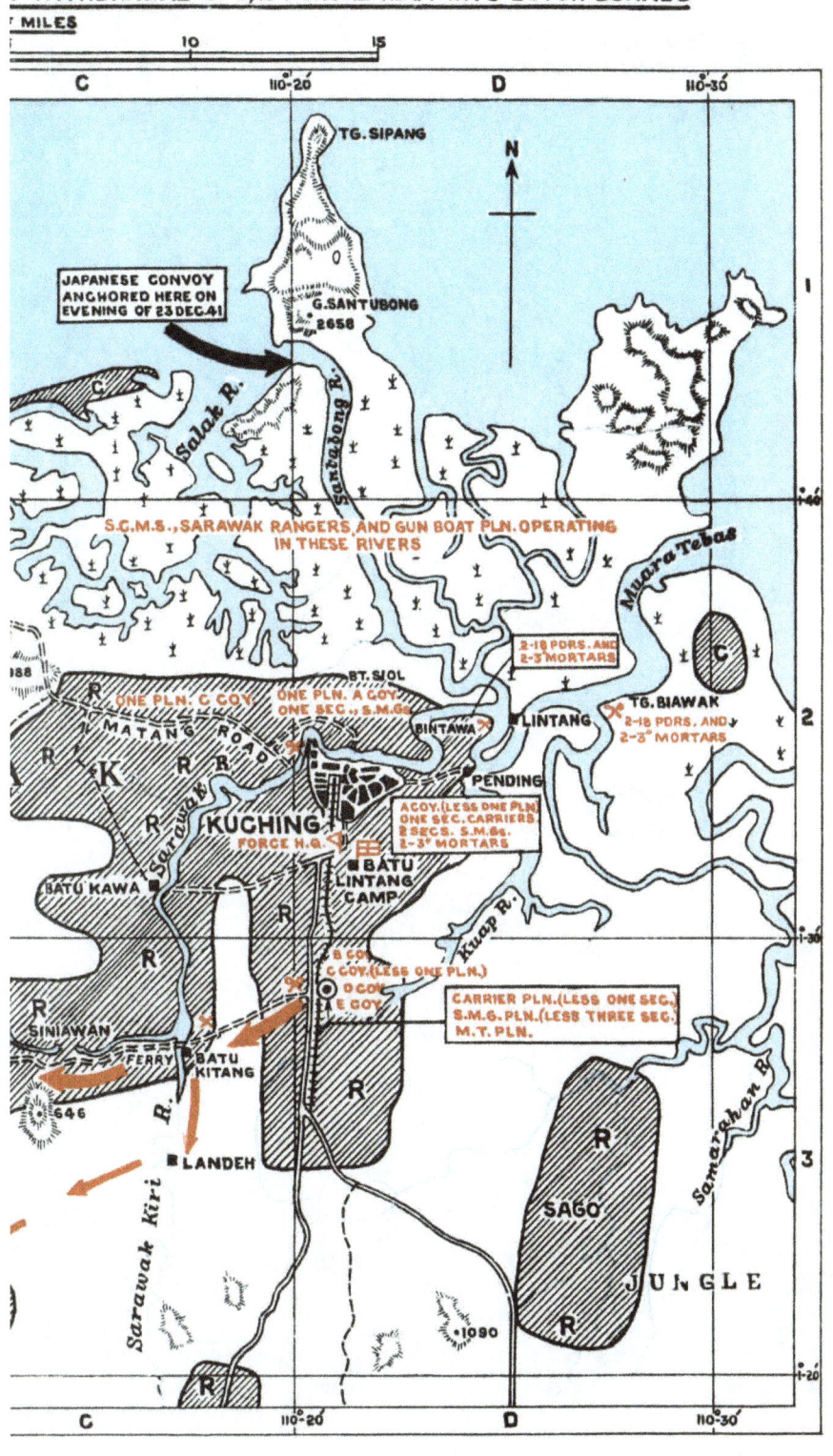

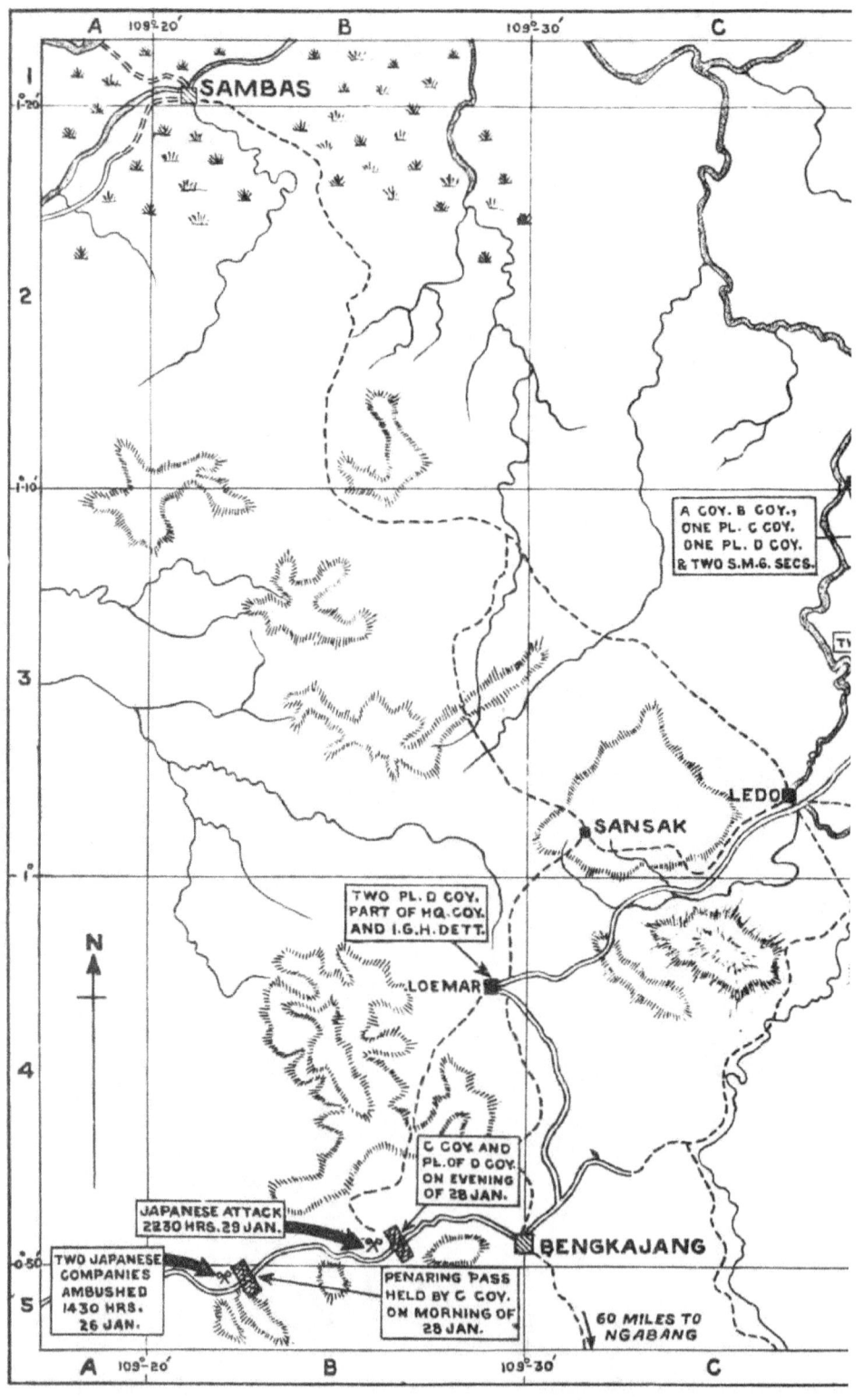

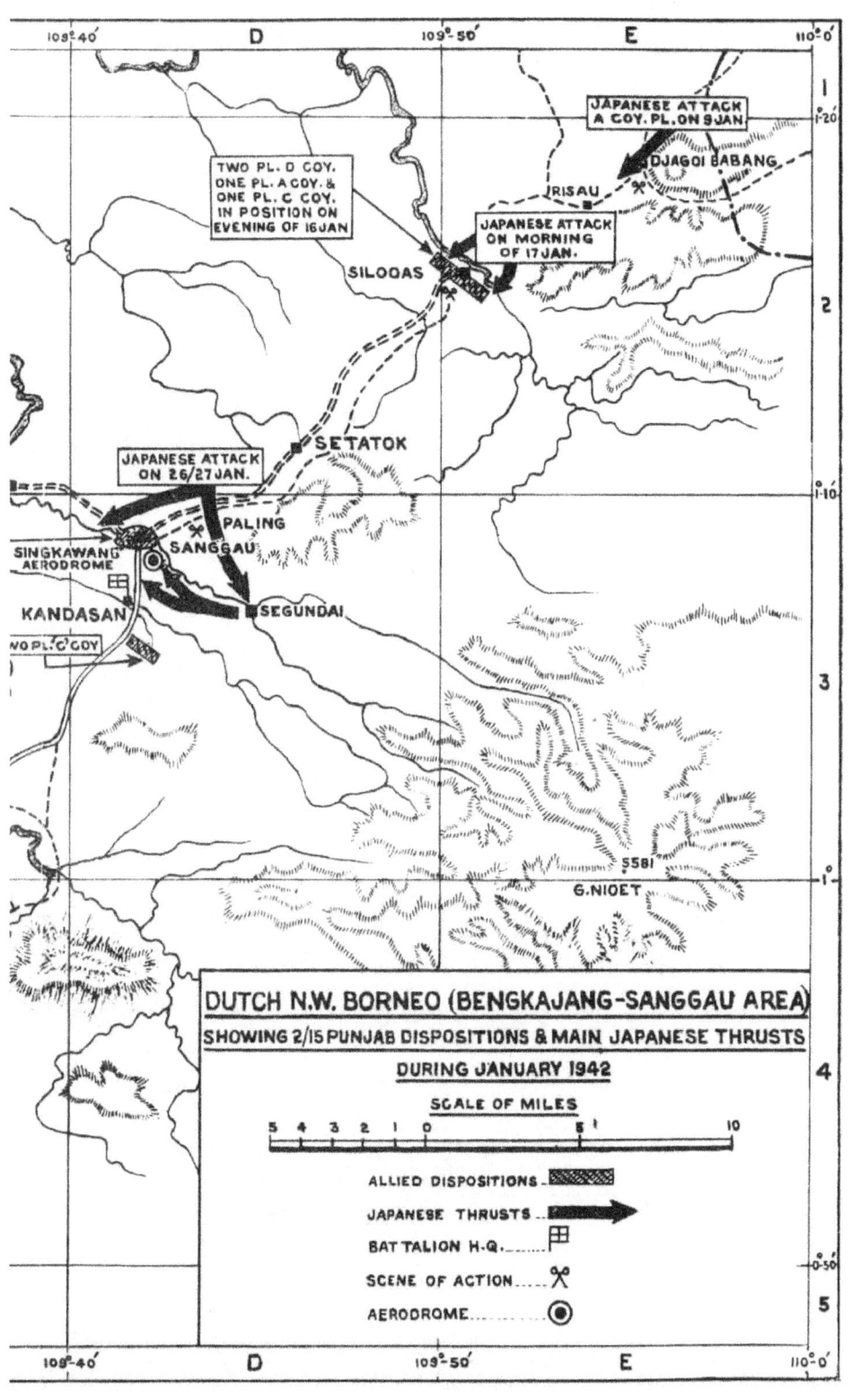

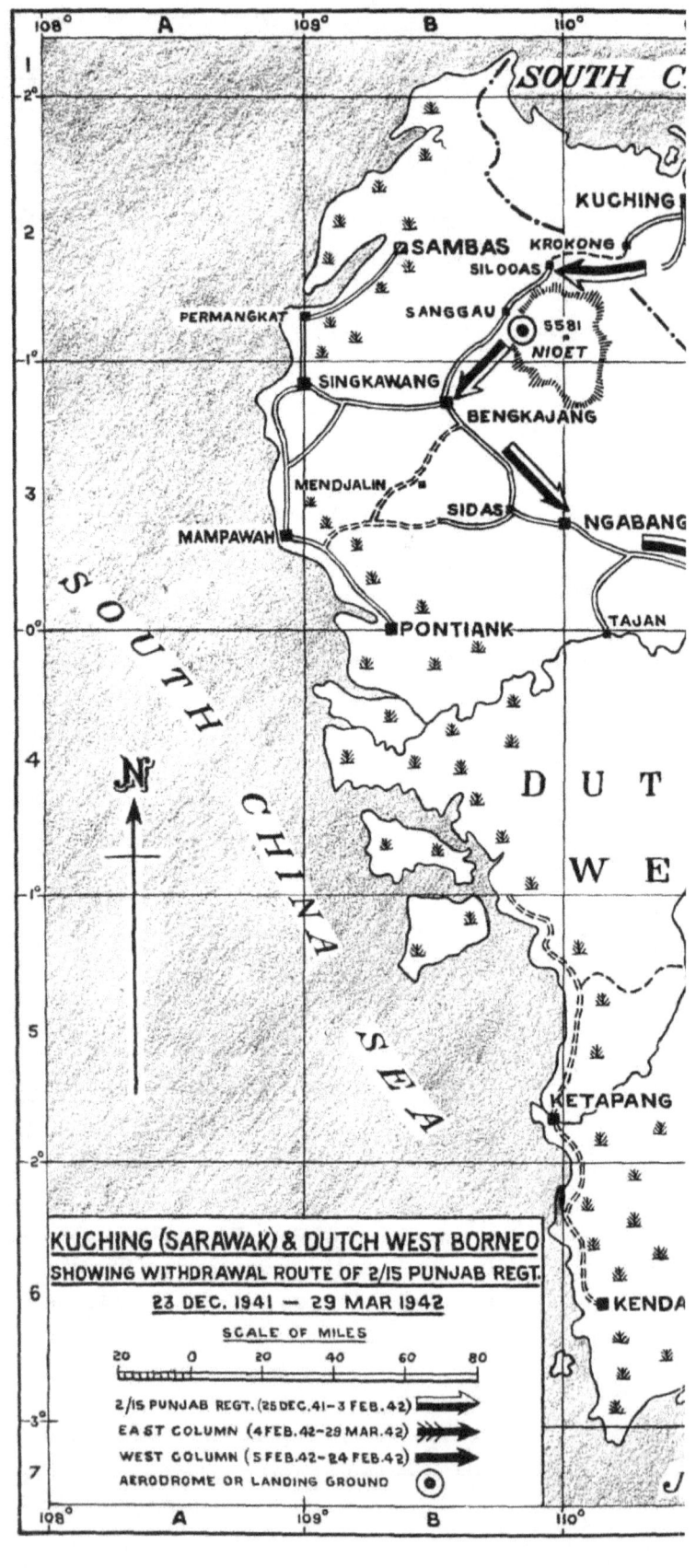

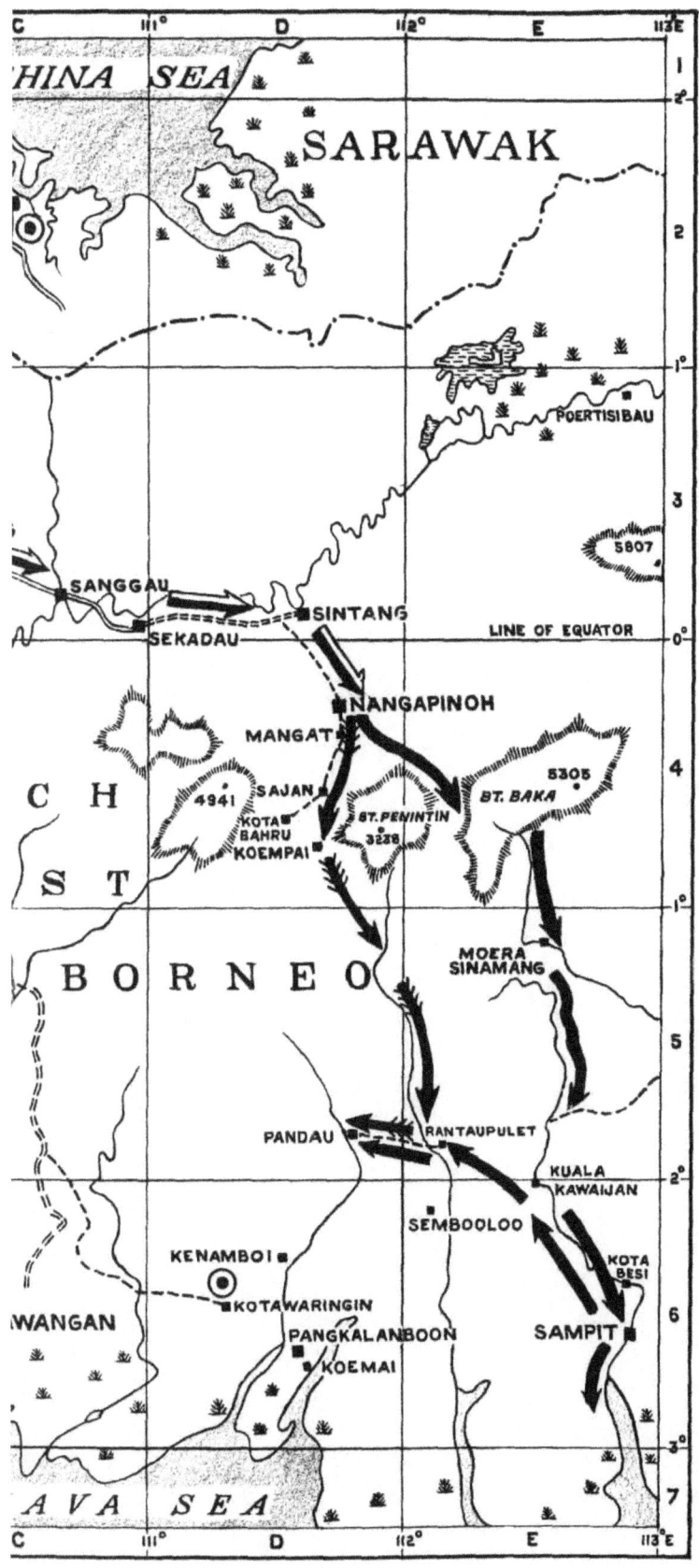

OFFICIAL HISTORY OF THE INDIAN ARMED FORCES
IN THE SECOND WORLD WAR
1939-45

THE RECONQUEST OF BURMA
Volume I

Maps and Sketches

The Reconquest of Burma Volume 1
List of maps

1. Upper Burma
2. Distribution of the hill tribes of Burma
3. Tiddim to No. 3 Stockade
4. Fort White—No. 3 Stockade Spur, showing Basha Hill
5. Loss of Fort White
6. Battle of Nankan
7. Bonchaung–Tigyaing Area
8. Tiddim sector, dispositions mid-November 1943
9. Tiddim sector, operations February and early March 1944
10. Troop dispositions in the Tamu sector, November 1943
11. Troop dispositions in the Tamu sector, end of February, 1944
12. Withdrawal of 17th Indian Division, 17-30 March 1944
13. The Japanese thrust in the North, March 1944
14. Operations on the Tiddim Road, 17-30 May 1944
15. Operations in the Palel sector: 5 April to 22 June 1944
16. The Litan Road, positions in mid-June 1944
17. The Iril Valley sector, thrust of 80th Indian Infantry Brigade, 7-22 June 1944
18. Reopening of the Kohima Road, 5 April-22 June 1944
19. Panorama from Punjab Ridge (478675) looking East
20. Detailed map of Kohima town
21. Recapture of the Naga village, 16 May-2 June 1944
22. Recapture of the Aradura Spur, 3-5 June 1944
23. Advance of 2nd British Division for the Relief of Imphal, 6-22 June 1944
24. Operations, Chinese Armies in India and 3rd Indian Division
25. Map of Indaw
26. Map of Mawlu
27. Bhamo Area
28. Wuntho–Indaw–Banmauk Area
29. Hopin–Kamaing–Mogaung–Myitkyina area
30. Capture of Mogaung
31. Defence of IV Corps HQ Area, being Appendix A to IV Corps Operation Order No. 7
32. Organisation of a Stronghold locality (Special Force)
33. Burma

UPPER BURMA

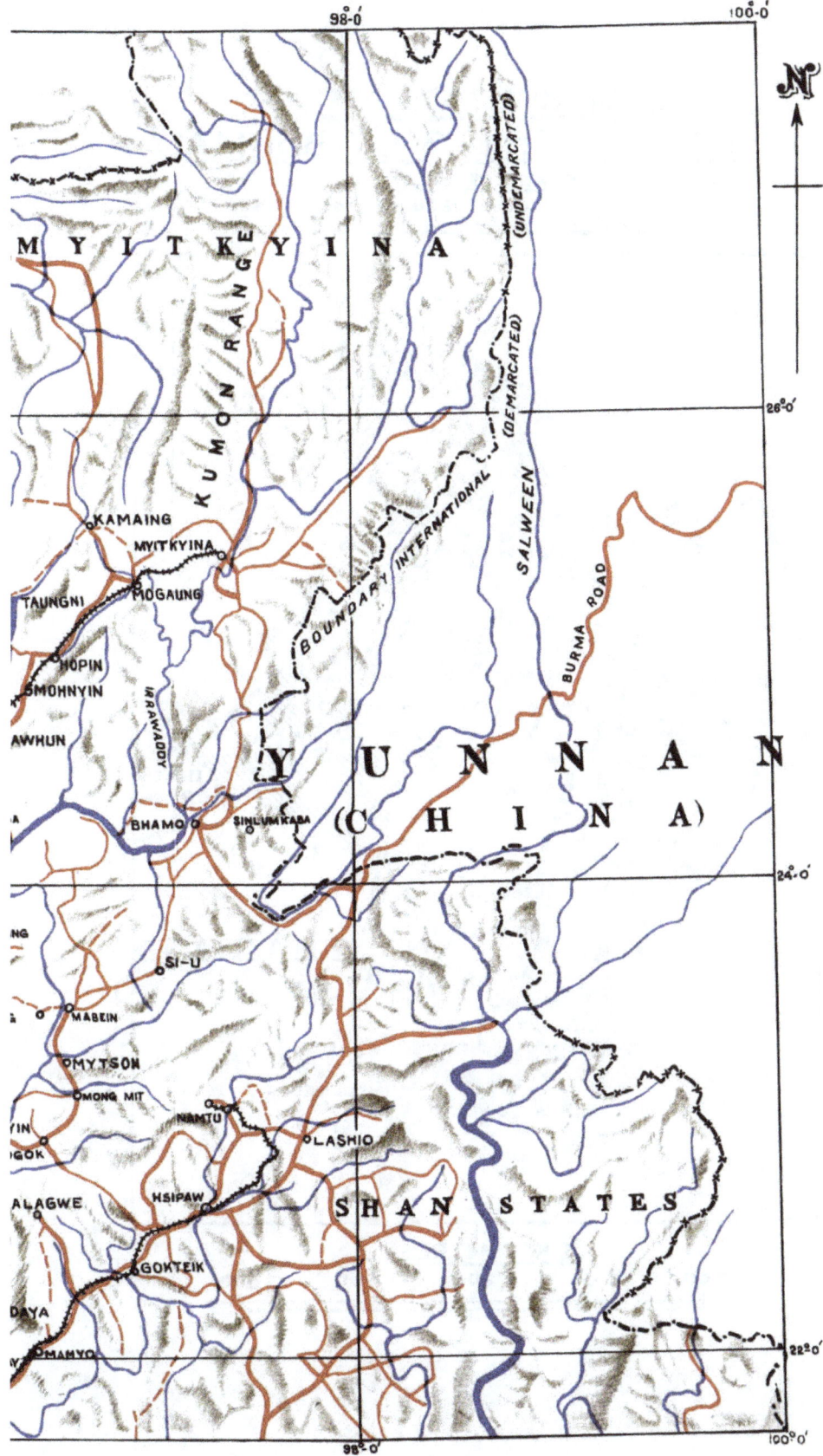

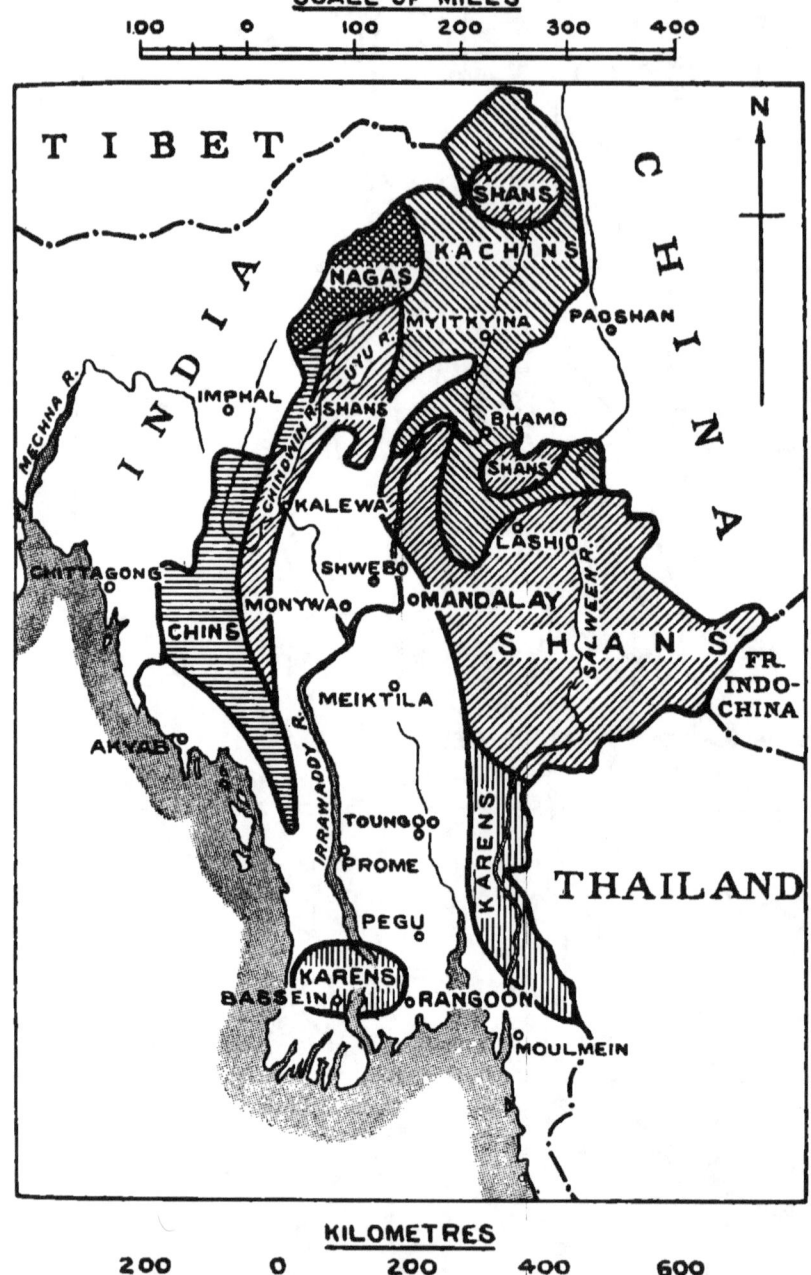

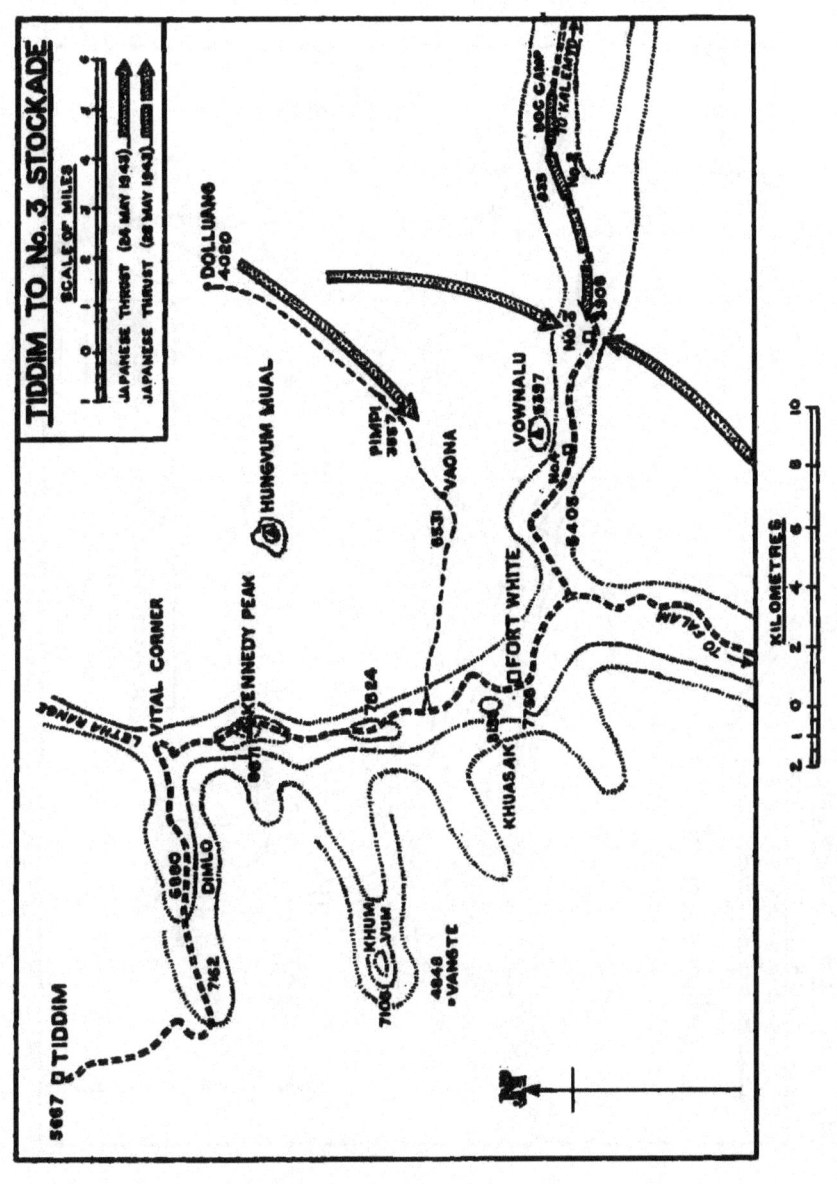

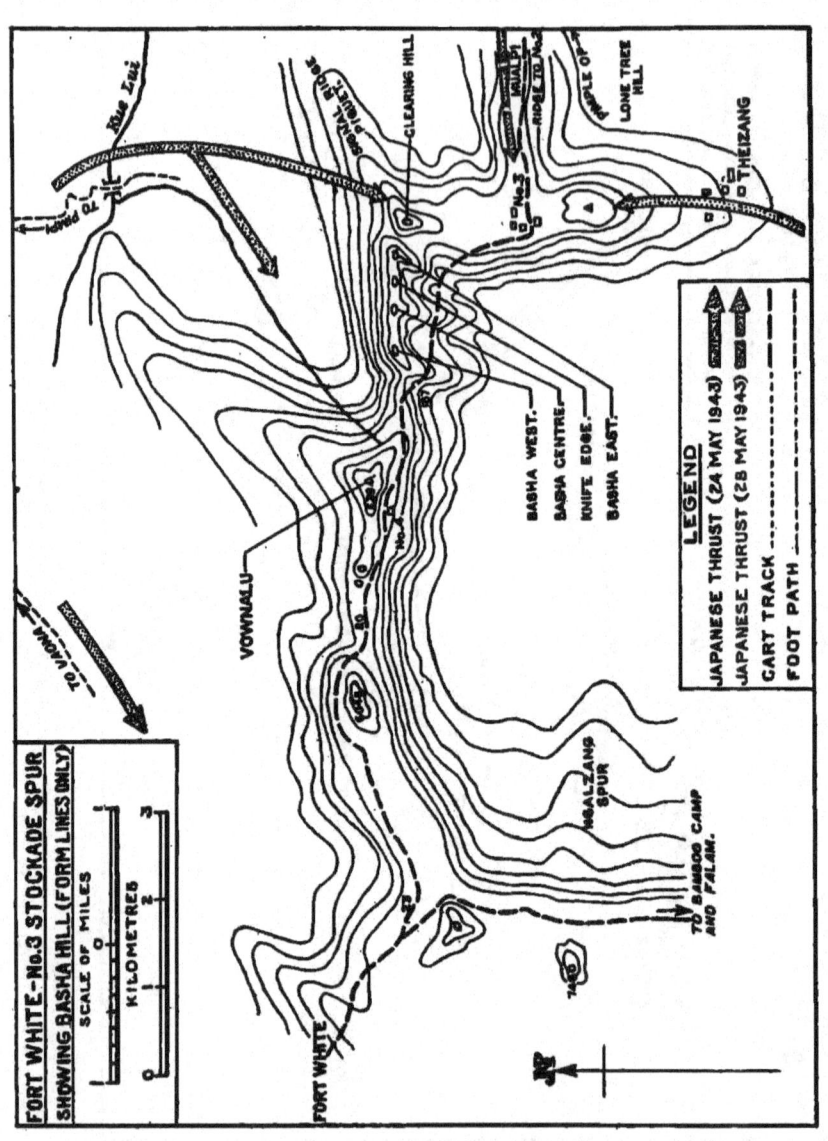

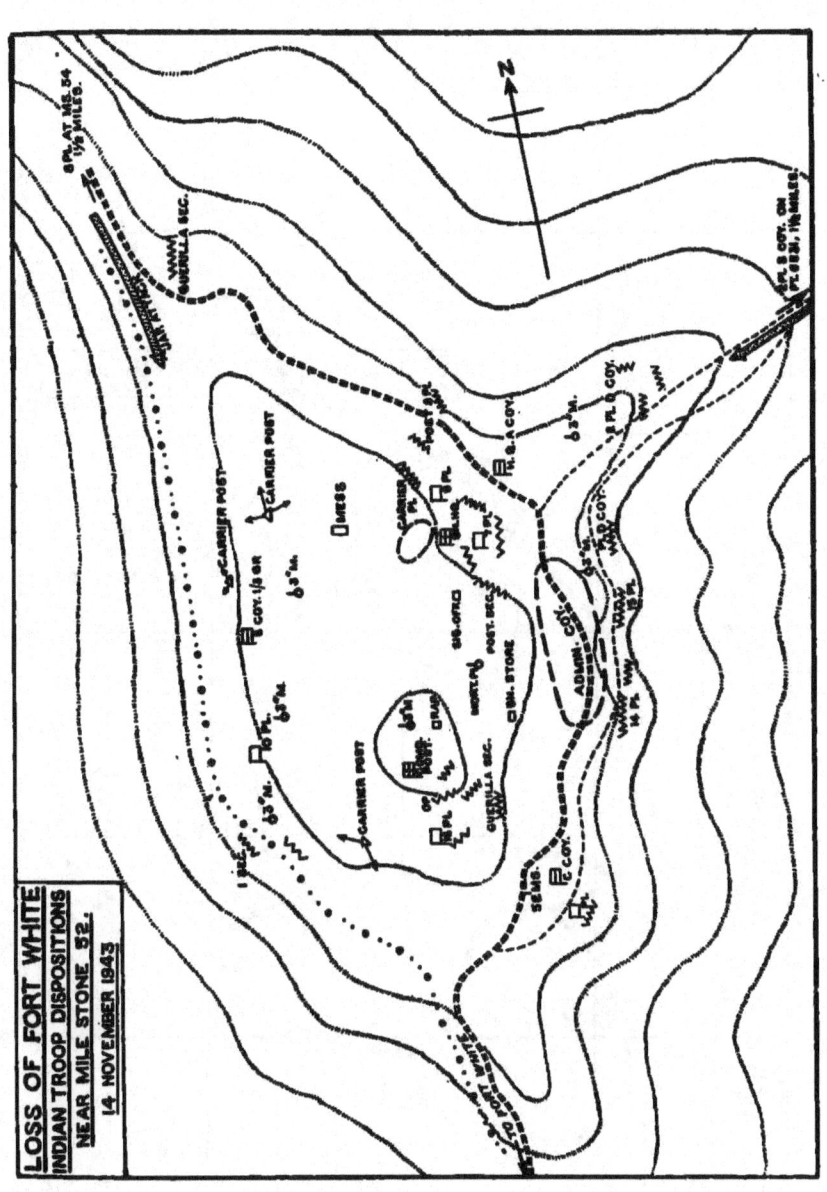

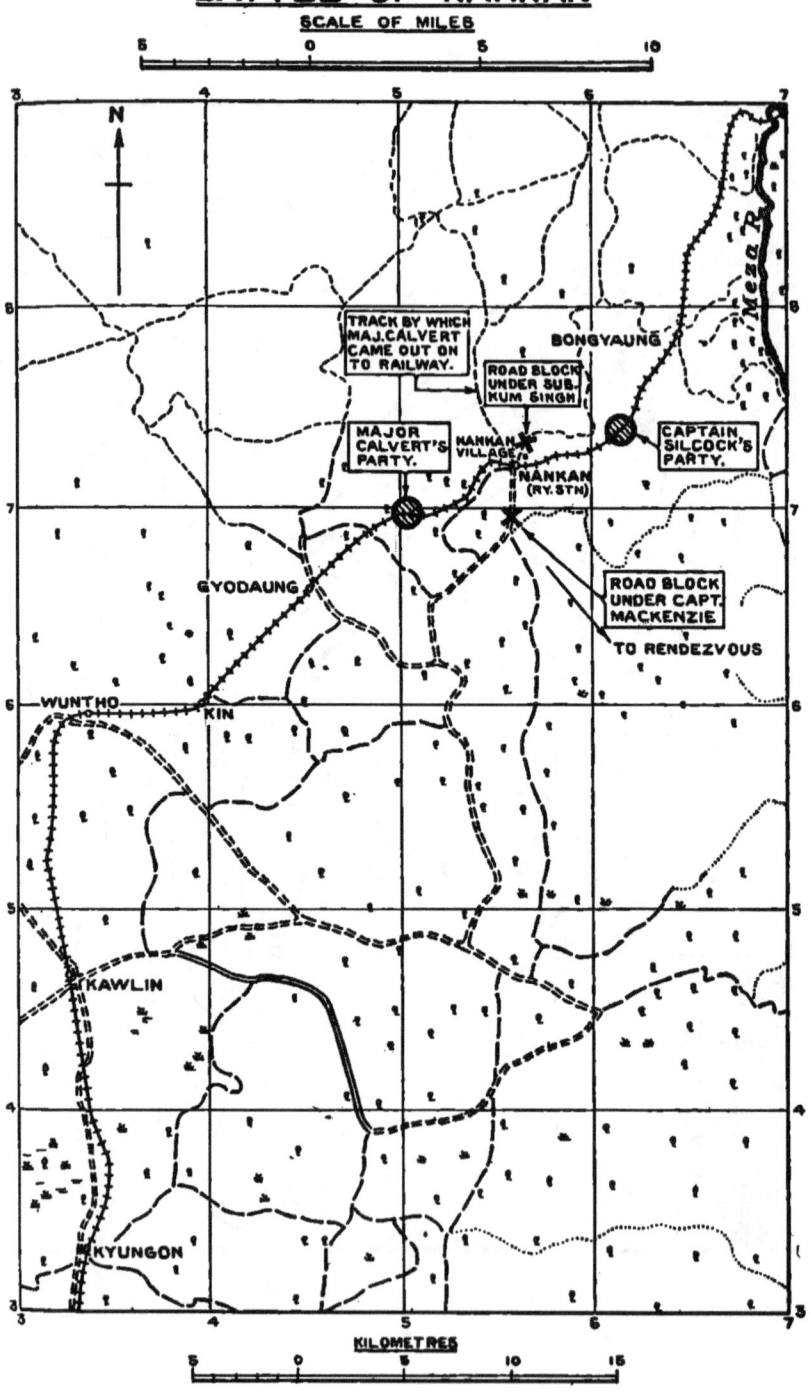

BONCHAUNG-TIGYAING AREA

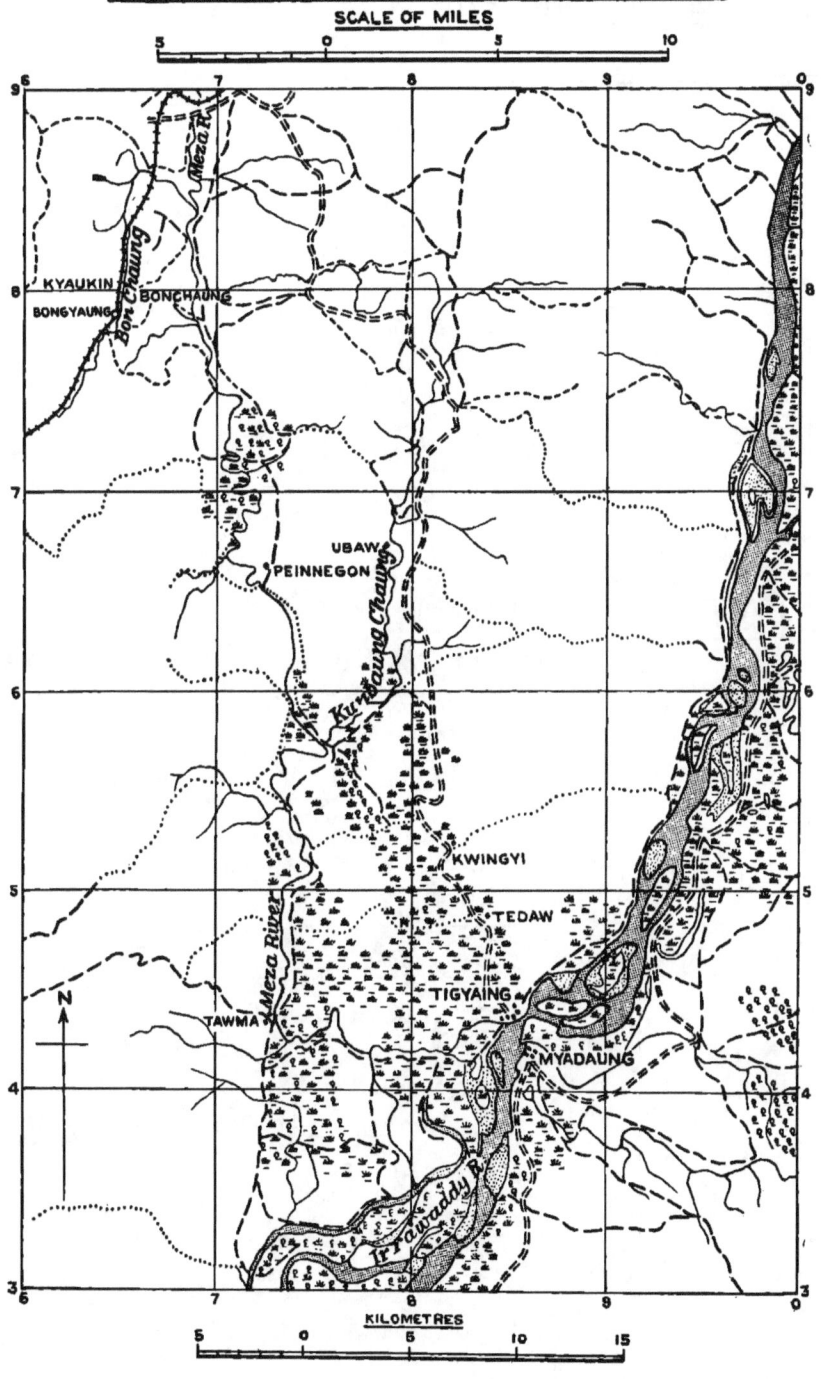

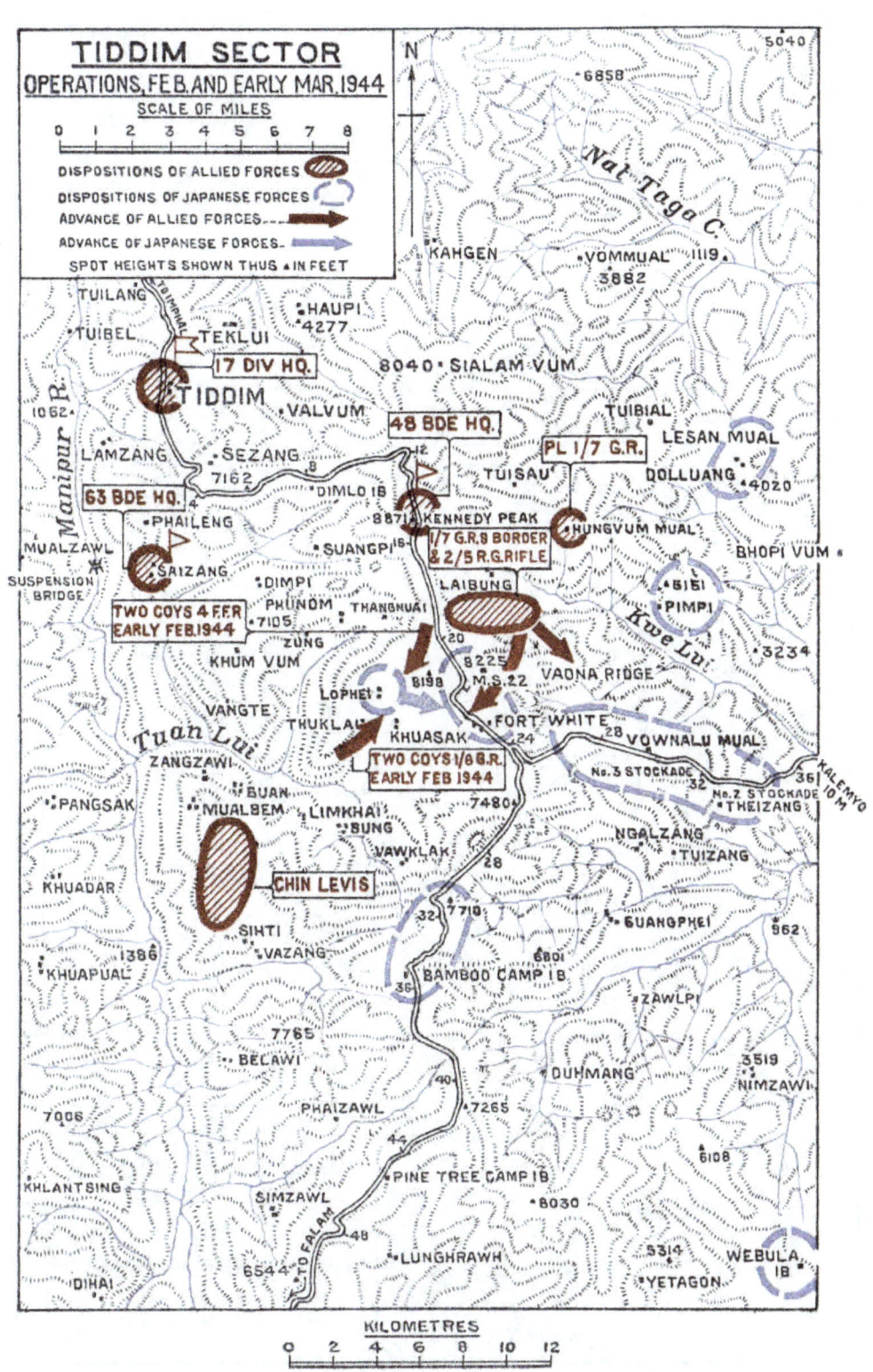

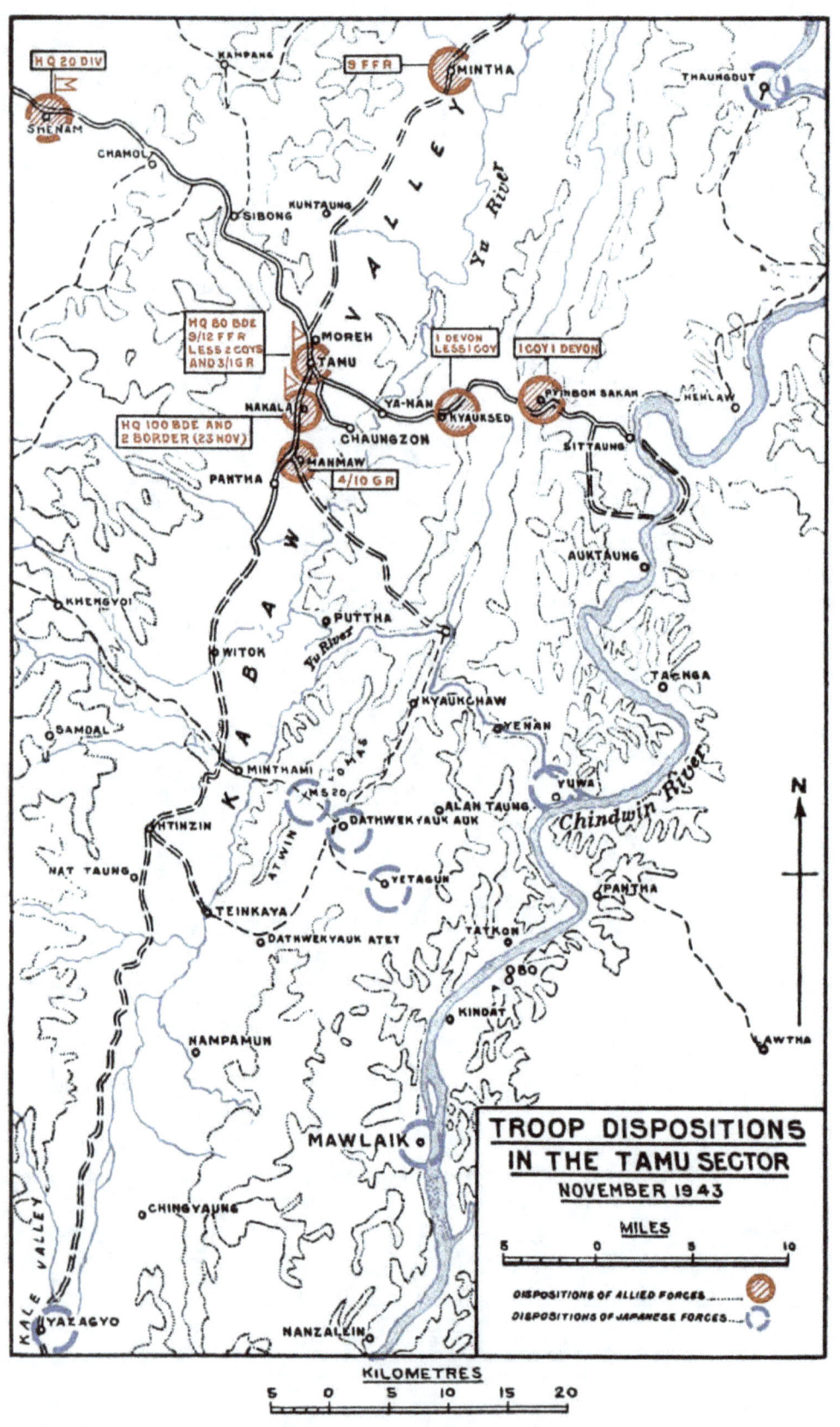

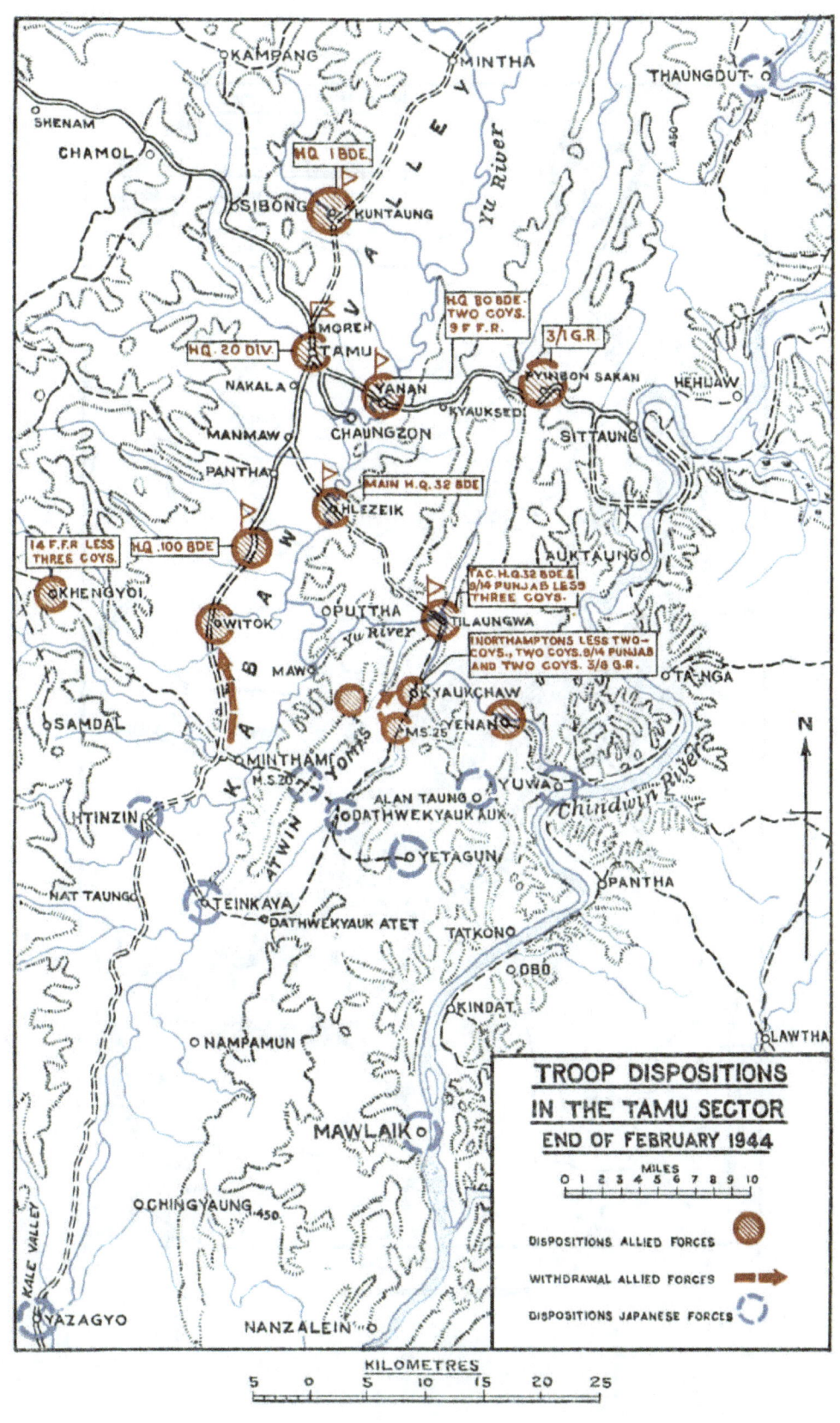

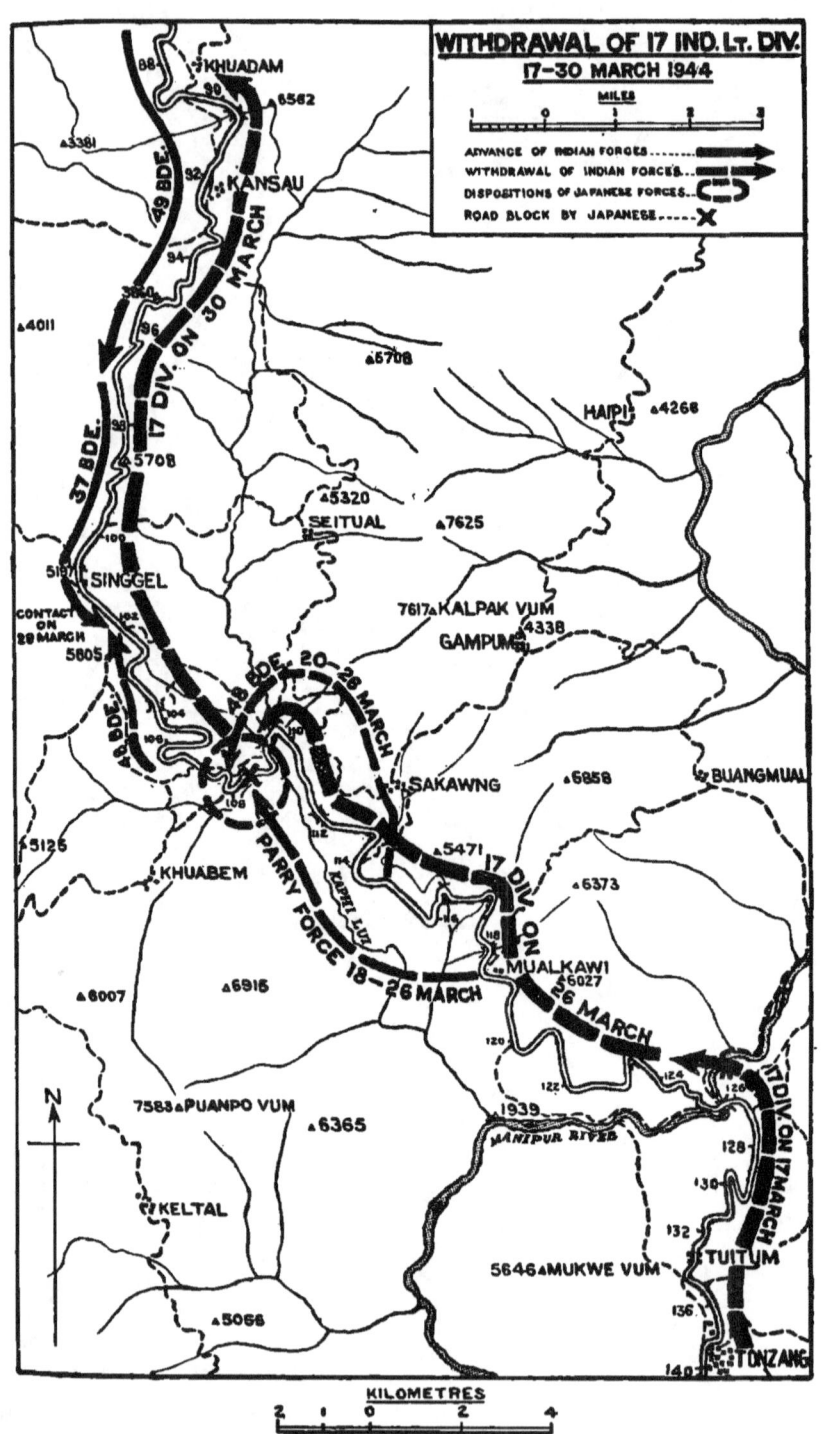

THE JAPANESE THRUST IN THE NORTH

MARCH 1944

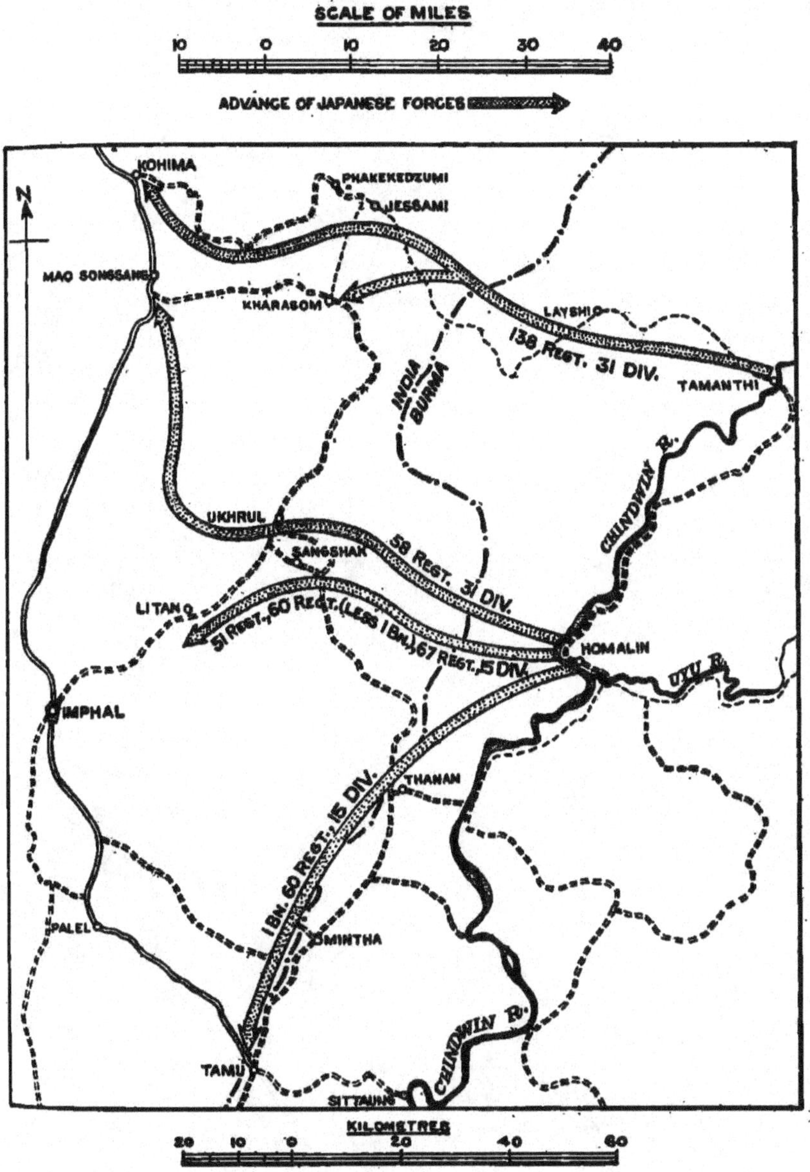

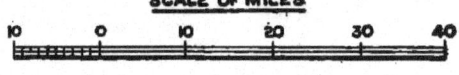

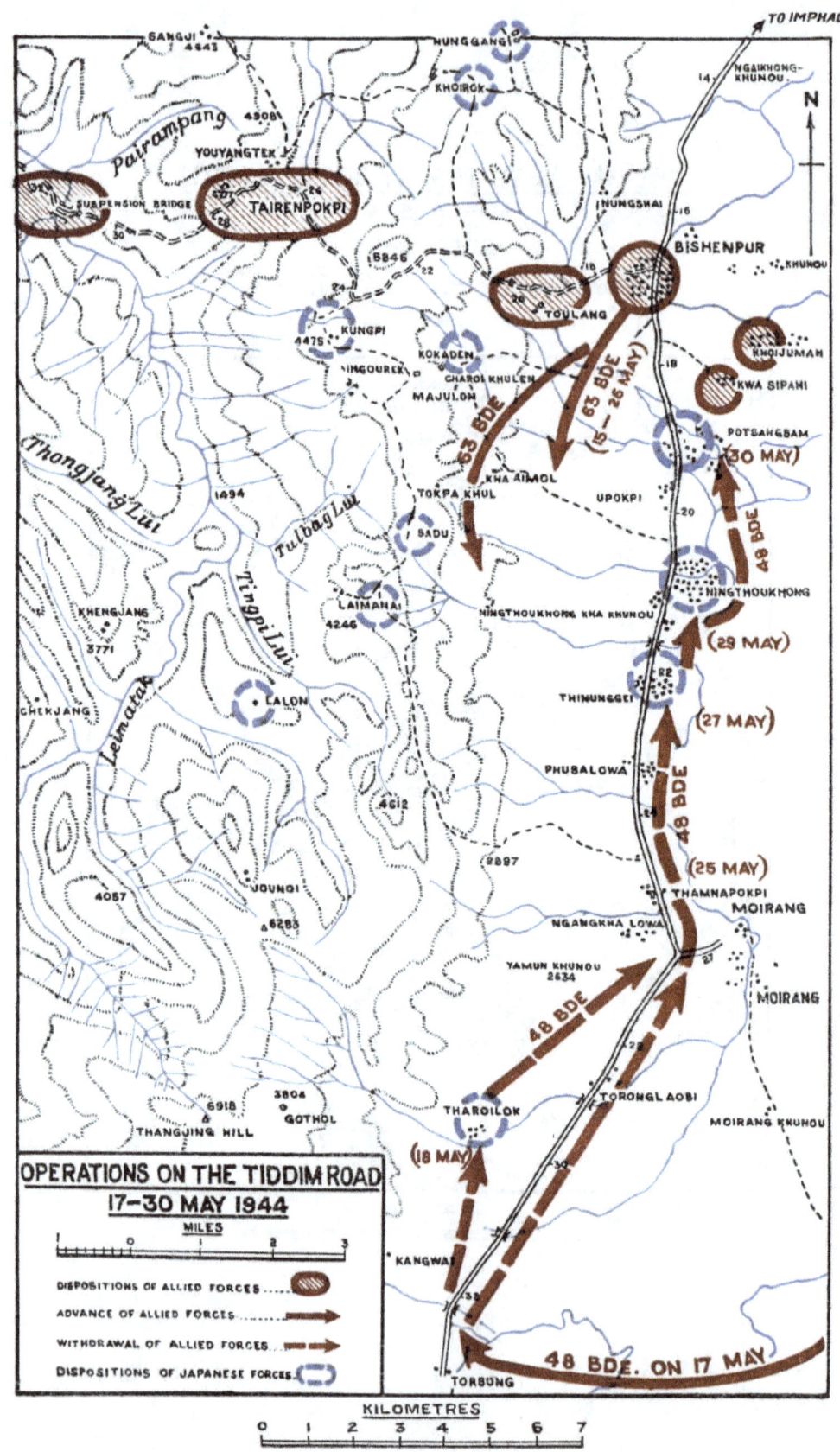

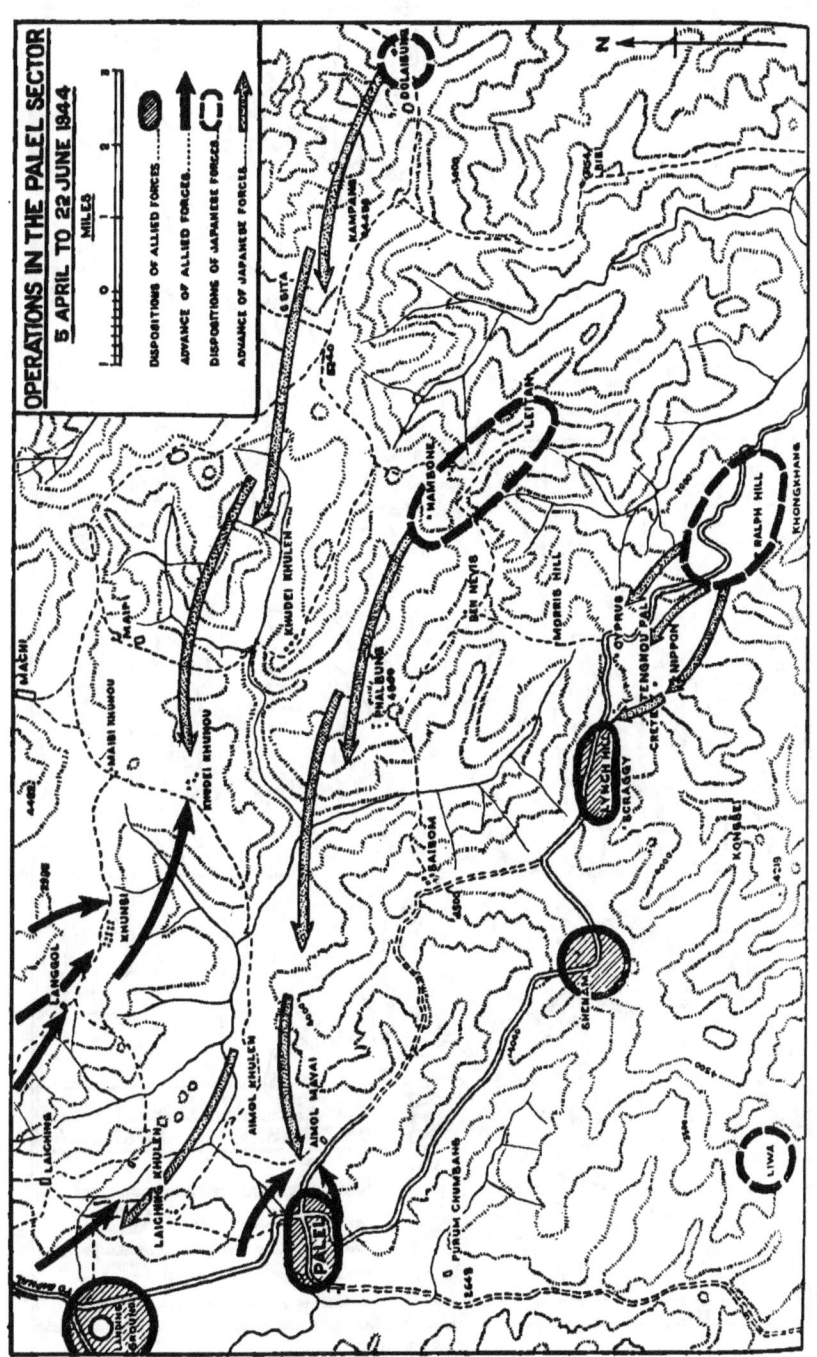

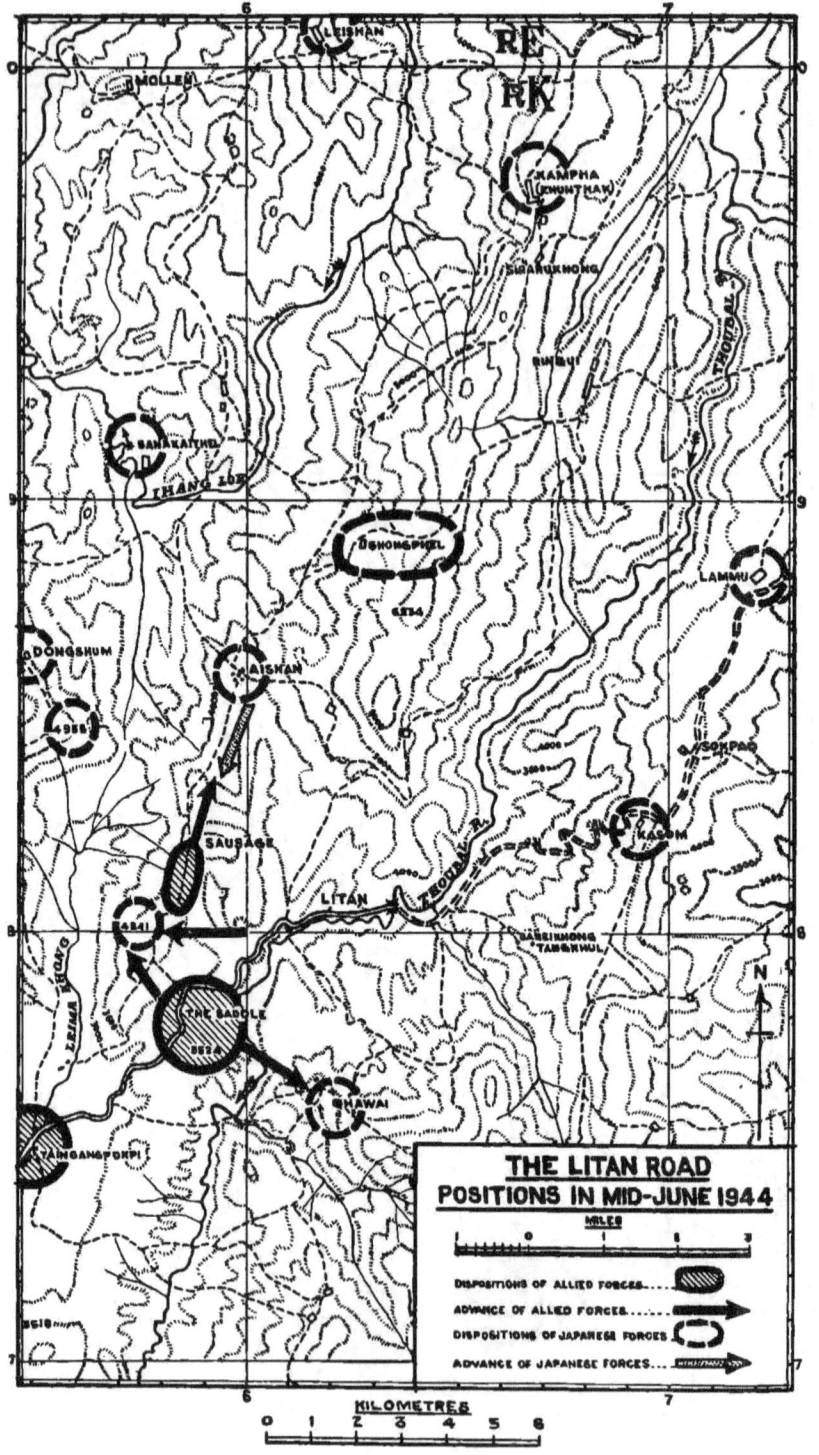

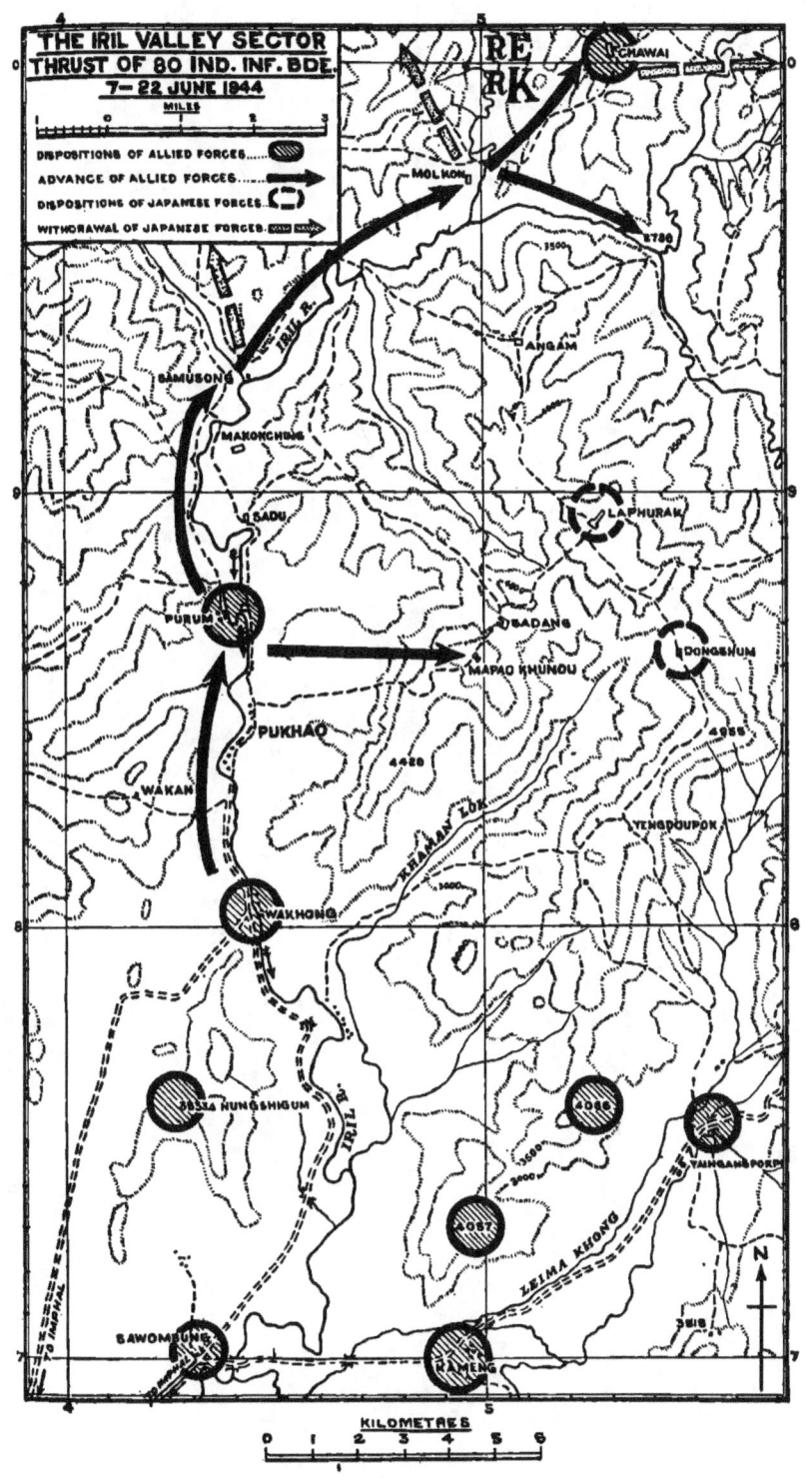

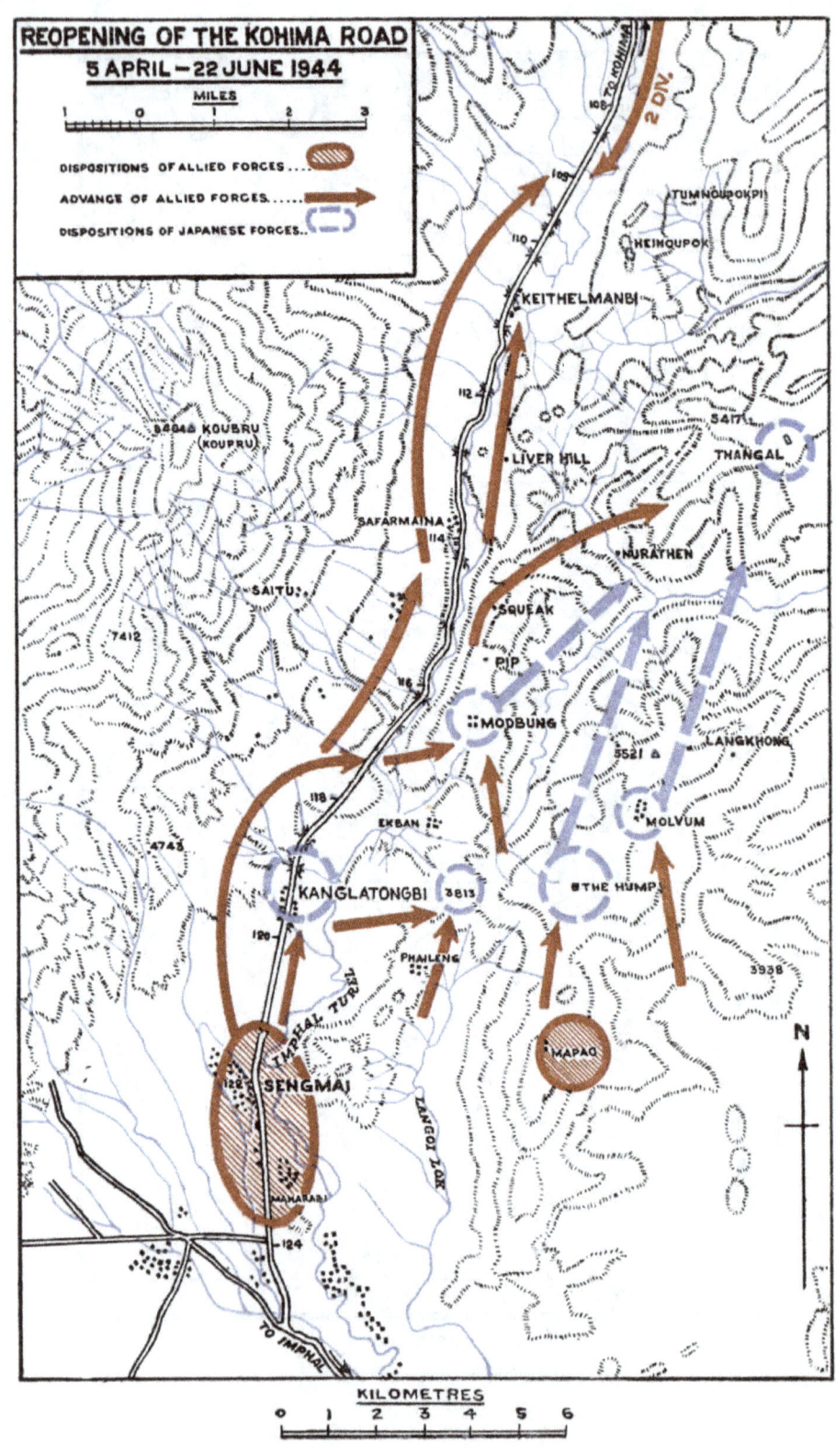

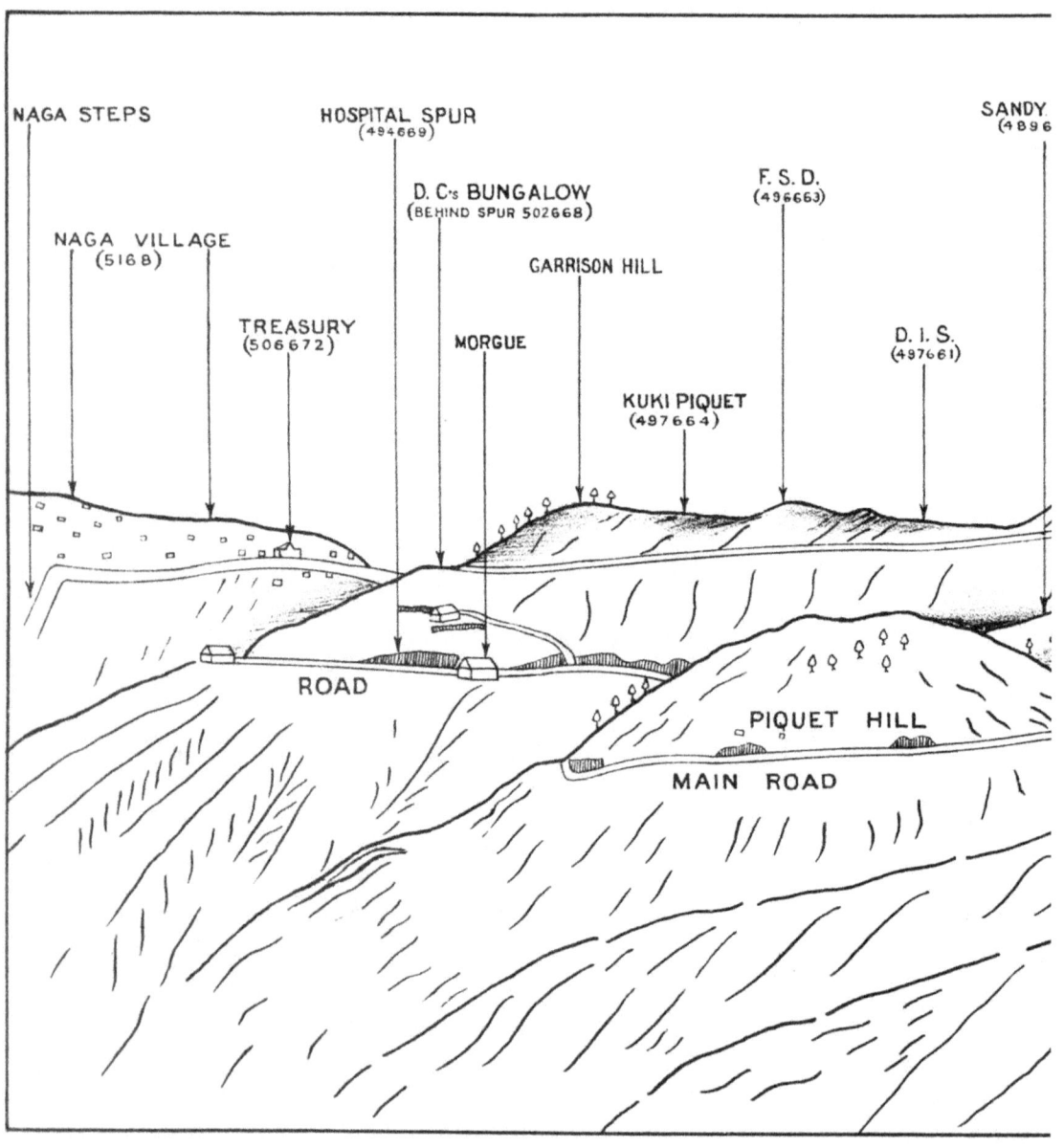

RIDGE (478675) LOOKING EAST

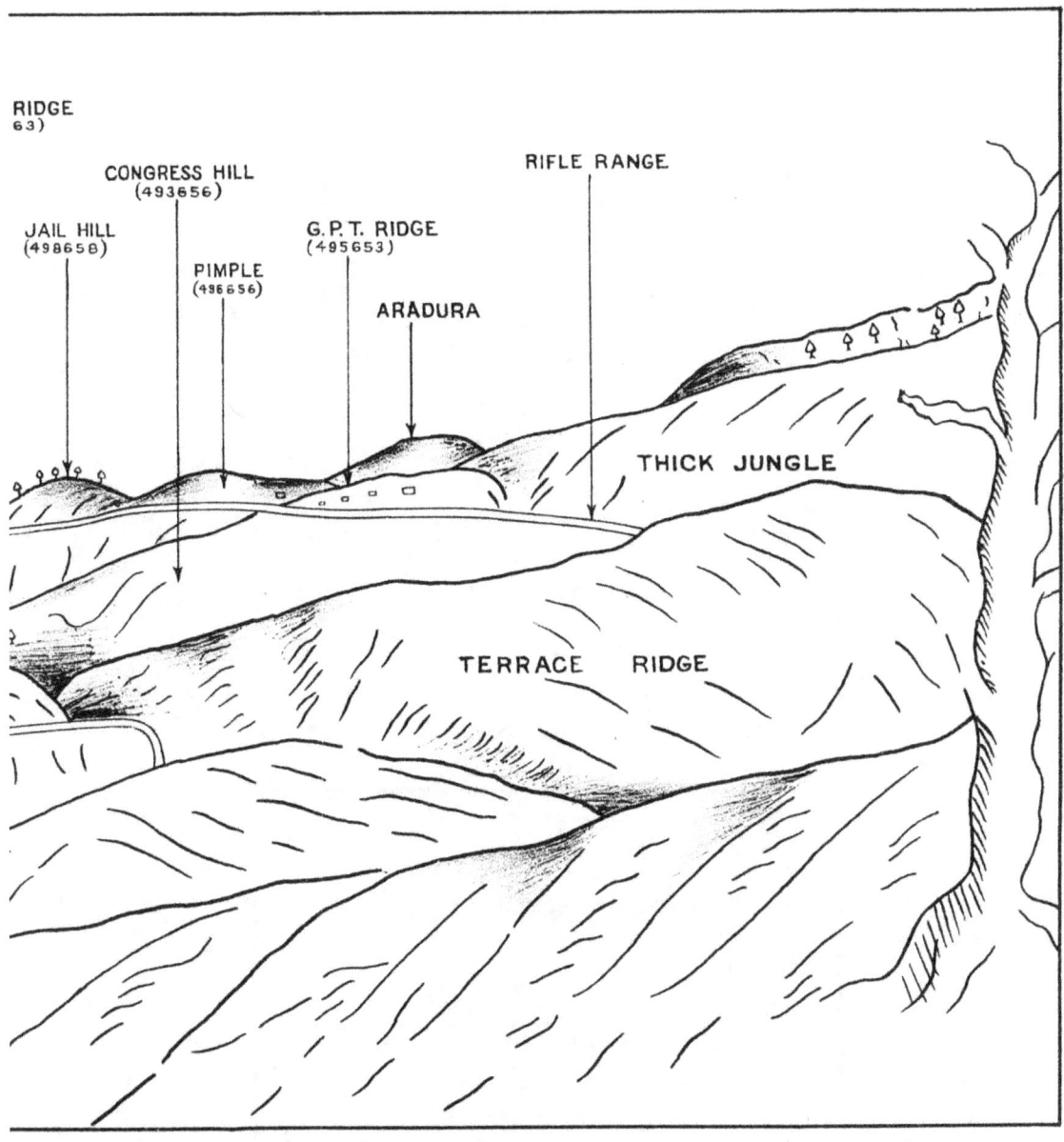

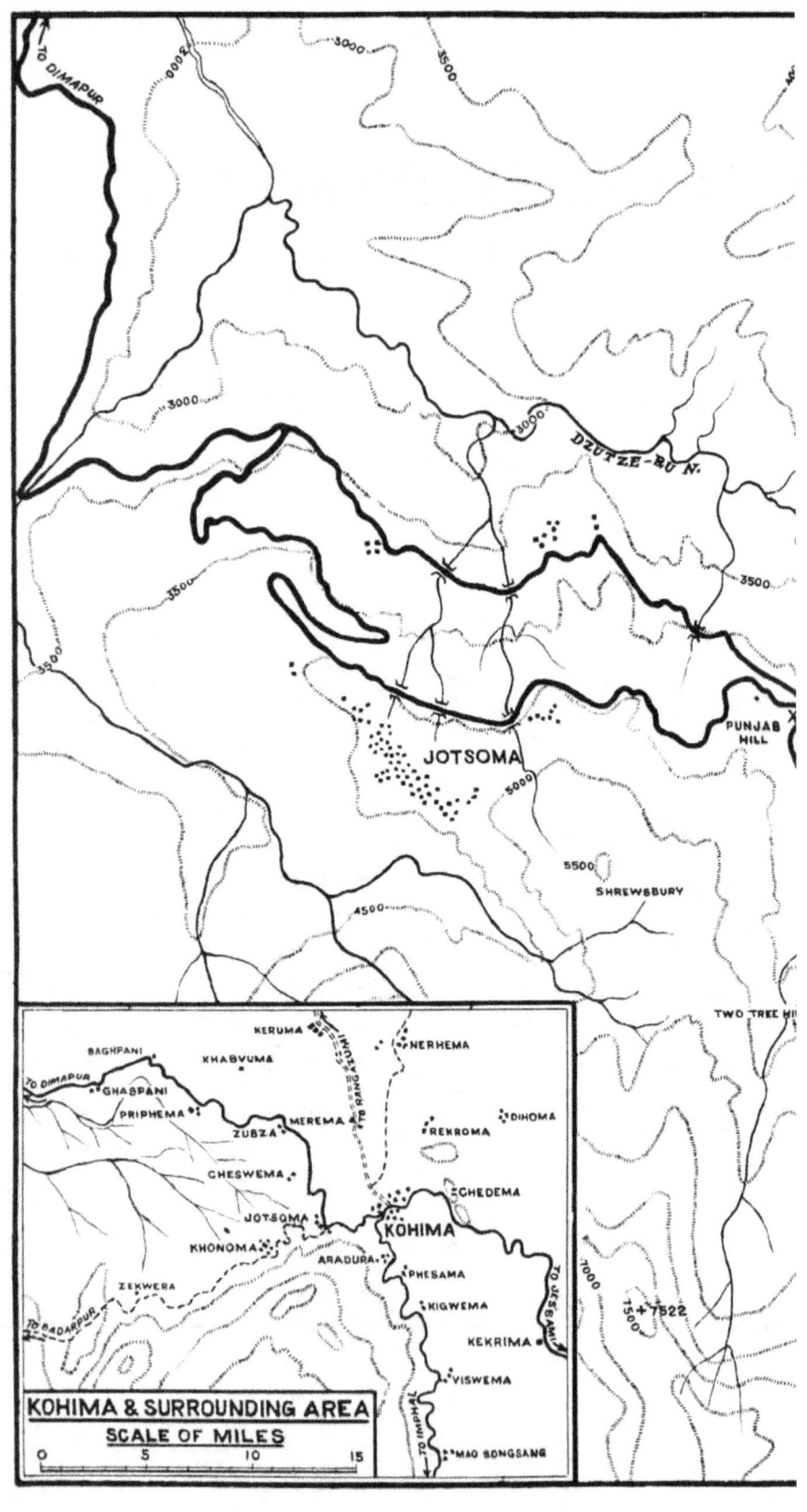

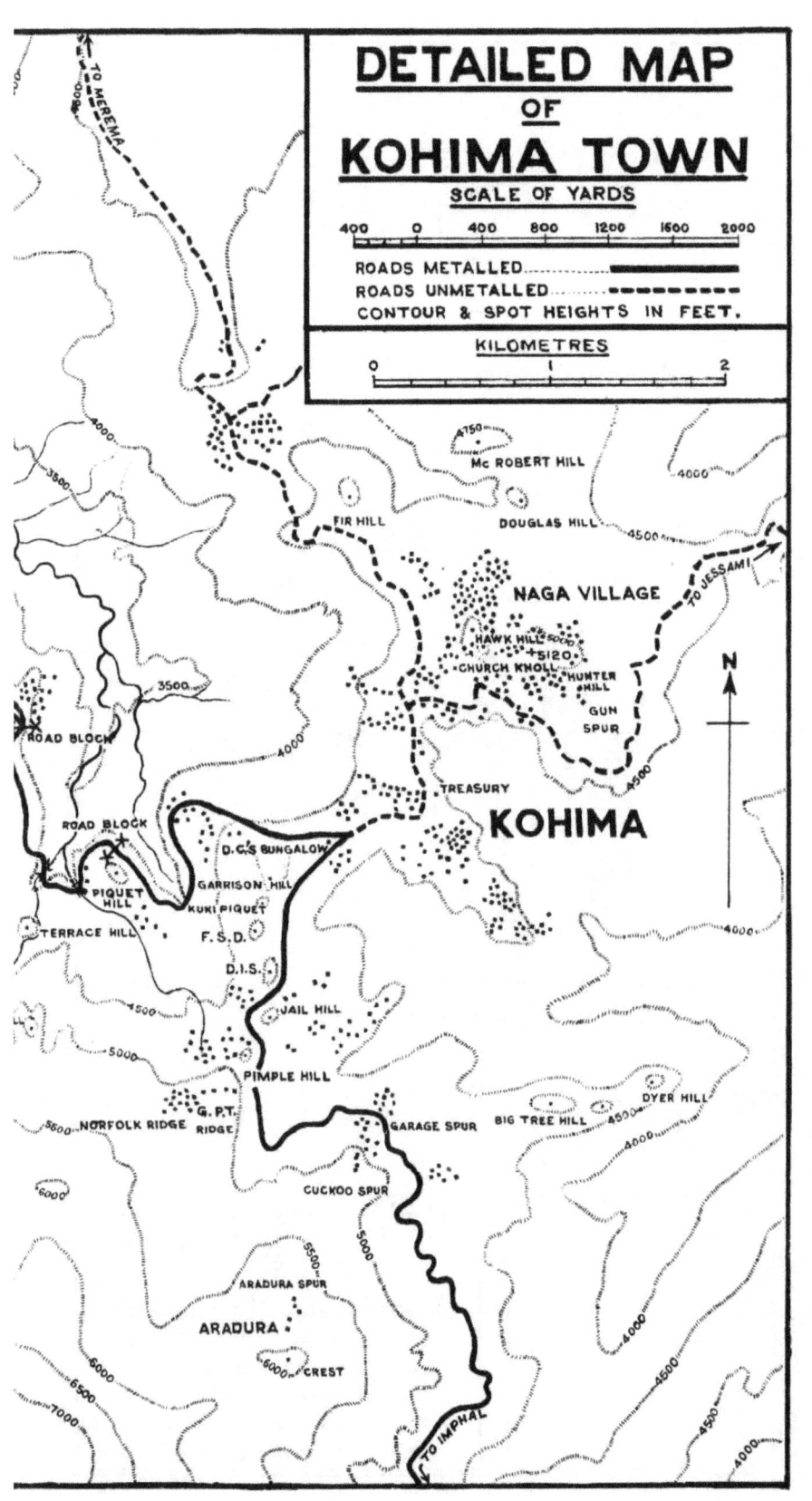

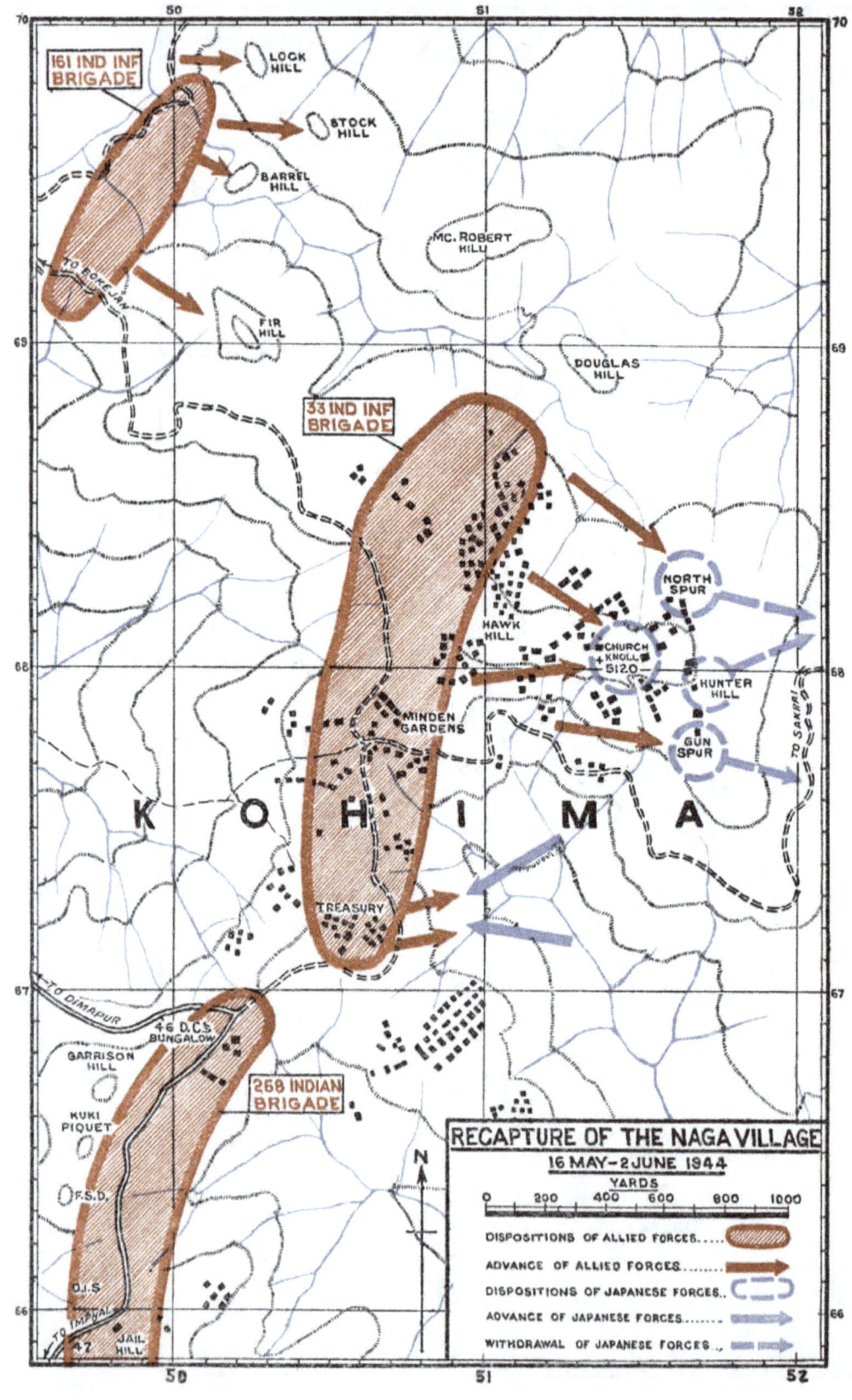

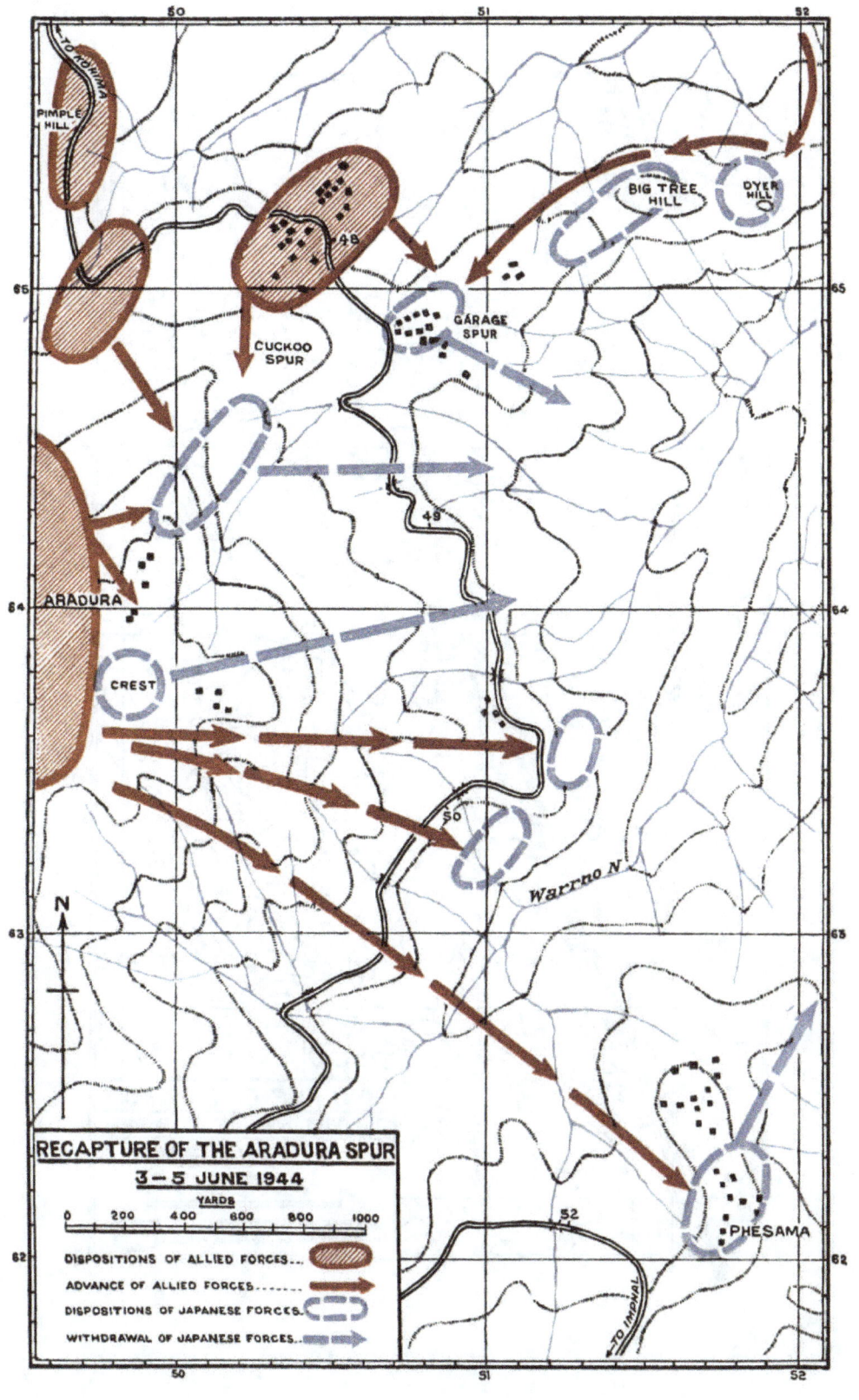

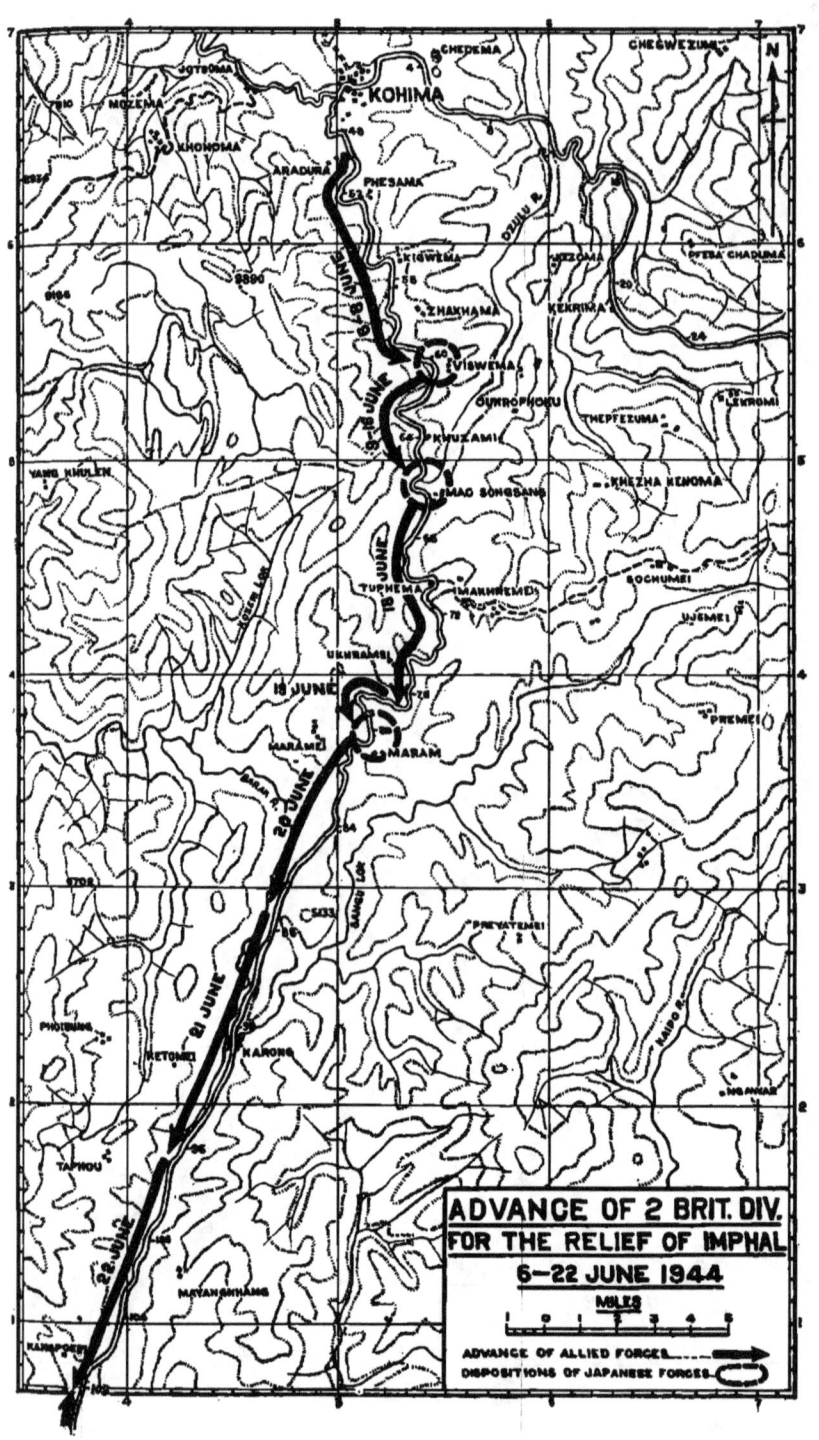

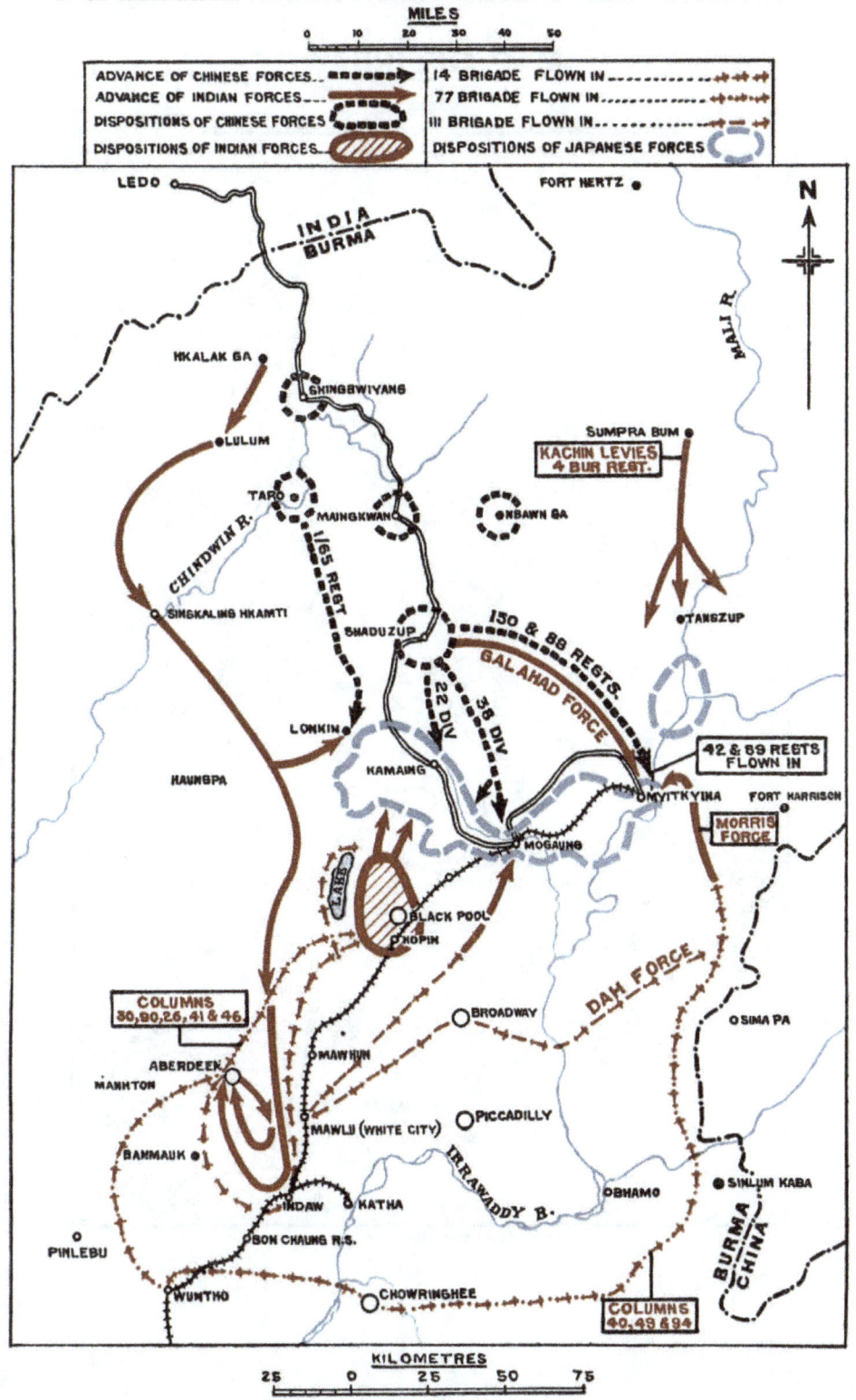

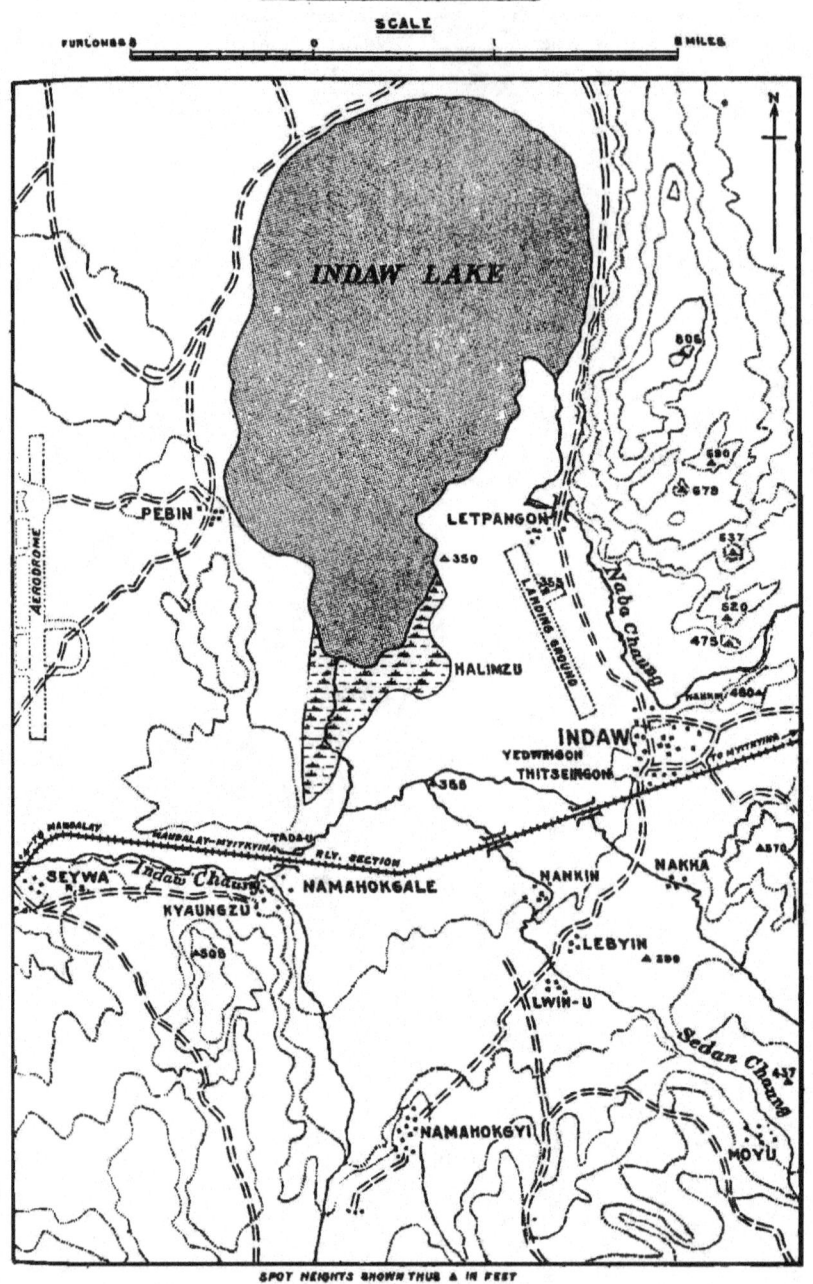

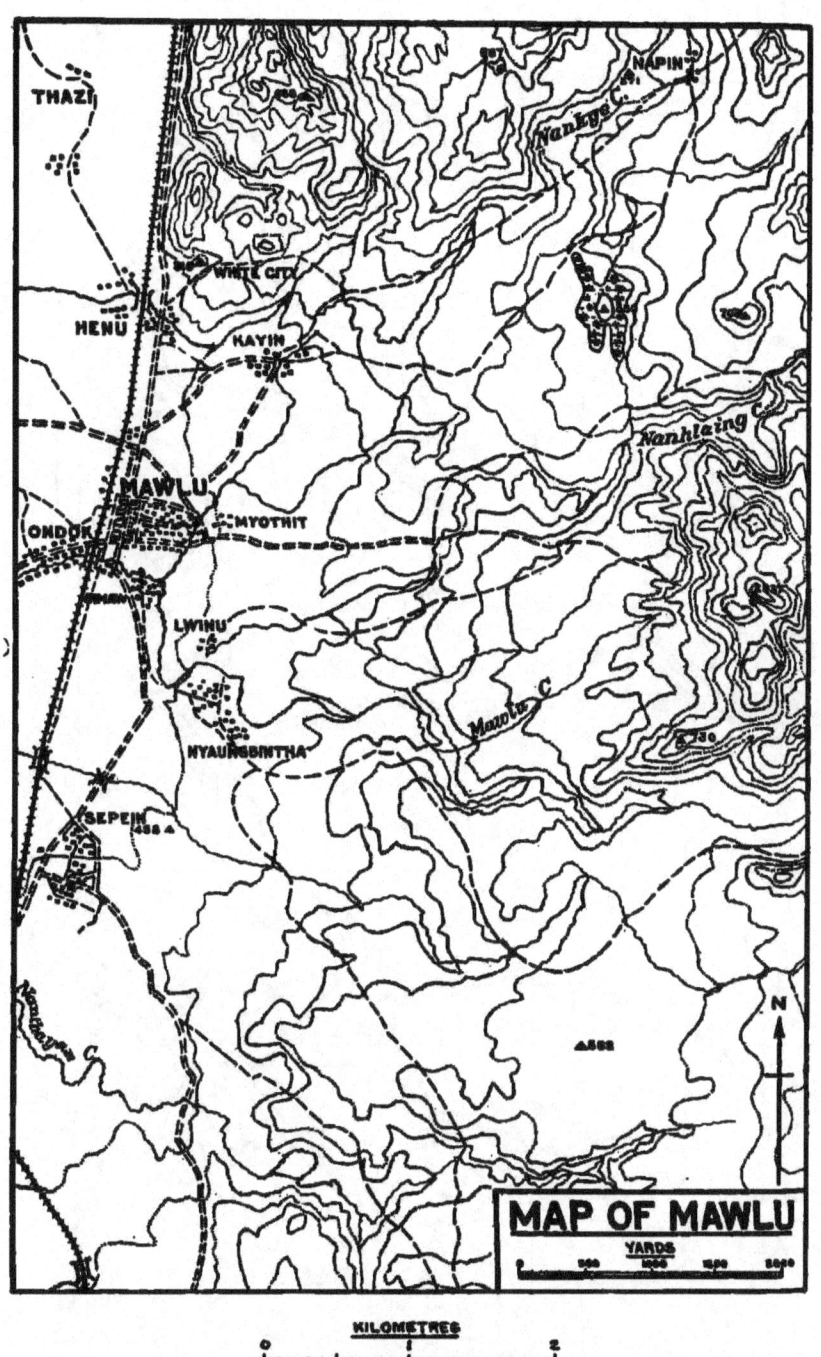

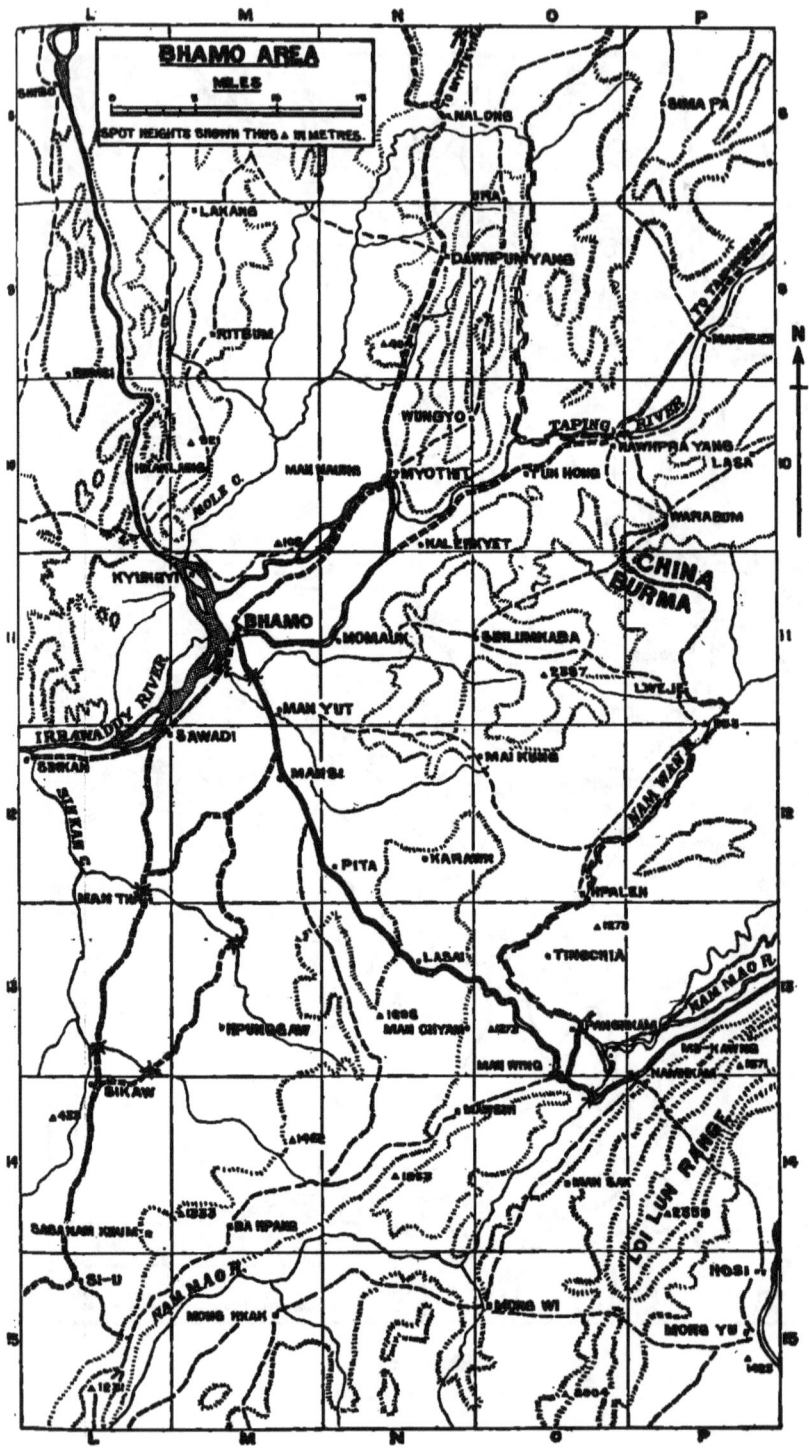

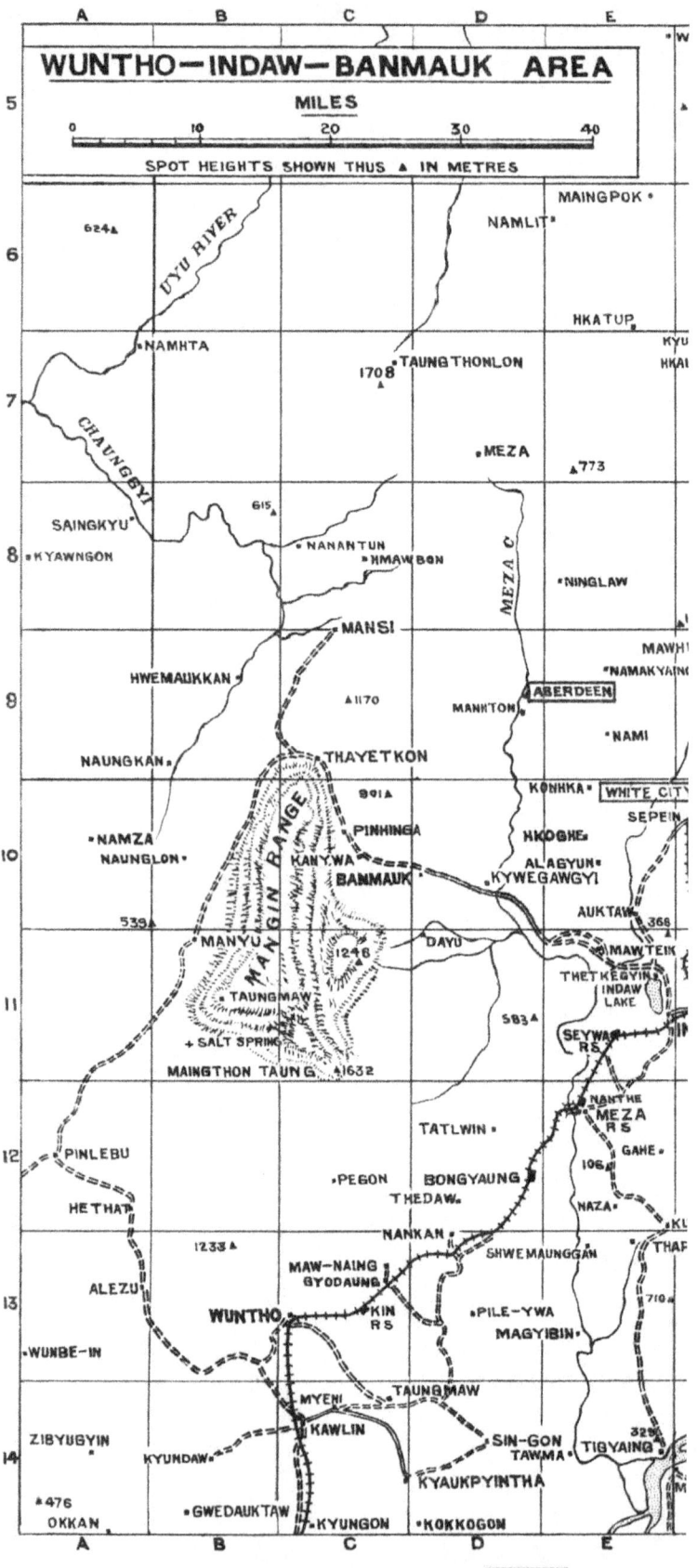

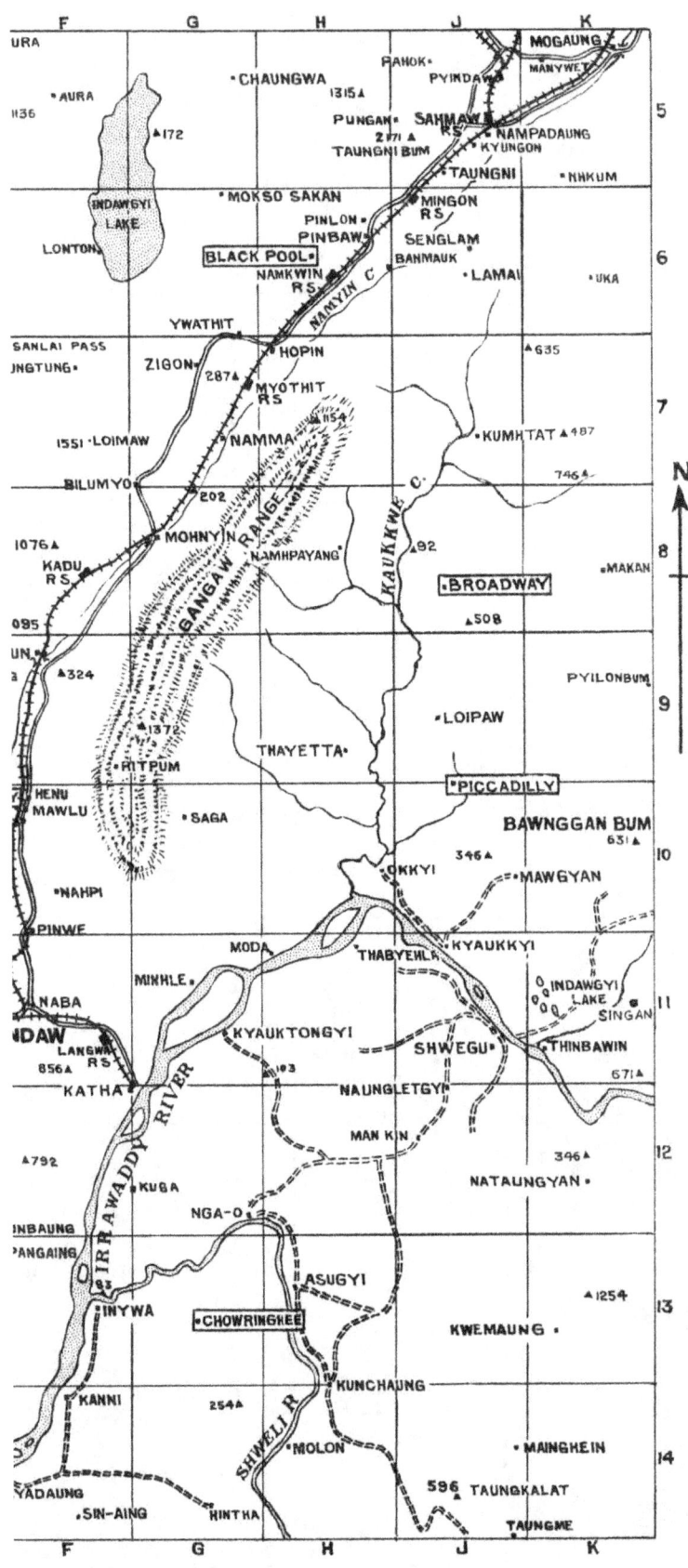

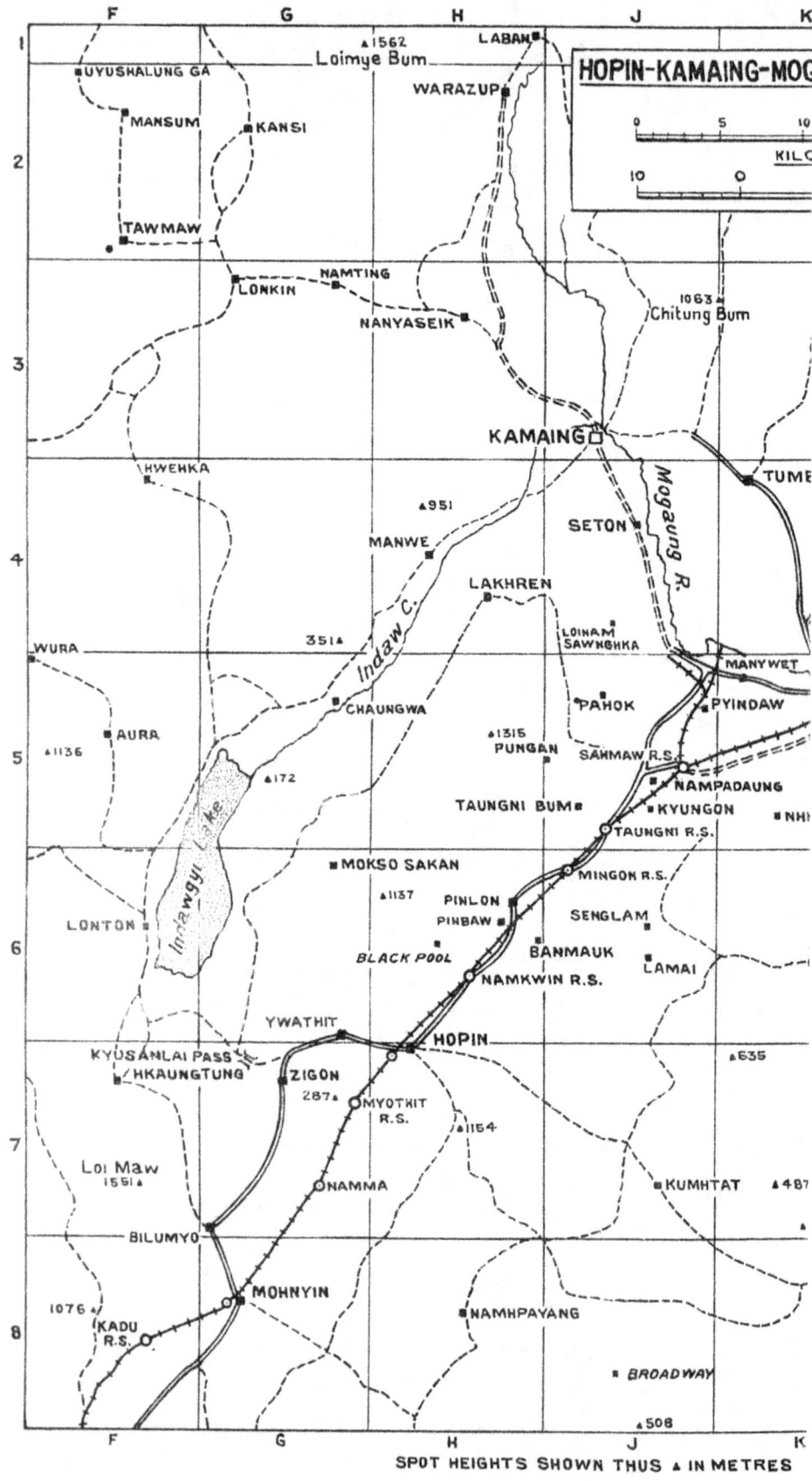

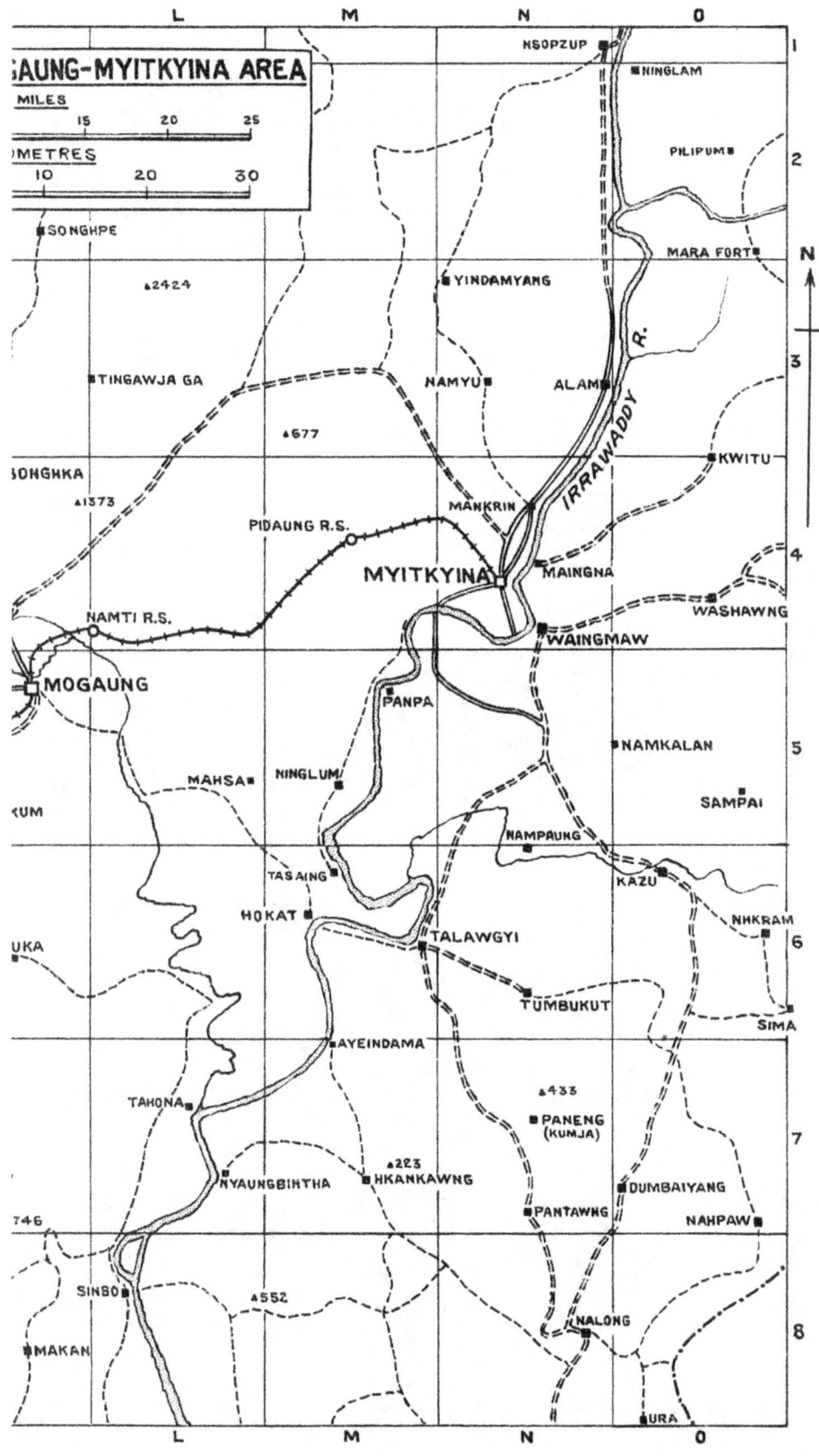

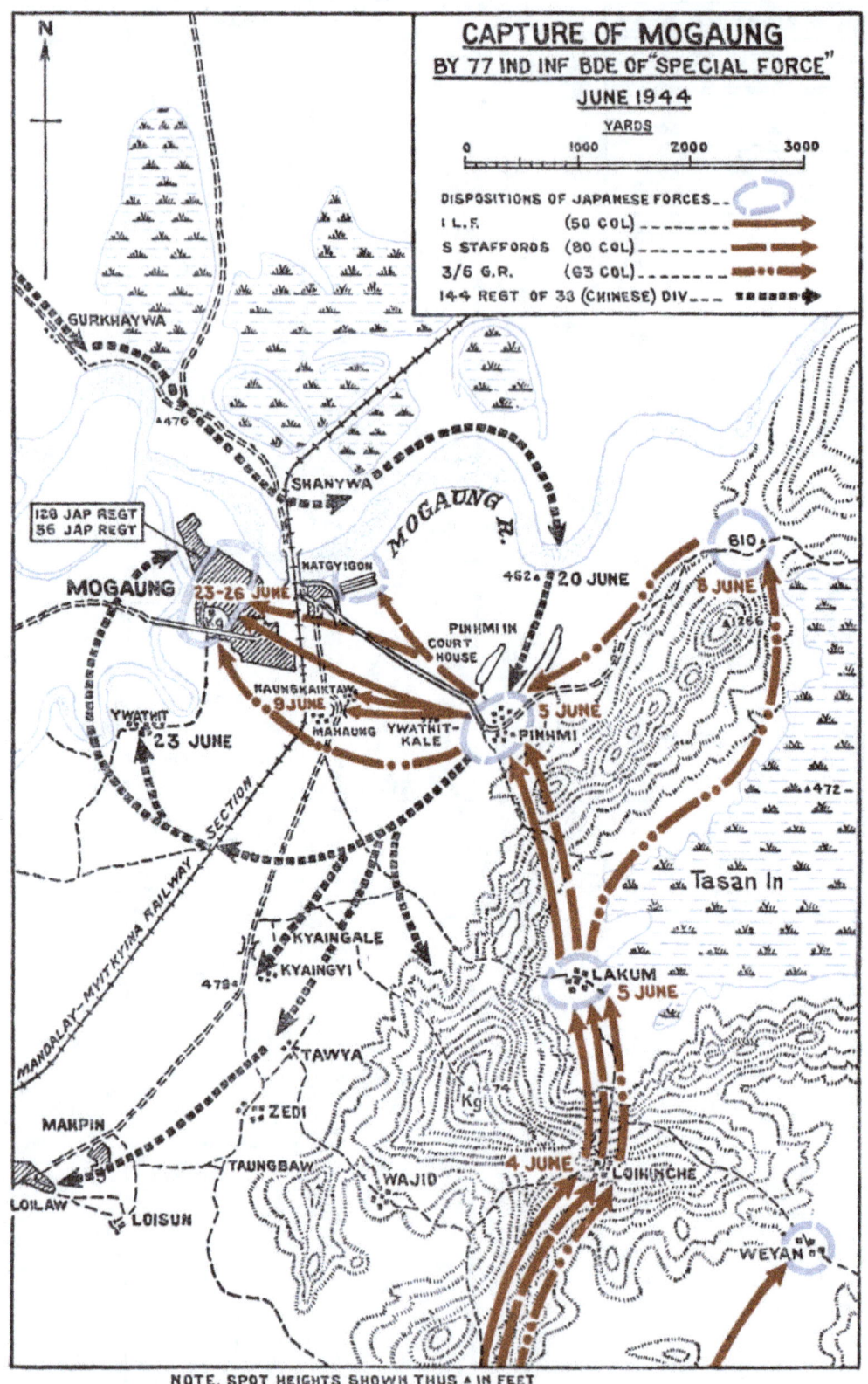

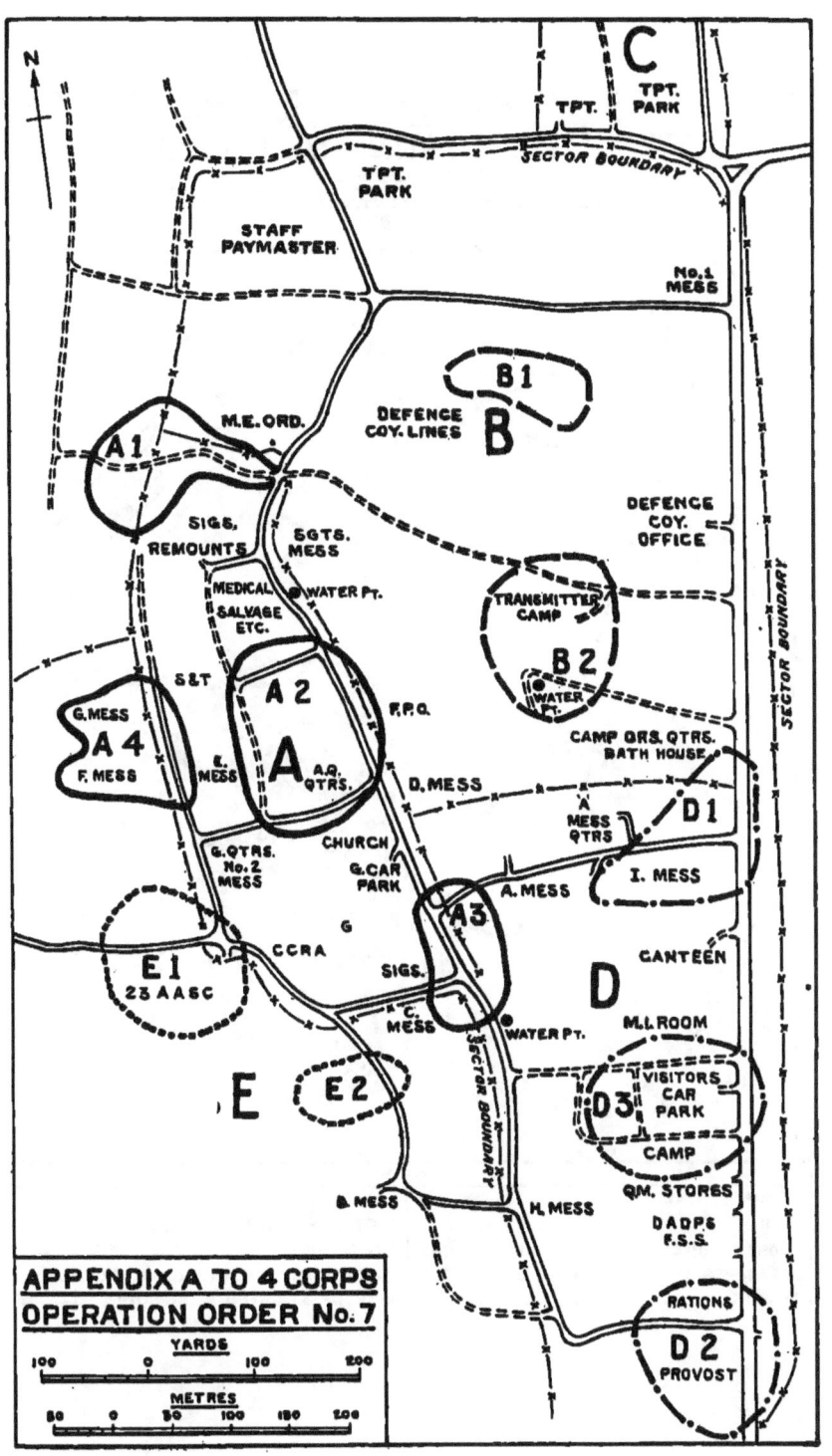

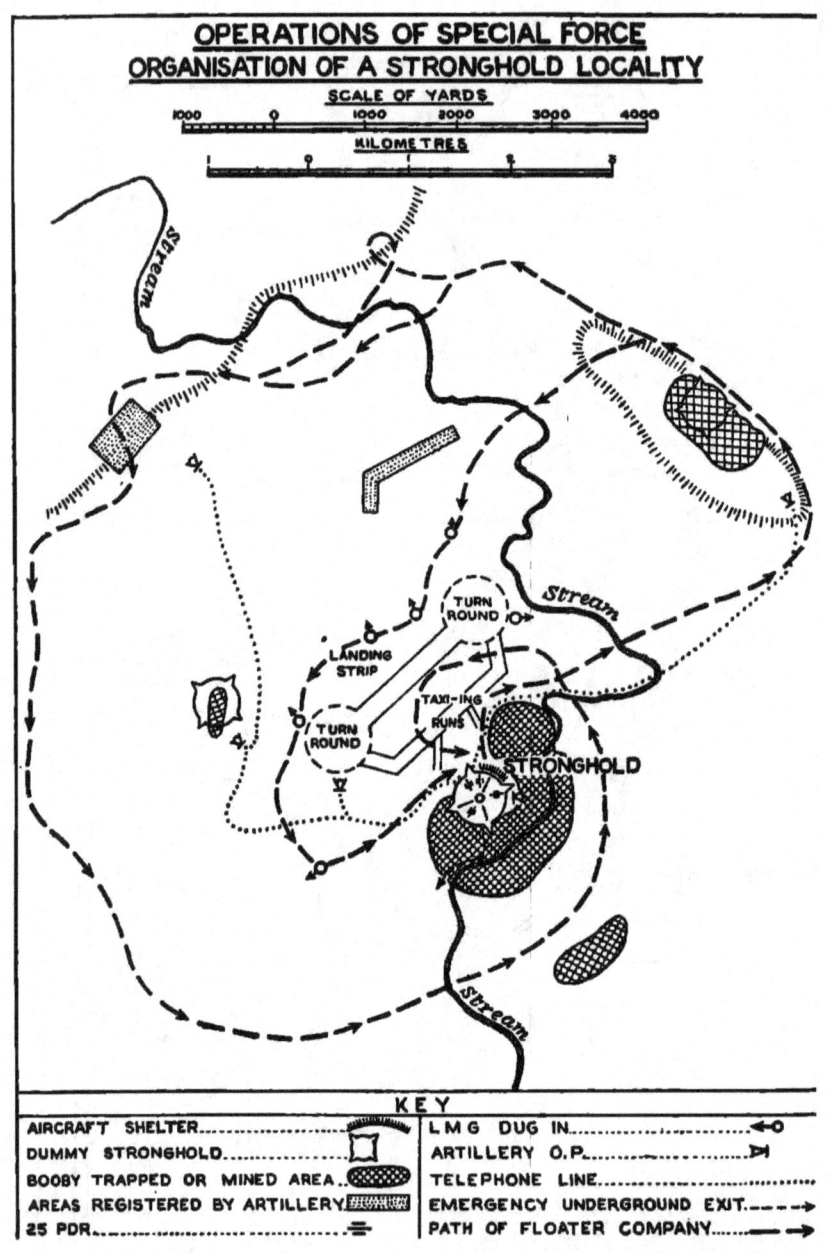

OFFICIAL HISTORY OF THE INDIAN ARMED FORCES
IN THE SECOND WORLD WAR
1939-45

THE RECONQUEST OF BURMA
Volume II

Maps and Sketches

The Reconquest of Burma Volume 2
List of maps

1. Burma (Central and Lower)
2. The advance on Ukhrul, 27 June-8 July 1944
3. Reopening of the Ukhrul road, 1-10 July 1944
4. The Tengnoupal positions on the Palel-Tamu Road, April-July 1944
5. The thrust to Sibong, 24-28 July 1944
6. The outflanking march by 123 Ind. Inf. Bde., 30 August-14 September 1944
7. Operations of 5 Ind. Div. against Vital Corner and Fort White, 2-8 November 1944
8. Drive to the Chindwin, June-November 1944
9. Fourteenth Army Plans, December 1944
10. Allied and Japanese dispositions, 24 December 1944
11. Allied dispositions (February 1945) prior to advance on Meiktila and Mandalay
12. Allied advance to the Irrawaddy, January-February 1945
13. The crossing of the Irrawaddy by 19 Indian Div. Mid-January to 20 February 1945
14. 20 Incl. Div. Operation to clear the north bank of the Irrawaddy, January-February 1945
15. 2 British Div. Operations to clear the north bank of the Irrawaddy, January-February 1945
16. Crossings of the Irrawaddy, January-February 1945
17. Crossing of the Irrawaddy by 20 Ind. Div., 13 February 1945
18. The crossing of the Irrawaddy by 2 British Div., 24 February 1945
19. The crossing of the Irrawaddy by 7 Ind. Div., 14 February 1945
20. Capture of Meiktila, 1-5 March 1945
21. 17 Div. consolidation in Meiktila, March 1945
22. Operation in Mandalay Arca, March-April 1945
23. Advance of Fourteenth Army to Rangoon, 26 December to 3 May 1945
24. Exploitation Phase, situation 7 April 1945
25. Battle of the Sittang bend, 7-10 July 1945
26. Japanese break-out from Pegu Yomas, 20 July to 4 August 1945
27. Burma

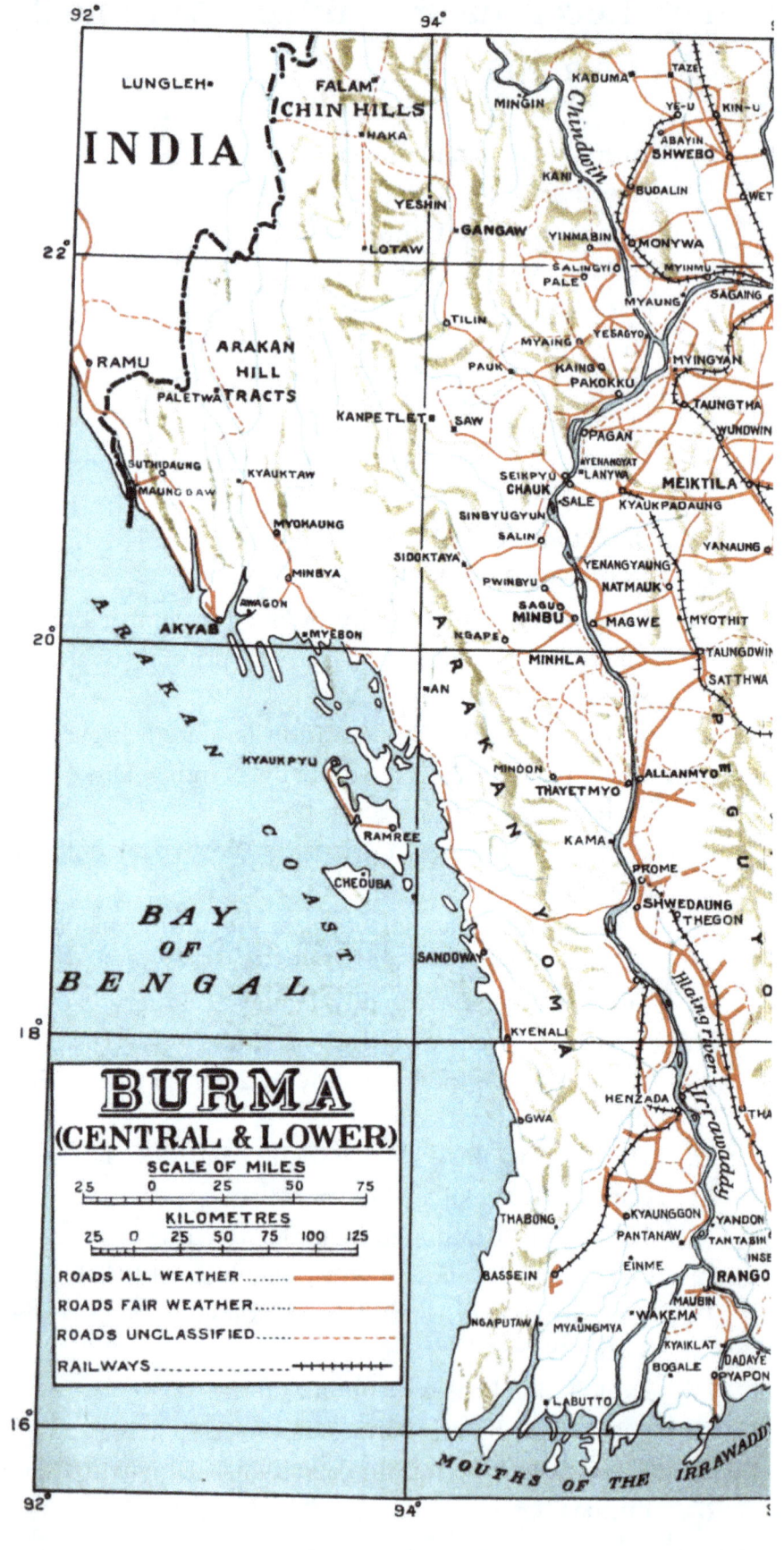

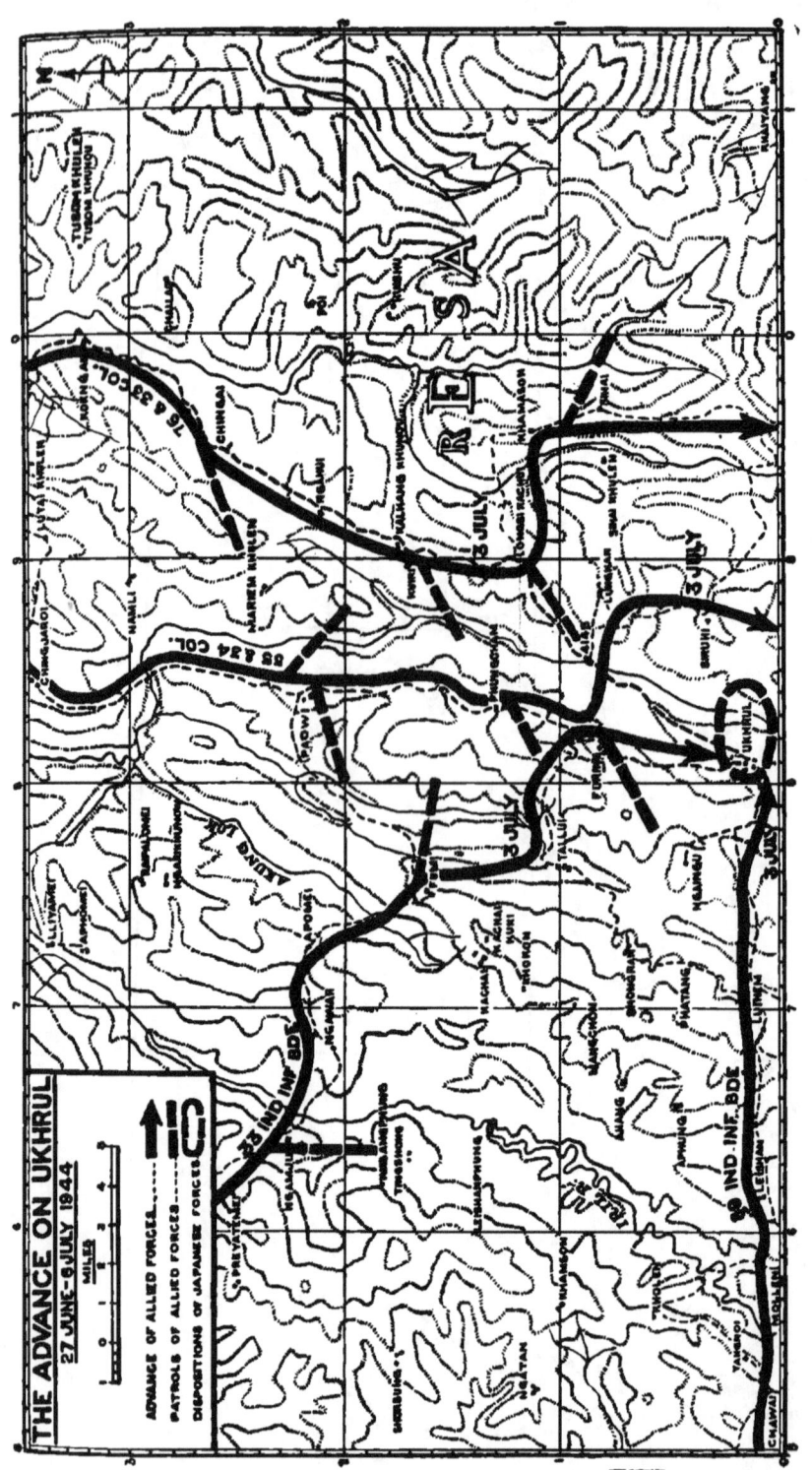

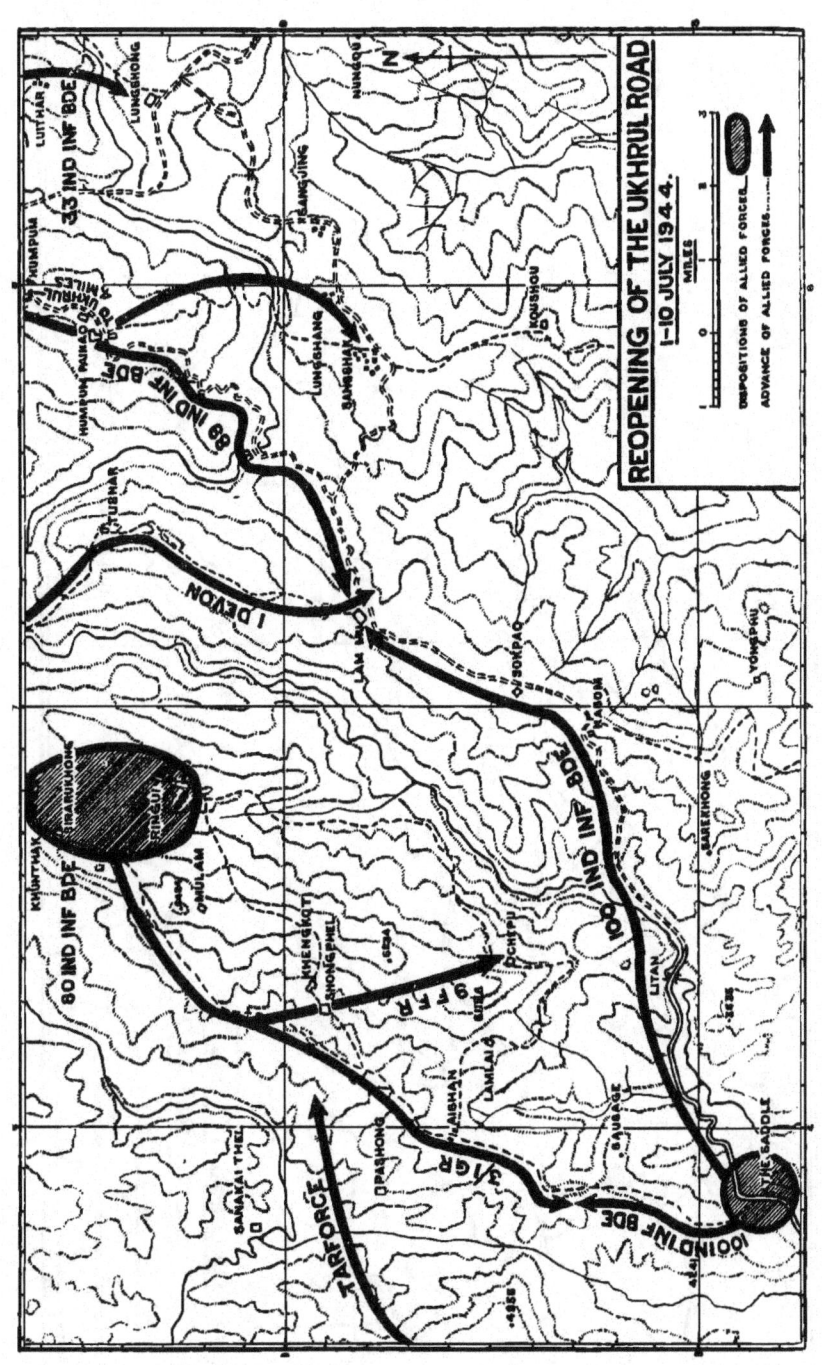

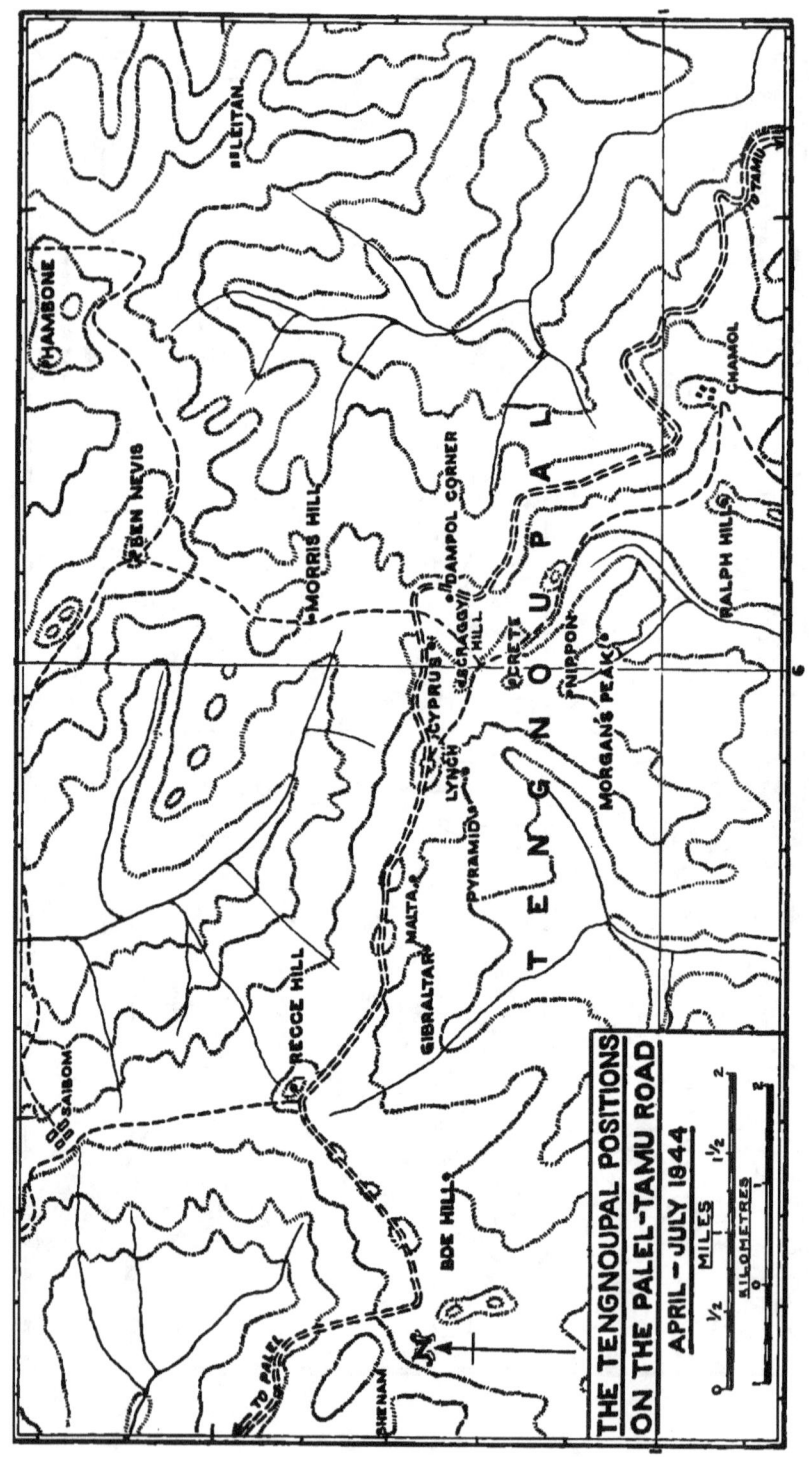

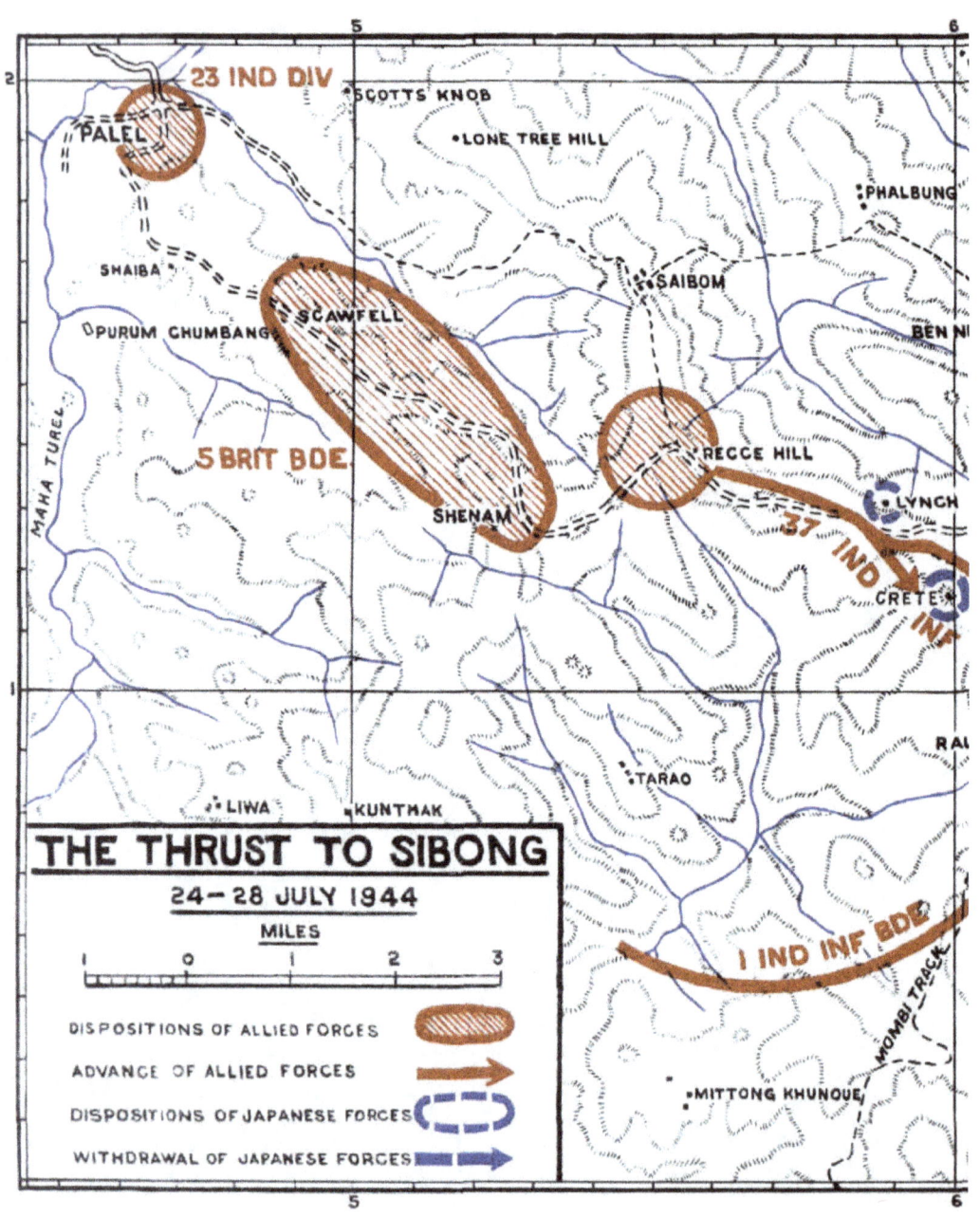

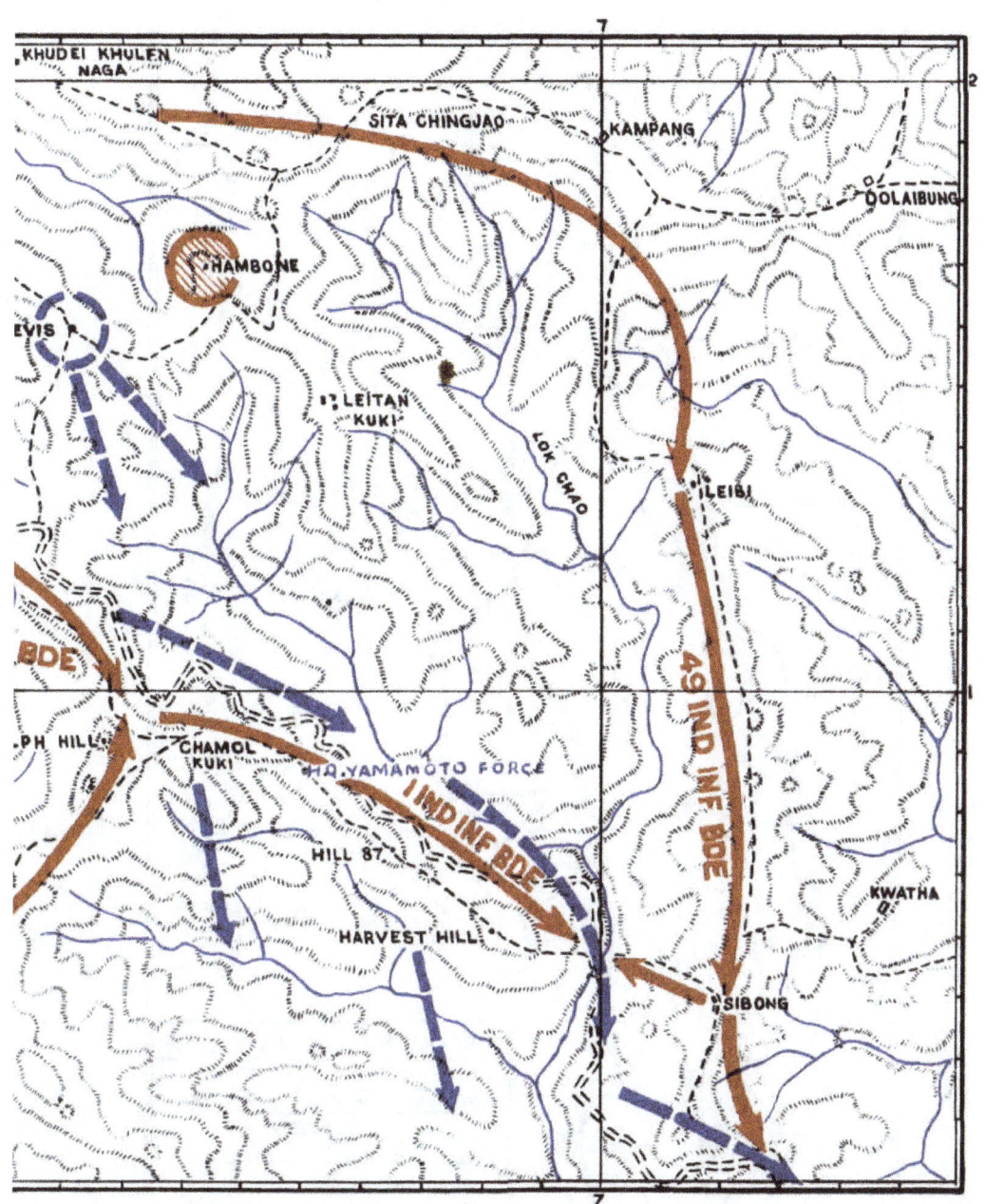

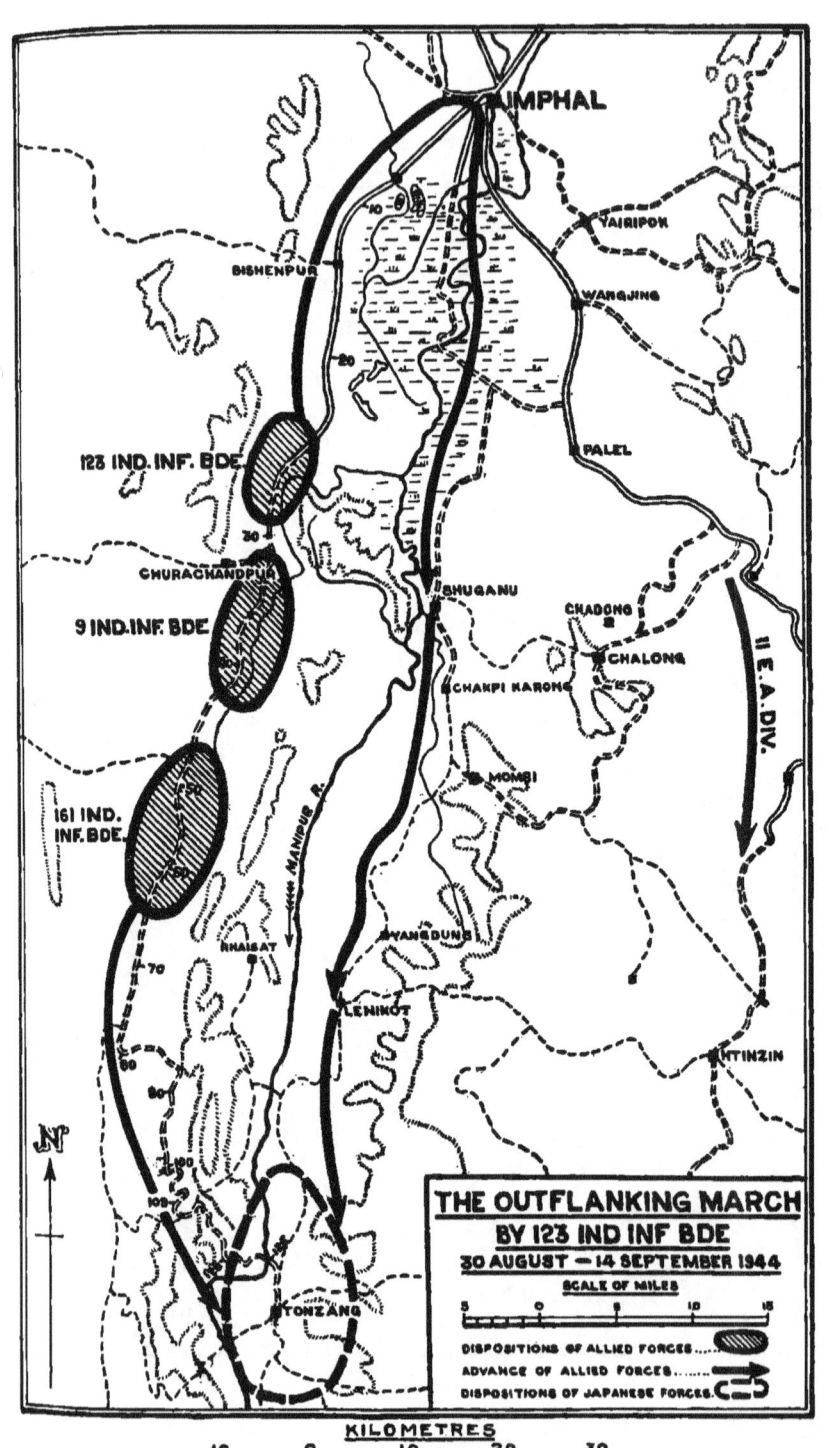

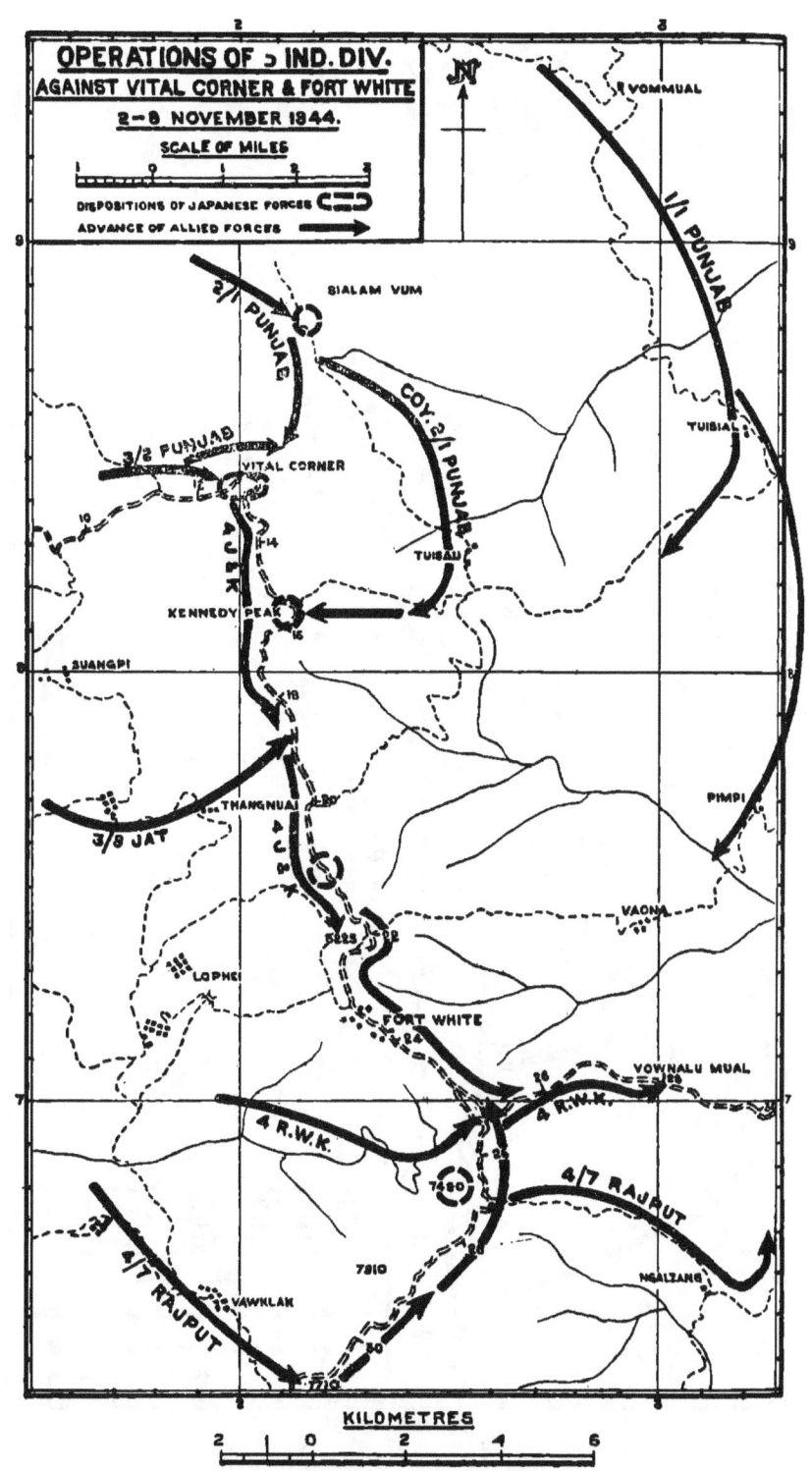

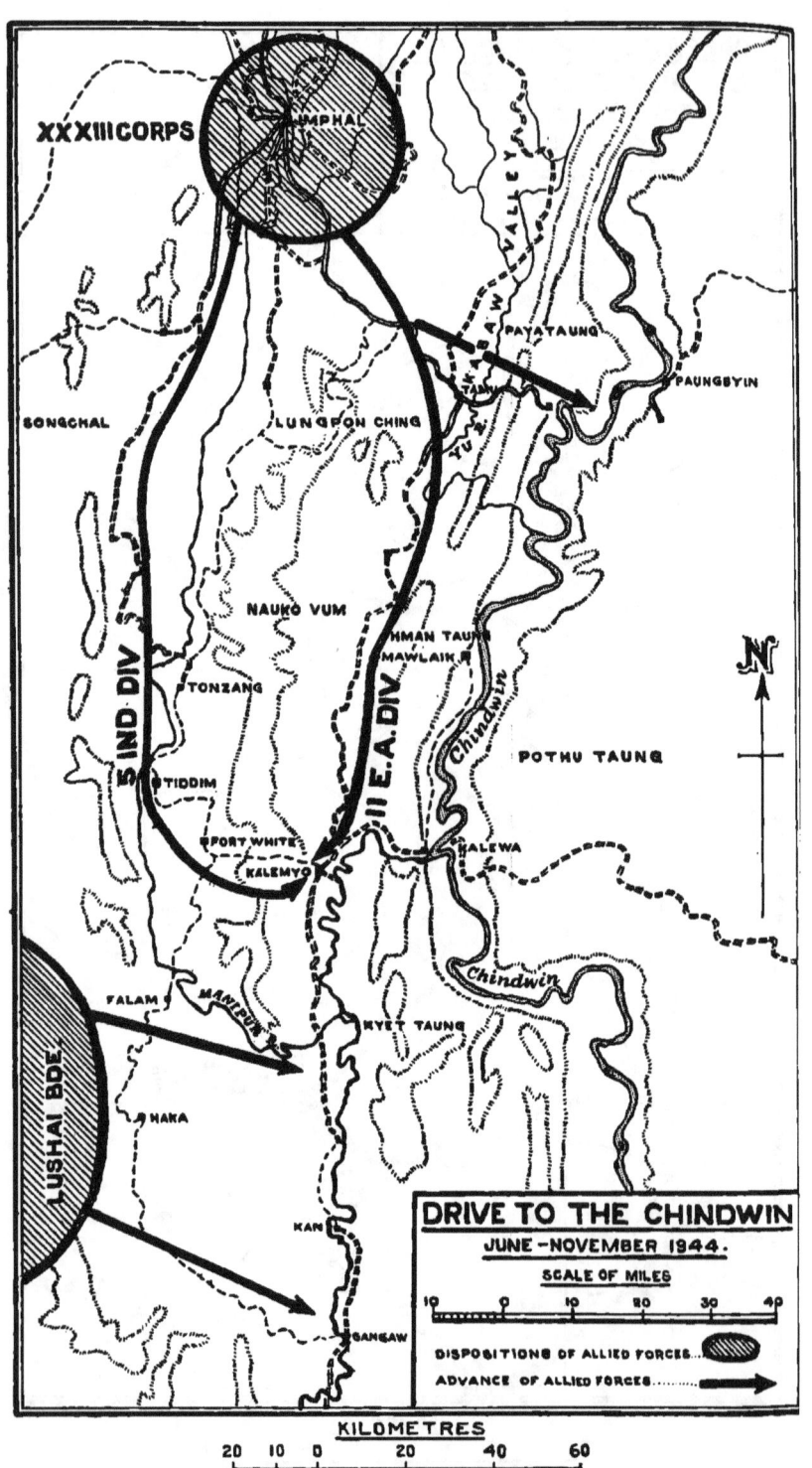

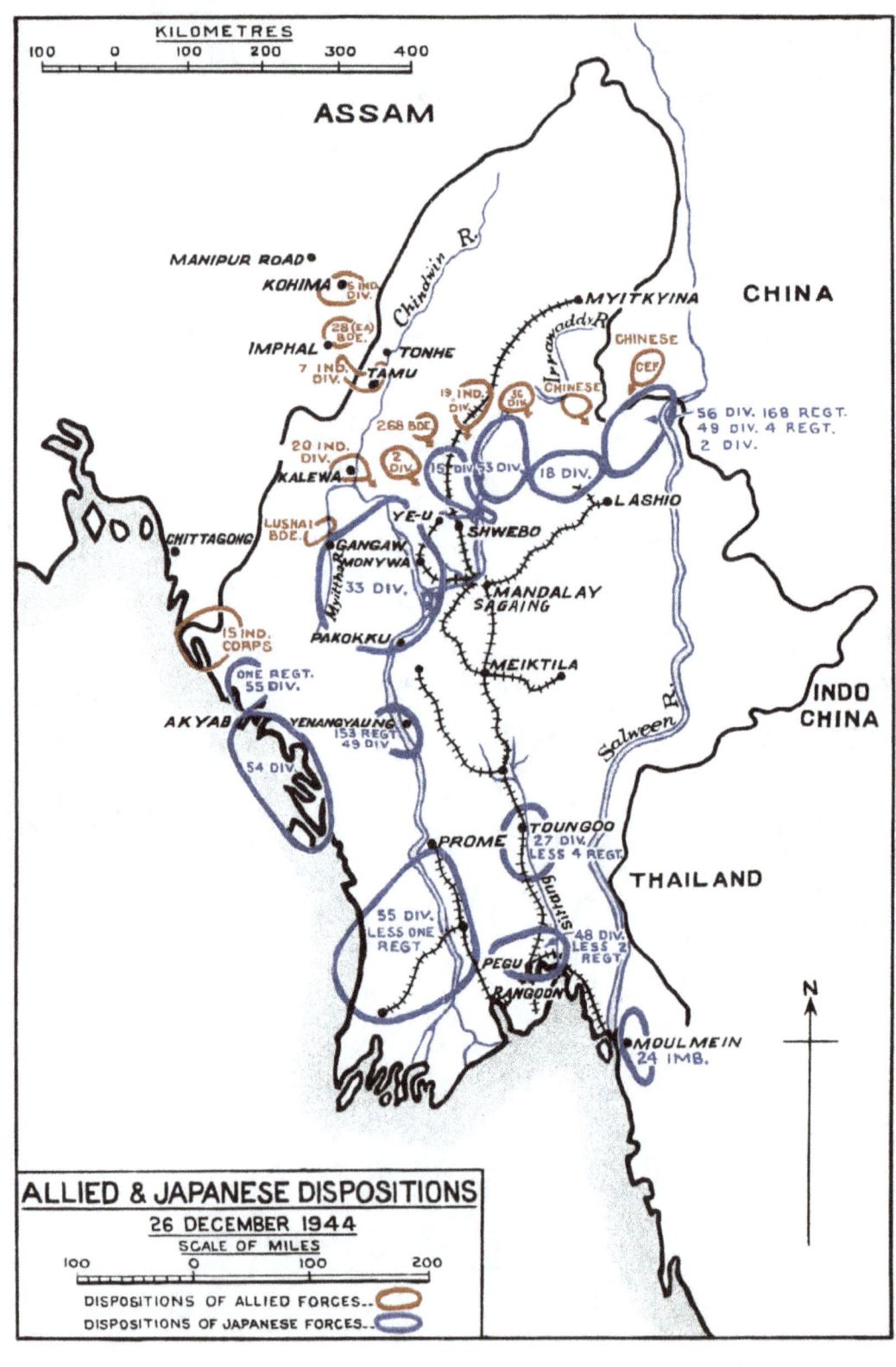

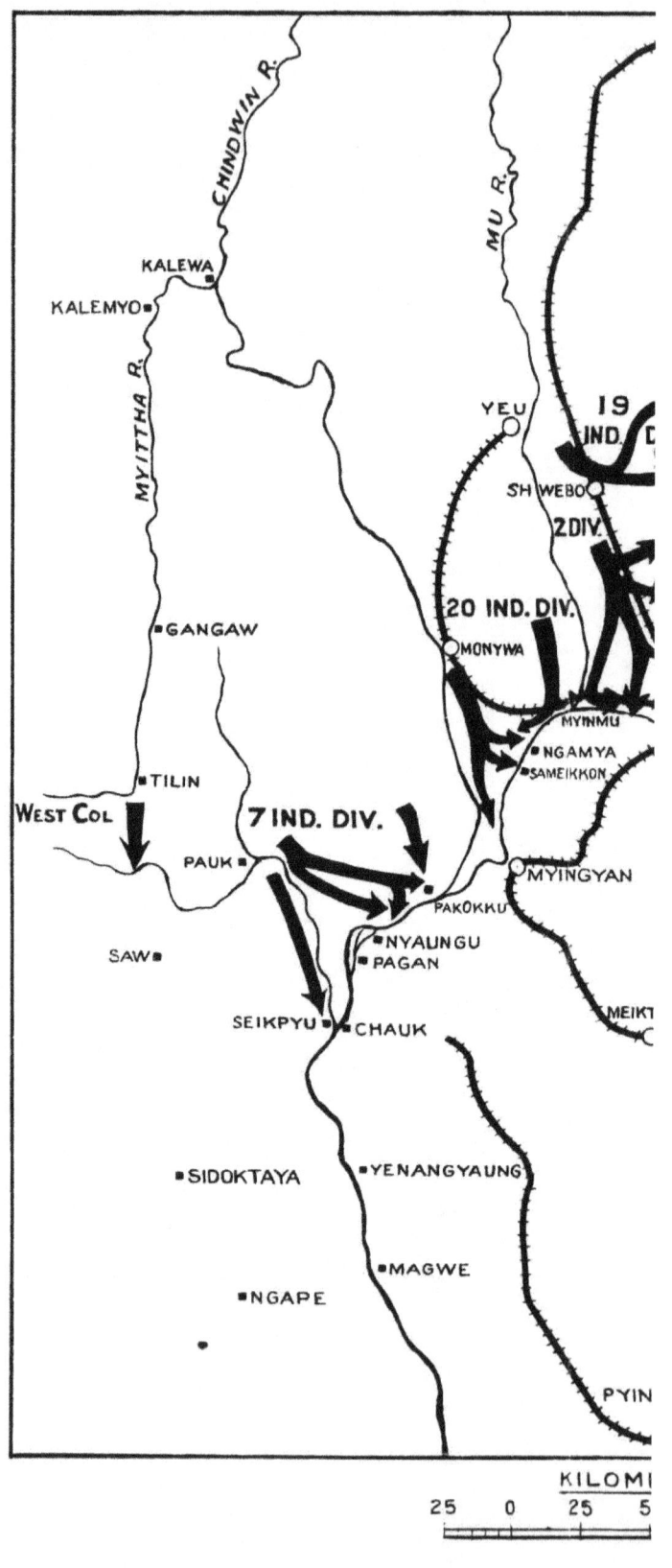

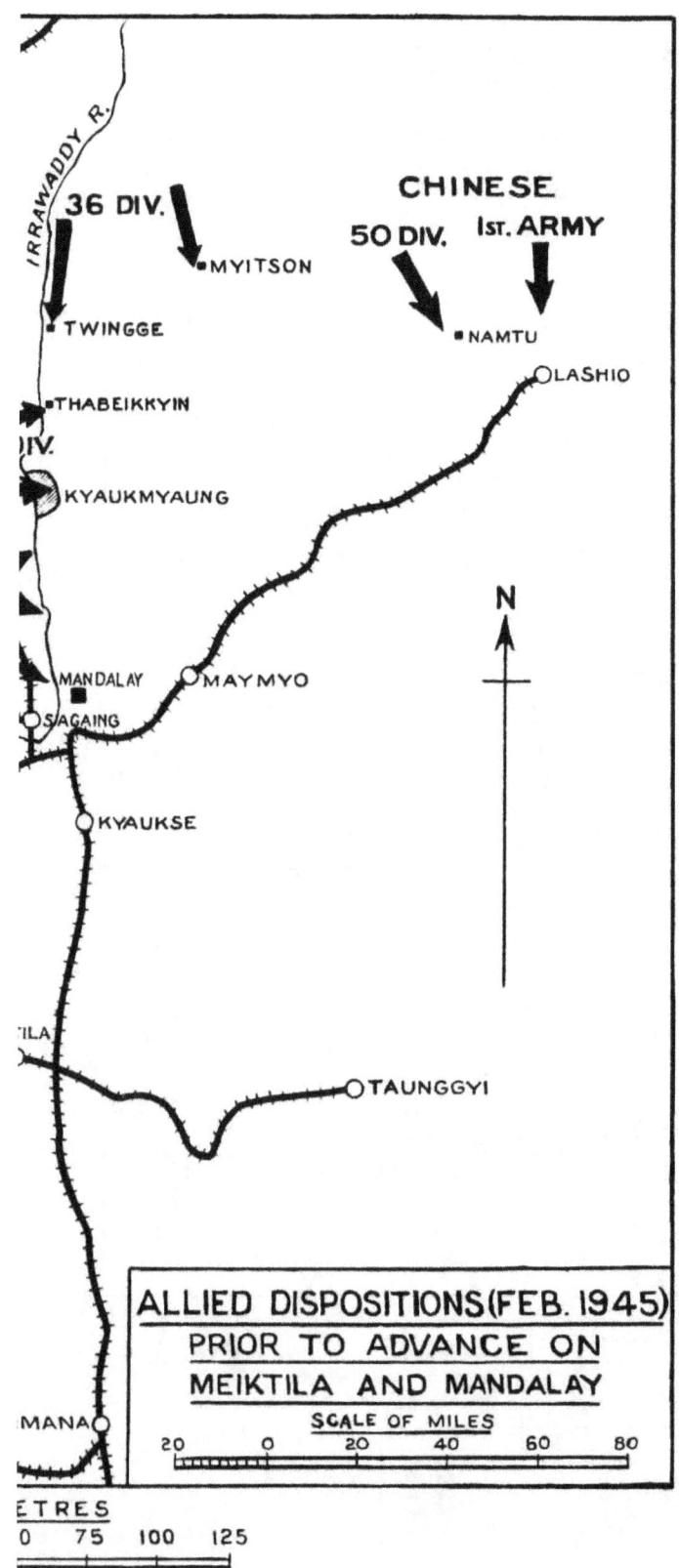

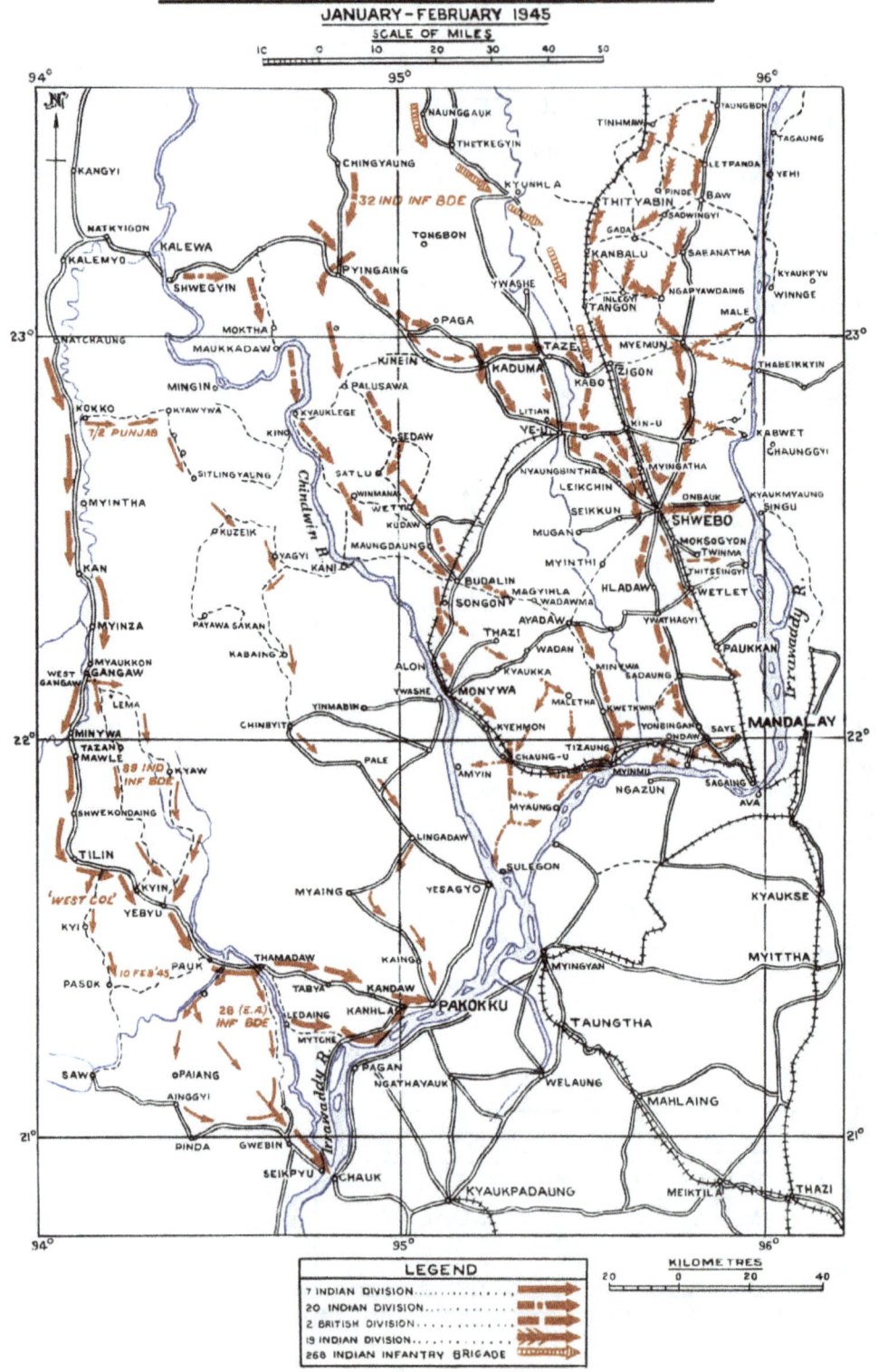

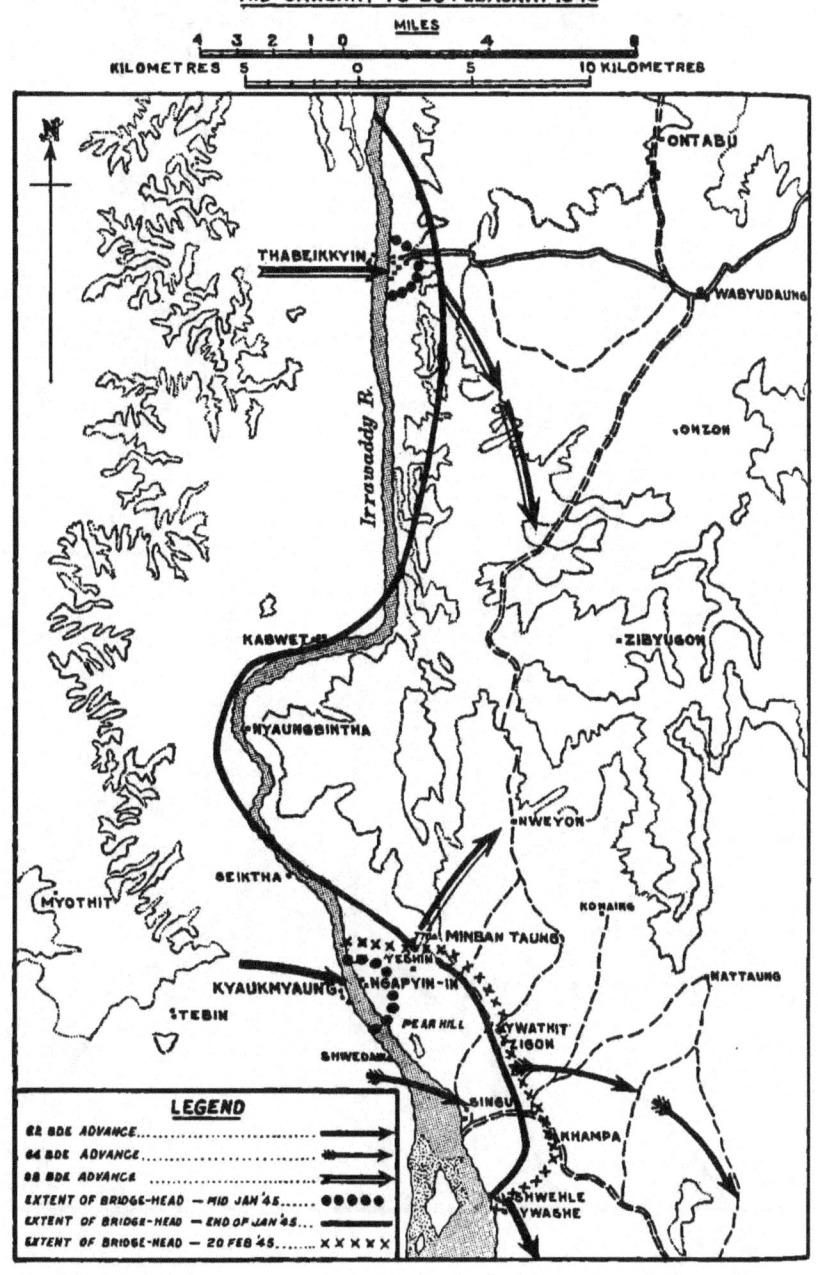

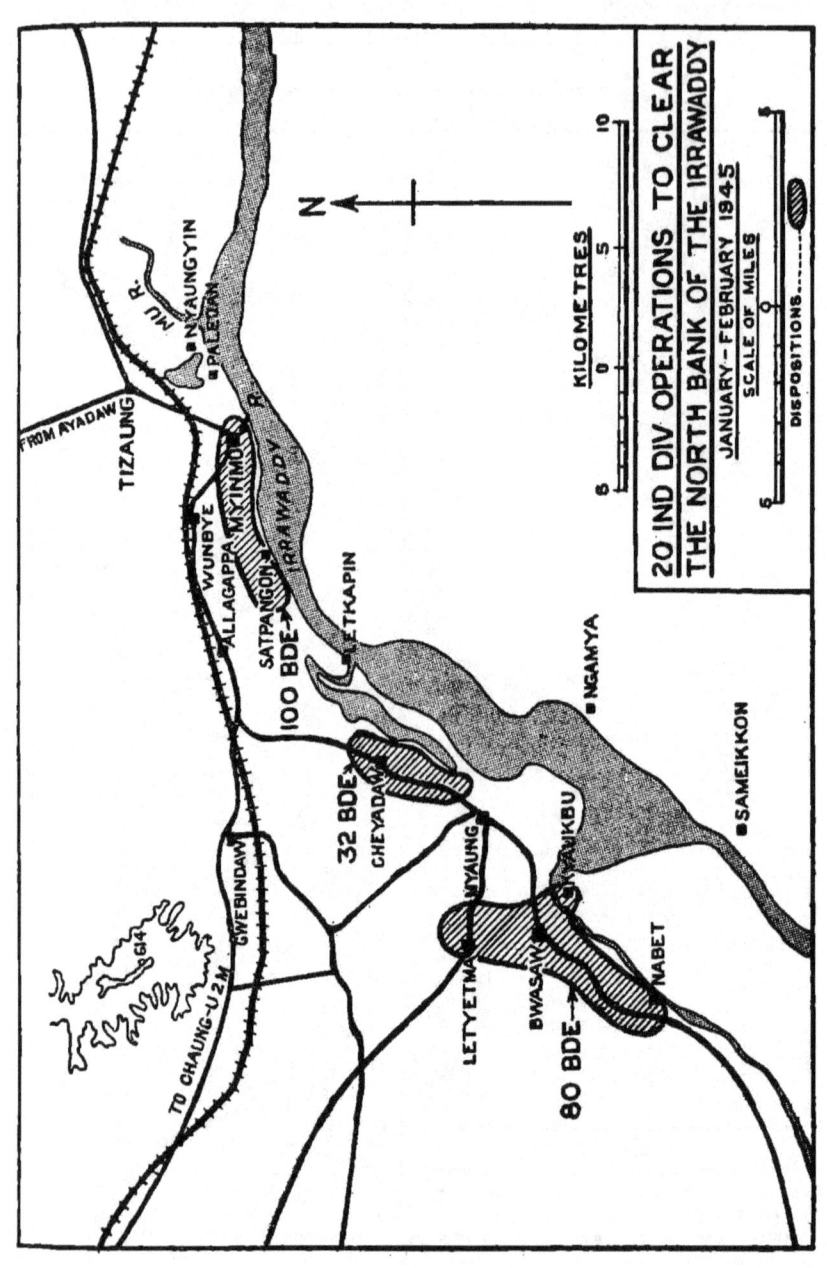

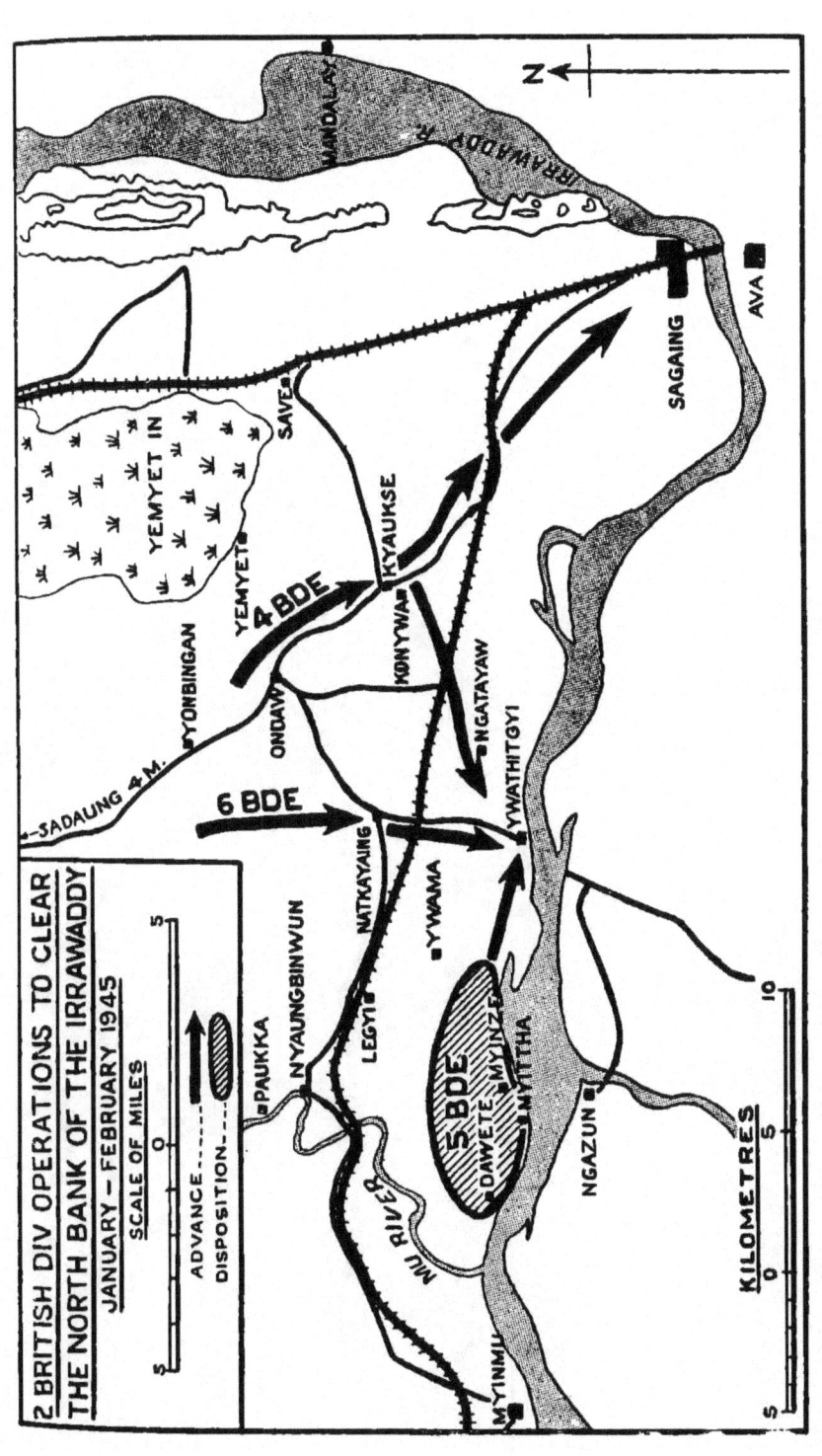

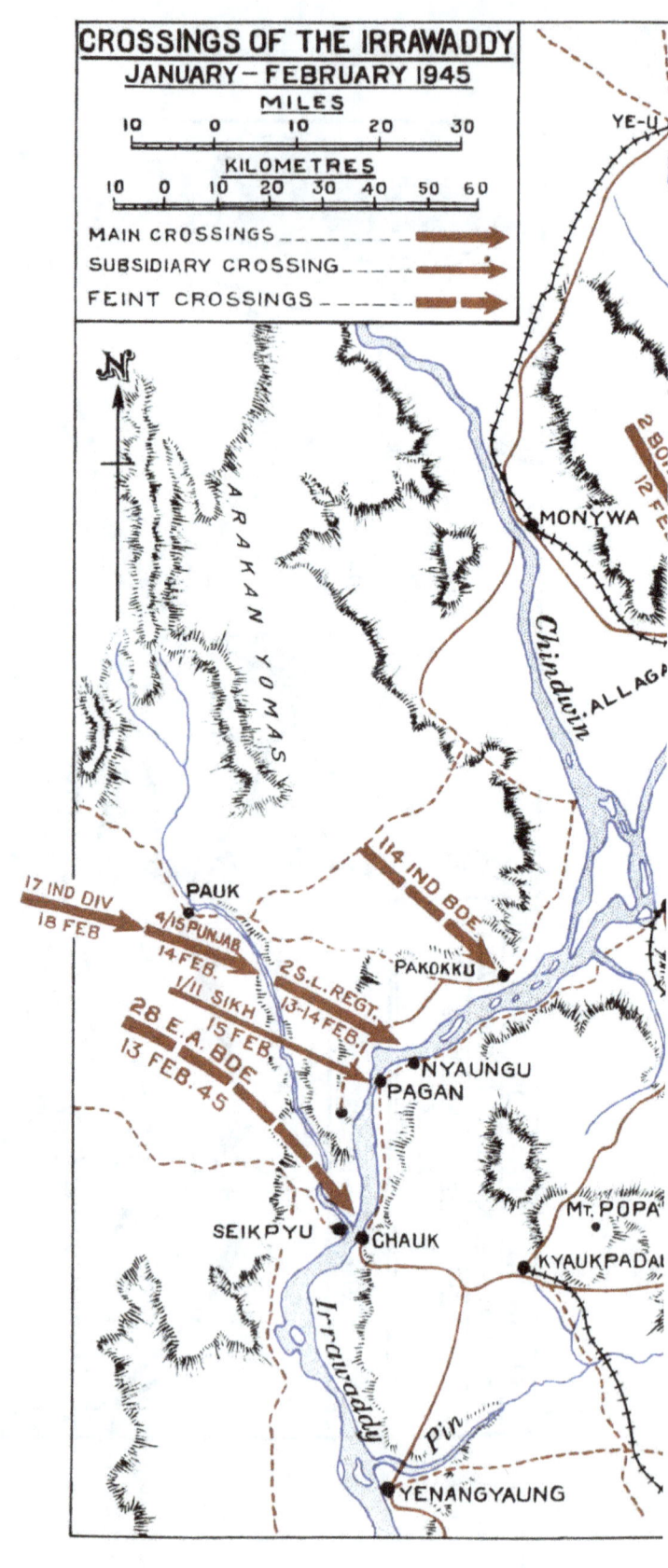

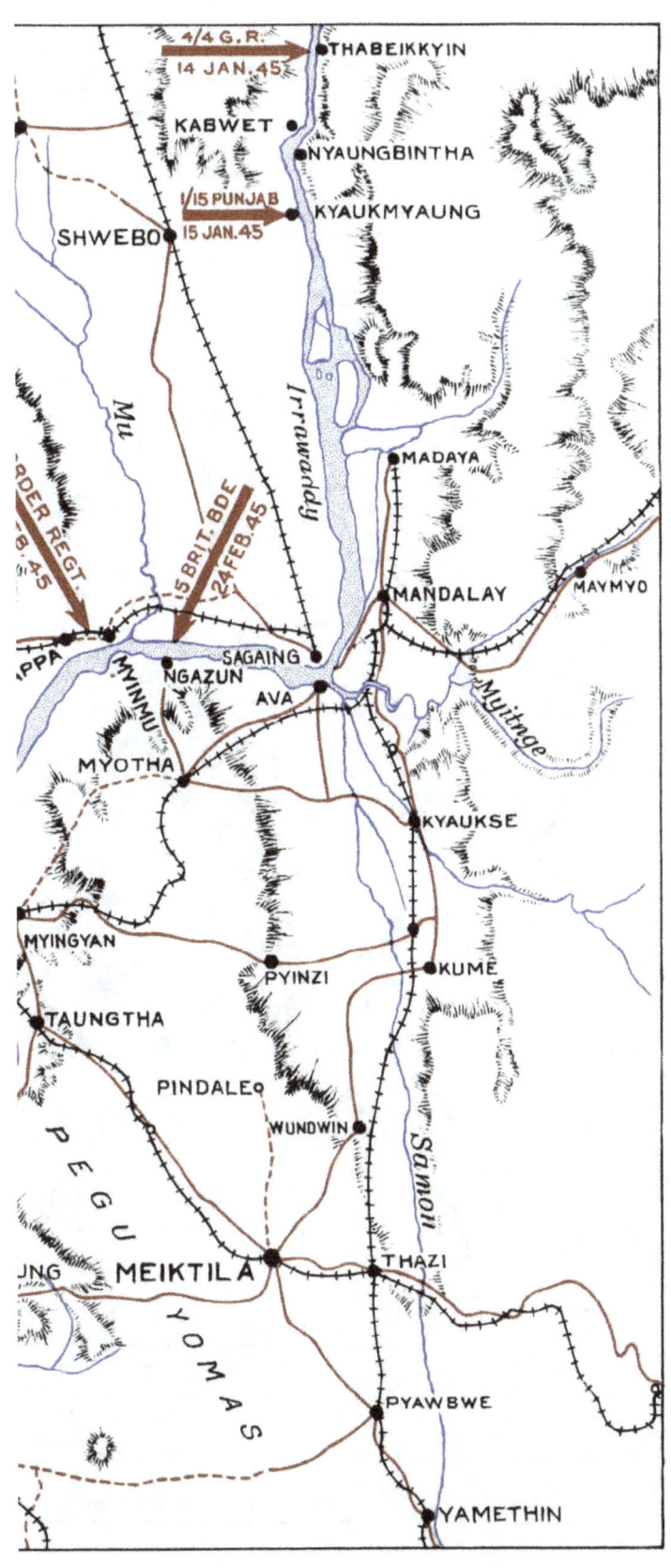

CROSSING OF THE IRRA

13 FEBRU

SCA

FURLONGS 8 7 6 5 4 3 2 1 0

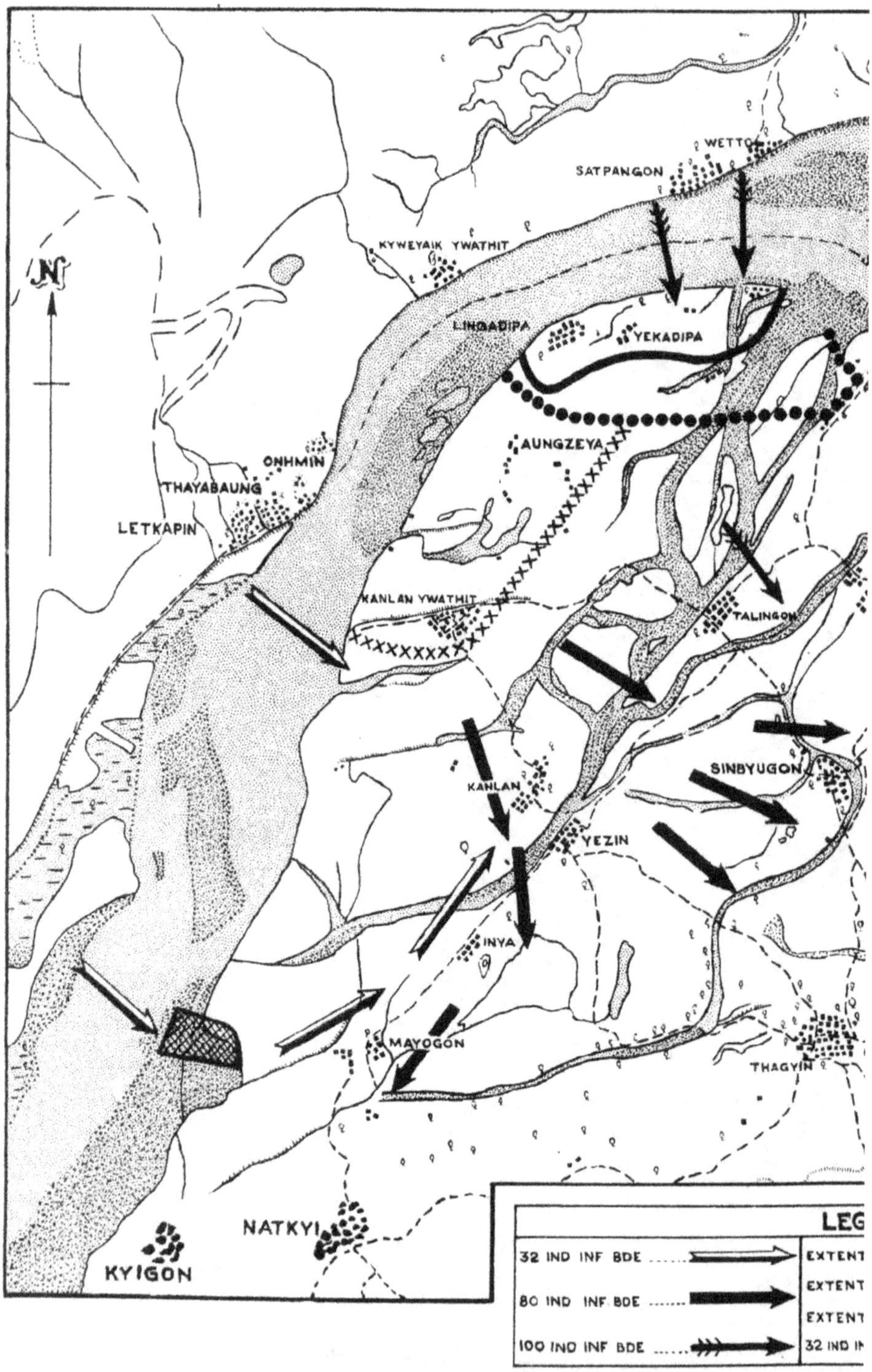

N
WETTO
SATPANGON
KYWEYAIK YWATHIT
LINGADIPA
YEKADIPA
AUNGZEYA
ONHMIN
THAYABAUNG
LETKAPIN
KANLAN YWATHIT
TALINGON
SINBYUGON
KANLAN
YEZIN
INYA
MAYOGON
THAGYIN
NATKYI
KYIGON
LEG
32 IND INF BDE ......
EXTENT
80 IND INF BDE ......
EXTENT
EXTENT
100 IND INF BDE ......
32 IND I

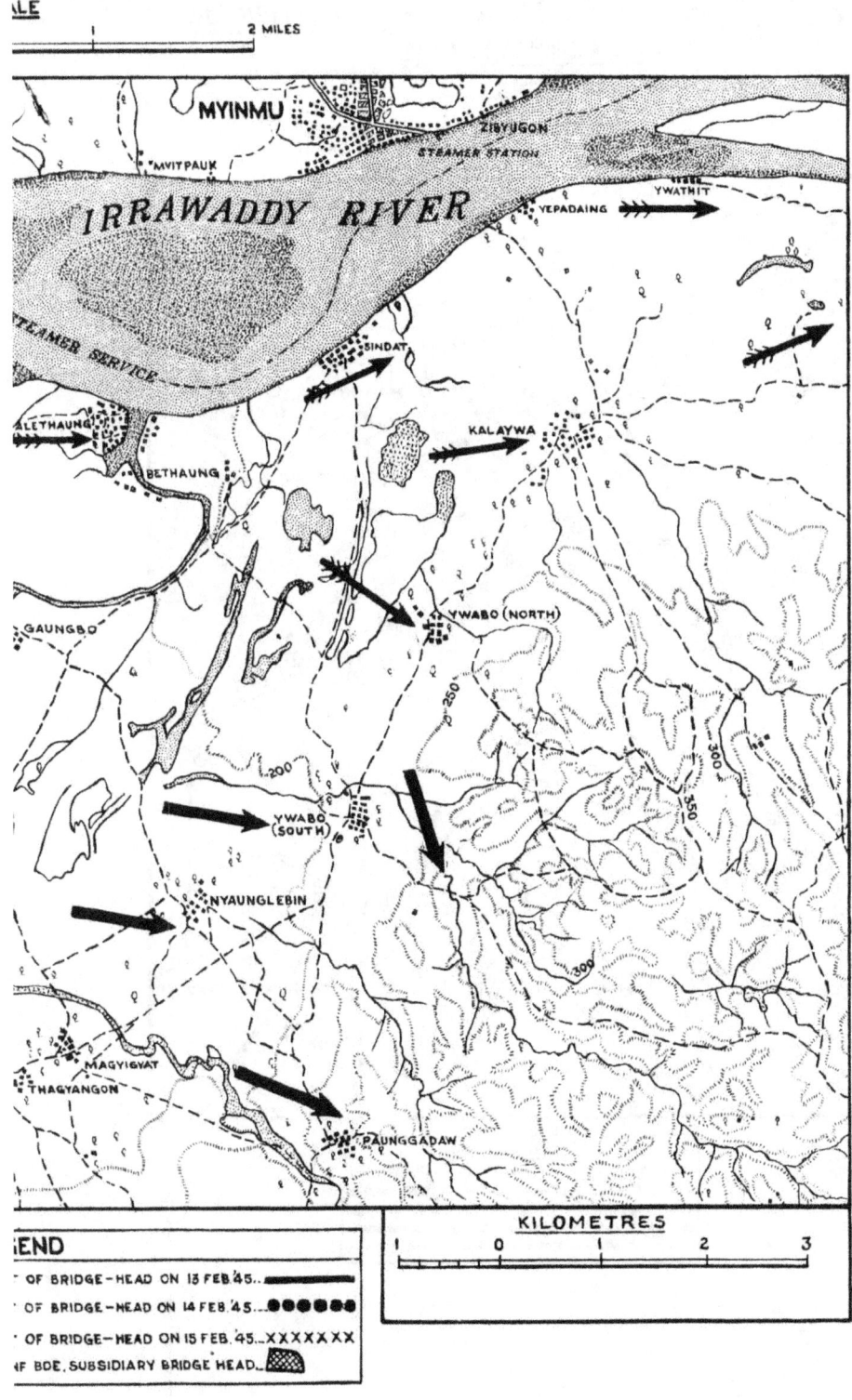

THE CROSSING OF THE IRRAWADDY BY 2 BRITISH DIV.
24 FEBRUARY 1945

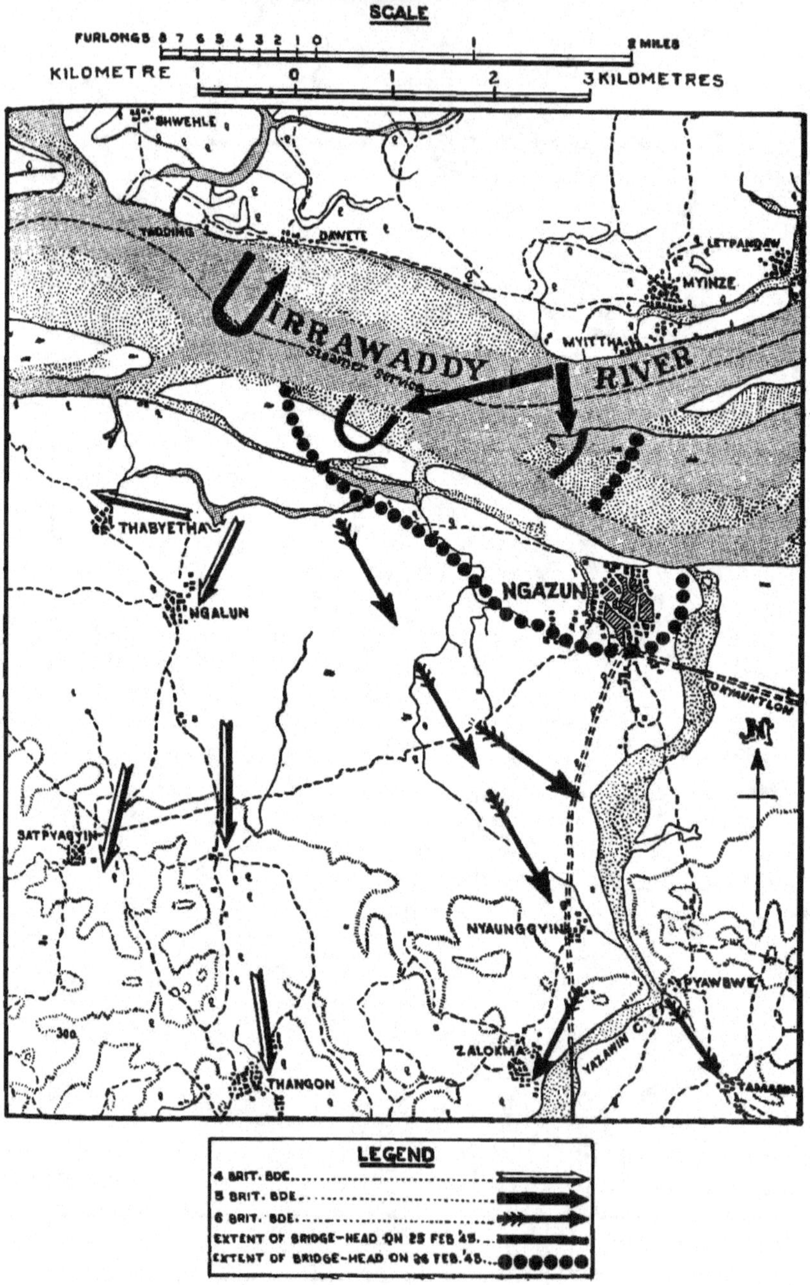

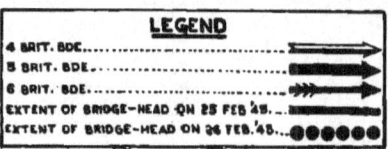

THE CROSSING OF THE IRRAWADDY BY 7 INDIAN DIV. 14 FEBRUARY 1945

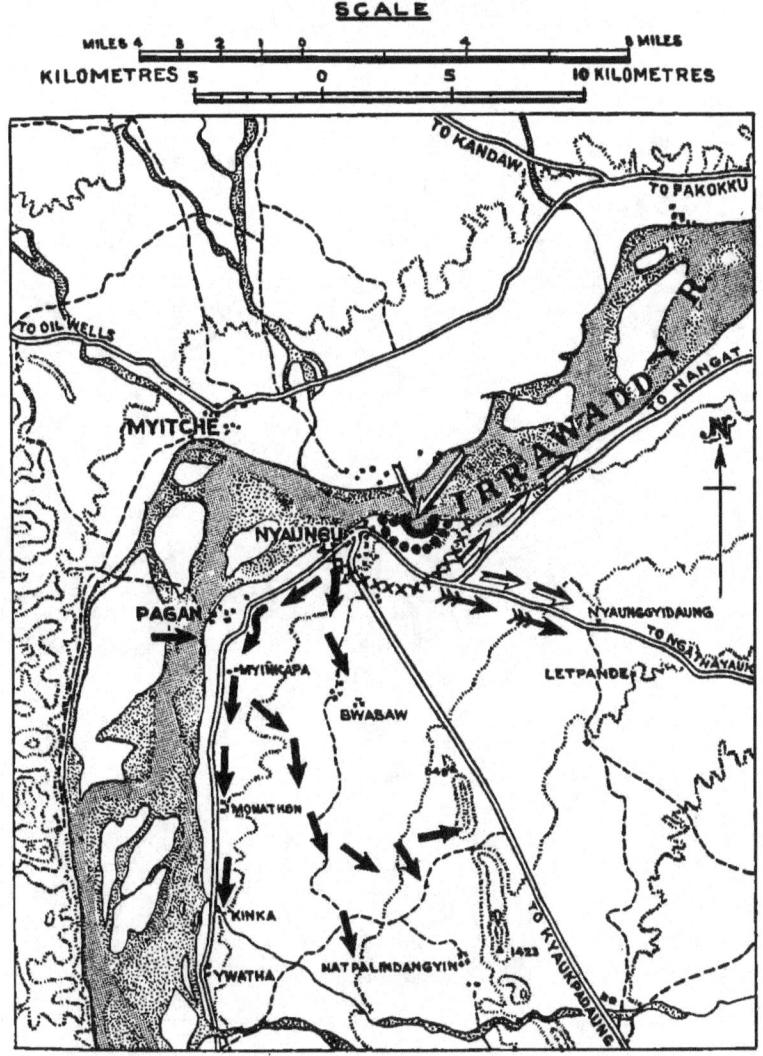

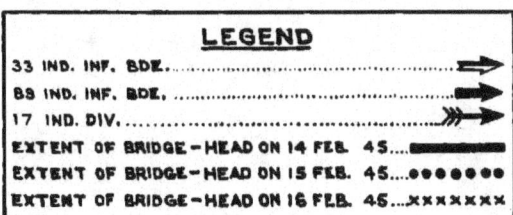

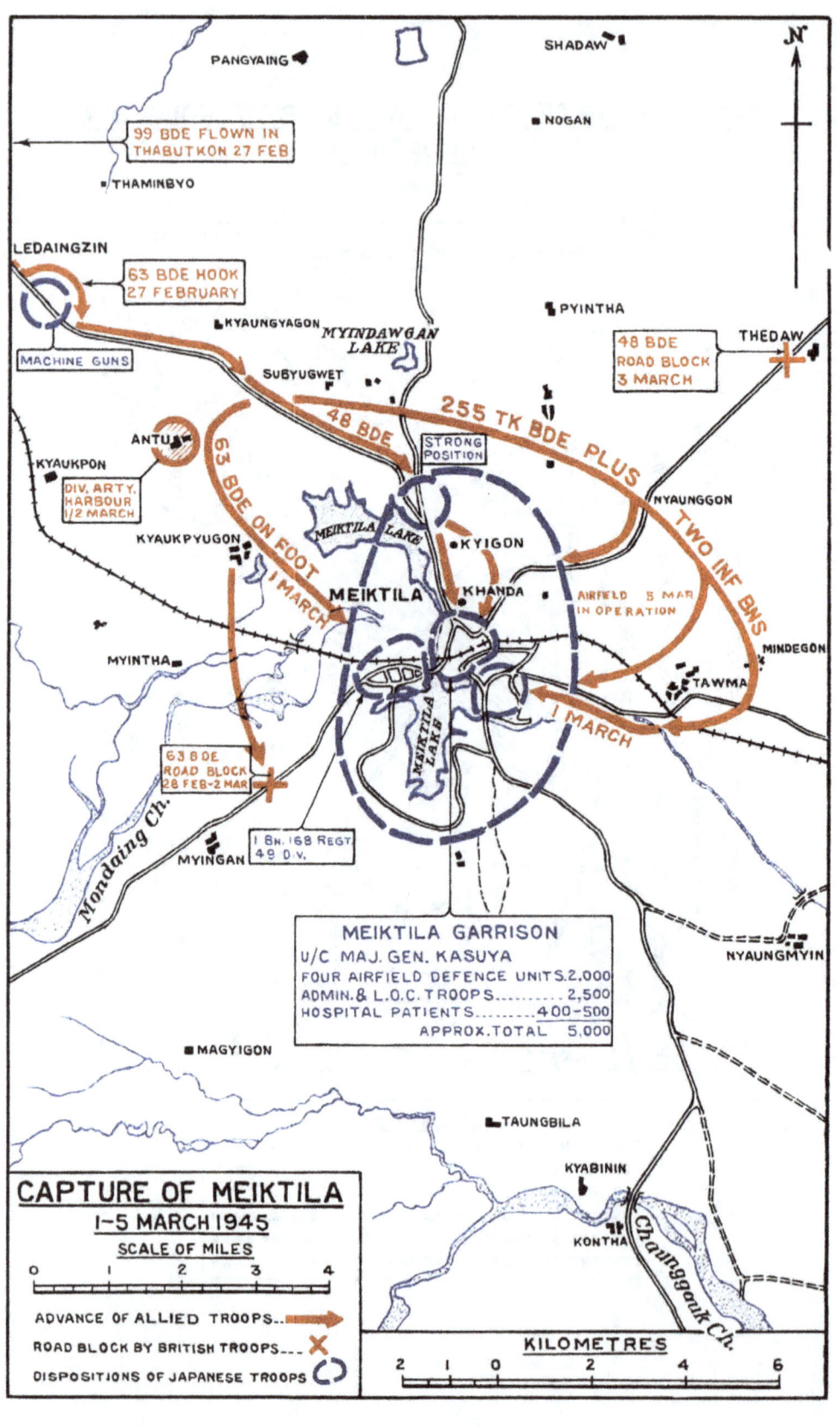

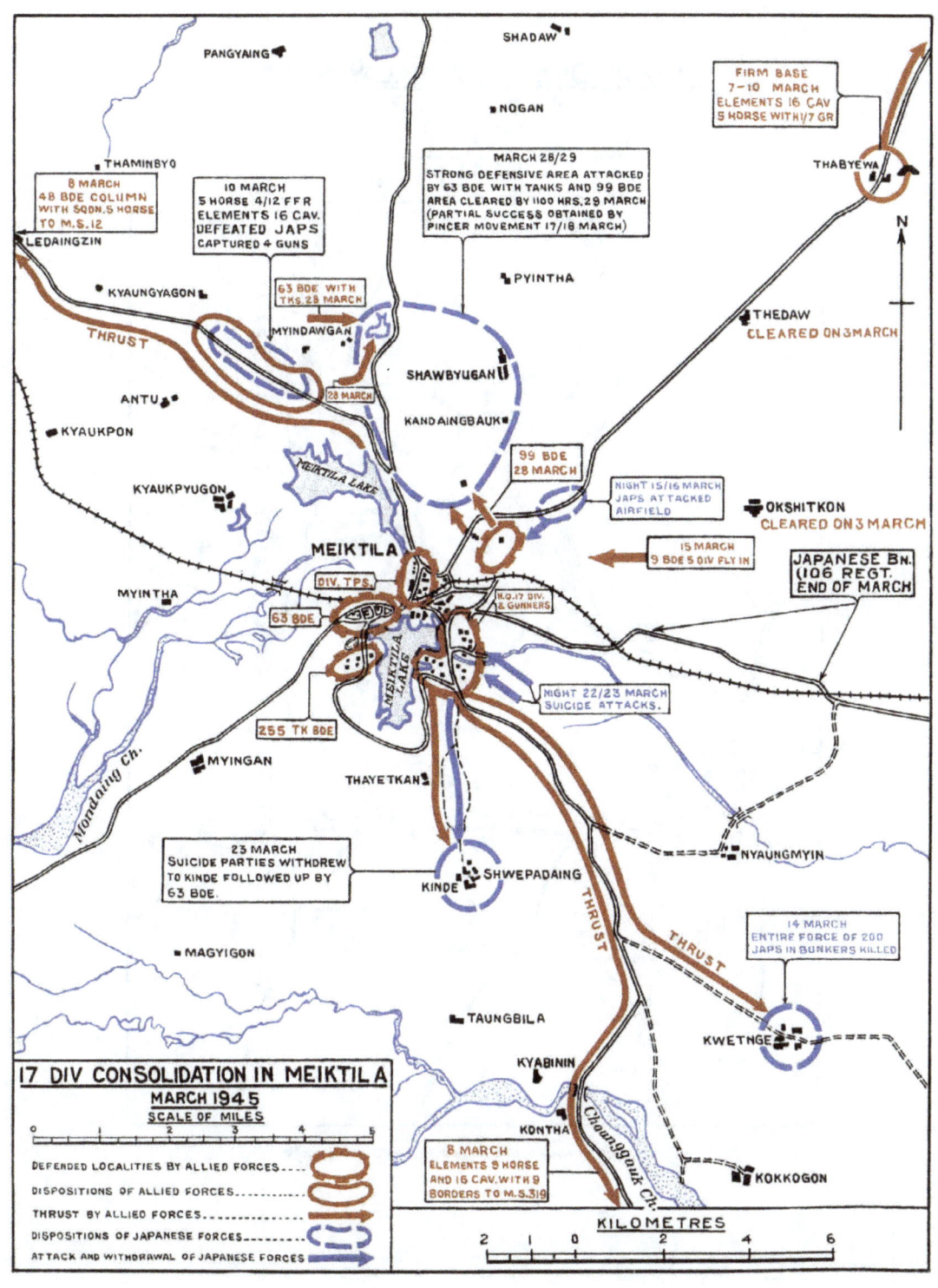

OPERATIONS IN MANDALAY AREA

MARCH–APRIL 1945

ADVANCE OF ALLIED FORCES SHOWN THUS ➡

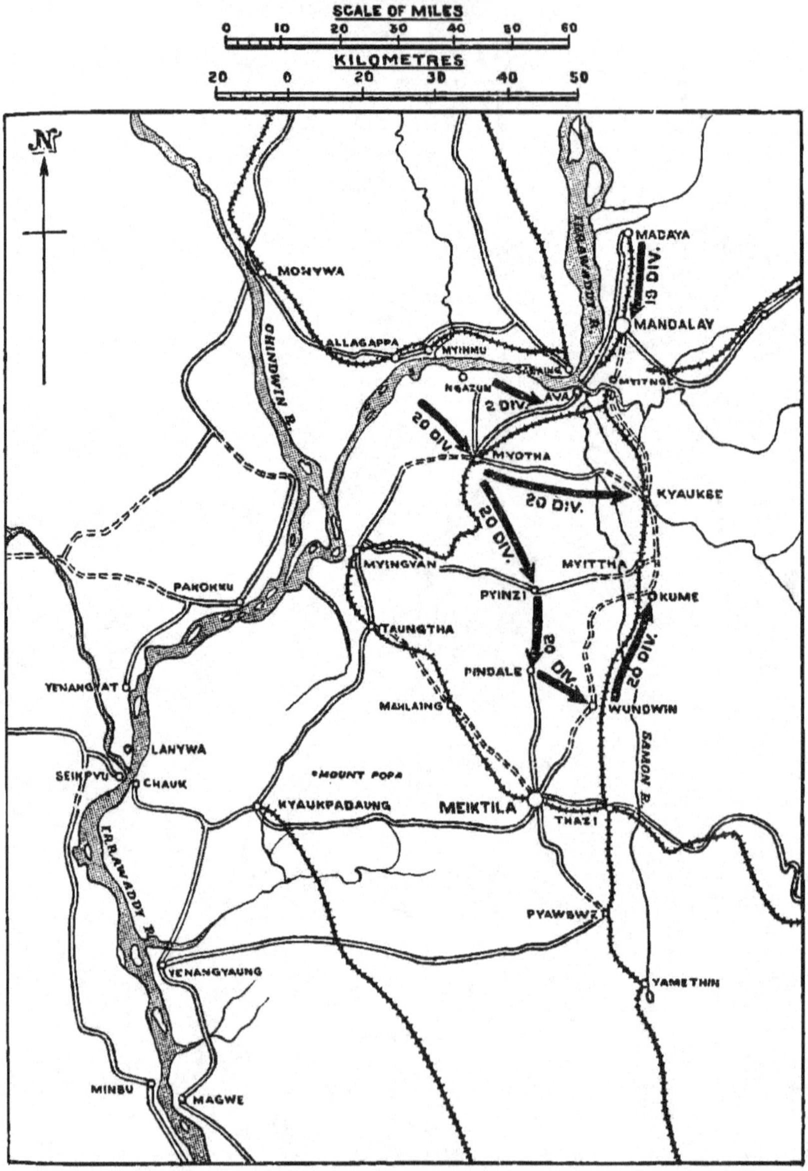

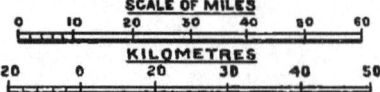

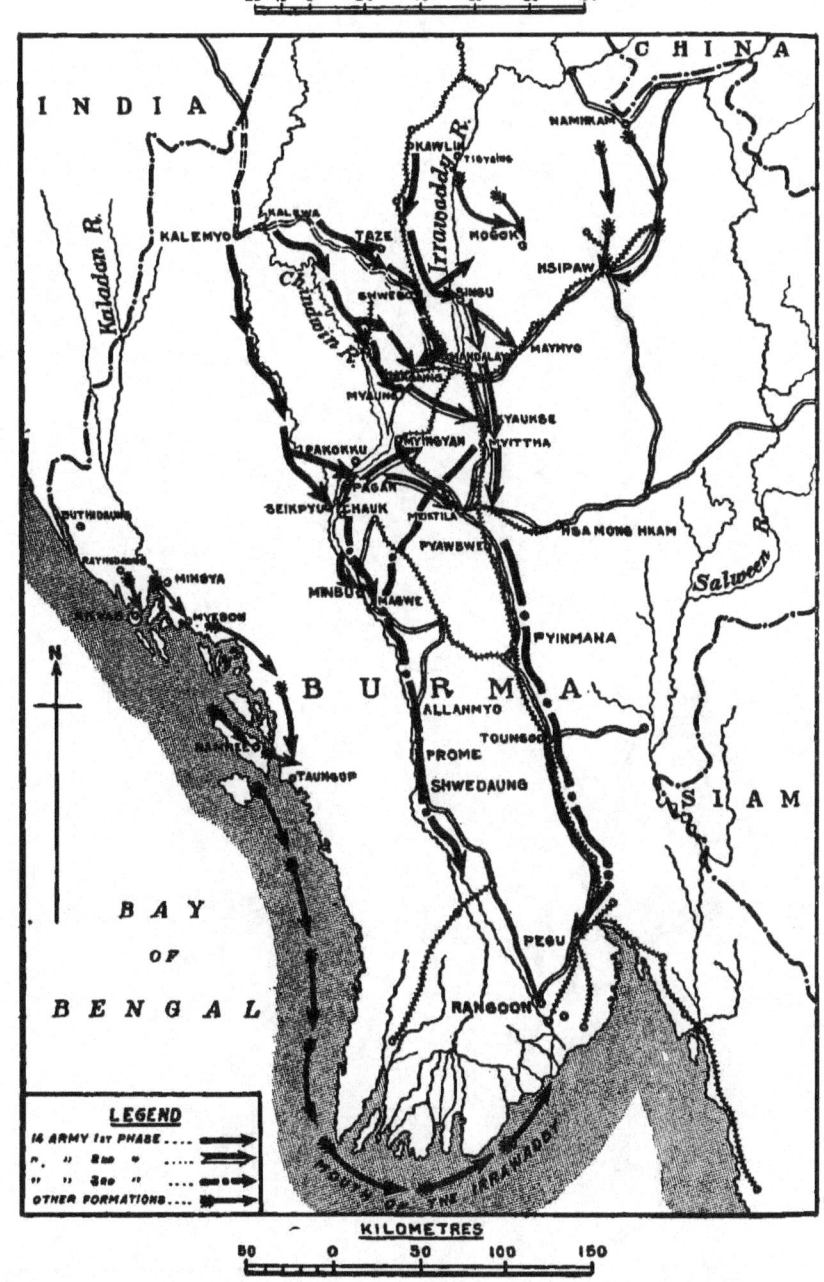

EXPLOITATION PHASE

SITUATION 7 APRIL 1945

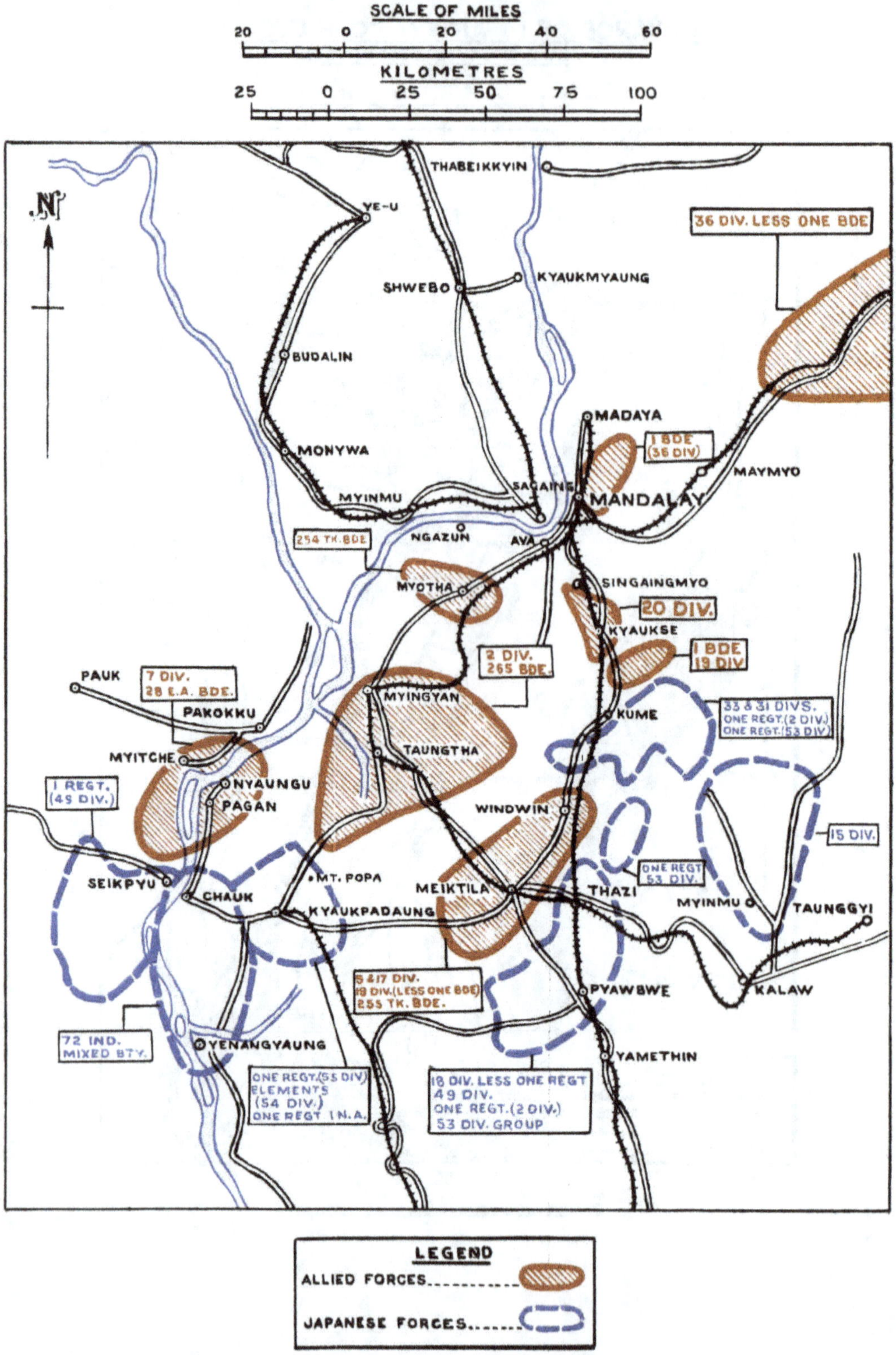

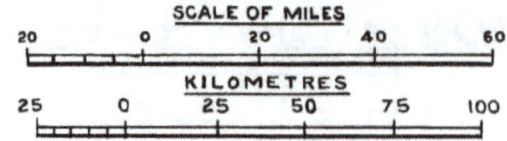

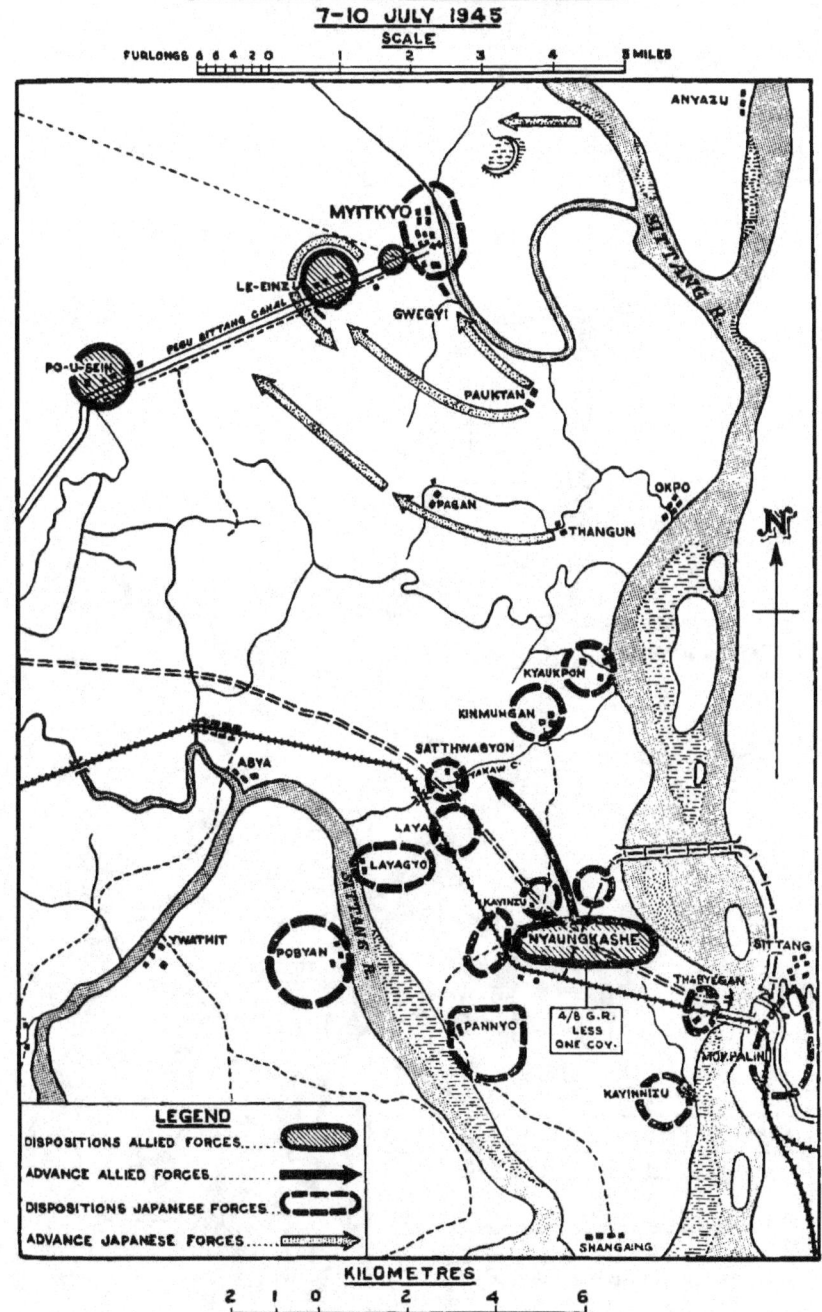

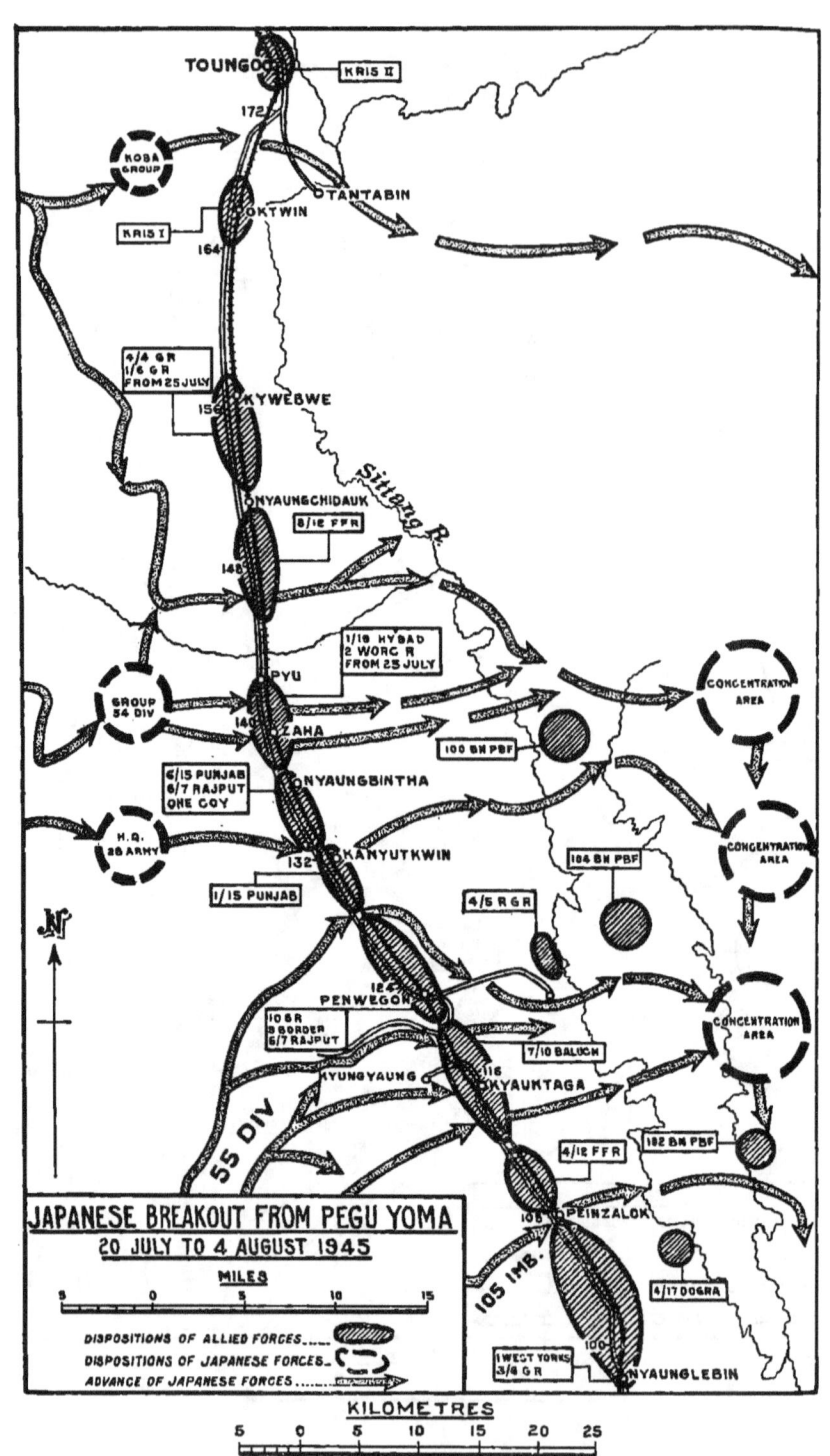

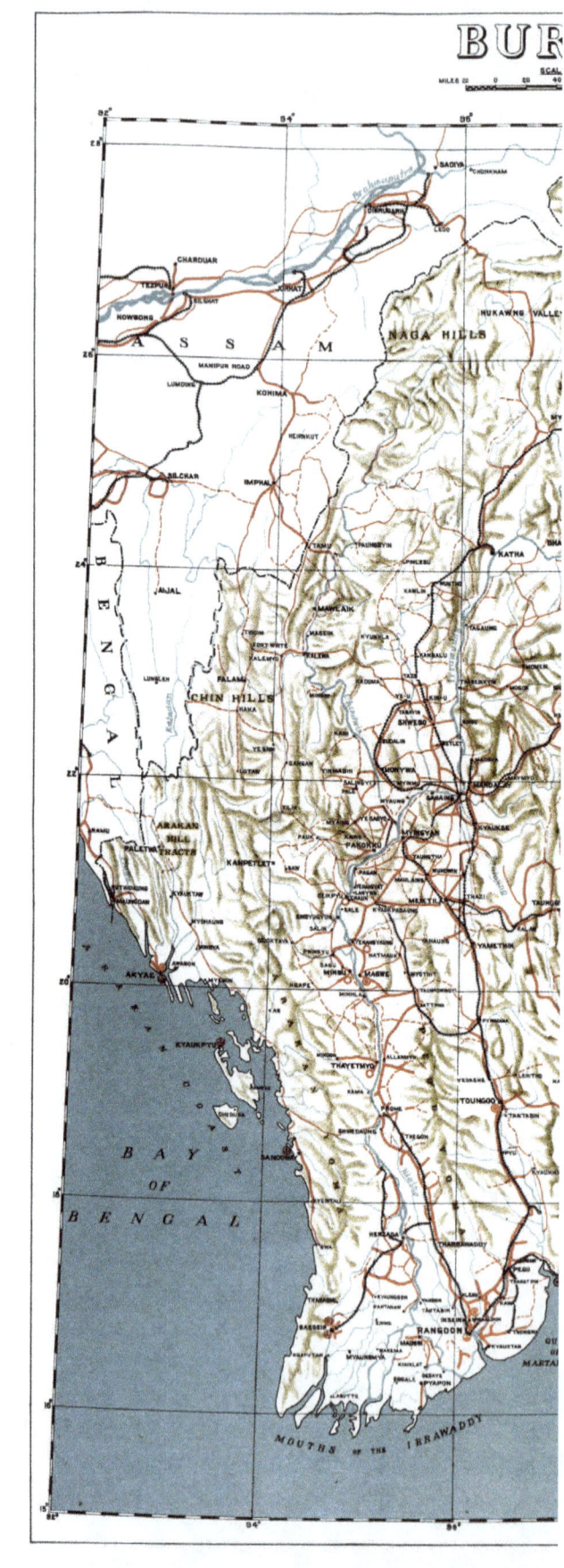

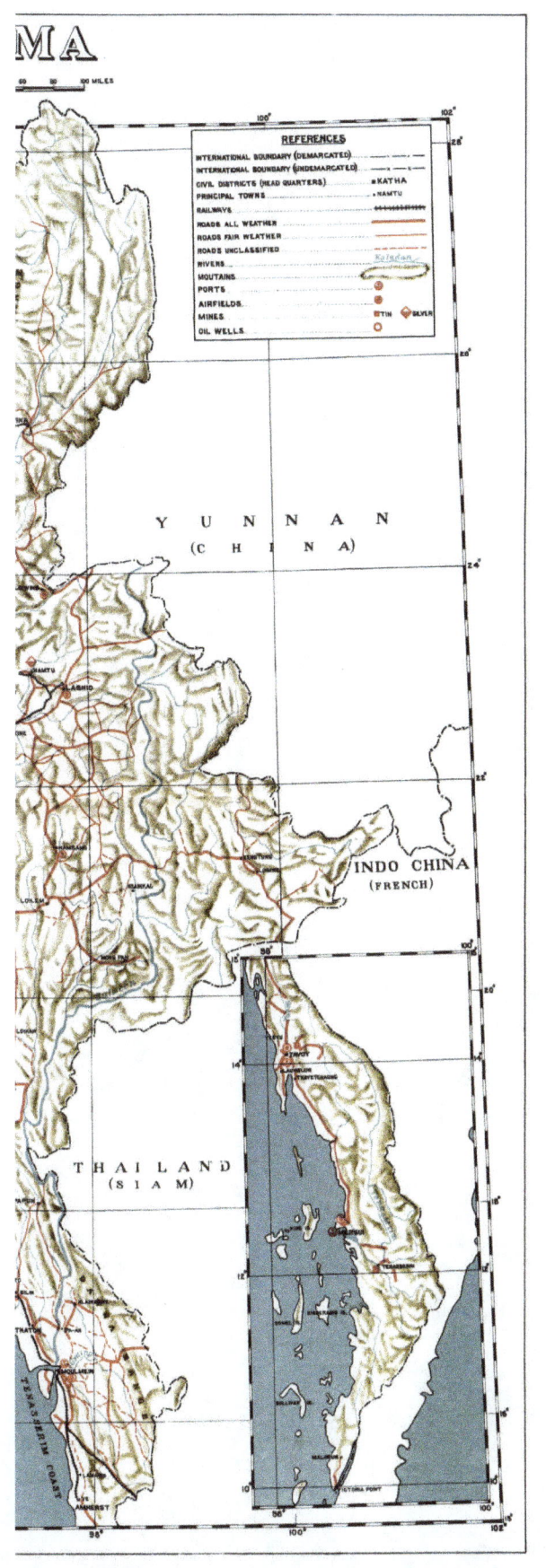

INDIAN DIVISIONS WON A FINE REPUTATION IN WORLD WAR TWO

Field Marshal Auchinleck, Commander-in-Chief of the British Indian Army from 1942, asserted that the British "couldn't have come through both wars (World War I and II) if they hadn't had the British Indian Army". British Prime Minister Winston Churchill also paid tribute to "the unsurpassed bravery of Indian soldiers and officers".

Between 1945 and 1947, the Director of Public Relations, War Department, Government of India, published a series of short publications covering the individual histories of the WWII Indian Divisions. They followed a consistent format, having between 44 and 48 pages within illustrated soft card covers. They have an average of 50 monochrome photographic illustrations, and each has a full colour centrespread depicting a scene from the Division's wartime operations (drawn by official war artists). They were printed at various presses in Bombay and New Delhi, and each contains at least one map.

As condensed histories they are useful – particularly those which relate to Divisions for which no other record was ever produced.

The British Indian Army during World War II began the war, in 1939, numbering just under 200,000 men. By the end of the war, it had become the largest volunteer army in history, rising to over 2.5 million men in August 1945. Serving in divisions of infantry, armour and a fledgling airborne force, they fought on three continents: in Africa, Europe and Asia.

This Army fought in Ethiopia against the Italian Army, in Egypt, Libya, Tunisia and Algeria against both the Italian and German Army and, after the Italian surrender, against the German Army in Italy. However, the bulk of the British Indian Army was committed to fighting the Japanese Army, first during the British defeats in Malaya and the retreat from Burma to the Indian border; later, after resting and refitting for the victorious advance back into Burma, as part of the largest British Empire army ever formed. These campaigns cost the lives of over 87,000 Indian service- men, while another 34,354 were wounded, and 67,340 became prisoners of war. Their valour was recognised with the award of some 4,000 decorations, and 18 members of the British Indian Army were awarded the Victoria Cross or the George Cross.

RED EAGLES
The Story of the 4th Indian Division
9781474537520

During the Second World War, the 4th Indian Division was in the vanguard of nine campaigns in the Mediterranean theatre, Egypt, Eritrea, Syria, Tunisia, Italy and Greece. The 4th Division captured 150,000 prisoners and suffered 25,000 casualties, more than the strength of a whole division. It won over 1,000 honours and awards, which included four Victoria Crosses and three George Crosses. Field Marshal Lord Wavell wrote: "The fame of this Division will surely go down as one of the greatest fighting formations in military history."

THE FIGHTING FIFTH
History of the 5th Indian Division
9781474537513

As described in much greater detail in Anthony Brett James's book 'The Ball of Fire', the division saw active service in East Africa, North Africa and Burma.

GOLDEN ARROW
The Story of the 7th Indian Division
9781474537506

The role of this division is also duplicated by a much larger work: the book by Brig. M. R. Roberts. However, this booklet gives a good account of Kohima and Imphal and the crossing of the Irrawaddy. In 1945, the division was flown into Siam, so becoming the first Allied formation to re-enter South East Asia.

BLACK CAT DIVISION
17th Indian Division
9781474537483

This formation was committed to Burma from the early days when the British were in full flight from the invading Japanese. It remained in Burma right through to the end, when the starving remnants of the Japanese Army were making their own desperate retreat.

ONE MORE RIVER
The Story of the 8th Indian Division
Biferno, Trigno, Sangro, Moro, Rapido, Arno, Senio, Santerno, Po, Adige

9781474537490

The 8th Indian Division started its overseas service in the Middle East in the garrisoning of Iraq and then the invasion of Persia to secure the oil fields of the area for the Allies, before moving to Italy in 1943. Landing at Taranto, it pushed up the length of the peninsula in a series of major battles: breaking the Sangro Line, forcing the Rapido and turning the defences at Cassino, breaking the stubborn German resistance at Monte Grande and, finally, forcing the Po River. It won four VCs, 26 DSOs and 149 MCs along the way. During the war the 8th Indian Division sustained casualties totalling 2,012 dead, 8,189 wounded and 749 missing.

TIGER HEAD
The Story of the 26th Indian Division
Arakan, Rangoon

9781474537452

This is a history of the division said later by the Japanese to have been the opponent which they most feared. The 26th held the Allied monsoon line in the Arakan during two such seasons, repulsing every attack launched against it. Later it made a series of leap-frog landings down the coast to clinch the issue in the Arakan. It was the first division to enter Rangoon, invading the city from the sea.

THE TWENTY THIRD INDIAN DIVISION
"The Fighting Cock Division"
Burma, Malaya, Java

9781474537469

The Fighting Cock Division is well recorded in the book by Doulton. This book gives coverage of the heavy fighting at the Kohima Battle, the capture of Tamu, the reoccupation of Malaya in August 1945, and then its strange role on the island of Java – concurrently disarming the Japanese garrison, fighting the insurgent Indonesian nationalists, and caring for 65,000 former internees pending the arrival of a new Dutch administration.

A HAPPY FAMILY
The Story of the Twentieth Indian Division,
9781474537476

One of the few Indian divisions in the 14th Army trained specifically for the war in Burma. Raised in Bangalore in 1942, it commenced active operations in late 1943 and served from Imphal through to the end. It established the 14th Army's first brigade-head across the Chindwin and its second such brigade-head across the Irrawaddy. Its final task was to round up the Japanese in French Indochina.

TEHERAN TO TRIESTE
The Story of the Tenth Indian Division
9781783317028

This History deals with the 10th Indian Div's exploits in Iraq (under Maj Gen "Bill" Slim) its role in the Libyan battles leading up to El Alamein, the following two years of garrison duties in Cyprus and Syria, and finally, its fighting services in the Italian campaign (from Ortona onwards).

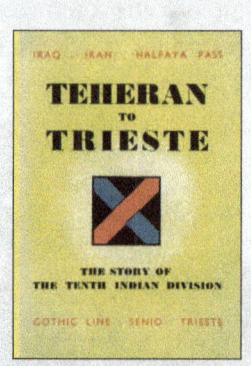

THE STORY OF THE 25th INDIAN DIVISION
The Arakan Campaign
9781783317585

Formed in Southern India in August 1942 for defence of that area in case of Japanese invasion, the "Ace of Spades" Division had its baptism of fire in Arakan in February 1944. It served throughout the remainder of that campaign the climax being the battle of Tamandu. Its victorious fight for the Kangaw roadblock was considered by many to have been the fiercest battle of the entire Burma war, while its liberation of Akyab was the first convincing proof to the rest of the world that the tide had turned against the Japanese.

DAGGER DIVISION
The Story of the 19th Indian Division
9781783317035

Raised in the late 1941, the 19th was the first "standard" Indian Division. Its troops were the first to breach the Japanese defence line in Burma and to raise the flag at Fort Dufferin. It crossed the Chindwin in November 1944, driving on to Mandalay and Rangoon during seven months of continuous fighting. The 19th's exploits are graphically described also in John Masters' personal memoir, *The Road Past Mandalay*.

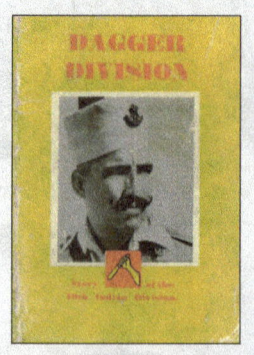

www.ingramcontent.com/pod-product-compliance
Lightning Source LLC
Chambersburg PA
CBHW080803300426
44114CB00020B/2815